Flip Flop

on the

Appalachian Trail

by Maribeth Crandell

Flip Flop

on the

Appalachian Trail

by Maribeth Crandell

ISBN 9781984204219

Cover art by Beno Kennedy
www.benoart.com

Photo of author by Dawn Adams, aka Zama

Dedicated to my father

who told me, early on, that I could do
anything I set my mind to.

The Appalachian Trail

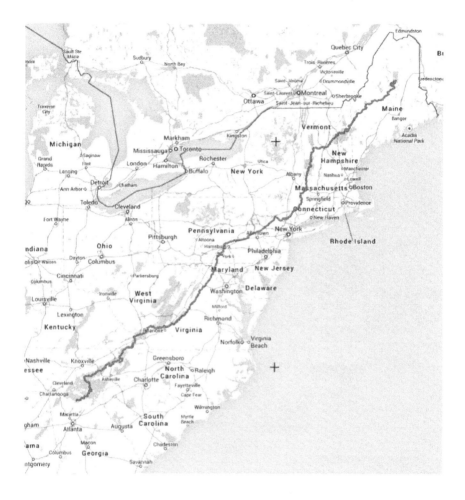

For an online interactive map with photos of shelters and other trail features and details, visit:

https://thetrek.com/thru-hiker-resources/appalachian-trail-interactive-map/

Acknowledgements

Thanks to my parents who were very supportive of this endeavor, as if they'd been waiting for me to finally get around to it. I always loved hearing their enthusiasm whenever I called home. They sent my mail drops along with letters that kept me connected to the family. Dad managed my affairs while I was hiking which freed me up to fully experience the trail. They gave me a good send off, met me part way, and helped me celebrate when I finished. They picked up the tab on numerous occasions and then encouraged me to write this memoir. They got me started, camping, hiking and practicing good outdoor stewardship at a very young age and I'll always be grateful for their guidance and support.

My sister Martha, after hiking the Appalachian Trail from Georgia to Maine, said to me in a heated moment that I never would, which of course was a challenge I could not ignore. So thanks Tortoise. I appreciate all the tips I got in her letters from the trail, conversations and the memoirs she shared with me. Her experience paved the way for my own.

Thanks to Kelly O'Rourke who has been my hiking and camping partner for over twenty years. Her loyalty, love and support are a precious gift. Her Seattle home was my launch and landing pad and the loan of her six-foot Thermarest at the end of my hike was very much appreciated. And thanks to Suzen and Brian O'Rouke for hosting me in style, not once, but twice, in New York.

I could not have done this hike without all those trail builders and shelter constructors and maintainers, mostly volunteers, who helped establish this trail, and who work to keep it open and accessible year after year. What they do is often taken for granted; their efforts not only make a thru-hike possible, they save lives, and I, for one, am eternally grateful.

Thank you to all the trail angels, the friends and family, who supported us along the way, offered housing, snacks, meals, transportation, laundry, phones and kindness on this 2,000 mile trek.

Thanks for putting up with the thru-hiker aroma and appetite to make us feel welcome.

Thanks to Tim in Monson, Maine for inviting me and other thru-hikers to join your Friday night hoe down in the general store. That was a highlight for me and I'm sure others loved it, too.

Thank you to the friends who helped me wrestle this manuscript into a book worth reading. Paul Crawford, retired National Park Ranger and son of an English teacher, not only helped edit but added comments in the margins that sparked ongoing story swapping. Jack Hartt, retired State Park Ranger with publishing experience, edited and helped put the text into something resembling a book. Linda Summers, an avid reader and fellow adventurer, was the first to read through the rough draft and offer her thoughtful insights and suggestions. Clifton Crandell helped edit and offered comments and encouragement.

I could not have done it without all of you. Thanks for coming along on this journey with me.

Introduction

"What was I thinking? It's not too late to back out. I could just turn around right now and go home." The voice in my head would not let me sleep.

"It *IS* too late. You've already told all your friends and family. You've bought your new gear, your food and supplies. You've trained for months. You've packed your mail drops and said goodbye. Now the only thing left to do is hike. Besides, you have no home to go home to."

We were in a roadside motel in Georgia. I woke before dawn in the stale, boxlike room I shared with my parents. They'd driven me down from North Carolina to see me off. Now, here I was with the last minute jitters, a great time for second thoughts.

A crack between the curtains let in a dim glow. I crept out of bed and peeked out trying to determine the time. The streetlights were still on but there was a hint of dawn on the horizon.

Lying down on the carpet by my bed, I began doing stretches, my morning routine. Yoga had helped me gain flexibility, strength and balance. Perhaps it would also help calm my nerves. My knees were pressed against my chest with my arms folded over them, pushing up with my legs while pulling down with my arms and taking deep breaths. In the faint light I saw my mother's face hovering over me.

"What in the world are you doing?"

I'm forty-seven years old. Obviously I'm having a mid-life crisis.

A few months before, I'd called it quits from a marriage that had been dangling by a thread. My husband, a stand up comic, was only moonlighting when we got married, but through the years he'd become successful… at comedy. He loved the limelight, craved the attention and each year spent more time on the road. Even when he was home, he was still in "Comedyland", editing videos, managing gigs, booking flights. He never unpacked. When people asked how long we'd been together he'd answer, "We've been married for ten years, but we've been together for four."

I worked full time supporting us both while he developed his career. As his career took off, so did he. He was married to his work. I was merely the housekeeper. I gradually packed my things and moved out. He seemed too busy to notice.

I got a house-sitting job on Whidbey Island where I'd lived before I was married, and slipped back into a community of old friends. I moved into the guest cottage behind the old farmhouse surrounded by fields and forests. The owners were gone for the winter. There were nearby trails that circled ponds full of ducks. I could walk a mile into town on a quiet lane. It was a nurturing place, serene and beautiful. I started looking for work, trying to start over. I had three months to reassemble my life before the homeowners returned.

One day a thought occurred to me. I had no home, no job and no family obligations. I was emotionally exhausted. This was one of the lowest points in my life.

Or, it could be the opportunity of a lifetime. It could be my chance to finally hike the Appalachian Trail.

I grew up in North Carolina, the fourth of five kids. On a family vacation in the Smoky Mountains we pulled into an overlook to admire the view. Getting out of the car, my attention went to a scruffy looking fellow carrying a pack. My mother asked him where he was headed. He responded with one word.

"Maine."

As we watched him disappear into the woods my mother explained that he was on the Appalachian Trail that went from Georgia to Maine. She said some people hiked the whole thing, from one end to the other, in one summer. The seed was planted. I was ten years old.

Our house was at the edge of town. I walked to school on a trail through the woods along with my siblings and all the neighborhood kids. On weekends, I went exploring with a knapsack imagining I was Daniel Boone following deer trails, or Jane Goodall observing birds and squirrels. In summer I worked on my grandparent's farm. And for a few weeks each year my parents hitched up the camper trailer and took us to visit National Parks and tourist attractions in forty-five states. My mom was a Girl Scout leader and my sisters and I were enlisted into the troop. I suffered through the meetings but thrived on campouts.

At college in western North Carolina, I studied education, recreation and biology and used any excuse to get out into the mountains. My favorite professor, John Mackie, helped me devise my own degree we called Environmental Education.

He occasionally invited his former students to come back and give presentations about the jobs they'd found after college. One of those students gave a slide show about the Olympic Rain Forest in Washington State. As I gazed at images of people dwarfed by the huge ferns and enormous evergreen trees, little bells went off in the back of my head.

That summer I took an internship in Olympic National Forest and got a ride to Washington State with Doug, a friend of a neighbor. On our way across country we camped out in the Tetons, Yellowstone and Glacier National Parks. When we arrived at my Forest Service camp near Forks, Washington, I moved into a bunkhouse and Doug left for his summer job in North Cascades National Park.

I lived on the Olympic Peninsula for five months burning slash and fighting fires. I felt like I was living in one of the tall tales of Paul Bunyan my mom used to read to us on camping trips. I was surrounded by lumberjacks, fighting fires, washing off in icy mountains streams, sleeping in a bunkhouse and eating in a cookhouse just like Paul.

That was one of the first in a long succession of outdoor jobs for me. I worked in city, state and national parks. I became a naturalist working with kids and led seniors on hikes. I worked on whale watching boats and natural history cruise ships. I was a trail guide from Southeast Alaska to the Columbia River Gorge. I didn't make much money but I racked up a lot of outdoor experience, stayed in shape and collected stories to share around the campfire.

These were almost all part-time or seasonal jobs which meant I made my money for the year in the few pleasant summer months. So even though I'd dreamed of hiking the Appalachian Trail for decades, I couldn't justify giving up most of a year's income for a summer of hiking the AT. Years passed. Time marched on. It was a "someday" kind of thing.

Then my sister went and did it.

Out of the clear blue sky, she just announced that she was going to hike the Appalachian Trail. The whole trail. She was a bookworm, not a hiker, and certainly not a backpacker. She'd worked in a hospital, about as far from a rugged outdoor experience as you could get. And that's probably what drove her to it. Her job was driving her crazy. She'd struggled with it for years, had become bitter and angry, anti-social and depressed. She had to get out. So, six months before her 50th birthday, she took a leave of absence, shouldered a pack and hit the trail.

She lived in Boone, North Carolina (elevation 3,300 feet) and was familiar with mountain weather, the seventy-five mile an hour winds on Grandfather Mountain, the snow that hit by Thanksgiving and stayed until Easter. Still she wanted to be standing on Mount Katahdin, the northern terminus of the Appalachian Trail on her 50th birthday in August, so she left in mid-February. Brrrrrrrrr!

Meanwhile, three thousand miles away in the Pacific Northwest, I tracked her every move. I ordered a trail guide and studied it almost daily. I tried to guess where she'd be and what she might encounter. I imagined the terrain, the weather, the hostels and shelters along her route. She avoided phones, would have nothing to do with computers, but wrote great long letters with stories of the trail and her encounters with fellow thru-hikers, hostel keepers and townsfolk. I sent care packages trying to anticipate things she might need at different points along the way. I threw in little bottles of shampoo, sunscreen, glucosamine, Deet, and essentials like... crossword puzzles and chocolate.

Toward the end of the summer I wrote asking if I could meet her for the last leg, to climb Katahdin and celebrate her 50th birthday with her. She wrote back disheartened. The trail through the White Mountains of New Hampshire is rugged. She had struggled through the challenging terrain, had trouble packing enough food and had fallen behind schedule. She was disappointed that she wouldn't be able to make it to Katahdin for her birthday. In the last letter I received from her, dated August first, she sounded defeated.

Communicating through letters makes for a slow conversation. It takes four or five days for a letter to cross the country from one small town to another. It takes even longer if one of those correspondents is hiking between towns for a week or so. She told me our Plan A, to climb Katahdin together on her birthday, wasn't going to happen. So I determined to come up with a Plan B. I'd fly to Maine to meet her anyway. I could at least be there to help her celebrate her 50th.

The only trouble was I didn't know exactly where to find her. She was somewhere on a thin line of trail that stretched for 282 miles in the State of Maine. Dad had an idea.

Before she left, she had packaged up trail food and supplies in a set of mail drops, labeling them for specific post offices along her route. She'd write a couple of weeks ahead asking our parents to mail the appropriate package to the appropriate post office at the appropriate time so that she could intercept it. Post offices kept these packages for at least a couple of weeks.

Dad called the post office in Monson, Maine, where they'd sent the last mail drop. He was told that she hadn't picked up her mail there yet. The Caratunk post office, thirty miles south, was just off the trail so she'd agreed to stop there, too. We found out she hadn't picked that mail up either. But she had picked up the mail from the previous post office in Stratton. So she was somewhere between Stratton and Caratunk. We'd narrowed it down from 282 to just thirty-seven miles.

I flew to Maine.

The Adventures of Tortoise and Slug

Driving a rental car through the Maine countryside I passed many sprawling farmhouses and barns all white against a green backdrop of forest and fields. It was hauntingly similar to the dream I'd had the night before I left Seattle.

In the dream, I was in an old, white farmhouse looking for my sister. I climbed the stairs and found a room marked, "Appalachian Trail". Entering the room I looked out the window and saw a group of backpackers coming into town. I ran downstairs, out the door and down the street. When I reached them they were huddled around a hiker who had fallen face down in a ditch. I reached down and pulled her up only to find my sister with the face of Raggedy Ann.

What a strange dream, I'd thought. I hadn't seen or even thought about Raggedy Ann and Andy dolls for decades. And now I was passing farmhouses much like the one in my dream.

The two lane highway was wet with recent rain. I pulled off when I saw a sign that read "Caratunk, Population 108". There were no schools, churches or stores on the main street so it was easy to find the post office. I went in and asked if Martha had come in to get her mail.

The post mistress smiled. We'd spoken on the phone the day before and my father had called again that morning.

"No, Martha still hasn't arrived." She gave me directions to the hiker's hostel just two blocks away. I drove another block and saw a young man with a backpack. Rolling down the window I asked if he'd seen my sister, *Tortoise*, her trail name.

"Yes," he said, "I shared a shelter with her last night. She should be coming along any minute."

What luck! I'd flown in from across a continent wondering if I'd have to wait a few days or if I'd catch up with her at all. Martha had written to me about people looking for thru-hikers on the trail, one headed north while the other headed south. All it takes is for one to step off the trail to pee and they could miss each other. But it seemed we were arriving in Caratunk just minutes apart.

I parked at the hostel and was greeted by Bailey, a huge yellow lab soaking up the sun on the porch. With his tail wagging, he introduced me to the owner, Paul, who said, "Yes, you can park here. Most of my clients don't have cars so there's plenty of room." Then I went back to the street and looked toward the trail.

There was a small figure in the distance coming slowly into town. I walked toward her, hopeful but unsure. Her dark hair hid her face. When I was finally, reasonably sure, I leapt up, hooted and started running toward her calling, "Martha!" Then I remembered to use her trail name, "Tortoise!"

She stopped and looked up. She looked behind her, then back at me. By then, I was close enough that she recognized me. Her eyes grew wide and her mouth dropped open.

It's hard to hug someone wearing a backpack.

"I didn't know you were coming. How did you know where to find me? I can't believe it!" which was the line she repeated throughout the day.

It was late August. She'd been hiking for six months and other than her fellow thru-hikers, hadn't seen a familiar face since April when family members met her in Virginia. Seeing me here in Maine, well, it was unexpected. I took her pack (which she said threw her off balance) and we walked on into town.

We stopped by the post office where the clerk greeted us warmly. Handing over her mail she asked, "Have you called your mother yet? They've called here three times, first father, then mother, then sister!" Martha just smiled.

We walked together to the hostel. I pulled my pack from the car and went to check in. We opted for an upstairs bedroom. The old house was full of antiques and collectables. In the hall I noticed a ladder back chair and stopped. There sat Raggedy Ann and Andy.

Martha got a shower and changed into clean cotton clothes I'd brought for her. We asked Paul where we could go for lunch. He mentioned a camp store a mile away. Then I reminded him that I had wheels. This opened up several possibilities. We put the top down on the convertible and drove seventeen miles to the slightly larger town of Bingham. On the way, I offered Martha a doughnut from the airport hotel where I'd stayed the night before. I ate half of one in the time it took her to finish hers so I gave her the other half of mine. We shopped for trail food in a small store and then went to a diner and ordered lunch.

Martha stood about five foot nothing and weighed a flat 100 pounds. After six months of hiking she was fit, tan and lean. She could eat anything and looked great. A few days shy of her 50th birthday, she could've passed for thirty-five.

We enjoyed our burgers. She finished hers and was well into her chips before mine was half gone. I gave her my chips, too. We topped it off with berry pie a la mode. Martha ate hers in half the time so I offered her half of mine. We walked around town stopping to pose next to a statue of a huge moose about the size of the one she'd recently seen on the trail.

I told her I'd reserved a campsite near Katahdin when we were thinking we'd be hiking there together. Now I suggested we spend her birthday there. They had a hot tub, canvas tents with beds and a pond where you could go out in a canoe. We could have a look around Baxter State Park and get a preview of Katahdin.

I'd been thinking about the trouble she'd had carrying enough food while going through the long stretches between re-supply stops in the White Mountains. I suggested we leave a food drop for her in the Hundred Mile Wilderness.

From Monson to Katahdin is actually 115 miles. There are only two access points and one was about thirty miles in at the trailhead to Gulf Hagas, a river canyon they call "the Grand Canyon of Maine". We could go there for a day hike and leave the food drop nearby. That way Martha would only have to carry enough food for six days instead of nine or ten. At first she resisted, but gradually warmed to the idea.

Martha suggested I hike with her for the next three days from Caratunk to Monson. Paul offered a shuttle service between the two towns so that afternoon I drove to Monson, left my car and caught a ride back to Caratunk in Paul's van.

Back in Caratunk thru-hikers had continued to come into the hostel. The bunkhouse filled. The guest rooms were taken and there were a couple of tents and hammocks set up in the yard. In late afternoon, Paul brought a big platter of steaming corn-on-the-cob out on the porch. Bailey searched in vain for leftovers.

That night Paul drove his van full of hungry thru-hikers to a nearby pub for dinner. Martha told me her daughter, a vegetarian, had made her promise to eat a salad at every opportunity. That night we gorged on chicken fajita salads. I ordered an extra double chocolate fudge brownie to go.

This was a favorite hang-out of the river rafting crowd that populated the area. The younger hikers were enjoying the lively atmosphere. Martha and I were more inclined to head back to the hostel for a good night's sleep in preparation for an early start in the morning. As soon as we stepped outside, a local asked, "Need a ride back to town?"

He was a river guide. Martha had a friend from the hospital where she'd worked who told her, "When you get to Maine, ask for Eric. Everyone knows Eric." Eric, her nephew, was a river guide, too, and sure 'nuf, this fellow knew him. Small world.

In the morning the dining room at the hostel was packed for an early breakfast. Juice, coffee and cocoa were available on the buffet. A lazy Susan in the middle of the big, round table helped disperse the French toast, fruit, yoghurt, eggs, bacon and home fries. Martha and I sat at a smaller table by a sunny window. I was amazed at how bold my sister had become in order to get a good helping of food. She would have to be. It was gone as soon as it hit the table. In between mouthfuls the hikers gushed with praise for the delicious and ample breakfast. When everyone had eaten we all took our dishes to the kitchen, loaded the dishwasher, wiped the placemats and swept the floor.

Martha and I brushed our teeth, used the flush toilet, hoisted our packs and said good-bye to Raggedy Ann and Andy.

Maine is a very wet state. We walked in the pouring rain. The trail was like a creek except where it climbed steep rock faces and became a waterfall. My shoes and socks were soaked, but my backpack and most of the rest of me stayed dry under my poncho. I'd packed my sleeping bag and clothes in plastic bags inside my pack. At least I had worn the right clothes, my quick-dry shirt and shorts. We were climbing almost 2,000 feet that morning so I was sweating, but when we stopped, we'd get cold, so we didn't stop for long.

We did pretty well under the circumstances, rain, elevation gain and my first day on the trail. At mid-morning we stopped at a bridge and Martha pulled out her trail guide. I pulled out the chocolate fudge brownie leftover from dinner and split it with her. Martha stuck some glasses on her nose. Both of the ear pieces had broken and the nose piece was held together with duct tape. She read the information she sought as the glasses slid slowly off the end of her nose. She caught them in mid air and packed them and the trail guide back into her pack. I asked if she needed a new pair.

She told me this was the second pair she'd had on the trail. She'd lost her first pair and couldn't read her trail guide without them. The only thing she had as an alternative was a little gadget I'd sent her for good luck that included a small compass, a whistle and a magnifying lens. She'd thought it was silly, but packed it anyway. Another sister, Sue, had given her a tiny LED key chain light which she also thought was frivolous, but in fact it probably saved her life.

She'd been hiking through deep snow on Roan Mountain on the Tennessee - North Carolina border. The wind picked up on the treeless summit and turned the snow into a blizzard. She pushed along in white-out conditions without stopping, trying to follow the trail to the next shelter. Darkness fell and she kept moving but her flashlight battery died. The only light she had was the tiny key chain light which guided her through the storm until she reached Overmountain Shelter, a cavernous and drafty old barn. She found the loft full of other hikers hunkered down in the dark. Martha crawled into her sleeping bag exhausted.

After about six miles, we stopped at a shelter for lunch. Martha whipped out her camp stove. In a flash, she'd cooked up hot ramen with tuna. She ate out of the pot while I ate out of the lid. We proceeded on.

In the afternoon the rain stopped. Four hikers we'd seen in Caratunk passed us. We had miles to walk in our wet clothes. She told me this was her rainiest day on the trail for a long time. I figured I'd brought the clouds from the Pacific Northwet.

After hiking twelve miles we arrived at a short stretch of dirt road. I noticed my legs shaking with fatigue. We came to a place where we had to ford a stream but before we did, I asked Martha how much farther we had to go. She consulted her trail guide.

"Three miles," she said.

"Then I need to sit down and rest." I had to take the weight off my legs for a while. We snacked and drank some water. Martha encouraged me saying how well I was doing for my first day on the trail. But soon we were getting chilled so we got up and had a look at the stream.

There was no point in removing our shoes as they were already soaked, so we stepped in trying to stay on the rocks that were higher though still underwater. The cold water was up to our knees and the bank was slippery on the far side, but after the stream crossing, the last three miles got easier. We were within 100 yards of the shelter when we had to ford another stream. I was discovering that on the AT in Maine, every trail starts and ends, and is often punctuated in the middle, by fording a stream.

When we arrived at the shelter the four thru-hikers were already there. I followed Martha's lead. We threw down our sleeping pads and sleeping bags to claim a spot. Then we removed our wet shoes and socks, rung them out and hung them up out of the way. Wearing flip flops, we went to get water from a nearby spring, came back, lit the stove and boiled our water. We made tea in my thermo mug, wrapped it in fleece and then started supper. In minutes our pasta was done. We polished it off with fig Newtons, snack bars with peanut butter, with tea and chocolate for dessert. As darkness fell we climbed into our bags and talked softly while others read or finished their dinner, cleaned their pots and hung their food bags.

I struck up a conversation with the fellow next to me who used to live near Whidbey Island while he was in the Navy. He talked about places he'd kayaked and mountains he'd climbed in Washington State. He was reading *Undaunted Courage* about the Lewis and Clark Expedition. We discussed other real life adventure books like *Endurance* by Shackleton and *The Long Walk* by Slavomir Rawicz.

Martha said our conversation was more interesting than your typical shelter discussions. As Martha and I talked softly between ourselves, I ribbed her about being a frail old lady. I could hear the fellow snicker behind me.

We woke at first light and quietly started breakfast. Martha didn't usually light her stove more than once a day, but for me she lit it for breakfast, lunch and dinner. We had oatmeal with raisins and brown sugar, English muffins with peanut butter and my favorite, chai tea. To top it off, Martha had a coffee nip. She likes to have "breakfast in bed" and put off packing up until the end. We left our flip flops on until the last moment when we put our feet into our soaking wet boots. We hoisted our packs at 7:30, last ones in and first ones out of the shelter.

Martha's trail guide said we'd have only thirteen miles that day and skies had cleared so things were looking up. We climbed a gentle slope to the top of Moxie Bald, a big, rounded rock of a mountain. There were faded prayer flags on the top flapping in a cool breeze hung between stunted spruce trees. From there we could see all the surrounding mountains and ponds. In Maine, what they call *ponds* look like lakes to me. But then their mud puddles are pond sized as I was soon to find out.

As we came down off the rocky summit, I stepped on to a smooth stretch of trail and sank up to my knees. Martha screamed, "Are you stuck? Can you get out?" I was a sloppy mess and broke up laughing. On the way down the mountain, as the mud dried on my legs, I repeated a mantra, "Boot-sucking, stick-grabbing, sock-stinking Maine mud!"

We stopped for lunch by a pond and found a big, flat rock for a dining room table. It was sunny and warm by then so we had to share the rock with three snakes and a chipmunk. Two other hikers came by but found another spot. We ate hot pasta, fig Newtons, snack bars and lemonade. I washed off my legs and tried to dry out my socks and shoes but it was pointless. We'd just be crossing another stream before long.

The sun was out but the trail was still muddy when we got to the east branch of the Piscataquis River. This was more than just a creek crossing. Fortunately, some hikers had just come from the other side and warned us that if you walk straight across you'll sink into a deep hole near the far bank and those hikers were a foot taller than us.

I went in search of a natural walking stick while Martha scoped out the situation. She found a gravel bar downstream and we crossed there getting wet up to our thighs. The current was strong and it was hard to keep our footing on the slippery rocks. With help from our sticks, we managed to stay upright. We learned a few things. It was the biggest ford we'd done yet.

Toward the end of the day we walked on a relatively easy trail alongside a rushing river. My shoulders ached. I had to stop and rest just a mile and a half from the shelter. Martha was very accommodating. She suggested I adjust my pack straps. She tugged here and there and that's all it took. It made a world of difference.

After thirteen miles the blue blazes leading to the shelter turned uphill. I leaned on my stick, my new best friend. We came into the shelter and lo and behold, it was empty. We thought we might have the place to ourselves, which we did, for about three minutes. Meerkat came in right on our heels. He dropped his pack and went off to jump in the river. Martha explained, "He's a Maineh and jumps into cold water anytime he gets the chance." A few minutes later Sugar Daddy arrived. Martha had met them before. Later another couple of guys came up and the six of us settled in. Sugar Daddy was going to the spring to get water and offered to get some for us, too. (Was that how he got his name?)

I went down to the river to clean up a bit using a bandanna to take a sponge bath. We made dinner, tuna and rice, fig Newtons, English muffins and snack bars with peanut butter, tea, and chocolate for dessert. (Note: I didn't eat all this but Martha did.) Martha and I lay quietly in our bags on one side of the shelter listening while the boys carried on a colorful conversation on the other.

Meerkat strung up a hammock, complete with mosquito netting. They discussed the stream crossing earlier that day and how it came up to their privates. Sugar Daddy had a tiny dictionary and looked up the word "turbid", reading the definition aloud for the betterment of all. Then he was asked to report on his attempts to woo a female thru-hiker a few days earlier. It was very entertaining.

We were up early and quietly made breakfast. This time I couldn't finish mine and offered it to Martha. She said I'd been trying to eat like a thru-hiker but it takes a few weeks of hiking for the metabolism to crank up that high.

My toes were sore from coming downhill the day before. She loaned me her toe nail clippers and urged me to take care of my feet. Her toe nails had fallen off months before and were just starting to grow back, a fairly common phenomenon among thru-hikers. I donned my last pair of dry socks for our walk into Monson.

As we prepared to leave the shelter, I risked embarrassing my sister by taking out my camera to capture the scene, a typical shelter at sunrise. To my surprise, other hikers followed suit. One fellow rolled over in his sack, saw what we were doing and in a groggy voice, called out, "Fuck you guys!"

Obviously, not a morning person.

We had just a six mile stretch into Monson, but though the trail was easier, and there was no significant elevation gain, we still had to ford a river, because, hey, we were still in Maine!

We stepped off the trail and onto a quiet road where we were picked up almost immediately by a local offering us a ride into town. As Martha jumped into the cab she instructed me, in hushed tones, to climb into the back of the truck and stay with our packs. Later she told me of thru-hikers whose packs had been stolen, ending their trip.

We drove by beautiful lakeside homes and cabins and passed a rock quarry full of water. The stone cliffs above were reflected in the pool below. It was a crystal clear, blue sky morning and Martha's 50th birthday.

When we got to Monson, we found my car and put our packs in the trunk. By then it was time for first lunch, or second breakfast, so we went to the lunch counter in the General Store. A frantic cook served us burgers while she fretted over some burnt fudge. Next to us was a basket full of oversized muffins. Martha grabbed two dark chocolate ones for her birthday cake.

After lunch we ambled down to the post office and got Martha's mail. A few other hikers were sorting through their mail drops in the parking lot. As we started up the street, Martha stopped in her tracks. There was Slips!

Slips and Martha had started hiking the trail on the same day down in Georgia six months before. He and his friends, Fits and Eats, had given Martha her trail name. She'd start out from the shelter bright and early each morning while they slept in. Then, being younger and faster, they would sprint past her during the day. They'd have a fire going when she'd drag herself into the shelter at night. They marveled at how they would cover the same distance day after day, the Tortoise and the Hares.

The Hares were more inclined to linger in trail towns enjoying the cold beer, hot food and the company of others. Tortoise, on the other hand, would re-supply, get a hot shower, good food, do her laundry and head back out at dawn. Thus, the Tortoise and the Hare arrived in the same town at the same time 2,000 miles from where they'd started. They had a delightful sidewalk reunion.

Slips told Tortoise that Eats had quit the trail and Fits had hurried ahead in order to make it to his brother's wedding in New York City the next week. Slip's brother was coming to give him a ride to summit Katahdin with Fits the next day and then go to the wedding. Then Slips planned to return to Monson to hike the Hundred Mile Wilderness and finish the trail.

He and Martha compared dates. He said upon his return to the trail he'd have to hike fast to catch up with her and summit Katahdin again.

He said he'd bring her some real bagels from New York City and leave them just ahead of her on the mountain with notes saying, "Only four more bagels to go!"

Slips told us he was walking one day and came upon a strange sight. "There's a privy right on the trail," he thought. Then he noticed movement on the other side of the trail. "That tree just moved!" He did a double take and found the "tree" was a moose! He was fumbling for his camera when he heard a snort behind him and turned to find that the "privy" was, too!

Slips was staying at the massage lady's house across the street. This hostel was not in the guidebook. She had a kitchen, a bathroom and a big room with mattresses on the floor where hikers could stay for free in exchange for doing a few chores. She was in the process of painting trim and fixing up the bathroom. You could do housework or weed the garden. He said she was a real nice lady.

We'd learned from southbound hikers on the trail that the other two hostels in town were in stiff competition with each other. Shaw's had put up advertising on trees and shelters in the woods. They served a legendary breakfast. There were also rooms over the launderette but they were more expensive. We'd come back to Monson later, but that night we had a reservation at the camp near Katahdin.

We settled into the rental car and drove to Millinocket to shop for supplies. We did laundry, got milkshakes and strolled through town. Martha tried on new reading glasses at the drug store. She told me she'd pretty much stopped reading which was shocking as Martha had always been a bookworm. I wondered if her battered glasses and the failing light at the shelters were contributing factors. She picked out a purple pair and threw out the old ones at the check out.

We drove on a long dirt road to the Penobscot Outdoor Center. The pavilion was full of young people drinking beer, watching the big screen and hottubbing. We'd been looking forward to the tub for two days, but at the moment, it was fully occupied. So we went to settle into our camp site where we had a canvas tent on a wooden platform.

Martha went off to find the privy while I worked feverishly stringing up balloons and crepe paper between the trees. I set out her cards and presents on the picnic table. By the time she returned, her two chocolate muffins were poked so full of candles they looked like well tanned porcupines. Her smile stretched from ear to ear. I took pictures while she blew out the candles.

She read the cards sent by friends and family and opened her gifts. Dad gave her a membership to the AARP. She had a gift bag with vitamins for 50 Plus, Tiger Balm, Emergency C with Glucosamine,

Seattle Chocolates, salmon sticks, and a baseball cap that said "Tortoise" on the front with the AT symbol. The back said, "Class of 2004". She was thrilled. She put it on immediately and wore it almost constantly for the rest of the time we were together. I cut her chocolate muffins into quarters. I ate one piece while she ate three.

Then we put it all away and went to get showers, wash our hair and have a long sit in the now abandoned hot tub. It felt good on her knees and my shoulders. So we weren't on top of Katahdin, but we had a nice view of it across the pond that night.

Baxter State Park is in the middle of nowhere at the end of the road and the trail. It is twenty miles from Millinocket, the nearest town, and roughly 2,175 miles from the start of the Appalachian Trail in Georgia. Less than a quarter of those who start out to hike the whole trail complete it. For those who do, reaching Katahdin is like crossing the finish line of a very long marathon. The hike to the 5,267 foot peak includes a 4,000 foot elevation gain which means not just walking uphill, but climbing up boulders the size of a minivan. From a distance it looks like one big rock, very intimidating, which is attractive to a lot of people in a masochistic sort of way.

Park staff have about fifty years of experience with thru-hikers finishing the trail here ready to celebrate by partying with friends and family. This explains why there are so many restrictions about entering and camping in the park. The park opens in mid-May and closes in mid-October, so you better finish your hike before the gate closes. Dogs are not permitted anywhere in the 204,733 acres of wilderness preserve. Thru-hikers traveling with a dog have to arrange to board the dog outside the park until they're done. There is a special camping area designated for thru-hikers called the Birches, with shelters and tent platforms. No more than twelve can camp there on any given night and no friends or family are allowed. If a thru-hiker cannot find a site and tries stealth camping, they risk a stiff fine and could be tossed out of the park. Thru-hikers are defined as someone who has entered the park on the AT at Abol Bridge, the South entrance, after hiking through the Hundred Mile Wilderness. So if you've hiked from Georgia and get a ride into town from Abol Bridge and then come back by car to finish your hike, you are treated as a day hiker and cannot camp at the Birches.

Anyone camping in the park has to have reservations and stay in designated sites. You have to pay with cash for any of these sites. Even day hikers cannot enter areas of the park if they're full. There are no paved roads, no stores, no showers, no phones and no electricity. And still they come.

We came to get a sneak preview. We paid $12 just to get in the gate where they gave us a long list of restrictions. We drove first to the ranger station at Katahdin Stream campground near the trailhead to Katahdin. Martha checked the log book reading notes left by many familiar people with congratulations and farewells. There was a bin under the counter full of used day packs that thru-hikers could borrow for their hike to the summit while leaving the bulk of their gear at the station. We saw the list of climbers that had signed in that morning. There was Fits who signed in at 7:30 while Slips signed in at 10:30. Both noted they'd planned to take the trail along the Knife Edge down the other side, something I knew Martha, who had a fear of heights, would avoid.

We started off for the Roaring Rock trailhead where her friends would be coming down, but we weren't allowed in until others had come out. So we found a picnic table by a pond and had a big lunch and a nap in the sun wearing our fleece, while the local Mainehs were swimming in the icy water nearby.

At 3:00 they let us in through the gate. We didn't find Slips and Fits but we got a good feel for the park and started thinking about how Martha would finish her hike and get back to North Carolina.

We returned to our campsite to make a salad and grill chicken over the fire. On an after dinner stroll we took a canoe out on the pond for a sunset paddle. I was looking for moose. We'd seen scat and tracks on the trail but I didn't want to leave Maine without a glimpse of the real thing. Martha was in the bow and said she spotted something swimming on the far side. The light was dim and she couldn't tell what exactly it was but thought it was probably a loon. I told her to keep her eyes on it as I paddled as fast and quietly as I could. She repeated that it was probably just a loon until we saw it move toward shore and come erupting out of the water as big as a horse with water cascading off its back.

"Okay," she said, "it's not a loon."

We glided up quietly as it stood among the trees close to shore and continued chewing, watching us and chewing some more. I was thrilled. After the moose retreated into the woods, we paddled back to the pavilion, soaked in the hot tub and went to bed really happy.

We had a big day planned. We were going to hike the Gulf Hagas trail and leave a food drop and trail magic while we were there. Tourist brochures called it "the Grand Canyon of Maine" but with all the lush vegetation and waterfalls it reminded us of Linville Gorge in the mountains of North Carolina. By leaving a food drop there Martha would not have to carry so much weight. The way she was eating, a three day food supply weighed a lot. We had plenty of food from her mail drop, birthday gifts and care packages. All we needed was a container.

We stopped at a diner in Millinocket, ordered hot chocolate and asked the waitress if she had an empty container. She looked around and came up with a plastic jug with a small lid. We could stuff the food in, but Martha would have to cut it open to get the food out.

We drove up a logging road to the gate house of the Iron Works and got a map. At the trailhead we loaded the container and made a label saying, "Please leave food for Tortoise." I just hoped the bears could read.

We had a smaller plastic tub with a screw on top which we filled with Tootsie Pops. Martha wrote on the lid, "Almost there! Congratulations Class of 2004." We both drew symbols on the top, her Tortoise and my new logo, a Seattle Slug. As we walked down the trail to meet the AT we came upon Sugar Daddy. He was chowing down on a pouch of tuna, first lunch. We gave him a Tootsie Pop and went on to find a place for our food cache. I found an old iron stove among the leaves and pulled the rusty door off. We propped it against a tree by the trail and left the Tootsie Pop container there, trail magic. Nearby, Martha found a hollow tree. We stuck her food drop container inside. We figured the stove door would be a landmark to help her find her cache. She made a note of it in the margins of her trail guide.

After the plastic containers were emptied, we figured it wouldn't be hard to find a day hiker to carry them out to a trash can. The parking lot for the Gulf Hagas Trail was just off the AT. We included a note to that end inside the container. Martha was a strong Pack-it-in, Pack-it-out kind of gal, so that was an essential part of the plan.

Back at the stream crossing by the trailhead we met up with Sugar Daddy finishing his lunch. He stashed his pack off the trail and started hiking the Gulf Hagas Trail with us, which added 8.2 miles to his Hundred Mile Wilderness experience. He soon flew by us and we found ourselves leap frogging with a family of Mainehs. A group of kids ran to the edge of the cliff and then ran back to get the adults. Then they'd run to the next cliff and back again, like walking with a Golden Retriever.

I'd forgotten that Martha does not like heights. In addition, after hiking the steep rock faces in New Hampshire and southern Maine her knees were shot. The bouldering, splashing through mud and my leaning out for views of the gorge were an ordeal for her. Due to an old motorcycle accident she had favored one leg over the other for the last 2,000 miles. She could only step down on her right leg and only step up on her left. One leg was slightly larger than the other. But she soldiered on and restrained herself from screaming when I got close to the edge for a look.

For lunch, we stopped on a flat rock in the sun just above the water's edge. A swarm of orange butterflies landed on our arms and legs, attracted to our sweat. With the waterfall, the sun shining down through the gorge, and the butterflies hovering around us, the whole scene was enchanting.

As we finished our hike, of course, we had to ford yet another stream. Before leaving, we went back to check on the container of trail magic. Four Tootsie Pops were missing. We felt good about becoming "trail angels."

Passing through Millinocket, we bought some chicken and salad and went back to cook our meal at camp. We added our instant rice and dined by the fire with our boots propped up by the coals to dry.

In the morning we started sorting. Taking everything out of the car, the mail drops, care packages, birthday gifts, and extra food, we laid it all out on the table. We made a pile for the Hundred Mile Wilderness and Katahdin, and another for the journey home. I packed up the stuff left over to mail back to our folks in North Carolina. This was the day to prepare for what Martha called her "afterlife", after she finished the trail.

There is no public transportation from Baxter State Park. You have to arrange for a ride or hitchhike at least as far as Medway to catch a bus. We figured since she'd be finishing on Labor Day Weekend, she shouldn't have a problem finding a ride. When she got out she thought she'd get a room at the motel in Medway. She could catch a bus the next morning from the gas station next door.

We put together a box of things she might like to have on her long bus and train ride back to North Carolina. Once she caught the bus, her pack would be stowed so we thought it would be nice to have a shoulder bag of things to keep at her seat. She could have a book, snacks, a water bottle, a sweater and her wallet. She was grateful for the clean cotton clothes I'd brought for her.

"But where are we going to put this package?" she asked. I suggested we mail it from Monson to the Medway post office.

Later, in Millinocket, we found an Army Navy store where Martha bought a fanny pack for the last leg of the trail. She'd had one when she started and found it very useful to keep small items like a camera and snacks handy wearing the pouch in front. Her first one wore out long ago but she was happy to find a replacement. At a thrift shop we found a shoulder bag that would work for the bus and train trip.

Then we drove to Medway to find the motel, bus stop and post office and check the feasibility of our plan. They were all within a mile of each other. But there was one hitch. The post office opened at 9:00 and the bus left the station at 9:30. Timing would be tight and there was just one bus a day. She decided to take a cab. She planned to get to the motel on Monday of Labor Day weekend, have a good meal and a bath that night. Then as soon as the post office opened on Tuesday she'd get her mail drop with her bus bag and clean clothes, and catch a taxi back to the motel just in time to change clothes, catch the bus and head home. She had a plan.

We drove back to Monson and checked in at the massage lady's house. A note on the door said, "Welcome Hikers". Inside were more notes. She was out hiking for a few days but there were instructions about chores that could be done in exchange for a night's stay. Martha needed a nap. I went out and got our laundry started and then went to the General Store to look for boxes in which to mail our packages. Tim, the store owner, was happy to help. I bought a bottle of maple syrup to include in the package to the folks in North Carolina.

After mailing Martha's package to Medway and the leftovers to North Carolina, I got the laundry and went back to the hostel. I was cleaning up the kitchen in exchange for my stay, when I met Walks Softly who said he was from Weaverville, North Carolina. That's where my best friend from college lives. She has three daughters and he knew their eldest who had been in all the school plays.

When Martha woke up we headed out for dinner at the BBQ place down the street. She'd been munching on chips and chocolate and then we ate a big dinner. I got a piece of apple pie and took it back to the hostel to eat later. Martha was so stuffed she had to lie down. I took a walk around, my last night in Maine. Monson is a picturesque village of quaint farm houses, steepled churches and rustic barns. I walked out of town toward the quarry as the sun hovered over the horizon and the warm colors glowed.

When I got back, I checked the fridge and found that someone had eaten my apple pie! It was Walks Softly and he was guilt ridden. I should have known better, the way thru-hikers eat. He apologized. We settled in for the night as other thru-hikers gathered outside to enjoy a beer around a campfire in the twilight.

In the morning Martha and I were up early and packed our things. We were the first at the breakfast counter in the General Store as the frantic cook was fretting over some chocolate cakes she'd burnt.

While Martha finished her stack of pancakes I wandered around the store and came upon a banjo and guitar in the back corner. Tim said there was a Hoe Down there every Friday night and we were welcome to join in. I play banjo but this one had six strings and was tuned like a guitar so I didn't quite know what to do with it. Tim gave us a sample of his twelve string guitar. He talked about the thru-hikers who had sat in with the locals in the past. We were disappointed to miss it, but on Friday night Martha would be in the Hundred Mile Wilderness and I would be on a jet flying back across the country.

After breakfast, I drove Martha south on Pleasant Road back to the trailhead where we'd entered town a few days before. Martha insisted on not cutting corners. Even though another road headed out of town to the north and met up with the trail three miles hence, she insisted on coming back to where we'd left it on the south side of town. She wanted to be able to say she'd walked by every white blaze on the AT.

We hugged, said good-bye and good luck and she started down the trail. Then she turned. "I feel like I'm abandoning you!" she said. I felt the same way. I took her picture by the first white blaze and another as she disappeared into the woods. After six months of hiking, the Hundred Mile Wilderness and a climb up Katahdin was all that was left between her and the end of the trail. Then a bus and a train would lead her to a soft bed, a hot shower and all the food she could eat.

Driving back into town, I came upon Walks Softly. I offered him a ride. He was heading to the other trailhead north of town. On the way I told him he could rid himself of all guilt if he'd do me one small favor. I wrote a note on a banana and asked him to leave it by the trail where Martha would find it when she got there in about twenty minutes. It said, "To Tortoise, Love Slug".

That was in August, 2004. Martha completed her thru-hike as planned and returned to North Carolina. Though Martha didn't want a computer, she accepted a laptop from Dad for Christmas and spent the next few months typing up her trail journal. She gave copies to a few close friends and family members. She's a good writer. We urged her to publish it but she wasn't interested. So I was even more grateful that I had a copy of my own.

She moved back into her rustic home in the mountains of North Carolina and tried to go back to work in her old job at the hospital, but she soon returned to her previous state of misery. Finally, she signed up to do trail work as a volunteer and met the man of her dreams, a Cajun cook and trail building expert from Louisiana who went by the trail name "LA Bear".

He was also a thru-hiker and as an employee of the Appalachian Trail Conservancy, he was steeped in trail culture. They fit together like two peas in a pod. I'd never known my sister to be so happy. But she continued to struggle with her job. So two years later, she left the hospital and vowed to hike the trail again, this time starting in Maine and heading south.

Maine doesn't thaw out until June so that's when most Southbound thru-hikers, or SOBOs, begin. It's more of a challenge because they start in the most rugged terrain when it's hot and humid and buggy. At the other end of their hike, in the Southern Appalachians, it gets pretty cold and snowy come November. That gives them a smaller window of good hiking weather. But she was determined and this time LA Bear would be meeting her along the way and cheering her on.

Meanwhile, out in the Pacific Northwest...

Natural Disaster

Okay, so maybe it was a bad idea, a naturalist marrying a stand-up comedian. I get up early and go for a run or a walk outside. He sleeps in till noon. He loves urban commotion, the spotlight, the crowds. I love the woods, the sound of birds, wind in the trees. I go to bed to read and turn out the light by 10:00. He stumbles to bed in the wee hours.

Delusional.

We'd met while working together on small natural history cruise ships in the Pacific Northwest. He was the Expedition Leader in charge of coordinating logistics with the ship's crew. After getting to know him I called him the "Exhibition Leader" as he obviously craved attention. He entertained at cocktail hour with skits from Monty Python or recited the *Legend of Sam McGee* which he knew by heart. He was full of mischief and a lot of fun.

I worked as part of a team of naturalists and historians, each with our own specialty. We'd point out birds, discuss whales, lead hikes, identify plants and share research. David introduced all of our talks and usually stayed to glean what he could from each lecture. Thus, he was good at dinner conversations with the guests.

We packed that summer with adventures, jumped into rushing rivers, flew over glaciers, watched Orca and Humpback Whales in Alaska. Near Sitka, a Grizzly approached me on the beach. Watching through binoculars from the ship David radioed, "It's been really nice getting to know you."

The naturalists had been sent ashore to check things out before the passengers were brought in by Zodiac. We spread out. I'd been watching the bear from the trees, standing still and quiet. David's voice on the radio alerted the bear to my presence. Now, I was something to investigate. I responded to David with a description of what I saw before me. The bear rose up on its hind legs and sniffed the air.

Our conversation alerted every other staff member carrying a radio and several things started happening at once. Two male naturalists on shore left the others and came around the point to stand with me. We raised our arms in the air and shouted, "Yo Bear!" According to the rule book, that is supposed to scare the bear away. But it just cocked its huge head and continued ambling in our direction.

The bosun, piloting a Zodiac full of passengers, steered as close as he could. All together they threw their arms in the air and shouted. They sounded an air horn but only got the bear's attention for an instant before it continued toward the landing where the five of us naturalists were gathering.

Grizzly bears can run thirty miles an hour, so if it had broken into a run, it would have overtaken us in about three seconds. We walked slowly and quietly so as not to trigger that predatory behavior.

Meanwhile, the captain had jumped into an empty Zodiac and sped directly to shore. Our whale expert, a small woman in her fifties, had drawn her only weapon, a can of bear spray. She aimed it toward the bear, ready to fire. As the boat brushed her leg she turned to the captain as if noticing him for the first time and asked, "Permission to come aboard?" We all climbed in and pushed off to watch the bear from a safe distance.

The next thing I knew, David had invited me to meet the folks.

It was a gorgeous summer day when we took the ferry up to Orcas Island in the San Juan Archipelago. We stood out on deck cruising by forested shorelines, looking out for whales, waterfowl and eagles. We found a ride to the end of their road and walked with our packs by horses and sheep. When I saw the Jag in the garage, I thought, "Oh no! They're not going to let me put my feet on the furniture."

We came in the front door and dropped our packs. A wide staircase led into the living room with two storey windows framing a view of the water. But his folks were hanging out in the kitchen with their feet on the chairs. I liked them immediately.

We spent our days hiking with their two yellow labs. We'd strip down and fly out on the rope swing and drop into the lake. We'd row out in the skiff and put in the crab pot for dinner, or help chop and stack firewood. Then, at the end of the day we'd gather for a great meal, sit back and talk into the night. I loved visiting his folks. So, out on the island when he put a ring on my finger, even though we'd only known each other a few months, I said yes.

I moved in with him in Seattle and got full time work in a city park. I supported him while he developed his comedy career. Then he supported me while I went back to school to get my teaching certificate. It was a partnership in the early years. As a budding comedian he was ambitious and hard working. But it's a career that's very demanding, a career that made frequent promises and just as frequently broke them.

I withered in the city. So we moved to a small town nearby, at the foot of the Cascade Mountains, and later to Whidbey Island so I could be among friends while he traveled. David was miserable on Whidbey. With his late night gigs he often missed the last ferry and had to sleep in his car. So we moved back to the same small town near Seattle just blocks from our first house.

Still, it wasn't really a question of geography, but compatibility. Our friends belonged to two distinct groups and they mixed like oil and water. In each place we lived I built a garden and just as it got established, we'd move, each garden abandoned. His work carried him across the country and occasionally overseas. He skipped out on birthdays, anniversaries and holidays with his family to do last minute comedy gigs.

We tried to talk it out and each time things improved for a while. But then we'd soon slip back into old patterns a little worse than before. I felt neglected, ignored. I didn't fit in with his urban friends or entertainment industry lifestyle. After ten years, I gave up. It wasn't what I considered a marriage. I asked for a divorce.

This wasn't uncommon for us. Our marriage had been a struggle from the start. The difference was that this time, it really was over. I was tired of trying to make it work. They say opposites attract, but they don't say they stay together.

In addition to my divorce, and at the same time, I had to evict a delinquent renter. We'd bought a second house a year before. It was in a neighborhood we'd always liked in Anacortes, on another island between Orcas and Whidbey. Though you could reach it by bridge, it was still too far from Seattle and the airport for David's frequent flights, so we decided to rent it out until the day when we might arrange to live there. It was just a few blocks from the water. We both loved being able to walk to the center of town to shop or run errands. David liked seeing the masts of the boats from the main street.

But our first renter never paid the full rent on time. We tried to negotiate and reason with her but the results were the same. She got further and further behind. It took months of legal maneuvering and finally the sheriff's knock on the door to get her to leave, which she did abruptly, leaving truck loads of stuff behind. We'd decided this house would go to me in the divorce, so David didn't help with the legal hurdles, costs or clean up. Without a job, I couldn't afford to live there either. I had to find a new renter, someone that would actually pay the rent.

I thought it was interesting that I kept having to deal with piles of garbage, truckloads of garbage, mostly other people's garbage.

When I started moving out of my house with David, my friend Mac said I could store my things in his shed. "It's almost empty!" he said. He was away when I arrived with a truck load of my things. I backed up to the shed and opened the door. It was piled high with a year's worth of recyclables. I had to break down boxes and move his trash out so I could unload my things. Then I filled the truck with stacks of cardboard, bags of cans, boxes of glass and newspaper, and take them to the recycle center. I figured it was the cost of the storage.

When I moved into the house sitting job on Whidbey Island, the owners had just cleaned out their basement and asked me to deposit several bags of garbage in their can over the course of the winter. I didn't generate much myself so there would be plenty of room in the garbage can. I filled my car with boxes of their old newspapers, cans and bottles and took them to the recycling center.

My evicted renter left behind piles of garbage and recyclables, too, plus old box springs, a dryer and a bunch of household items. Legally, I couldn't keep any of it. So I put it on the nearest public property, the sidewalk out front, where she could have retrieved it if she had arrived before the neighbors.

All this garbage seemed like the outer manifestation of my inner clean-up project, deciding what in my life I really wanted to keep and what needed to be evicted. Breaking free of life's garbage is a lot of hard work. I had stored my things and all that I had with me was what fit into my small car. I would start all over.

There are pauses in a person's life when everything familiar grinds to a halt. This had never happened to me more distinctly. I was standing at a threshold, a clear line between past and future. As I considered what might come next, what job I might pursue, where I might live when this house sitting job ended, what new relationship I might eventually find, I realized that the door was wide open, the slate wiped clean. This was my opportunity to finally hike the Appalachian Trail!

Making a Plan

I went to the woods because I wished to live deliberately,
to front only the essential facts of life, and see if I could not
learn what it had to teach, and not, when I came to die,
discover that I had not lived.

Henry David Thoreau, Walden

I wrote in my journal;

I've always been intrigued by the idea of submersing myself in
wilderness. The Appalachian Trail is pretty tame in places. There are
lots of other people on the trail and towns a week or so apart. It's not
like walking across Alaska. But I think it will pose plenty of challenges,
some with people, some with weather or terrain, some with my own
abilities and fears. But I've always wanted to do it.

One big attraction is to simplify life down to as little as possible.
No hummy, buzzy things, no phones, no TV, no computers, no traffic,
no little lights glowing from all corners at all hours.

Maybe I'm running away from responsibility. Maybe I'm running
toward a dream. Maybe it will be good therapy, or escapism. There are
so many negatives in my life, a failed marriage, no job, no home, no
plan, except this. So I focus for short stints on getting a divorce from
an inaccessible husband, evicting a delinquent renter and then study
the prospect of walking 2,175 miles by myself with as little on my back
as possible. I feel like I am finally getting something right.

I got organized. My goal was to get everything in order so that I
could start hiking by the first of March just three months away. But a
lot of things had to fall into place first. I kept my intentions to myself.

I began getting up before dawn and doing yoga, then walking
several miles in the winter wind and rain on back roads or woodland
trails seeking the steep terrain. My clothes would get soaked.
Temperatures were freezing, but I stayed warm as I walked. When I got
home I could take a hot shower and change into clean, dry clothes, a
luxury I knew I would not have on the trail.

I read books about the Appalachian Trail. One was written by Earl Shaffer the first thru-hiker. He'd come back from World War II with a heavy heart and a lot on his mind so decided to take a walk.

The trail had been created from a dream in 1921 to a reality in 1937, but was still a bit rough. He hiked the trail for the first time in 1948, before there were many shelters or hostels or good maps or signs or bridges. No one thought it was possible to walk the entire length of the trail in a thru-hike. But when he finished, he convinced a panel of experts from the Appalachian Trail Conference that he had actually hiked the whole thing. Later he hiked it again from the opposite direction, another first. And on the 50th anniversary of his first hike, he hiked it for the last time at seventy-eight years old. He had some recommendations for others who might follow.

> *Good planning, a sturdy physique, exceptional determination, and ingenious adaptability are essentials on a long strenuous foot journey... Above all, do not underestimate the difficulties involved or overestimate your own capabilities. Both good luck and good management are necessary.*

I'd been trying to find a thru-hiker's account that might closely resemble my own situation. I found a book written by a blind man who hiked the trail with a seeing-eye dog, a book by a young man who hiked with a group of other young men. And finally I found a book written by a woman, but in the first chapter realized that she'd hiked the trail when she was half my age and had her boyfriend along to curl up with on cold nights or share the weight of her pack, not to mention the added security.

The memoir I found that most closely matched my own set of circumstances was the unpublished account written by my sister, Martha, after her trek. I read that one twice.

I also had a collection of her letters from before her trek and those written while on the trail. They listed her equipment, several ways to set up a tarp, debates over walking sticks, foot wear, stoves, sleeping bags, maps and guide books, places that lacked good water, which shelters to avoid, as well as her experiences in different hostels and trail towns.

Her letters were spiced with the vocabulary of thru-hikers referring to Southbound and Northbound thru-hikers as SOBO's and NOBO's. Those who hike part of the trail going north and the rest going south are Flip Flops. Those who hike continuously back and forth are YOYOs. MUD was short for mindless ups and downs. SUD meant steep ups and downs, and PCC stood for pointless creek crossings. Blue Blazers are those that take easier side trails, Yellow Blazers hitch-hike around sections, and Aqua Blazers are those that raft the Shenandoah River that parallels the AT instead of hiking that section.

I'd been buying, weighing, testing trail food and practicing with my new camp stove. I didn't have a set of kitchen scales at my cottage so I took food into the grocery store and weighed it on the produce scales. I had to try to find as much variety, nutrition and flavor as possible but was limited by my cooking equipment, one pot with a lid, one spoon, a camp cup and a water bottle. There were lots of gourmet backpacking pre-made dinners, "just add water", but that would be expensive on a long hike. I steered more toward the bulk food aisle. Oatmeal, pasta, nuts, raisins, dried potatoes and beans with packets of tuna or chicken and various condiments to try to make them interesting. I picked up extra packets of mustard, soy sauce, relish, parmesan cheese, chili peppers, salt, pepper and sugar when I ate at fast food restaurants and coffee shops. I'd carry enough hot chocolate mix to wash it all down.

For New Years Eve, my faithful friend, Kelly, agreed to accompany me on an overnight hike to the Olympic Hot Springs. The Olympic Peninsula is famous for big trees and rain and this trip was no exception. But it was just a short two mile hike in and then there'd be the hot springs! It couldn't be that bad. Could it?

We walked in through a drifting mist swirling among the evergreen giants. At the camping area we pitched our tent and threw our bags inside. Crossing a log bridge we peered into the gorge below. We could barely hear each other speak over the roar of cascading Boulder Creek. On the far side we investigated several steaming pools nestled against the cliff surrounded by tall trees and found we had the place to ourselves. We chose a pool at the base of a rock face with dripping moss. Leaving our clothes under the branches of a tall cedar, we slid into the murky bath and soaked while listening to the constant drip of the rain forest around us. It was late afternoon when the light faded from the canopy high above us.

We dried off a little and put on our clothes while still glowing from the hot springs. That warmth soon ebbed as we crossed the creek, returned to camp and started making dinner. As darkness fell the rain gained momentum. This was rainforest rain, a real soaker. Huddling under low branches we wished our pasta would hurry up and cook already. We compared rain gear. Neither of us was dry. We discussed stoves and all their complicated parts and ate hurriedly. After cleaning our pots we rushed into the tent and climbed into moist sleeping bags. We figured it must be midnight somewhere, wished each other Happy New Year and went to sleep early.

At first light we packed up and headed for the hot springs to warm up. My bag was over twenty years old and showing its age. I'd shivered through most of the night even while wearing several warm layers. My raincoat wasn't really waterproof and my boots weren't either.

After a nice soak, we got out of the pools, dressed quickly and headed down the trail. The rain stopped, but the wind picked up. With wet hair and damp clothes it sucked out what little heat we'd retained from the hot springs. I was relieved to get to the car, the heater, and the café in town where we ordered a big, hot breakfast. Kelly still claims I was trying to kill her. (She'd made that claim on several previous adventures.)

It was that trip that convinced me to cough up the dough for all new gear. It wasn't just a matter of comfort or fashion. It was a matter of survival.

Beyond Backpacking

One day while bringing the mail into the old farmhouse, my eyes fell upon a book on the shelf, *Beyond Backpacking* by Ray Jardine. Jardine was legendary. My sister had told me about his unorthodox gear and approach to hiking. They called it *the Ray Way*. He hiked the Pacific Crest Trail annually and hiked the Appalachian Trail just for comparison. He'd adventured in Alaska and was known by rock climbers in Yosemite for his inventions and techniques. I took the book over to my little cabin and dove in. The comments written by others said his suggestions sometimes seemed a bit extreme, but every thing they'd tried had worked well. When I told my sister I'd found this book where I was house-sitting, she said, "It was meant to be."

That book became my Bible. My goal was to keep my pack weight down to a quarter of my body weight or less. For me, that was thirty-two pounds fully loaded with food, fuel and water. My old pack weighed 4 pounds with nothing in it! I gave it away to a bigger, stronger friend. I researched equipment and then went shopping. As I weighed and tried on packs I couldn't help but overhear conversations between sales people and other customers.

"This pack is a good size for a weekend outing," said the clerk with a tone of authority, "but if you're going out any longer, you'll need this bigger one."

The customer nodded gravely at the salesman. He was the expert, was he not?

"Bull!" My inner voice shouted. "You carry everything for a weekend that you'd need for a week or two or a month, except you'd bring more food or re-supply along the way. You don't need a frame. Let the contents of your pack provide the structure. Just keep it light and be careful how you pack it. You dress in layers of quick dry clothing. You rinse out a shirt one day and wear it the next. If it's cold, you don't change clothes. You just add layers and keep moving. You carry the smallest pack you can and minimize the weight and you can enjoy your hike more, no matter how long you're out there."

I was already sounding like a thru-hiker, very opinionated about gear, except that I had yet to try this out and the whole monologue took place in my head.

I made several spread sheets on my computer, a list of the legal steps required to evict my renter, a list of procedures for my divorce, things to buy for my trek, their estimated weight, the estimated cost of my hike, an estimated timeline and a list of addresses for mail drops. I was a real multi-tasker, a project manager. Whenever I could check anything off my lists, I felt a big sense of relief and accomplishment. I was making progress, moving toward my goal.

My new pack weighed just ounces when empty, not pounds. I bought a new sleeping bag with a compression stuff sack to make it fit in my small pack. They said it would keep me warm down to ten degrees. It was only fifty six inches long. Since I'm just five three I would fit nicely and it's lighter. I wouldn't carry a tent. There are usually shelters or hostels, but I'd carry a nine ounce tarp, line and stakes that weighed less than a pound, just in case. I got a lightweight Titanium cook pot and a Whisperlite stove. Walking the trails around the Island I broke in a new pair of boots.

I decided to do a Flip Flop. I'd had a good summer job for over a decade leading hiking tours in Olympic National Park and the Columbia River Gorge. The job would be my only income for the year. So I planned to start my AT hike early in the season in Georgia. I'd travel north going as far as I could before I had to fly back to the Northwest to work.

My summer hiking tours involved leading day hikes, with a small pack, staying overnght in lodges and eating good meals. My summer break would be a chance for my body to recover with enough activity to stay in shape to finish the trail. At the end of August, I'd fly back to the AT in Maine and head south. I looked forward to hiking through New England in the fall.

Letting the Cat Out

I stopped job hunting. I cleaned up my rental house and found a good renter who signed a year long lease. I was making progress. Eventually I began to share my secret.

For almost a decade, I'd been getting together with two girlfriends for a hike each month. Kelly, Linda and I always had a great time together, hiking, backpacking and kayaking. When I told them I'd finally decided to do the Appalachian Trail after so many years of just talking about it, they threw me a party.

They came up to Whidbey Island on a gorgeous day in February. Most folks know that it rains a lot in the Pacific Northwest, but if you pay close attention you'll find that there is typically a week in February, just before we're all about to slit our wrists or jump off a bridge, when the sun comes out and we're saved! We had such a day.

It was sunny and warm. We walked Ebey's Bluff, my favorite trail on Whidbey Island. Sitting on a 400 foot bluff we looked out over the water. To the south we could see 14,000 foot Mount Rainier looming over the far end of Puget Sound. To the north we could see the glow of Mount Baker in its lofty station near the Canadian border. And across the water we could see the quaint Victorian seaport of Port Townsend. The entire snow capped Olympic Range stretched out behind it with the crown of Mount Olympus dappled in blue and white.

Those summits, Mount Olympus, Mt. Baker and Mt. Rainier, were the pinnacles of my home. They'd been the points of my compass for thirty years. A winter appearance of all three at once was a good omen. I felt as if they'd joined the party to wish me good luck and farewell.

The thought had occurred to me that I might not return. There are risks we take so often that we give them no thought, anytime we get into a car for instance. But this 2,000 mile trek on an unfamiliar trail had many unknowns. I had thought about the possibilities, the potential hazards, wild animals, weather, terrain, and perhaps the most unpredictable... other people. I might have problems with my equipment or my own abilities. I'd never tested my body like this before. When I expressed some doubts to my friends, Kelly looked perplexed.

"Why wouldn't you make it?"

I appreciated her vote of confidence, but reminded her that only about twenty percent of those who set out to walk the entire trail in one season actually finish.

"I might get sick, or have an accident and break a leg or sprain an ankle, or worse." No matter how well prepared I might be, there was a strong possibility of failure.

But we put those thoughts aside. Sitting in the tall grass at the top of the bluff, we soaked up the mid winter sun, shared a thermos of tea and visited with passing hikers and their dogs.

Returning by the beach, both women picked out a tiny pebble for me to take along on my trek. I said, "Some friends you are, weighting me down with rocks!" Those pebbles rode in my pack and anchored me to home.

After our hike, we returned to the cottage. Kelly and Linda created a festive fondue farewell dinner. Steve, an old friend from Portland, was in town and came by to wish me well. But we still had more food than we could eat, so we invited the owners of the cottage who had recently returned home to the big farmhouse. It was a fun and messy evening full of story swapping and laughter.

I asked Steve, "If you were going to go hiking for six months, what one thing would you be sure to bring?" Without hesitation he answered simply, "A car."

Everyone departed one by one. I was expressing my last minute doubts to Steve saying I wasn't sure if I'd trained enough or how well I'd do on the trek. His words stayed with me on the trail whenever I needed to psyche myself up for my next big challenge.

"Piece of cake."

I wrote a song about that later.

Piece of cake, piece of cake,
My stomach flutters and my old knees shake,

My heart's a pounding like a big earthquake,
But my hiking buddy says, "Piece of cake."

When I first left the old North State,
I had good reason to hesitate,
The trail I was walking crosses 14 states,
But my hiking buddy says, "Piece of cake."

Broken

Though I'd asked David for a divorce in early October, he didn't deal with it for months. He was busy producing a big DVD of himself, a five camera shoot in a downtown Seattle night club. Then there was the holiday season where he made big bucks traveling all over entertaining at corporate parties. So it wasn't until late January, when his schedule opened up, that he began to focus on the divorce.

I'd heard about other people's divorces. There are a lot of legal steps and some take a while. People go to counseling, work with a mediator, get a lawyer. They dicker things out for months or years. I met one woman who lived separated from her husband for decades before proceeding to a divorce and then the legal process took several more years.

I'm not that kind of girl. Once it's done, it's done. After waiting for months for David to turn his attention toward the divorce, it took only a few weeks for us to hammer out an agreement.

We worked out the details at the kitchen table with lists of assets, columns of numbers and a box of Kleenex. When it got really hard, we took a walk in the woods, then came back to start again. Once we'd worked it out, we had a lawyer draw up the papers. We met in his downtown office and signed the agreement. The documents would be filed with a judge and at least one of us would have to be present in court six weeks later. I hoped to be hiking by then. David agreed to go.

That night we walked the wet streets to our favorite restaurant, split a steak and the check, and walked home together. Just before midnight, I drove him to the airport to fly to his next gig. With tears in our eyes we kissed good-bye. Our marriage had ended.

I think each individual has an idea about how their married life will be. I expected we'd love and support each other. I expected we'd work as a team. I expected it to last. The marriage becomes a third being. It's not one person or the other. It's not even the two combined. It's another entity altogether. That third being was dead. It was sad to say good-bye.

That night I slept alone in our house, an old familiar feeling. I played the piano. It had belonged to David's grandmother so it would remain with him. I'd been learning a new song, *Caledonia*, a song of farewell. It was my way to grieve. The following morning I drove myself to the airport, left the car for David's return and departed for the Appalachian Trail.

Base Camp, Carrboro, North Carolina

When my sister hiked the trail, she wasn't very communicative with the family. She doesn't like phones and refuses to leave messages on answering machines. She'll write letters, but says her email address is "nevergonnahappen.com." She packed up her mail drops, sealed them and left them with my folks with the estimated dates for mailing them to a list of post offices along the trail.

Many thru-hikers use mail drops as a way to re-supply trail food and goods they'll need along the way. My folks were happy to send her packages upon request. In return they got a letter from the trail every two or three weeks and a total of four phone calls in six and a half months. My parents had a guide book and a map they used to track my sister's progress. They watched the weather channel and saw how snow storms hit the mountains in early spring and rain flooded the rivers in the summer. But they got little word from Tortoise.

I've heard that it's a mother's job to worry. Well, my mom was exceptionally good at it. Over the course of the summer, mom developed strange symptoms. She got stomach aches and nausea. She couldn't eat. She felt lethargic but couldn't sleep. She had heart palpitations. She went in for tests, but the doctors couldn't find anything wrong. This went on for months. Finally, they told her it was in her head. The day Tortoise completed her hike, mom miraculously recovered.

So, when I flew back east, I brought my supplies and equipment and laid it all out in my parents' den. Mom went shopping with me to finish gathering what I'd need. I showed my parents my water treatment system. I involved them in measuring and bagging food and explained the nutritional value of corn pasta over refined white flour. I showed them how my stove works, explained that my new sleeping bag goes down to ten degrees, showed them my Thermarest sleeping pad, laid out my quick-dry hiking clothes and first-aid supplies, and sorted my mail drops. Mom helped me collect odds and ends to put in them: safety pins, Zip-lock bags, mailing labels. Dad bought me a new pocket knife. Mom contributed her flip flops and umbrella. They were fully involved in preparing for my departure.

Just before I left, mom treated me to a haircut. The hair dresser told me if I bought this mousse I could style it. I said I wouldn't be using any mousse. She suggested I use a blow dryer to make it go this way or that. "No," I said, "I'll be hiking for the next six months. I won't have electricity, a mirror, a brush or a comb, and I'll probably be wearing a hat most of the time." She kept cutting.

Each night we watched the weather report on the evening news. The forecast for my departure was good. Northwestern Georgia had remarkably warm days for February. I threw my arms in the air. "Yes!" It looked like I'd get an easy start.

The family gathered for a farewell dinner with siblings, nieces and nephews. The next day my parents drove me down to Georgia. It's a long drive. At sunset we checked into a motel. That night we watched a documentary on PBS about a ship and crew that got stuck in the ice in Hudson Bay 200 years ago. Some resorted to cannibalism. None of them survived. After a while my Dad turned to me and asked, "Should we be watching this?"

The morning dawned sunny and warm. We went out to breakfast and I ordered steak and eggs knowing that breakfast would be oatmeal for the foreseeable future.

It's not a straight shot to the trailhead. We had to stop and ask directions twice. I found the place names difficult to pronounce, and then I'd have to listen carefully to decipher the thick Southern drawl, but we finally made it to Amicalola State Park.

There's a big set of scales at the ranger station where hikers were weighing their packs. I didn't want to know. I used the flush toilet. It would be the last one for a while. We looked at the exhibits, checked out the books and maps.

I bought a post card to send to Tortoise. She'd been in Louisiana camping with her boyfriend. I wrote a quick note and mailed it from there. It felt weird to have said good-bye to the whole family except the one person who had hiked the trail before.

I signed the register with my new trail name, "Scout". Now it was official. I had picked this name out of my favorite book, *To Kill a Mockingbird*. In the book and the movie, I loved the characters, especially Scout. She reminded me of my up-bringing in the hot, muggy south. I'd spent summers on my grandparent's farm, driving a tractor in the tobacco fields, fishing with granddaddy, shelling butter beans with grandma, eating her fried chicken and homemade biscuits, drinking lemonade and sweet tea, swinging on a tire swing with my cousins, wearing bib overalls, getting sweaty and dirty.

I went to college in the mountains, hiking whenever I got the chance. I loved the old cabins in the hills, the fall foliage and the winter snows. I'd studied Appalachian History and worked as a National Park intern on the Blue Ridge Parkway. But I'd lived in the Pacific Northwest longer than I'd lived in the south. This trek was a way to reconnect with my roots.

Besides the connection with Scout in *To Kill a Mockingbird*, I was also a pretty good Girl Scout when I was young and had grown up to become a hiking guide which seemed like added justification for the name. A friend embroidered the name on a hat for me, "Scout, Class of 2006".

I'd been thinking about this trail name phenomenon. Every thru-hiker had a trail name, whether you picked one for yourself or were named by others. Even if you insisted that your name was just Jim. You'd be called, "Just Jim". Some trail names referred to an event and each time you introduced yourself you'd be inclined to re-tell the story as in the names "Mickey One Sock" or "Donkey Love". Others just sounded cool like "Feather" or "Bluebird". When I introduced myself as "Scout", I rarely had to explain. *To Kill a Mockingbird* was well known in the south.

I figured when people start out to thru-hike the Appalachian Trail, they know it's going to take a chunk of time out of their lives. They'll be leaving a lot behind, a job, a family, a home. So to introduce themselves like they normally would, "I'm Jason, the bus driver," or "Ms. Brennan, the math teacher," or "Jessie, the mailman," or "Olivia, the barista". We might say, "I live in that house by the hardware store," or "in that gated community" or "in that apartment complex". None of it really applies on the AT.

On the trail, everyone starts on a level playing field. You walk with people, share shelters, sleep in bunks next to people you might never bump into off the trail. So you leave it all behind, including your name, and you become someone new. You belong to a distinct group. You are now a thru-hiker. Your new address is the Appalachian Trail. I'd just walked away from a name, a house and a title. I liked my new name, my new address, my new role.

There were a few others at the ranger station, some big guys with big packs, a young couple, and a woman with legs like tree trunks and strawberry blonde hair wearing a seasoned pack. She seemed to be watching everyone and smiling. I noticed the names of hikers who had signed the register ahead of me. Four young men had signed in writing that their destination was "Katadin". I studied the word. Isn't there a silent *h* in there? Somehow it made me feel a little less intimidated and the 2,000 mile target a little less daunting. I mean, we might actually make it despite all our imperfections.

I bought a map and shouldered my pack. My parents took my picture, hugged me good-bye and I excitedly started up the approach trail for Springer Mountain.

The AT Proper

There are options on the trail. Some people drive up an old service road to get within a mile of the top of Springer Mountain and the official start of the Appalachian Trail. I hiked the approach trail, 8.8 miles from the ranger station. It's not that I'm trying to prove anything. It's just that the service road was rough and rutted. My elderly parents drove a small car. Besides, I felt like hiking, which is a good thing when you set out to walk 2,000 miles.

March first was a warm, sunny day. I was anxious to get started, full of adrenalin and solar powered! My pack was stuffed, at full capacity, but it didn't slow me down. I've led groups of hikers for twenty years keeping track of twenty people on a trail. This time I was on my own and I was elated! I could go at my own pace! I didn't have to wait for anyone, or struggle to keep up. I didn't have to worry about anyone but myself. It was liberating. I was free!

I made good progress climbing the steep slopes of red clay up Springer Mountain. The glitter of mica at my feet added to the excitement with each step. I passed other hikers who had stopped for water or to check their maps. A couple of young men sat by a trail sign. One looked red faced and tuckered out. I stopped briefly to chat. They'd been in the military together but hadn't seen each other for a while. I moved on and passed another couple by a waterfall along with the woman from the ranger station with the tree trunk legs.

After hiking for a few hours I saw some comfortable looking rocks and stopped for a rest. I took my boots off and propped up my feet. I'd read that airing out your feet, shoes and socks at breaks can help prevent blisters. Propping up your feet allows the blood to move into the rest of your body, which is supposed to be a good thing.

In a box at the top of my pack was a special "power cake" I'd made before leaving my parent's house. It was packed with raisins, nuts, oats and molasses. Fuel food! I'd stuffed it into a pasta box to keep it from getting squished. Breaking off a piece, I leaned back against a boulder to eat.

The woman with the tree trunk legs caught up and sat down with me. I offered her a chunk of cake. While we ate she told me she had thru-hiked the AT years before. This time however, she was just out for a few days to see the new class of thru-hikers. Her trail name was Dutch Apple as she was from Holland. After a short break we set out together.

As we hiked upward, she told stories of other hikes she'd done. Not only had she hiked the Appalachian Trail, she'd also hiked the entire Pacific Crest Trail, and the Continental Divide Trail, each over 2,000 miles long. No wonder she had legs like tree trunks! She'd hiked the Triple Crown!

Though it was fascinating to meet a Triple Crowner on the very day that I was starting the AT, I realized my initial enthusiasm had dwindled. For one thing, her achievements far overshadowed what I was just beginning to attempt, so it was a bit intimidating. Second, I had been so thrilled to be hiking at my own pace before she joined me, and now I was modifying my pace to stay in step with her and carry on a conversation. And third I'd been staying with my parents for a week where there is non-stop noise, TV and talking, and I'd really been enjoying the subtle sounds of the woodlands and my own thoughts. Walking with Dutch Apple, I was subjected to endless chatter. I began to drop back and let her move ahead. The conversation died. I was back in my own personal reverie as I approached the top.

Hearing voices not far ahead, I looked up in time to see a small figure darting behind a tall, bearded fellow with a notebook. Dutch Apple had just stepped past them and looked back at me smiling. That little glimpse a fraction of a second earlier told me that my sister, Martha, aka: Tortoise, was here! At first I couldn't believe it. I thought she was in Louisiana. But I knew what I'd seen, even if only for a moment.

"I see you up there!" I called out. And her face popped out from behind the larger man, grinning broadly. I greeted her, surprised and delighted. The bearded man, a Ridge Runner, wanted me to register and told me that dozens of thru-hikers had come up to start the trail that day. It was the first of the month, a popular time to begin. He was taking a survey or something. But I barely greeted the man before I turned back toward my sister.

Martha had taken the service road in her four wheel drive pick-up and walked the rest of the way to the top. I didn't think she knew I was starting that day, but I had already learned that these serendipitous encounters were not uncommon on the trail. I'd surprised *her* in Maine three years before. Now, on my first day on the AT, she'd surprised *me*!

"I brought you a cake," she said, as I followed her to the first shelter not far away. She'd hung her food bag from the bear line. I took off my pack as she lowered the bag and retrieved the cake. It was a small round layer cake with chocolate frosting and written on the top it said, ".02 down 2,174.4 to go".

Dutch Apple hovered nearby. The lure of cake was strong and this looked much better than my "power cake". Dutch Apple volunteered to take a picture of the two of us. Though Martha hates having her picture taken, she managed to pose beside her clever cake with a little less than her usual scowl. We cut it with my new pocket knife and shared it with the other hikers at the shelter.

Martha had brought her pack and planned to spend the first night with me at this shelter, but it was early yet, just mid-afternoon. I wanted to hike further. She said the next shelter was a dump, but both of us carried tarps. I convinced her that I needed lessons on how to set mine up. She caved. We walked down to her truck by the service road and then on to the Stover Creek shelter which, as she'd said, was a dump. We set up our tarps in a clearing by the creek curtained by rhododendrons and tall evergreen trees.

Martha catered dinner, a package of pasta and sauce for me and Ramen noodles for her. It was hard for me to eat all of mine but she urged me to eat as much as I could. "You need to keep your weight up," she said, which was an entirely new concept for me and one that I appreciated for the duration of my hike.

We shared the rest of the cake with the hikers at the shelter, which included Dutch Apple, again. As it got dark and the temperatures dropped we crawled beneath our tarps and slid into our bags. A nearby stream sang us to sleep.

Through the night I heard the roar of the wind high up on the mountain and was glad to be in this protected ravine. In the weeks to come, I became well acquainted with that bitter, cold, mountain wind.

In the morning we ate our oatmeal and packed up together. She wished me luck. Then she walked south 1.6 miles back to her truck and I turned north with 2,172 miles to go.

Magic

At the ranger station I'd bought a map. It folds up like a fan, like most road maps, but this map is of the Appalachian Trail. It is nine inches wide and fifty-two inches long. At first, I couldn't unfold that map all the way. I opened it just enough to see the section I was walking at the time. It was overwhelming to think about how far I had to go, so I took it one step at a time, shelter by shelter, day by day, fold by fold.

I figured I'd walk maybe ten or twelve miles a day at first. I had all day with nothing else to do. My pack wasn't heavy and I was in reasonably good condition. I had a lot of hiking experience, but I had done very little backpacking since college and that was ancient history. But you never know until you actually try. I'd hiked over eleven miles the first day. On my second day, I determined to find out just how far I could go.

It was a cool morning with thick fog and seemed only to get more cold and damp as I walked along. I saw Dutch Apple and others from time to time, but mostly hiked alone. When I reached the Hawk Mountain Shelter at mid-day, I stopped for lunch. Other hikers came in couples or alone. The shelter filled as the fog turned to drizzle.

Resting, with my pack off, I got chilled so it wasn't long before I started off again.

I was just behind a couple who were finishing a Flip Flop they'd started the fall before. They'd hiked from the north end of the trail in Maine to somewhere in Pennsylvania. Now they were heading from Georgia back to where they'd left off. Soon, I passed them as they rested just off the trail.

Looking down a steep hill through the trees I saw an intersection of dirt roads up ahead. There was an old pick-up truck with coolers and camp chairs behind it and men's voices talking and laughing. I slowed my pace and looked on to assess the situation. As a lone woman hiker I had to wonder, "Is this trouble, or is this trail magic?"

I could wait for the Flip Flop couple to come up and head down with them, safety in numbers, they say. But when I noticed a pack lying on the ground, and heard the good-hearted laughter, I determined it was magic and proceeded cautiously on.

I'd heard of trail magic from my sister and from books. It was sort of magical that my sister had met me unexpectedly on Springer Mountain with a cake. But this was my first experience of getting kindness from a complete stranger, intended for thru-hikers, like a 2,000 mile long cheering section. It's a phenomenon I've only experienced on the Appalachian Trail. It was truly magic and it was just the beginning!

Otto and his German Shepherd, Raven, were veteran thru-hikers who were there to greet the class of 2006. As I approached, another hiker, Cedar Moe, brushed off his hands and reached out to introduce himself. Otto got busy making us grilled cheese sandwiches on his Coleman stove. Now this was fine hospitality! I dropped my pack as instructed, and poured myself a cup of orange juice from the cooler. As we visited, other hikers joined us. The Flip Floppers arrived. Then the Jolly Green Giant and Compass came up.

Cedar Moe asked where I was headed for the night. I answered vaguely, partly to protect myself and partly because I wasn't sure. "I'll know when I get there." I said. Otto smiled and nodded approvingly.

A couple of young men approaching from the hillside above caught our attention. When they looked down and realized they'd come upon actual trail magic, they broke into a run waving their hiking sticks in the air. One had a mass of red hair and let out a loud hoot and a holler. Together they made a wild rumpus and came to a screeching halt by the coolers. Otto grilled more sandwiches which they ate with gusto. The redhead introduced himself as Sunshine but we said, "No. You looked more like an Orangutan storming down the trail with your arms waving over your head." It was unanimous! One day out and Sunshine had a new trail name.

Stealth Camping

I hiked on, part of a migration of hikers heading north. In the afternoon I stopped to rest sitting in a dry ditch full of leaves, I propped my feet up, took my shoes off and reached into my pack for some "power cake". Despite the protection of the pasta box, it looked a bit deformed, but still tasted good.

Jolly Green Giant approached with Compass and stopped to chat. Compass had earned his trail name by starting off in the wrong direction. Now he was having problems with blisters. He looked miserable. His friend, the Giant, smiled at my words of encouragement, but seemed a little disappointed at having to slow his pace to accommodate his friend. They both worked at an outing goods store in Atlanta and came with all the best gear. Good gear is helpful but doesn't guarantee that you'll complete your hike. A number of people each year drop out in the first few days.

When I reached the sign for the Gooch Mountain Shelter there were a couple hours of daylight remaining. At the turn-off I passed two Army veterans who were struggling with packs that must've weighed eighty pounds each!

I looked over toward the shelter 100 yards away. There were already a dozen hikers gathered there, and I knew more were on their way. Consulting my guide book I figured I'd come thirteen miles so far, not bad. But I could keep going, I wasn't tired. The next campsite was at Woody Gap about four miles away, but there was also a road there. I'd read about locals coming out to the trail and hassling hikers that were camped near roads. Just to be on the safe side I'd decided not to camp within a mile of a road. I thought it might be a good night to try "stealth camping".

I continued on and didn't see any other hikers. They'd all stopped at the last shelter or had been ahead of me and moved on to the next. About an hour before sunset I began looking for a place to sleep. Not a shelter or a campsite, just a flat place, off the trail, protected from the wind. I was looking for a place where I could pitch my tarp close to the ground, lay my sleeping bag beneath it and crawl inside. I was looking for a place where I could sleep undetected from the trail.

I found such a place about a mile from the up-coming road crossing. It was an old, overgrown road bed with plenty of small saplings so I could tie up my tarp with lots of dry leaves for a mattress. I set up my sleeping spot laying my poncho on a thick bed of leaves and stringing my tarp between the saplings. Then I took my dinner back to the trail about thirty yards away. I checked my guide book and discovered I'd gone over fifteen miles that day.

Stealth camping includes stealth eating, so I didn't cook dinner. I didn't want to attract wildlife with the scent of hot food or the sound of a stove. Animals are attracted to campsites and shelters where they can score an easy meal. But if you're stealth camping, where it looks like no one has camped before, neither man nor beast expects to find you. I watched the sun set and ate the power cake out of the box (though by now it was getting thoroughly schmooshed and loosing its appeal). As darkness fell I hung my food, crawled into my sleeping bag and tried to sleep.

The wind roared all night and I was thankful to be tucked into a low pass. Still it sounded like a procession of freight trains echoing through the hills. I was glad when the dark night finally began to yield to the coming day.

The morning was frigid and I hated to get out of my sleeping bag. I put on all my clothes before climbing out. When I finally started packing up, I decided to hike on to the picnic area at Woody Gap before making a hot breakfast. As I packed I saw the Flip Floppers pass by on the trail, but they didn't see me.

I hiked the next mile and found a picnic table out of the wind and in the sun where I could make a pot of oatmeal and thaw out a bit. A steady parade of hikers passed by on the trail below. As I ate I could pick out some familiar faces. Some of them would be with me for months. I packed up my things and fell into line.

A Family Forms

I hiked on in the cold wind all day, but the sun was out and carrying a pack uphill warmed me. I met another veteran thru-hiker going south. Stump-knocker stopped to comment on how I wore my fleece vest backwards. If I was hiking downhill on the shady side of the mountain, it was easy to put it on to keep my front warm while my backpack kept my back warm. I could slip my vest off as I climbed a hill in the sun and tuck it through my pack strap. Though it may have looked odd, it worked well for me.

In a ravine, out of the wind, I came upon a man doubled over with his hands on his knees. His pack looked huge and heavy. He wore jeans and a denim jacket lined with sheepskin. As I approached he straightened up and looked at me with a red face and labored breath.

"Are you alright?" I asked.

"Just catching my breath. I'll be fine in a minute."

He was obviously embarrassed that I'd found him at a weak moment. I gave him an encouraging smile and moved on.

The Blood Mountain shelter is a little rock house with a small open window letting in precious little light. It seemed gloomy and foreboding, maybe even haunted. I was glad that it was mid-day and I could put miles between me and this place before dark. Later I read that Blood Mountain had been named after a fierce battle between the Creek and Cherokee Indians which had stained the rocks red with blood.

I knew I must be near a road because I started to see hikers without packs and people walking their dogs. They struggled up the boulders as I cautiously stepped down.

I heard cars go by before I came out of the woods at Neels Gap. It was the first paved road I'd seen in three days, a pretty isolated spot but it was bustling with activity on this sunny afternoon. I thought briefly about taking a short break and then moving on, but my "prove something" voice got overpowered by the voice shouting, "Hot shower! Warm bed!"

The sprawling stone structure had a visitor center, an outfitters store, and a hiker's hostel with a stone terrace out front. The trail went through a breezeway between the buildings. There I found a hiker's log book and wrote down the words of the song that had been stuck in my head since I'd started hiking three days before.

Hurry up sinner, make your legs pound,
I'm running on the top, I'm running underground,
I'm running away, away, away,
To a place I know that I'll never be found.

I turned toward the outfitters where a few packs rested against the wall outside, but they were just a few feet from the cars in the parking lot. I kept mine on. There were several people inside, tourists, hikers, salespeople. I felt the eyes of an older man looking in my direction, but as I looked up he turned away. I looked around at the room full of gear, trail food, post cards and then made my way to the counter to register for a bunk at the hostel. The older man approached the other end of the counter at the same time. The clerk started toward him, but he objected.

"Don't you think you should help the lady first? She's carrying a pack."

I thanked him for his unexpected courtesy, registered and went to settle into the hostel. In the bunkhouse all sixteen bunks were almost full. I was assigned to an upper bunk just above a young woman whose trail name was the Tortoise. (No relation.) Bluebell, a middle aged woman from Texas, was the only other woman there. She was traveling with a few Southern gentlemen about her age. They were a bit concerned about their knees and blisters. I gave one of them some Second Skin for a bad blister. He gave me a Snickers bar in exchange. Most everyone else were young men in their twenties. Bluebell acted like a den mother to them all.

In the living room, one "old timer" with a long beard sat quietly in a corner. He was a veteran thru-hiker named Pirate with years of experience not only thru-hiking, but living in one hostel or another. There are those that never really leave the trail. Hikers got good advice and trail information from him like a guru surrounded by his disciples. He didn't use a bunk that would be occupied by a paying customer, but was used to sleeping on the couch or the floor wherever he was. It brought to mind a joke I'd heard.

"What's the difference between a thru-hiker and a homeless person?"

"Gortex."

Two young men stood out among the rest. They had other trail names but came to be more commonly known as Dumb and Dumber. They were eighteen or nineteen years old. They'd heard about the trail on Tuesday and started hiking it on Thursday. Between them they had $80 which they'd spent on Rock and Roll jeans so they'd look cool hiking through the forest. Their gear consisted of one backpack with a broken strap, one gallon sized milk jug for water, and one sleeping bag which they'd squeeze into together.

Other hikers at the hostel donated spare supplies and equipment, but in the end, the staff at the outfitters called their parents to come get them. I felt bad for them, but had to agree, especially this early in the spring with snow a certainty, they were a danger to themselves and others.

Neels Gap is three days from the start of the Appalachian Trail. Many hikers who start the trail in Georgia intending to hike to Maine find that they're really not cut out for thru-hiking. They get crippling blisters, can't sleep in the shelters, their backs complain loudly and this is their first good opportunity to jump off. The year I hiked the trail 1,150 people started the hike in Georgia and seventy-five bowed out at Neels Gap, three days later.

For those who are determined to continue, the staff at the outfitters provide a critical service. All you need to do is ask, empty your pack onto the floor, and the helpful staff will assess your equipment, free of charge. They'll tell you what you really need and what you could send home. They might suggest that you purchase a few things that you're lacking or exchange a weighty item for something lighter that serves the same function. They probably make a few sales this way, but thru-hikers benefit, too. It's extremely helpful to minimize pack weight and maximize the uses of whatever you decide to carry. After three days of backpacking, you have a good idea of whether you need this service or not.

After checking out the place, I went to the rest room and washed out a few things in the sink. I'd only been on the trail for three days and couldn't justify doing a whole load of wash. Apparently other people could. When I tried to get a shower the water pressure was next to nothing and the temperature was ice cold! Back in the bunkhouse, I strung up a bear line over my bunk and hung up my quick-dry shirt and socks. I lounged in my Polyprope long johns, gym shorts and fleece.

While I was in the shower, the others got together and called in a big pizza order. When the delivery arrived, they crowded into the common room to watch a video and eat. I had a microwave potpie from the outfitters, but had seen the movie before, so after eating, I stepped outside to the phone booth to call my folks. The wind was freezing cold and I was lightly dressed, so it was a quick call.

Mom told me she'd written my cousin Nancy to let her know I'd be in her neighborhood soon. I double checked my guide book.

"I'll be there in three days. Could you give her a call for me?" I was moving a little faster than my original estimate.

Back inside I went into the bunkroom. On a bunk by the door sat the grey haired fellow that had let me go ahead of him at the counter. We introduced ourselves. He said he was Silver Streak and he was from Michigan. His daughter, a marathon runner, had challenged him to hike the trail so here he was. We talked a little before I retired to my bunk. Sleeping in that room of sixteen people were some champion snorers. I spent the evening writing and reading and then put in my earplugs to sleep, happy to be out of that ferocious winter wind.

The next morning was cold and windy but the sun shone bravely through the bare branches of the trees. I made oatmeal and packed my bag but was hesitant to leave. The hostel was so nice and warm. To justify my delayed departure, I did some yoga stretches. A lithe young man from the Midwest did yoga, too. When I asked his name, I thought, "Wait 'till I tell the folks I was doing yoga with Superman!"

Inevitably, I had to get out in the cold. It took a long time to convince myself, but it's true. It almost always looks worse from the inside. Once I got started, the exercise kept me warm and I made good progress. First I passed Bluebell and her gentlemen friends. Then I leap frogged with Silver Streak, Cedar Moe, Superman, Jolly Green Giant and a guy named Rick, who had yet to find a trail name.

About mid-day I was walking with Silver Streak when we came across a plump, young man sitting on a rock in the sun. His pack looked huge. He even had a pair of snow shoes strapped to the top.

"You must be Tom," I said. He looked surprised but nodded. "Thanks for carrying those snow shoes." Now he looked really perplexed. Silver explained.

"We heard about you from Pirate. He said as long as you're carrying those snow shoes, it won't snow." Tom nodded again. He didn't say much, but later we found out that he hailed from Connecticut and that he liked snow.

Before leaving Carrboro, mom had asked if I needed a walking stick. I'd never used one in all my years of leading hikes in the Northwest. If I felt the need temporarily, to cross a stream or muddy area, there was usually a stick on the ground I could use. She'd gotten a walking stick for a recent trip she took to Mexico to see migrating butterflies. Hers was a red one from Walmart with a compass on top of the handle that always pointed southwest. She offered to loan it to me. I told her

I thought I could manage without it. I was beginning to regret that decision.

People often compare the Appalachian Trail with the Pacific Crest Trail. The PCT runs from Mexico to Canada along the spine of the Sierra Nevada and the Cascade Range. The AT seems tamer, connecting the dots of mountain towns from Georgia to Maine. The highest peak is only 6,600 feet, not very impressive compared to the PCT which is much higher, longer and more remote. But I'd read that a thru-hiker on the Appalachian Trail climbs and descends twice as much as the PCT. They compared it to going from sea level to the summit of Mount Everest and back more than sixteen times. It takes a toll on the knees and ankles. A thru-hiker without a walking stick is rare. Looking around on the ground I found a stout branch that I adopted as my own.

In those first few days on the trail, I bonded with my stick. We became loyal companions traveling together every step of the way, despite the fact that I repeatedly left it behind as I started walking each day and grumbled as I went back to get it. No matter how many times I left it, my stick always waited patiently for my return.

At a scenic overlook several hikers had stopped for a break. I met Mickey One Sock, another seasoned thru-hiker who was out to meet this year's hatchlings. He pointed out the nearby peaks and told stories about the area. My sister had mentioned meeting him. He had a warm smile and an encouraging word for everyone that came by. He said, "I may not be the fastest thru-hiker, but I like to think I'm the kindest."

On and on we went, but at the end of the day I stopped along with Silver Streak, Cedar Moe and Rick. We didn't know exactly where we were but there was a good spring nearby and a level clearing by the trail with a fire circle and a pile of branches. There was enough room for their three small tents and my tarp among the rhododendrons. We pulled out our four separate stoves and made our four separate dinners.

Cedar Moe spilled a little water on the ground from his packet of tuna which got all of our attention. Bear bait. To his credit, Cedar tried to dig up the dirt affected by the spill, carried it down the trail and tossed it into the woods, which may have confused the beasts a bit, but not much. Now we were expecting company. We hung a bear line up in a tree and tied all our food bags to it. Tooth paste, chapstick and anything else that smelled interesting had to be hoisted ten feet up and five feet out.

Rick invited us all to participate in some after dinner fun. He'd brought along a variety of miniature game boards, dice and cards. I said if I could play from inside my sleeping bag I'd be up for it. But as the temperatures dipped with the sun, we all burrowed deep into the relative warmth of our separate sacks, tents and tarps.

That night was pitch black. There was no moon and no wind. I was awakened by the sound of something sniffing around the edges of my tarp. Half awake, I rustled around in my sleeping bag to let whatever it was know this tarp was occupied. The sniffing ceased. It moved through our camp. I was happy it was moving away from me.

In the morning Cedar reported he'd heard scratching in camp where the tuna water had spilled. He'd unzipped his tent and found himself face to face with a big Georgian black bear!

At breakfast we discussed Rick's possible trail names. How about Dice Thrower? No. Gameboy? No. What about Yahtzee? He liked it. It stuck.

Angels

In the morning we were packed and almost ready to go when up came Superman and the Jolly Green Giant. The six of us walked on together... more or less. Silver and I were twice the age of the four speedsters. They'd move ahead on the trail but waited for us at trail crossings. After sixteen miles, we all ended up in the Tray Mountain shelter, famous for its sunsets. The view seemed to go on forever, ridge after ridge, but as the sun slipped behind the mountain, and the air grew chill, I retreated to my sleeping bag.

The next day the guys moved out early, anxious to get a spot at the legendary Blueberry Patch hostel. I'd arranged to meet my cousin Nancy at the same road crossing. I knew she wouldn't be there until after work which gave me plenty of time to sit in the sun and read while having lunch. Tom walked up, but didn't seem interested in dining with me. He slogged on at his usual pace.

In mid-afternoon I arrived at Dick's Gap and US Highway 76. There was a picnic area where a couple had stopped. They seemed pleased to offer me a ride the three and a half miles to the hostel. When I arrived I called my cousin and told her where I was. It would be an hour or so before she finished work and could come by to get me.

Most of my hiking companions had accepted a ride into town to get lunch at an All-You-Can-Eat restaurant, a big attraction for thru-hikers. Cedar Moe had stayed behind to read and relax. He gave me a tour of the converted garage hostel and introduced me to the donkeys in the field out back. I was sampling the home made zucchini pickles from the refrigerator when the boys returned.

Each hostel has a unique character. This one was famous for its kind hospitality and incredible blueberry pancake breakfasts. I remembered a letter my sister wrote from here. She'd arrived in a snow storm. They wrapped her up in a blanket while they washed her clothes. For me, it was a balmy spring day.

Cousin Nancy drove up and greeted me warmly. She wanted to meet everyone. When I introduced her to "Superman" and "the Jolly Green Giant" she could barely keep from laughing.

Nancy is the very manifestation of Southern hospitality and treated me like a queen. We'd grown up together, but as adults lived 3,000 miles apart and hadn't seen much of each other for years. Her husband, Clay, met us at a restaurant in town where we ate chicken fried steaks and mashed potatoes. Afterward, at their house, we sat by the fire talking. Nancy had supplied me with a cozy sweat suit to wear while my hiking clothes spun around in the washer. Outside the wind blew snow down the mountain. I was grateful to be inside by the fireplace with a comfortable bed in the next room.

Nancy was working as a hospice chaplain driving all over to visit people in their homes. She knew all the back roads in a wide area through the mountains. Clay brought out a map that showed where those roads intersected the Appalachian Trail. Nancy saw that she could pick me up again after just three more days on the trail. I gladly accepted!

I told them they were now official Trail Angels, but they'd never heard of such a thing. When I explained about Trail Magic and Trail Angels, Nancy determined to join their ranks. In the morning she made breakfast while I sent emails to family and friends. She took me to get groceries and bought treats for my hiking companions. Then she took me back to the trail. Afterward, she started carrying bottled water and juices in her car and offering rides to backpackers she found at trail crossings. Her halo sparkled!

Spring Break

Back on the trail, I soon caught up with Silver Streak and Tom who by now had gained the trail name Tank. It seemed to suit him, slow and heavy. I'd only caught a glimpse of the twenty-somethings. They'd leapt out of the car from the hostel just as I'd arrived at the trailhead. But once we started hiking, they left us in the dust (or more accurately, snow), fueled by blueberry pancakes and youth. Silver and I followed in their wake.

We spread out, hiking at our own pace, stopping and passing, leapfrogging all day. For me it was the ideal sort of companionship, knowing someone was nearby, but not tripping over each other. I could take time to look around, and on this shimmering day, I did so often. There was a light dusting of snow on the ground and a mesmerizing rime ice in the tree tops. The rattle of bare branches drew my attention into the canopy. Every tiny twig was encased in ice sparkling like crystal in a brilliant blue sky.

We arrived at a shelter late in the day. In the log book the guys had left a message saying they'd gone to the next shelter. Silver and I pushed it the last five miles over roots, rocks and a 2,300 foot climb and caught up with them at the Standing Indian Mountain shelter just before dark. It had been a tough seventeen and a half mile day and the youngsters were shocked (as were we) that we'd made it. Cedar Moe boiled some water for my dinner as I rigged up my tarp. Superman helped us string up a bear line and asked, "Did you train before coming out here?"

D-Rock misread a sign that warned, "Hikers Beware! Bears hunting packs. Use extreme caution." He thought it read, "Bears hunting IN packs!" A scary thought. But the humans had the bears outnumbered at this stop.

Besides being the start of thru-hiker season, it was also spring break. There were sixteen people at the shelter that night. Five lovely co-eds from Chicago delighted the young men with their company. D-Rock got absolutely ga-ga about one. As darkness fell he made a lot of noise stomping out into the woods to gather huge limbs and logs for a fire. We hadn't had a fire on the trail before, just our camp stoves. It was too cold to stay up after dinner so we would all burrow into our sleeping bags as soon as the sun went down. His brilliant fire brought everyone out to socialize.

The young ladies, like a row of fresh flowers, sat on a log huddled close together. The young men seemed restless, buzzing around them like bees. Silver Streak sat down right next to them and said, "I've been hired by your fathers to come out here and keep an eye on you." They giggled shyly and the boys smiled.

The girls slept in their own large tent. At sunrise the tent was quiet while the boys packed up and headed down the trail. D-Rock left poetry in the shelter logs for days knowing they would follow.

Silver and I caught up to the boys at a shelter at mid-day. D-Rock had brought a bag of apples which he shared with the rest of us. I was amazed that anyone would carry such weighty cargo, and then share it after all that work. Later, he and Cayenne were low on food. Other hikers shared their goods. What goes around comes around on the trail.

D-Rock hailed from Baltimore. He had fiery red hair and wore a twisted bandanna like those worn by gang members. Being a small town girl myself I wasn't entirely comfortable around him and had kept a little distance, but I was fascinated by the tattoo that covered his entire left arm. I got up my nerve and asked if I could take a picture of it. He proudly pulled up his sleeve to display a beautiful, full color Geisha expertly etched into his skin. After a few days of hiking together on the trail, the edgy urban dude didn't seem so scary.

The young men outpaced us, but Silver, Tank and I carried on. In the first week, we crossed from Georgia into North Carolina. One down, thirteen states to go. We climbed Mount Albert, the first peak over 5,000 feet high. We put our first hundred trail miles behind us. We were beginning to form a family.

At the end of the week, we met Crutch, a former thru-hiker who had intended to hike again that year but tore a ligament. The doctor told him, "No hiking for eight weeks." So Crutch became a trail angel. He set up a table near a trailhead and served up fruit and sandwiches to thru-hikers. We were planning to go into Franklin, North Carolina. He used his cell phone to call for a shuttle service that met us at the next road. Silver and Tank checked into a hiker-friendly hotel. I called Cousin Nancy to tell her where I was. She'd pick me up after work. Then we went to an All-You-Can-Eat buffet nearby.

I piled a lot of salad on my plate and went back for more. Silver had two salads before going back for meat and potatoes. Tank had two huge plates of meat, just meat. I kept kidding him about his lonely, neglected salad plate, but he just grinned.

Nancy picked me up a little later. The weather report forecast thunderstorms that night and then a week of clear, warm weather. This was perfect timing for going through the Smokies. They'd recently had a lot of snow but this meant that by the time we got there the snow would be melting. I spent a stormy night in the comfort of Nancy's mountain home sitting by the fire swapping stories. As I crawled into a king-sized bed and turned out the light, the thunder rolled, lightning flashed, rain pounded on the windows, and I gave thanks to be inside for the night.

Sleeping with Married Men

After another three days of hiking in the woods, Silver and I came upon the Nantahala Outdoor Center. It was buzzing with activity. The restaurant was on the left, the outfitters on the right, motel rooms, cabins, dining halls were all around. People in kayaks were dipping and gliding, shooting the rapids of the Nantahala River that ran through the middle of it all. Compared to the quiet woods this place was like Disneyland.

Silver and I had an agenda. We each wanted to find a bunk, pick-up mail drops and eat what we'd started calling "real food". We approached the desk and asked for a place to sleep. We were given a couple of options. Would you like a bunk room for two, or bunk with other hikers. We'd experienced snorers on the trail and opted to take a bunk room for just two.

"Would you like one bed or two?" she asked. We both blushed.

"Two bunks, please." we answered awkwardly in unison. When she asked for a name, address and credit card, I stepped back. "You better fill out the form," I said. Since I was in the midst of a divorce, the answers to seemingly simple questions had become complicated. I slipped Silver some cash to cover my half.

We spent the afternoon calling home and picking through our mail drops. Crossing the parking lot we saw a curious sight. It was Superman… in an SUV. His father had come to meet him which gave him the opportunity to do a thirty mile slack pack. He was planning to hike from the Nantahala Outdoor Center to Fontana Dam while his father drove around carrying his pack. This was one of many stunts of this Super hero. Superman, we came to find out, was a sprinter. He'd hike overnight, great distances and at high speed, just for fun. Then he'd get to a town and party for days. Though he was among the faster hikers I knew, he ended up finishing the trail late in the season, which reminds me of another bit of trail wisdom:

"The first one to Maine loses."

The next day as Silver and I had breakfast in the restaurant, along came Tank, fully loaded as usual. I ran outside to invite him to join us but Tank declined. Not even the smell of bacon could detour him. He kept walking, slowly and surely, ever onward.

Back on the trail later that day we met a woman who seemed to be living in a shelter. Her clothes were drying on a line out front. We stopped for lunch. She offered us a Snickers bar and in the course of conversation began reciting Robert Frost.

Whose woods these are, I think I know.
His house is in the village though.

I joined in.

He would not see me stopping here
To watch his woods fill up with snow.

She continued,

My little horse must think it queer
To stop without a farmhouse near.
Between the woods and frozen lake,
The darkest evening of the year.

He gives his harness bells a shake
To ask if there is some mistake.
The only other sounds the sweep
Of easy wind and snowy flake.

We finished together,

The woods are lovely dark and deep,
But I have promises to keep
And miles to go before I sleep,
And miles to go before I sleep.

Silver gawked at us open mouthed. Two women in the woods reciting poetry was outside his realm of experience. Beyond being hiking partners, we had only glimpses of each others lives.

In the first few days of hiking together I'd learned that his wife and daughter operated a beauty salon. His other daughter, the marathon runner, was a physical therapist. Up until now, most of Silver's outdoor experience had been gained on hunting trips. He ran his own electrical contracting company with help from his sons. The love of his life, besides his wife, was his young grandson. He missed both of them terribly. He leaned right politically and among his ten essentials was a Bible.

In the afternoon I reached a field where a dirt road crossed the trail. There was a huge white circus tent and outside was a flag flapping in the breeze that said simply, "Angel".

I went in and found Bluebird and Abandon finishing off their hot dogs. The Angel's name was Apple. He apologized for running out of hot dogs but scurried around searching for other offerings. Bluebird and Abandon thanked him and moved on while I sat down in a folding chair. Apple served up a soda and chips, a Snickers bar and of course, an apple. He'd hiked the trail before and from then on had spent his vacations from work each year in this tent on the trail offering food and sometimes shelter to hikers. We talked as I enjoyed his generous provisions and then continued down the trail smiling. I'd never experienced Trail Angels before, but it was definitely something I could get used to.

As darkness fell, Silver and I arrived at the Brown Fork Gap shelter. It was overflowing with hikers. Everyone was busy getting water from the stream below or making dinner, gathering wood or tending the fire. I stepped up to the shelter platform to see if there was room for me to sleep inside.

I met him lying down in the dark. I could tell by his voice that I'd like him. He introduced himself as Firefly.

"Oh good," I said, "I've been looking for fire flies!"

I met him again about a half hour later.

"Hi, I'm Scout. I don't believe we've met."

"I'm Firefly."

"Wait a minute. Isn't that you lying down there?"

Either he was a clone or a ventriloquist. It was hard to tell in the darkness that the sleeping bag in the corner had been vacated, but the voice of the man standing beside me was the same.

Firefly was exactly half my age, a tall, dark and handsome young man from Alabama. His soft southern drawl, relaxed and upbeat manner made him easily approachable. He had a quick wit and a mischievous twinkle in his eye. He soon became our company comic. He was observant, insightful and easily entertained. Firefly, Silver and I became a trio with Tank coming and going intermittently. I don't know why he hiked with us. He was certainly strong enough to hike much faster, but he seemed to like our company.

Unlike Tank, Firefly liked to talk. In fact, he was one of the few hikers I could converse with while hiking. The more he got into conversation, the slower he'd walk, until I was almost stepping on his heels. If I wanted to continue talking and walking, I'd have to find an opportunity to step around him and set the pace. Otherwise, we'd still be hiking long after dark.

I found him fascinating. Growing up, he said, his parents were always fighting. He'd spent a lot of time with his crazy Cherokee grandmother. Since his parents divorced they didn't seem close to him. He'd suffered from ADD as a kid and couldn't sit still. He'd taken medication for it through school, but the trail suited him and he left the meds behind. He had plenty of energy, enjoyed meeting new people and exploring new places. He was fun to be around, with enough life experience and maturity to be able to contribute insights on serious issues as well.

Firefly had been married for six months to a drop dead gorgeous Latina woman who, without warning, would break into terrifying hysteria. When they got divorced, heavy-hearted Firefly immediately went to hike the trail. It was late in the season so he started in Maine intending to hike south to Georgia. He had only been on the trail a few days and was about fifty miles from the nearest town when he acquired his trail name. He lit himself on fire.

It's a curious thing about alcohol stoves. In the daylight, the flame is nearly invisible. He was sitting at a shelter about to make dinner. He lit his stove but it seemed to have gone out. So he began to add fuel, only to discover in a flash, that the fire was still very much alive. As he saw the flame leap up toward his fuel bottle and realized his mistake, he waved the bottle frantically trying to pour the fuel out on the ground. In an attempt to try to dodge other hikers sitting nearby, he splattered fuel across his own shoulder and down his back. His synthetic shirt caught fire and before he could throw himself in the creek, he had 2nd degree burns. Unable to wear his pack, he hugged it, hiking until he reached the nearest road and got a ride to a hospital.

After a two week hospital stay, he recouped in a hiker's hostel in Millinocket, Maine. Then he continued hiking south. The hospital bills had taken a toll on his hiking budget. He made it through several states before his money ran out. Over the winter he worked construction jobs, saving up to start again the following spring. Now he was heading north.

The Smokies

Approaching the Great Smoky Mountains National Park, we arrived at a huge, new shelter known as the Fontana Hilton by Fontana Dam. It was cushy compared to the others, with enough room for twenty hikers. A nearby restroom offered flush toilets and running water, a real luxury. At the edge of the dam not far away was a visitor center and around back, showers! I dug into my pack and pulled out a tiny bottle of shampoo and a tiny bar of hotel soap. The shower was a big spout in the middle of a large, cold room. I got in and out as fast as possible. A bunch of guys using the men's shower asked me for soap which I gladly relinquished.

Outside, other hikers gathered. Coconut Monkey was met by his family and girlfriend. They were taking him off the trail for a few days to celebrate his twenty-first birthday. He was a track star, lean and fit, so we had no doubt that we'd see him again soon.

A shuttle service offered rides to the resort nearby. I caught a ride and tried to find some trail food in the small gift shop without much luck. I ended up dining out with a couple of Georgian hikers at the fancy restaurant on top of the hill. There were white linen table cloths and crystal glasses. They ordered fried green tomatoes. I was embarrassed to admit, growing up in the South, that these were the first I'd ever tasted. This sort of fine dining was a splurge but it would be a week before I could eat out again and my trail cuisine was limited, to say the least.

That night tucked into my sleeping bag I wrote in my journal by the light of my headlamp. The guys in bunks all around me talked, snored, farted, and eventually got quiet. The next day we would enter the Smokies, the first big challenge for NOBO's and everyone was getting psyched up for it. Starting early in the spring as we had, snow was expected. We'd heard there were accumulations of five feet on the peaks. But the reports were good. The snows of the past few weeks were melting and the forecast was clear.

We started the day with a hike across the top of Fontana Dam, a massive cement spillway on the threshold of the national park. It seemed totally foreign to our feet to walk on this mountain of smooth cement. On the far side as we started up the steep trail and filtered through the woods, we thinned out. At the first shelter I sat against the sunny south-facing wall to have lunch. There were lots of college students coming and going, stopping to talk.

Silver and Firefly went ahead. I thought I'd catch them at the next shelter, but when I arrived, there was no one. I checked my guide book. It was another 3.5 miles to the next shelter but the sun was low. I hurried on. When I arrived the shelter was nearly full, but Silver had thrown his sleeping bag on one bunk and his sleeping pad on another to save me a spot. I was grateful.

In the Smokies the shelters are three-sided rock structures with two rows of bunks, up and down. A heavy tarp was tied across the front of the shelter with big rocks holding down the bottom edge. Cruise, Applesauce and Salsa were gathering wood and starting a fire in the fireplace at one end of the shelter.

Cooking inside was frowned upon. It would attract mice or larger animals, so I stepped outside to make dinner under a covered porch. It was already getting really cold and the wind was picking up. I peered around the side of the shelter to find a young couple, acting silly as they prepared their meal. He was dressed in a big, black down coat and ski hat. She had a pink one, also with a matching hat. "College students," I thought. "They aren't serious hikers."

After dinner at sundown, we either snuggled deep into our bags or sat within a few feet of the fire. There was room for only three on the bench by the fireplace, and if one was Salsa, there was room for only two.

We were at just under 5,000 feet in early March and it was cold. The wind not only magnified the chill, but it howled all night. As the sun went down, it was as if someone had released the Hounds of the Baskervilles that rampaged across the ridges, snarling and tearing at the edges of our tarp. I endured these nights, sleeping fitfully, always grateful to see the first light of day.

After another day of hiking, Silver and I stopped at a little shelter with some young members of a volunteer trail crew. We'd already passed other crews on the trail clearing the winter blow down. Most of the 2,000 mile trail is maintained by volunteers and we depended on them to stay on course, hike safely and make good time. We thanked them heartily.

A young woman on the crew asked, "What was that strange, low, vibration we'd feel as we walked through the woods?" I'd been taken by it, too. It was so close sometimes it felt like my own heart pounding and I had to put my hand on my chest to make sure I wasn't having a heart attack. Once I'd ruled that out, I came upon a more reasonable conclusion.

"It's the mating call of a grouse," I told her. "It's low enough to be out of the hearing range of their main predator, the Great Horned Owl."

Silver looked at me, and then at the woman and told her, "I'm traveling with a naturalist."

I looked at Silver and then at the woman and added, "I'm traveling with an electrician. A lot of good that will do me."

When I chanced to encounter these grouse, or the much larger wild turkeys, coming around a bend in the trail, there was a sudden and terrifying flapping of wings that sounded like a helicopter taking off and I'd nearly jump out of my skin!

We shared the shelter that night with some college students on spring break who stayed up late, talking loudly, drinking and telling dirty jokes by the fire. In the morning we didn't apologize as we took down our tarps letting in the bright sunshine and the cold wind. Neither did we tiptoe around making breakfast with our little gas stoves. Mine, ironically called a "Whisperlite", sounds like a Boeing 747 taking off. The students moaned and rolled around in their bags as we packed and left the shelter just after dawn.

That day we climbed the cement tower atop Clingman's Dome. At 6,643 feet it's the highest point on the Appalachian Trail. The view was obscured by snow flurries and a brisk wind. After taking a few pictures we got moving to stay warm. The trail was covered in ice and snow. It was enchanting with each tiny tree limb entombed in crystal, but it was treacherous for walking. We each took a tumble, Silver, Firefly and I, but none of us hurt more than our pride. Firefly got a good laugh out of our lame attempts to stay upright.

That night we met up with another shelter full of hikers. There was the couple with the down jackets. I learned they were indeed thru-hikers from Portland, Oregon, Zama and Lug. When I commented on her pink jacket, Zama responded, "Oh, do you like my pink and puffy? Pink is the new black, you know."

She and Lug were both thirty-one. They'd been asked to accompany Zama's mom as she attempted to hike the trail in her 50th year. But her mom had problems right from the start. Within the first two weeks she had crippling blisters, a twisted ankle and finally got off the trail with a broken arm.

Zama and Lug had made all the arrangements to hike for six months. They'd left jobs and home behind, saved their money and obtained all the gear they needed, so even though her Mom couldn't make it, they decided to continue. What the heck?

It was after dark. We had all eaten our dinners and closed up the tarp for the night when a troop of four large, loud men with huge packs burst in. One even carried a pillow on top. They looked around for vacant bunks and then one proclaimed, "We have four bunks reserved so some of you are going to have to go!"

Excuse me? If they had asked nicely, we would've all moved over and made room. We would've welcomed them in and helped make them comfortable. I was floored by their rude behavior. But before I could recover from the shock, I heard some whispering between Zama and Lug. Then Zama kindly said, "We'll go outside. We were feeling a little claustrophobic in here anyway."

In the Smokies there is a reservation system for the shelters. They keep four bunks open for thru-hikers, but there had been a computer glitch which resulted in that shelter being overbooked. Still, there are nicer ways to approach your shelter mates.

It was literally freezing cold, dark and blowing like banshees out there, but Zama and Lug quickly packed up their gear and went to pitch a tent outside. They instantly became legendary among their peers, winning the award for most gracious hikers on the trail. Meanwhile, the four newcomers got the cold shoulder.

The next day, Silver Streak, Firefly and I checked our guide books and maps and decided to hike our first twenty mile day in order to get out of the high country and into some warmer climes. Silver showed us his elevation chart that indicated a gradual drop and smooth decline all day. We set our sights on the Crosby Knob Shelter.

Late in the day as we climbed yet another icy slope we questioned the accuracy of Silver's elevation charts. He had shared them with us since the start but we'd found them to be misleading. It was as if someone had turned the long thin pages sideways and drawn a slightly wiggly line that coaxed our feet into our boots with the promise that today's hike would be easier than the day before.

I checked my guide book. It gave the elevation for springs and shelters along the way, which told another story. We'd be hiking plenty of ups and downs between 5,000 and 6,300 feet that day. The important thing was that the shelter we chose for the night was at a mere 4,700 feet and consequently warmer with a forest for shelter instead of being perched high up on a ridge.

Late in the day, Firefly and I were together when we reached the side trail to the shelter. Just at that moment, a Wolf sprang up the trail coming right at us!

He was dressed in a one piece outfit and carried a very small, light pack. He seemed extremely friendly and came down to the shelter with us "talking a blue streak!" as my mother would say. He told us how he traveled so light, and how many times he'd hiked the trail, back and forth, and how he had special permission to climb Katahdin anytime of the year when it's normally closed to hikers for the winter. He went on and on. As he talked, Firefly and I nodded our heads and inflated our sleeping pads. We nodded our heads as we pulled out our sleeping bags. We nodded our heads as we made our dinners and ate our food. We nodded as we sat back with cups of cocoa. Still Wolf talked on. Firefly seemed honestly curious about this strange beast that had occupied the shelter with us, more interested in his need for attention than his current topic of conversation. Thus, Wolf directed his monologue primarily toward Firefly.

As he talked, time passed, light faded and I grew concerned about Silver. I knew he'd planned to meet us at this shelter, but what was taking him so long? He should have been here an hour ago. It was almost completely dark by the time he showed up. He was a bit harried after making a wrong turn and exhausted after putting in an extra few miles before correcting his error. It had been a very long day. I served him a cup of chocolate-mint cocoa to warm him up, get some calories into him and to celebrate St. Patty's Day. We all slept better that night, even though we were sharing the shelter with a Wolf.

The next day was almost all downhill. The frosty forest was mystical. We stopped to listen to conversations between owls asking, "Who cooks for you?" "Who cooks for you?" which got us thinking about food. We were headed for the Standing Bear hostel just outside the park. We looked forward to sleeping inside, getting showers, heat, a bunk and town food! And the elevation would be just 1,850 feet! Ahhh... We'd made it over our first hurdle.

"Ladies First"

We reached Standing Bear hostel at mid-day and dropped our packs. The owner, who bore a strong resemblance to Tommy Lee Jones, showed us around. It looked like the whole compound was made of salvaged building materials. There was the rough bunkhouse with a wood stove where the guys would stay, the lovely cabin built right over the creek with French doors and a loft for me, the root cellar full of trail food we could buy, the little hut that served as a laundry with a desk, computer and internet access, the adjacent camp kitchen, and what I'd been waiting for, a shower house with clean towels! That's when I heard the magic words from my companions:

"Ladies first."

I thoroughly enjoyed my first hot shower in a week and wore my dirty clothes inside. I soaped up with them on and then again after removing them. When I emerged the guys stepped in to do the same while I strung up a clothes line outside. The afternoon still had some warmth in it. But within the hour the sun had slipped behind the steep horizon and into an early dusk. With the sun went the warmth. I grabbed my things from the lovely but chilled private cabin and claimed a spot in the bunk house with the guys. It had a wood stove. Privacy is one luxury I could give up in exchange for heat.

The little wood stove in the center of the bunk house was promising but it was missing one key ingredient... wood. I looked around the place and found a stash of logs under the porch, all too long to fit into the stove. Sprocket, a hiker and friend of the owner, got a chain saw and bucked up the logs while I split them. I'd lived many years with only wood heat and was handy with a hatchet. Silver and Firefly seemed impressed. They helped carry the wood inside and soon we had a good fire going. I strung up the clothesline between the bunks and our laundry finished drying as we huddled by the fire.

A local stopped by and offered us a ride to the nearest restaurant. It was more like a gas and sip but we weren't complaining. We got a hot meal and headed back to the bunkhouse where we stoked the fire and enjoyed the warmth swapping stories as the night grew cold outside.

In the midst of this happy scene came the other woman. She had driven all the way from Michigan seeking out this remote cabin in the dark. When she drove up, Silver's eyes lit up like headlights. He ran outside and then brought her in to show her around. After a moment, he turned to us and said, "This is my wife, Marilyn."

Shock! Awe! We'd been invaded by aliens! Just about everyone we'd met in the last three weeks had been on the trail. Suddenly here was someone from that other world, one we'd willingly left behind.

I offered my hand saying, "Hi, I'm Maribeth." which sounded completely unfamiliar. Firefly and Silver exchanged looks. There was a moment's hesitation. Then Firefly shook her hand and introduced himself as "Eric". So the secret's out! We had other, ordinary sounding names.

Silver had arranged to take a break from the trail and go home for a few days. He had a family to connect with and a business to manage. His daughter was running a marathon and he wanted to be there to cheer her on. He'd be back in a week and promised to catch up with us. He grabbed his pack and just before following Marilyn outside, he gave Firefly a look that said, "Take care of Scout while I'm gone."

Sleeping Around

I didn't really choose my trail family, but once we'd started traveling together, I chose to keep them. From the first day I met Silver when he let me go ahead of him at the outfitters, I knew he was a courteous gentleman. He saved me a spot in shelters on several occasions, and let me take the first showers when we reached the hostels.

Firefly had proven to be entertaining, intelligent and insightful. He was energetic and engaging with other people we met, and he added comic relief to our hiking experience.

Hiking with a happily married man and a man half my age allowed me to hike as a single, middle aged woman with some degree of protection. People have often asked if I was scared of bears, but after three decades of wilderness experience, the conclusion I'd drawn was that the scariest animals out there are human. I've studied wildlife enough to know how to avoid trouble, but humans are hard to predict. Hiking with Silver and Firefly made me more comfortable than I would've been traveling alone.

When Zama and Lug joined the family I also benefited from the luxury of having another woman at the shelter. I've observed that men, even crazy, young, obnoxious men living out in the woods for months on end, tend to moderate their behavior when there are women around. Being "older" women (meaning over thirty) we may have reminded them of their mothers or teachers or other female authority figures.

Zama was known for her cooking. She and Lug ate like royalty every night while the rest of us drooled. Lug and Firefly shared a similar playful spirit. Both Zama and Lug were modest, kind and generous, even though we continually and mistakenly referred to them as Zug and Llama.

Tank wandered in and out of our family. He was the youngest, just nineteen years old, and the quietest. As we hiked we reported to each other if Tank spoke more than a sentence or two that day. He was like our quiet kid brother, or youngest son. It seemed that Silver and I had become like parents of this flock.

Many hikers formed groups but ours was the most diverse I'd met. We had a representative for each decade from the teens to the fifties. We hailed from Washington, Oregon, Michigan, Connecticut and Alabama. Our trail family opened up and reached out to other thru-hikers who I called our extended family. Cruise, from Virginia, and his cousin Applesauce, from Florida, Salsa, Cedar Moe and Pogue from Tennessee, Superman from Illinois, Jolly Green Giant from Georgia, Messenger and Braveheart from North Carolina and a host of other hikers migrating north through the seasons.

Firefly and I slept well in the warm bunkhouse. When we awoke it was another story. The uninsulated building had become a refrigerator overnight. We got up and packed early. Sprocket popped in and said someone had dropped off a bag of potatoes and invited us to breakfast in the camp kitchen. He served up farm fresh eggs and a pile of hash browns and sent us on our way fully fueled. We hoisted our packs and were just heading out when Zama, Lug, Cruise, Applesauce and Salsa arrived. We left the place to them and said we'd see them in Hot Springs in two days time.

That morning we crossed Max Patch, an exposed mountain top meadow. At over 4,600 feet it was covered in snow with a brisk wind. Firefly said in summer it was a popular spot for weddings, but our procession was not as formal or as slow. We walked quickly to get back into the cover of the trees.

At the shelter that night we met two SOBO's still trying to finish a hike they'd started nine months before. Bemis and South Paw had actually met Firefly in Maine when he'd started his ill fated hike the year before. They had some scary stories about trying to hike through deep snow on Mount Rogers in Virginia. They'd done some extended work-for-stays at certain hostels and were finally closing in on the finish line. They both welcomed and dreaded reaching the end.

We, on the other hand, were just beginning.

First Day of Spring?

In the morning Firefly and I started north together but it wasn't long before the temperatures dropped and rain began to fall. I told him to go ahead while I stopped to put on my long johns. We were aiming for Elmer's hostel in Hot Springs, North Carolina, eighteen miles away. I figured Firefly was twenty or thirty minutes ahead of me but as the day grew colder there was no question that either of us could stop without getting dangerously chilled. The trail led across the top of Bluff Mountain, elevation 4,686 feet, where I climbed up icy stone steps to a thin ridge. I paused to take in the view. Icicles clung to the shrubbery and frost covered the landscape far into the distance. As rain began to fall, I moved on. The rain soon turned to sleet and finally snow.

I had read about hiking with an umbrella and this was the first time I tried it. My mother's folding umbrella was small enough to fit into the side pocket of my pack. It not only kept my upper body dry and blocked a cold wind, it also provided a tiny amphitheatre for my voice with the percussion of rain as my back-up band. It was silver colored so I sang into it as I walked:

Bring me lil' water Silvie,
Bring me lil' water now,
Bring me lil' water Silvie,
Every lil' once and a while.
Every lil' once and a while.

As the snow came down in fat flakes and mixed with the mud on the ground, the trail became a trough of slush. My shoes and socks got soaked. The damp and cold wicked up my pants to my thighs. I had to keep moving. I had to stay positive. I had to make it to Hot Springs. I sang.

Singing in the snow,
I'm singing in the snow.
What a wonderful feeling,
Just nine miles to go.

Though he couldn't stop and wait Firefly was apparently thinking of me. I was following his tracks and now and then he left a sign in the snow. He made a five foot circle here. He spelled something out there. And further on... were these dance steps? I appreciated his encouragement. It was good to know I wasn't really alone. At least I didn't *feel* alone.

When I looked through the bare branches of the trees and saw a cluster of little rooftops and a row of toy school buses far below, I willed those buses to get bigger. It seemed to take hours, but gradually they grew and at long last I found myself stepping down stone steps onto a road in the tiny town of Hot Springs, North Carolina.

I followed the trail blazes right down the sidewalk along the main street to the Post Office. Opening the glass door, I folded my umbrella, and asked for my mail drop. As I waited, I noticed a pool was forming around me on the floor. The clerk returned and passed the package over the counter frowning as she noticed it, too. I mumbled an apology. She gave me directions to the hostel pointing back the way I'd come.

It felt all wrong to go south after three weeks of going only north but I forced myself to back track expecting to see a sign. The slushy snow was still falling when I asked a woman hurrying by on the street who said, "It's the big white house on the corner." But it seemed there were big white houses on every corner.

Walking in the direction she'd pointed I came upon a dark, neglected looking Victorian with overgrown shrubbery and water cascading off the roof. It wasn't until I got up on the front porch that I saw a handwritten note on an index card duct taped to the door jam saying, "Use the kitchen door." I went around the house until I found Firefly's pack on the back porch, a confirmation. Dropping my pack next to his, I stepped inside.

There sat Firefly by a big, old stove polishing off a plate of leftover pancakes. A tall man behind a central counter pushed a bowl of soup in my direction. I pulled up a stool and began to spoon the goodness and warmth into me. He and Firefly were talking but the words didn't register. It was a comforting sound, like a murmuring creek or birds singing in the woods. It didn't have to mean anything. I didn't have to understand it.

As I ate I stared at the tall man's shirt. There was a design and symbols around it. I'd recently gone back to school to get my teaching certificate so I knew that these symbols were letters. Very slowly, through the voice of my literacy instructor, I heard, "Letters form words. Words have meaning." Gradually I realized these words said, "Pike Place Market".

Pike Place Market, I repeated inwardly. That sounds familiar. Eventually the thought crept into my mind, "Hey, Pike Place Market is in Seattle." And a moment later I realized, "Hey! *I'm* from Seattle."

I figure if you can spell hypothermia, you probably don't have it.

I'd made it to Elmer's Sunnybank Inn. Elmer wasn't there, but his staff was welcoming. After the soup, they pointed me toward a heater in the hall. Firefly and I draped our wet coats, socks and shoes over some ladder back chairs to dry. Then we were given what seemed to be the required tour. I hated to leave the heater, but I didn't want to be rude.

Our host told us that this was the house where the "Songcatcher" lived. A musicologist named Olive Dame Campbell lived there while she collected and recorded authentic mountain music around the turn of the century. The last century. I'd seen a movie about her years before. So, of course, our tour included going into the music room which had been closed off and was frigid. I thought it ironic that the only unheated room in the house was full of musical instruments. I didn't think Miss Olive would approve. As much as I like to sing and play music, the lure of the piano, guitar and banjo could not compete with the gas heater in the next room.

We were taken upstairs where several doors opened onto a long hall. I was shown to a sunny room at the front of the house with two beds. One was occupied by a sleeping woman. Firefly got a room near the back. Most of the rooms were empty when we arrived, but it was clear the house could hold a lot of hikers, and as the night wore on, it did.

Returning down the stairs Firefly nodded toward the bathroom saying, "Go ahead. Take your time."

I got a towel and took a long hot shower. Then I went upstairs and climbed in between flannel sheets under a thick layer of quilts. The mattress was like a giant feather pillow that wrapped around me. My body radiated warmth and my muscles relaxed. I fell into a comatose sleep.

Waking well before dinner, I found my clothes had dried, all but my shoes, so I got dressed, retrieved the banjo from the music room and hung out in the parlor by the gas stove. More hikers came in: Cruise, Applesauce, Salsa and a little later, Zama and Lug arrived.

Firefly approached me with a troubled mind. He'd received word that a woman he'd dated a time or two was coming to meet him there. She'd sent him a care package with all his favorite things, a bottle of whiskey, a box of cigars, some homemade brownies. I told him it sounded good to me, but he was clearly uncomfortable. It was evident that he did not intend to maintain a relationship with her while he was on the trail. Apparently this woman had different ideas.

We'd heard that the food served here was vegetarian, organic and mostly grown on Elmer's farm just outside of town. Hikers could work for their stay by helping on the farm… weather permitting. I was really looking forward to dinner, but could hardly stay awake until 7:00 p.m. when they finally called us to the table. They passed around hearty vegetarian lasagna and crusty homemade bread. The meal was good for body and soul. We all had our fill. As we ate, more hikers arrived and the crew quickly got them warmed and fed.

One of the staff sitting at the head of the long table reported that he'd read that 75% of Americans were extroverts. But on the Appalachian Trail it was the reverse. Thru-hikers were 75% introverts. That made sense to me. You'd have to enjoy solitude to go hiking for six months. Though there were many thru-hikers on the trail, I spent most of my time hiking alone. Then again, I enjoyed the company of my trail family as we gathered at the shelters and hostels in the evenings.

After dinner we moved into the parlor swapping stories. I played softly on the banjo enjoying the rocking chair and the warmth of the heater. It was 9:30 and I was on my way to bed when the last two half frozen hikers arrived. They'd walked thirty-one miles to get there, not their original plan. The hosts jumped up with a sense of urgency to get them hot tea and soup. Now the Inn was stuffed with grateful hikers, a refuge from the winter storm.

I celebrated the first day of spring by "taking a zero", meaning I would walk no trail miles that day. The bed was too warm and comfortable and the mountains too snowy and cold. I'd been hiking for twenty-one days straight and was ready for a break. I went to the library to catch up on emails, did laundry and bought supplies in town. I enjoyed strolling down the main street, in and out of shops, getting a few supplies and calling home. I walked from one end of town to the other, which didn't take long.

At the north end of town, I found the Hot Springs Spa from which the town got its name. My trail guide said the hot springs had attracted visitors since the 1700's. A detention center and prison of war camp was built there during World War I for Germans and German-Americans. They enjoyed the 105 degree mineral baths so much that many of them stayed. Old literature claimed the waters were therapeutic and could "bring vigor to a wasted frame" which sounded inviting. But in the 1990's the springs were bought and converted to an upscale spa, a luxury most thru-hikers could not afford.

Back at the hostel I met Firefly and his visitor. They'd arranged to shuttle her car to Devil's Fork Gap, a day's hike away. They'd hike together from Hot Springs to the car and then part company.

My roommate, Juliangelo, a young artist from Chicago, offered me some of her lotion. When I looked in the mirror I found out why. My face had become so red and wind chapped, it was peeling. It took several applications through out the day before my skin returned to normal.

Juliangelo was traveling with her dog, Thoreau, a beautiful and spirited husky, who slept on the back porch. She wouldn't be traveling on with us just yet. She had to tend to some business in town. Besides, she told me, "I love that big, cushy bed."

After having a relaxing day off, I packed my bag in anticipation of an early departure in the morning. I had a good nights sleep and woke ready to go. The day dawned cold and clear but "precipitation" was in the forecast. I wanted to put as many miles behind me as I could before that "precipitation" hit the high country.

But first breakfast! At the long table we passed around rhubarb compote, yoghurt, stacks of pancakes and maple syrup. The host asked us all to tell something about someone else at the table that the rest of the group might not already know. When it was my turn I mentioned that Firefly was a movie expert. The host grinned.

"A movie expert is he?" Firefly shot me the evil eye. I sank down in my chair.

The host challenged Firefly to name a movie for every other letter in the alphabet while the rest of us went around the table filling in movies for the letters in between. Firefly didn't falter. He named old movies, obscure movies and recent blockbusters without discretion. Not only could he name the movies, but he could name the stars, the directors, the year they came out, Oscars won and their social significance, if any. It took all of the rest of us to fill in the letters between.

Even with a belly full of pancakes, I managed to squeeze behind the chairs in the dining room, settle my bill and grab my pack to be one of the first out the door that day. As I walked through town, itty bitty snowflakes twinkled like fairy dust in the morning sun. Though they lasted for only a moment, they foretold what was to come.

Big Bald

At the end of the sidewalk, I crossed the river and climbed the ridge, then paused for a last look at the tiny town of Hot Springs before heading into the hills. The going was easy and I was rested so I made good time. At 1:30 I reached the first shelter. It was small with only enough room for five hikers to sleep. I knew there would be twice that many coming from the hostel, so I pushed on to see how far I could go. I caught up with Lug and Zama at about 4:30. They were filtering water by a stream and said they planned to camp nearby. The next shelter was just five miles away and I had plenty of energy and daylight so I hiked on. I ended up going twenty miles that day and had the shelter to myself. I left this little rhyme in the shelter log that revealed my transition to trail culture.

The weather was mild, the trail was kind, so I made it here in damned good time.

I got here just a bit 'fore dark, cooked up some beans and let out a fart.

Scared the roamin' bears away, slept peacefully till the break of day.

Now I'm off to Erwin town where I'm sure I'll see you folks around.

The next day I hiked a leisurely thirteen miles and was joined at the shelter by my favorite trail couple, Lug and Zama. A New Yorker, Woody Crow, joined us a little later. Explaining his trail name he said a friend told him he looked like a combination of Woody Allen and Russell Crowe. Personally, I didn't see the Russell Crowe part. Lug and Zama pitched their tent outside the shelter and made dinner at the picnic table in front of it. While writing in the shelter log I overheard their conversation.

Zama asked, "If you were a noodle, what kind of noodle would you be?"

Without missing a beat Lug responded, "I'd be a broad noodle."

"Like an egg noodle?"

"Like lasagna."

"I'd be a Penne noodle." added Zama.

Later, I heard Zama say, "I don't know if I'm getting tan or just dirty."

Woody Crow was planning to do a thirty mile day starting at 5:00 a.m. He needed to get to the Post Office in Erwin, Tennessee to pick up a mail drop before they closed at noon on Saturday. Otherwise, he'd have to wait until they opened again on Monday. He apologized in advance for his alarm clock.

Late that night some locals came up the trail. From deep in my sleeping bag I could hear voices, a man and a woman. It sounded as if at least one of them was drunk. They fumbled around with their tent, talking loudly and disturbing the peace. Finally, they got quiet.

Hours later from the depths of my dreams I heard a distant rooster crow. It kept crowing over and over though it was still pitch dark. I didn't think there were any farms nearby, but the crowing continued… until Woody turned off his alarm clock.

He emerged from his sleeping bag and turned on his headlamp. I turned in my bunk to face the opposite wall. He rustled around in his pack, made his breakfast, packed his gear and finally headed out. As he left the shelter I opened one eye. In the light of his headlamp I saw there were three or four inches of snow on the ground and big, fat flakes were falling lazily through the trees.

I lay in my bag for a while thinking about the snow. As the day dawned white and cold, I got up, made breakfast and consulted my guidebook. I wasn't fond of winter camping or hiking in the snow. Lug and Zama came into the shelter to hang up their wet tent that had collapsed in the night. I told them of my revised plan. Instead of hiking to Erwin in three short days, I'd do it in two long ones and spend the night in the Bald Mountain Shelter at over 5,000 feet. They wished me luck. I shouldered my pack and set out following Woody Crow's footprints in the snow. Thus began one of my most trying days on the trail.

The snow continued to fall all day. I was okay as long as I kept moving. I climbed in elevation until I got to a bald, a high open meadow. Out of tree cover, the wind was suddenly much stronger and the snow blew sideways. The white blazes that marked the trail were on weathered fence posts but the whiteout conditions made it difficult to see from one post to the next. Woody's tracks disappeared under the snow drifts. I held my umbrella to the side to block the combined force of snow and wind and peered ahead into a shimmering curtain of white.

The trail was a deep trench full of snow that I could feel more than see. If I walked on the actual trail, I'd sink in up to my knees, so I tried to stay on the grassy edges, but they were uneven. I staggered like a drunkard at the edge of the trail. A few times I was in near panic when I could see neither blazes, nor foot prints, nor detect the depression of the trench. I strained to see any clues ahead. Inching my way forward feeling with my feet, I stumbled along. I talked myself through it knowing no one would follow me past the last shelter and the people ahead had no idea I was coming. I was on my own.

Finally, I reached the protection of the trees again and breathed a sigh of relief. I picked up my pace until I came upon the next bald mountain top where the struggle began anew.

This happened three times that day. Each time, my progress slowed. Crossing the last bald, I knew if I lost the trail it would take a while to circle the field and find it. I was running out of daylight and couldn't afford to lose anymore time. I had no tent, only a small tarp for shelter. At last, I got into the trees again and relative safety. I uttered a grateful prayer to the Universe. Suddenly my energy was renewed and my state of mind was positive. I bolted ahead trying to make up for lost time.

At dusk, I arrived at the shelter after a nineteen mile day and found a man called "Wayfarer". He looked to be about seventy, sitting comfortably having dinner in expensive looking gear. I immediately thanked him for leaving his tracks. Woody had passed him, so Wayfarer's tracks had led me to the shelter. The temperatures were well below freezing and my boots were soaked through. I added layers of warm clothes as quick as I could and removed my boots and socks which immediately froze solid. I tucked myself into my sleeping bag and made a hot dinner. Reluctantly, I got out of my bag just long enough to hang my food and pack from the rafters and then hunkered down again. That night the temperatures dropped into the teens.

Around 1:00 a.m. the shelter host arrived. Mice are common in AT shelters but this was a special encounter with a fellow that commanded respect. He wore a black fur coat with distinctive white stripes down his back. We used our best manners and asked him to leave but he had other ideas and followed his nose around the shelter. Wayfarer was on the upper bunk at the opposite side of the shelter from me. He'd left his gear on the bunk below. When the skunk approached his cooking pots, Wayfarer shooed him in my direction.

"Wait a minute. Could we talk this over first?" The skunk was fast approaching my bunk. It was then that I discovered yet another vital use for an open umbrella. I used it with gentle persuasion to keep the skunk at bay. My efforts were successful, but he still didn't leave.

The skunk's attention then turned to my pack, hanging from the rafters. I'd hung my food in a separate bag with a tight drawstring hung on a mouse baffle (a tuna can turned upside down with a string through the bottom tied to a stick. The drawstring of a food bag can go around the stick and the mice cannot go around the tuna can suspended from the rafters). But the intruder seemed more interested in my empty pack. At least I thought it was empty. The varmint dove in head first leaving the dangerous end ready to fire. After some shuffling around, he emerged with a frozen tube of nut butter I'd apparently forgotten was inside. He threw it out onto the plywood floor and chased it around the shelter. It sounded like someone slamming a hockey puck against the walls, drumming it on the floor and sliding it from one corner to the next. Wayfarer and I tried to keep the skunk in the spotlight of our headlamps. I held my umbrella like a shield. I would've gladly offered up the treat in exchange for a quiet night's sleep. Finally, after about an hour of enjoying the spotlight, our shelter host lost interest in the rock hard tube and left us to burrow down into our bags until dawn.

The next morning it was agonizing to transition from my warm cocoon to the frozen world outside. I was becoming adept at clothing myself inside my sleeping bag and put on as many layers as possible before exposing myself to the freezing temperatures.

There were eight or ten inches of snow on the picnic table. At least I wouldn't have to go to the spring for water. But first I had urgent business at the privy. I grimaced as I shoved my feet into frozen boots and raced through the deep powder to the outhouse. The walls were two feet short of the roof, good for ventilation. When I peered in, I found six inches of snow on the toilet seat. It was a chilling experience and wasn't long before I was bounding back to the shelter again.

I melted snow to make oatmeal as Wayfarer emerged from his bag. He asked when I'd started my hike and then warned that I was going too fast. He actually used the phrase, "Stop and smell the roses." I looked out at the foot of snow on the ground with more fat flakes coming down and said, "I don't see any roses, Wayfarer, but when I do, I'll be sure to stop and smell them."

By 8:30 I was on my way to Erwin, Tennessee following a subtle trench left by Woody Crow the night before. The white blazes were difficult to see because snow was clinging to all the tree trunks making it look like every tree was covered with white blazes. The drifts had swallowed Woody's trail in a few places, but it only took a minute to find it again. I was led by clues like a log on the ground with a three foot section missing. I was aware that my friends would follow, and I did not want to lead them astray.

Gradually, as I dropped in elevation, the snow grew thin. I came around a corner and suddenly there was color! Green, brown and grey! I walked in and out of snow as the intermittent stretches of color became more frequent. The sun would come out and then the sky would darken to a metallic grey and it would snow or sleet again. The trail was mostly gentle downhill and I started thinking of these easy stretches as "free miles". I'd earned them and now I got to take advantage of them, so I lengthened my stride and cruised the last sixteen miles toward Erwin.

Passing under heavy snow-laden rhododendrons, my umbrella kept the snow from sliding down the back of my neck. As I walked I began to sing,

Winnie the Pooh doesn't know what to do.
He's got a honey jar stuck on his nose.
He came to me asking help and advice
And from there no one knows where he goes.
Well I wandered much further today than I should,
And I can't seem to find my way back to the woods…

Just then I came upon a couple with two small boys that had camped out in the snow the night before. They looked miserable, at the verge of tears really, but were taken aback to see a woman walking down the trail alone, wearing her coat backwards, carrying an umbrella and singing. I stopped to pass the time and hoped my buoyant mood would be contagious. (Thinking back now, it might possibly have been more disturbing than comforting.)

As I walked down the mountain, I eventually left the snow behind. The sound of a distant train whistle told me I was nearing a town. It wasn't long before I saw the Nolichucky River far below. At 5:00 p.m. I stepped off the trail and crossed the road. Just then a car stopped and a man offered me a ride into town. I was only going a mile to the

Holiday Inn where I was to meet my folks the next day, but I accepted. As he dropped me off at the door, he offered to come back in an hour and take me to dinner. Immediately, I was reminded that I was a lone woman and must remain cautious. I thanked him for the ride, but graciously declined the invite to dinner. Besides, I couldn't wait an hour to eat.

Whenever I walked into a town, I had loud voices inside my head arguing.

"First let's soak in a hot bath."

"No way! I have to get a good, hot meal!"

"But I'm so tired, I need a bed!"

"And for God's sake, girl! When are you going to wash your stinking clothes?"

As I made my way to the front desk at the Holiday Inn I knew that very soon all my needs would be met.

"How are you today?" the clerk said with eyes on his desk.

"Much better now that I'm here," I answered.

He looked up then, saw a half frozen hiker carrying her pack, and a startled look crossed his face.

"You won't be doing so well when I tell you this is Nascar Race weekend in Bristol. All the hotels in the area are booked solid. We only have one room left and its $279 a night."

I was shocked. In the guide book it had said the usual price was around $65. I told the clerk I had to take it because I'd arranged to meet my parents there. He felt terrible so dropped the price to $179 and signed me in.

I went up to my room, changed into my cleanest shirt and washed my face and hands. (No, Zama, it wasn't a tan.) I thought I'd go to the burger joint next door, get some take out and come back here to eat it while I ran a hot bath. Then I'd call my folks and tell them I was off the trail a day earlier than expected.

As I was about to leave the room, I went to the window to draw the curtains. Three floors below, something caught my eye. Down in the parking lot a couple was leaning into their car unloading some stuff.

"Hey," I thought, "that's *my* stuff!" I looked closer at the car. Yes, it was a Prius. Then I looked at the couple. Goodness! Those were *my* parents! I couldn't believe they were here early, too. We'd arrived at the same place just minutes apart.

I stepped off the elevator just as I heard the clerk turning them away. It was gratifying to see the change in their expressions as I interjected, "But you could share my room."

It was a wonderful reunion. All of us had been traumatized by our travels through the snow. We immediately went next door for burgers and root beer. When we got back to the room I had a good long soak in the tub. We ate popcorn and watched a movie on TV which kept me up much later than usual. Finally, I fell asleep in a big, clean bed. I was blissfully happy.

Miss Janet's

Early the next morning I dressed in the clean clothes my parents had brought, snuck out of the room and took the elevator down to the lobby. My boots were still wet and I'd looked forward to wearing my old familiar sneakers that day.

When I got to the lobby I found a great buffet breakfast only provided during Race Week (in an effort to justify the elevated prices). The manager, who was serving the food, saw me come downstairs with shoes on but then approach the buffet in my stocking feet. When she asked I told her I'd been hiking the Appalachain Trail and my parents brought my tennis shoes, but my feet had swollen and wouldn't fit into them anymore. She smiled and said she'd heard I was here. She cut the price of our room in half for the second night.

My parents came down and joined me for breakfast as I went back for seconds. Then Dad and I drove to the trailhead and picked up my buddies who were just coming down from the last shelter. We gave Firefly and Wayfarer a ride to Miss Janet's hostel in town. Zama and Lug stayed at the hostel across the road from the trailhead. Applesauce and Cruise were surprised by their parents who showed up with a picnic though it was still snowing outside. They invited us to join them, but we were already satiated. I heard later that they followed the hikers, stopping in trail towns with a car full of extra food, clothes and first-aid supplies offering comfort and assistance to any thru-hikers who traveled with Cruise and Applesauce.

We went back to the hotel to get Mom and then drove into town to meet Firefly for lunch at a diner near Miss Janet's. Firefly had told me how he'd been dreaming of fresh produce. He fantasized about going to a good grocery store, pulling a stool up to the produce counter and stuffing fresh fruits and veggies into his gaping maw. He ordered broccoli, potatoes, green beans and corn. But when his plate arrived, all the produce he'd been so anxiously awaiting came deep fried. He eyed the plate in disbelief. There was a moment of silence. Then we all offered to share our food with him.

My father had been terrified as he drove over the mountains in the snow, but we offered no sympathy.

"Were you in a heated car?" we asked.

"Well, yes, but..."

"Was there a paved road beneath you?"

"Well, yes, but..."

"Did you have a cell phone with which to call for help in an emergency?"

"Well, yes, but..."

"Okay then!"

At the restaurant Firefly told us about his hike over Bald Mountain. He had arrived at the last shelter the night before and found Wayfarer with his gear spread across the entire shelter. Firefly was hiking with Cruise, Applesauce and Salsa who moved into the sparse room left in the shelter. Just before dark, Zama and Lug arrived and asked if there was enough room for them, too. Wayfarer answered, "No."

The others hung as much gear up as they could on nails along the wall to make room. Wayfarer did nothing to accommodate them.

That morning at Miss Janet's, Wayfarer had taken a long, hot shower and then spent most of an hour preening himself in the bathroom while other hikers waited. He was not making any friends.

After lunch we took Firefly back to Miss Janet's. The rundown house in the old part of town had a long row of worn out boots that adorned the front porch. Walking sticks decorated the doorway. We went inside to visit with the other thru-hikers. My parents met Superman, Yahtzee and the Jolly Green Giant whose thick, curly hair had gone wild.

"Who does your hair?" my mother asked as she looked up admiringly.

"A whole team of beauticians follow me down the trail," he answered straight faced while fluffing up his 'fro.

The place was stuffed with hikers. Some had been there for several days waiting out the snow. Others were just leaving to get back on the trail. There were packs and gear strung up to dry on the porch and in the laundry room. Sleeping bags and blankets were thrown across the couches and floor in the living room. A comedy show was on TV in the corner. A puppy that someone found abandoned on the trail was carried for two days until it arrived at Miss Janet's and was adopted. The chaos of dogs and people was a bit crazier than Elmer's had been in Hot Springs.

Miss Janet promoted "slack packing" from Erwin, up and over Roan Mountain, a formidable challenge well over 6,000 feet and especially treacherous in snow. Shuttles to and from the trail were easy to arrange so one could leave one's pack at the hostel and hike all day with a borrowed day pack meeting the van for a ride to the hostel for the night. It sounded like a really good idea to me, especially with the possibility of more snow in the forecast. I told Firefly I would spend the day with my parents and be ready to hike again on Monday.

We had an easy day. I did my laundry while soaking in the hotel hot tub smiling up at the mountainside covered in snow. That evening we went out to a nice restaurant with a view of a river gorge. The place was popular among rafters but in this wintry March weather, it was nearly empty. We ordered barbeque, veggies and coleslaw. As we waited for the food to arrive, we looked the place over. A wall of local attractions displayed an account of an incident that many people in Erwin would like to forget, the story of Mary, the killer elephant. Or how Erwin became known for hanging an elephant until dead. It was a gruesome tale.

Historians have documented the facts that led up to the horrible event. It was in September of 1916 when the circus came to town. This little circus had been roaming the south for decades, first by wagon and then by train. Mary was their first elephant and for twenty years had never been any trouble.

Unfortunately, that summer the long time elephant trainer had to leave the circus. He was replaced by another animal trainer and a new man who'd been recently hired to assist. While leading the elephants to a watering hole, Mary was attracted to a watermelon on the side of the road. She went for it. The assistant trainer prodded her sensitive ear with a bull hook and Mary became enraged. She turned on the trainer, knocked him down and flattened his head with her foot. The town folk were terrified. They tried to shoot her but the guns of the day were not powerful enough. The elephant was arrested and later hung and buried at the railroad yard. This is the event that stands out in Erwin's history. I found it disturbing. We turned the conversation to other things and tried to focus on our food.

Returning to the hotel after dinner, my parents watched TV while I packed for an early departure. I unwound toilet paper from the roll in the bathroom estimating at least three days worth. That went into a Zip-lock bag with a small bottle of hand sanitizer which I'd keep in the right pocket of my fleece vest. The left pocket would carry my head lamp and bandanna. I zipped the pockets shut. The vest was the warm layer I'd put on when chilled on the trail or when I reached the shelter each night. When I snuggled down in my sleeping bag, my vest became my pillowcase. Any clothes I took off before going to sleep were stuffed inside my vest for a pillow. I'd always have my headlamp handy at night. In the morning, I'd put my vest on and make my way to the privy with my toilet paper and hand sanitizer already in the pocket.

I packed food in bags and spread them across the bed to assess my rations before loading them into my food bag. Then I emptied my first-aid and repair bag out across the blanket. Alcohol swabs, safety pins, band-aids and blister block, a patch kit for my sleeping pad, Benadryl, aspirin, Neosporin, a roll of athletic tape and gauze pads. I had fuel for my stove and water treatment drops. I carefully packed everything in their places. My pack was light. It had no frame inside or out, so it was essential to pack it carefully. When I was done, my pack was about the size of a pillow case and carried no more than thirty pounds.

As I finished, I turned and found my Mom had been observing me. She looked up at me and said just one word, "Amazing."

Just before bedtime the phone rang. It was Firefly who said he had a surprise for me. Then I heard Silver's voice on the phone. It was a little disorienting. We'd hiked together for two weeks. Then he'd disappeared while Firefly, Zama, Lug and I had hiked on through thick snow and freezing temperatures. And suddenly he was back stepping in again as if he'd never left. This became a pattern with Silver.

He had checked into Miss Janet's and had a plan for slack packing the next day. Firefly, Zama and Lug would all start hiking north together where they'd left off at the edge of town. I asked my parents to drop Silver and I off north of town, which was on their way home. We could slack pack south together twenty miles back into Erwin and stay at the hostel again the next night. I agreed to meet Silver at Miss Janet's in the morning.

When we arrived at 9:00 a.m. the house was utter chaos. One group of hikers were getting ready to get back on the trail, but had to wait until after breakfast. Other hikers were still coming in out of the snowy hills. Bunks were a hot commodity. Firefly, who was leaving, took my pack and threw it up on the top bunk, pulling his own pack down. "You can have my bunk." he said.

I introduced my parents to Silver who said something like, "It's been a pleasure to hike with your daughter. She always acts like a lady."

A curious comment, I thought. What, if anything I'd been doing lately would be considered "lady-like". No doubt it was meant to reassure my folks, though I'm not sure it did. It would give them something to talk about on the long drive home.

Silver was chomping at the bit to get started. He'd already packed one of the loaner day packs from Miss Janet's collection. He offered one to me. I threw in some food, water, an extra layer for warmth and a first-aid bag. Then we hugged Firefly good-bye. We'd see him on the trail.

My folks took us by a fast food place so Silver could get a breakfast sandwich before we headed for the trail. Silver told us that Tank sent his snow shoes home from Hot Springs and the day after, it had snowed. So, it was all Tank's fault!

At a wide place where the road crossed the trail, we pulled over and Silver and I got out. I thanked my folks for being good trail angels and gave them each a hug. They took our picture as Silver and I started out to hike the trail back to town. I was glad they'd had a chance to meet a good swath of the thru-hiker community. From then on Mom would ask about each of them by name and occasionally would get on the phone to speak with them directly.

For the next few days I sent emails to them from Miss Janet's. The first day, Silver and I had hiked several miles but had a tough time trying to figure out where we were and how far we had to go. We were now hiking south and meeting thru-hikers as they continued north. We met up with Applesauce, Cruise, Salsa and Pogue. Pogue had taken a side trip from the Smokies into Gatlinburg, Tennessee. It's a hopping tourist destination that attracts some hikers and repels others. Pogue had a new haircut, a four inch Mohawk. He said he got it on a dare on Saint Patrick's Day. One look at that hair-do would drive all the snakes out of Ireland, or any other country. I'm pretty sure alcohol was involved.

As we compared maps with our fellow hikers, we determined that we were going much slower than usual because of the foot of snow on the ground. If we continued with our original plan to hike twenty miles at this pace, we wouldn't finish until long after dark. But there was another option. Miss Janet was going to meet another group of hikers at a road crossing about five miles ahead. We could hike an eleven mile day today and do nine the next, going back to Miss Janet's for a warm bed in between. Silver reluctantly agreed.

Now we had no need to rush. I stopped at one shelter and made a snow man sitting at the picnic table. I called it "Raymond eating Ramen". Later, we came upon Yahtzee, Woody Crow, Bluebird and

Abandon. I gave them each some chocolate, a gift from my folks. When we arrived at the road crossing we met up with Superman, Juliangelo and Thoreau who were waiting for Miss Janet's rattletrap van. Thoreau, being a husky, thoroughly enjoyed the snow. At the end of the day we determined it had taken us six and a half hours to go just eleven miles.

Back in Erwin, just before going out to dinner, Jolly Green Giant arrived at the hostel. He was the biggest and strongest amongst us. He started out that morning from the same road crossing as Silver and I only he headed north with a full pack. He got over Roan Mountain in three feet of snow by brute strength. When he came out on a road at Carver's Gap he met a man taking pictures. The man, "Tarheel", had written the first AT guide book in 1979. He asked Jolly, "What in the hell do you think you're doing?"

Jolly replied, "Hiking to the next shelter."

Tarheel informed him that he'd never make it before dark and offered to take him anywhere else he wanted to go. So he returned to Miss Janet's for the night. Jolly's account of his day left us feeling like we had indeed made the right decision. He had no tracks to follow and repeatedly got lost and then found the trail again. When he got back to town he was shaking with exhaustion.

We were all hoping the expected rain and rising temperatures would clear the way for our forward progress. No doubt there would be a lot of mud and slush in the days ahead.

We were within a week of the Virginia border, but first we had to get out of Erwin, Tennessee. It seemed to some of us that Miss Janet's was a black hole. If you walked too far, her van would intercept you and bring you back. It was a party house with dinner shuttles to Johnson City, a nearby college town and late night drinking in the kitchen. Videos were watched non-stop in the living room. I slept with earplugs.

In the morning no one seemed in a rush to get going. There were now about a dozen people staying in the house. Miss Janet recruited help with breakfast. Others did laundry, vacuumed or swept, but nothing seemed to help the slow departure of the shuttle van to take us back to the trail each morning.

If you wanted to do a work-for-stay, Miss Janet had plenty of projects for you. I was talking with Silver in the bunk room when Miss Janet came in with a hiker explaining how she wanted this light rewired and that light relocated. She asked the hiker if he'd had experience with electrical work. He seemed hesitant. I looked at Silver who has a crew of electricians working for him wiring hospitals and shopping malls. He gave me a look that said, "Don't say a word."

The next morning at breakfast Miss Janet asked a question as a conversation starter. "If Robert Redford made a movie of the Appalachian Trail, who would you want to play your part?"

Without hesitation Silver spoke up, "Old blue eyes, Paul Newman."

I could see a slight resemblance. I pondered that question for days after and eventually composed a song.

O, Miss Janet asked a question of the hikers gathered round.
We discussed it over breakfast and then everyone left town.
But the question lingered with me as we hiked along for days.
I began to see my trail mates in distinctly different ways.

If Robert Redford made a movie of the Appalachian Trail
Who would you want to play your part,
Who would you want to prevail?
Johnny Depp, or Leonardo, or Matthew McConaughey
Sandra Bullock, Katie Hudson, oh, or Angelina Jolie!

When the question came upon me I responded in a pinch,
Keira Knightly in the morning, in the evening Judy Dench.
And perhaps there'd be some drama
And perhaps there'd be romance.
Kathy Bates would run the hostel with an element of chance.

Making up songs was a fun way to pass the time while hiking. I would finish this song months later.

The next day we finally summitted Roan Mountain. It was bright and blue and the top was bare and sunny. We met Zama and Lug and gave them each an apple which they thought was more precious than gold. On the way down the snowy slopes we met Firefly coming up. It was a steep climb for them and a precarious drop for us with plenty of snow and ice still on the slick trail. I admired them for sleeping in the shelters on such cold nights and continuing their northbound trek fully loaded. The small day pack I'd borrowed from Miss Janet's was heavily loaded with guilt. The gifts of apples relieved me of some of that burden.

Once we got down in elevation the snow disappeared and we walked in slushy mud for a while, but the last ten miles were clear, bare and dry. We took a break at Hughes Gap where Miss Janet left some trail magic for us, sodas, chips and chocolate cup cakes in a bag hanging from a tree.

There was also a wild boar that had been shot nearby and wrapped in a tarp. I'd heard warnings of these fierce, nocturnal creatures, but this was the first one I'd seen. We all got a good look. It was huge, blonde and had tusks about four inches long. Miss Janet's dog had come along with us and Juliangelo had her husky, Thoreau. The two dogs had been cohabitating well at the hostel, but they got into a vicious tussle over the boar. Bruno had to kick them apart. They hiked on leashes at opposite ends of the group the rest of the afternoon. We ended the day where my parents had dropped Silver and me off with no snow in sight. It's amazing what a difference a couple of days can make.

At the hostel that night Silver and I plotted our escape from Miss Janet's. The next day she'd drop our group at Carver's Gap and we'd hike north over the Humps. Miss Janet persuaded the eight of us who planned to hike on the next day to leave our backpacks in the van so she could take them up to the next hostel at Highway 19-E. We reluctantly agreed. The gentle slopes that lay ahead carrying only a borrowed day pack would make it an easy day indeed. Or so we thought.

Overmountain

Crossing the Humps went well. It was a beautiful day. The sun quickly melted the remaining snow. Climbing the trail between grasslands and rocks I could see the striations of ice on stone reminding me of the glacial history of western North Carolina. When I studied biology at nearby Appalachian State University, I'd learned that during the Ice Age, glaciers had moved into the Southern Appalachians pushing before them many species of plants and animals. Consequently there were more varieties of trees found here than in all of northern Europe. Most of them were hardwoods that had bare branches at this time of year, but the dry leaves that were emerging from under the snow attested to the diversity in pattern, shape and size.

But the Humps were mostly treeless, bald mountain tops accented by golden grass, shrubs and rocky outcrops. I was exuberant as I made my way easily along this open corridor appreciating the views of the distant hills and the line of hikers before and behind me. When I came upon the Overmountain Shelter I remembered that my sister, Tortoise, had had a very different experience. Instead of a pleasant day like this, she had struggled through a blizzard. Darkness fell as she pushed on and finally arrived at this old barn where she found shelter from the storm.

In the morning, prying herself out of her warm sleeping bag she wrote in her journal, "Boy, am I glad I live in the warm, sunny south."

As I toured the barn, now deserted, I found the shelter log and looked at the recent entries. I was surprised by an entry from Firefly who liked to read the logs but not write much. He had "found his voice" at last describing a lively gathering of hikers the night he'd spent here and of his own wild imaginings. I looked forward to catching up with him for more details. No two hikers experience any part of the trail the same way.

Though I crossed the Humps on a warm spring day, there were still patches of snow here and there. At one point I was stepping down from a snowy bank when my foot slipped. All my weight came down on my twisted knee. One thing I learned on the trail is if you have a problem, it's best to stop right then to deal with it. I bent it, flexed it, dug into my pack and got out my ace bandage, wrapped my knee and continued a little more slowly and cautiously than before.

Most thru-hikers carry two walking sticks. My sister calls them bi-polar. She and I walked with one, mono-polar. I like to have a hand free so I can get my water bottle out or adjust my clothing without stopping.

But there are advantages to walking with two sticks. If I'd had two sticks when I slipped, I probably wouldn't have twisted my knee. But then my companions had a touch of frostbite at the end of the day, where as I, walking with one hand in my pocket, and the other on my stick, routinely switching back and forth, did not.

That day we passed a cemetery. The plastic flowers had been blown by winter winds off the graves and up against the fence along the trail. I picked up a plastic bouquet of faded yellow roses and stuck them into the straps of my pack. Later I saw others with plastic blue violets. It seemed like a wish for spring, but it was dreadfully slow in coming.

We were headed for the next hostel, the Mountain Harbor B&B at US 19-E. Where the trail and the road met, there were piles of garbage, a real dump. We walked down the side of the road a little ways and soon arrived at the hostel.

Miss Janet had dropped our packs off earlier that day so we went to retrieve them. The owners explained that you could choose between sleeping in the hostel, or springing for the deluxe accommodations at the B&B. Only one of us took the B&B, Trail Mix. She obviously loved hiking the AT. She'd hiked it twice before and knew it well, served on an AT planning committee, dressed in stylish hiking skirts and leggings and didn't seem to worry much about spending money.

I, on the other hand, had to watch my expenses. Besides, all the fun folks were in the hostel. The owners had greeted us at the gate. Their goats had the run of the steep front lawn. Horses grazed below. They walked with Trail Mix toward the "big house" and pointed me in the direction of the barn.

I approached the well worn structure from the gate. Going inside the dark barn, the dense, earthy smell of mud and manure filled my head. I carefully watched my step in the shadows. I looked around for a light, or any sign of human habitation, but it all looked like horse stalls to me. I was wondering if this was where I was supposed to sleep and was trying to adjust my expectations. Then my rational mind spoke up saying, "You must have made a wrong turn." So I went back out into the daylight and walked around the back. Sure enough, there were steps leading up to a spacious deck that looked out over the barnyard, a little stream and the forested mountainside beyond.

Inside was a pleasant, though a bit snug, common room. The guys, Superman, Pogue, Silver and Yahtzee, were upstairs in the loft where there were four mattresses on the floor. Juliangelo and I would share a king-sized bed in an alcove curtained off from the main room. Wayfarer, who came in last, was not happy about the only option left, sleeping on the couch. We all got showers and the guys ordered pizza. While they waited, I was making pasta at the kitchen counter when Trail Mix showed up to cook her own dinner. The B&B provided only breakfast.

She liked to talk. She prepared her meal as if she were hosting a cooking show. I glanced around for the cameras. She explained every step out loud. Was she speaking to me? Was I interested? I sat down at a table nearby and propped up my feet to eat pasta out of my pot. Trail Mix continued her cooking monologue at the counter.

The next day I woke up to four legs stuck straight up in the air. Sometime in the night, Thoreau, the husky, had snuck into the middle of the bed. Fine by me. It just made us a little warmer. Some got an early start and set out for the next hostel twenty-four miles away. I took my time staying for breakfast at the B&B. All day I leapfrogged with Trail Mix who told me about each waterfall and landmark before I got there. There were no surprises, no sense of discovery. It was irritating. I dropped back and let some distance fall between us, but kept running into her and her running commentary until I'd drop back again.

At about 5:00 I arrived at the shelter where I'd intended to stay after an eighteen mile day and there was Wayfarer and Trail Mix settling in. At the picnic table out front were Superman and Pogue taking a break before moving on to the hostel still six miles away. Silver and Firefly were just ahead of them. With just a little encouragement I decided to move on, too. They took off and I followed in their wake.

Just as I left the shelter it started to rain, so I employed my umbrella. The trail led down a steep mountainside which troubled my knees so I slowed my pace. As darkness fell, I turned on my headlamp and walked on finally reaching a rain streaked paved road. A porch light lured me to a house across the street where I asked directions to the hostel.

"Which hostel?" they asked.

I wasn't aware that there were two, but answered, "Kincora". The directions were easy and just a half mile away.

When I made it to Kincora, Superman announced my arrival from the front porch. Firefly immediately vacated a comfy chair. I dropped my pack, Applesauce handed me a plate of hot food and Silver passed me a cup of cocoa. Zama and Lug, Cruise, Applesauce and Salsa, Bluebird and Abandon, Firefly and Silver, the gang was all there. Almost. Superman asked if I'd seen Pogue.

"No," I said, I hadn't. "Isn't he here with you?" Pogue had been hiking between Superman and me when we left the shelter six miles back, but had yet to arrive. We were starting to get worried. His brother had come to meet him and had been waiting for hours. Thirty minutes more went by. It was well after dark before Pogue's damp form appeared in the doorway. All eyes turned. Conversation stopped. Suddenly he was hit with a thousand questions at once. When he got a chance, he responded with an amazing tale.

He'd come off the trail onto the black top road and turned in the wrong direction. He came upon a building where he saw several people inside and figured he'd found the right place. So he walked around the house looking for a door. In the dark and rain he slipped on a ramp and slid right into the backdoor which burst open and dumped him inside. He found himself on the floor surrounded by beautiful college co-eds looking down at him in amazement. He explained that he was lost. They asked if he was all right and offered him food and shelter.

"So what are you doing here?" teased Firefly.

After eating a plate of hot food, Applesauce asked how I was feeling. I'd hiked twenty-four and a half miles, the last few in the dark and rain.

I said, "My upper half is happy, warm, dry and fed. But my legs may never forgive me."

I got a hot shower and climbed into an upper bunk Silver had saved for me. Unfortunately, I had forgotten to take my "Vitamin I" (Ibuprofen) before climbing up there and I was too tired to climb down and back up again. I felt achy and thought it would keep me awake, but I was wrong.

My legs were mostly recovered by morning and I felt fine after a second hot shower. I was always amazed at how quickly my body recovered after extra long days on the trail.

Lug and Zama had been given a ride to town and came back with breakfast for all. They made French toast, eggs and bacon, hot cocoa and orange juice, Sunday brunch for thru-hikers. This was the first time we would benefit from their exceptional generosity and culinary skills but it would not be the last.

It was a bright morning. The sun had come out and after a phone call, Bluebird had great news. He'd just been accepted for graduate school at MIT. He and Abandon would have to hurry to finish the trail in time for fall quarter. We toasted his bright future with fresh orange juice.

I realized my fleece vest had come untucked from my pack strap on the way down the trail in the dark. Fortunately, it was returned to me the next morning by none other than Trail Mix. I thanked her profusely as the vest was a key component in my hiking wardrobe and had sentimental value as well. She told me how it was soaking wet from the rain and how heavy it had become and how she determined to bring it to me though it was a huge effort on her part requiring enormous self sacrifice... Zama, overhearing this exchange, gave me a look with one arched eyebrow. I stuck it in the dryer and left as soon as it was done. Trail Mix stayed behind.

Knee Party

Leaving Kincora, I took it easy walking just eleven miles to the shores of Watauga Lake. My knees were still complaining from the night before. They would no longer allow me to squat with my pack on, a serious complication. I was wearing an ace bandage to add support to my injured knee and began to negotiate with both knees as I walked promising if they'd just get me over Mount Rogers, the last of the high mountains in the Southern Appalachians, I would throw them a party. I really didn't know what a Knee Party was but I thought I could come up with something. This was just the start of many months of conversing and negotiating with different body parts.

I passed through the enchanting Laurel Fork Gorge where the trail drops steeply to follow a ledge just above the rushing river. It was easy to see why there was a blue blaze high water alternative that followed the top of the gorge. A little more water in the river and you'd need fins and gills to get through.

In the afternoon I stopped at a picnic table next to Highway 321. I'd sent word to my nieces in Boone that I would be crossing this road today but I saw no sign of them. I sat and read for a while hoping they would come, though it was an hour's drive from town. After a while I moved on. There would be another chance to meet them in a few days. I arrived at Watauga Lake Shelter in mid-afternoon and soon heard a familiar voice.

"Honey, I'm home."

It was Firefly coming up just behind me. Together we moved into the shelter. When our trail family arrived at a shelter we usually swept it out before unpacking. Brooms stood in the corner of most shelters. This particular shelter had also been stocked with goodies. I took the Cheese Nips while Firefly claimed the Vienna sausages. We saved the mini-marshmallows for Lug and Zama knowing they were carrying hot cocoa mix.

Firefly took the shelter log and began to write. After the party at the Overmountain Shelter when different hikers had brought in a box of wine, beer, weed and even a very small battery operated stereo, his writers block had come unblocked. He was brimming over with ideas of what to write in the shelter logs. Firefly was the source of many mind ticklers and thought provoking questions like, "See the underwear in that tree over there? How would McGyver get them down?"

I used to love watching McGyver on TV saving the day (and usually a damsel in distress) with chewing gum, duct tape and paper clips. From then on, when we would puzzle over a problem, someone would inevitably ask, "What would McGyver do?" It always brought a smile and got our creative ideas flowing, though it seldom actually provided any solutions.

That night around the campfire as we were finishing dinner, a hiking party emerged from the woods. Superman, Pogue, Krispie and Janetor arrived after a detour hitchhiking to McDonald's for dinner. Superman and Pogue had noticed a couple of pudding cups in the creek just before they reached the shelter and were digging into them, delighted at their find. Zama had set them in the creek to cool while she and Lug ate dinner. I looked over at Zama who shook her head, indicating I was not to say a word.

Just then, by the firelight something scampered up a tree nearby. It attracted all our headlamps at once which must have frightened it so it FLEW to the next tree. A flying squirrel! The first I'd ever seen. We'd seen turkeys, grouse, snakes, deer, bear, vultures, a skunk and lots of shelter mice, but this was something unexpected and remarkable.

April Fools

The next day I hiked another easy day, just thirteen and a half miles, and ended at Iron Mountain Shelter with Zama and Lug. It was warm and dry and I planned to sleep in a soft pile of leaves outside the shelter. Two young guys came up around sunset, Chronic and Hatterass Jack. They were shocked that I'd sleep on the ground. Obviously, they'd never tried it. They moved into the shelter saying they were planning to get up early so they could walk into Damascus twenty-six miles away. They wanted to be in town to watch a basketball game the next night.

As darkness fell, I looked up from my book and noticed that clouds were rolling in. I called over to the shelter and asked them to save some room for me, just in case. An hour later the first tiny sprinkles fell. There was lightning on the horizon. I grabbed my stuff and high-tailed it to the shelter just before the deluge. We stayed up watching the storm with lightning, thunder and torrential rain. Lug put his cook pot on the picnic table to save a trip to the spring in the morning. We rarely got storms like this in the Pacific Northwest. Our rain usually came in the form of a constant drizzle. This storm was exciting!

Between the rainstorm and the mouse circus in the shelter that night, we didn't get much sleep. Chronic and Jack got up at 4:00 a.m. to start their hike into town. They rustled around making breakfast and packing gear for an hour before they left. When Zama woke up she realized her head was where her feet had been when she laid down but couldn't remember turning around. It had been a restless night.

Zama's Mom was planning to meet them in Damascus that day so they left the shelter at about 8:00. I left a little later and leap frogged with them all day. In late afternoon I was resting in a shelter doing some stretches when they came up looking badly shaken. I asked what had happened. Zama said Lug had walked into a tree.

"You mean a low branch?" I asked.

"No," she said, "a tree trunk. He hit it so hard it knocked him flat."

Zama said she'd had a hard time getting him back on his feet again.

I had never heard of anyone walking into a tree trunk in broad daylight which struck me as hilarious. I almost burst out laughing, but they were both so serious. I tried to at least look grave and concerned. They sat down with me in the shelter and had some water and a snack. Eventually, I decided to go all the way into town with them. It had been an easy day walking on old farm roads and logging trails and all the hikers I knew would be there. So we headed down the mountain to Damascus.

I arrived just before dark. The small town was quiet. I strolled down the sidewalk through a park. Crossing the street I noticed a newspaper box. The day's headlines caught my eye. *Tornadoes Sweep through the Midwest - Killed 11 in Tennessee.*

As I walked down the main street at dusk, all the shops were closed except a bicycle shop just ahead that was well lit and full of people. It was surreal. A man I didn't know swung the glass door open and invited me inside. Cautiously, I ventured in, remembering it was April Fools Day and wondering what sort of mischief this might be. There were platters of food on the counter and coolers full of drinks, and there was my extended trail family eating dinner and laughing with more people I didn't know. This was no mischief. This was Nirvana!

I learned that Cruise lived in nearby Abingdon, Virginia and used to work in this bike shop. His family and former employers were throwing him a party and any thru-hikers who happened to be in the neighborhood were invited. I dropped my pack and went out to look for Zama and Lug. When they arrived I got a plate of food and a glass of lemonade. I thanked my hosts and sat down at a big table next to Firefly. I couldn't help but notice the shocked look of Chronic and Jack who stared at me from across the table as if seeing a ghost.

The last time I'd seen Firefly he was leaving Iron Mountain Shelter with a plan to do some "cowboy camping" and sleep between shelters. I asked how he'd fared in the storm. He told me when the rain started, he'd grabbed his gear and hurried to the next shelter, but it was full and all were asleep. Instead of bothering them and squeezing in, he hiked on through the pouring rain with the trail lit by frequent lightning. Finally, he'd made it to the "Holiday Inn", the smallest shelter on the trail. My sister loves it. It's just her size. But for Firefly, it was miserable. His six foot frame crossed it diagonally and still stuck out the side. He had not slept much at all so he enjoyed this hospitality in Damascus all the more.

I asked about Silver and was told he'd gone to the hostel at the church a few blocks away. After walking twenty-six miles, I knew if I sat too long I'd stiffen up, so when I was done eating I thanked my generous hosts again and made my way to the hostel.

By that time it was dark, but the streetlights made the church easy to find. I walked around back and into the former parsonage where a sign read, *The Place*. The old home had large rooms, tall ceilings and wooden floors much worn down by hiking boots. The screen door squeaked behind me as I made my way through the dark kitchen. There was the usual unkempt mess of hiker's snacks in Zip-lock bags and trail food left out on the counters. It was quiet, but there was a light on in the next room. I walked in and found Silver reading alone. When he saw me, his face lit up. He slapped his knees laughing saying, "I knew it! I knew you'd make it."

I was perplexed. He said he'd asked those young fellers, Chronic and Jack, if I was going to come into town tonight and they'd said, "Oh, no, she'd never make it." Silver had bet them I would.

I said, "If you get any money out of this, you better take me to dinner."

It had been a long and satisfying day, but my bones were tired and the wooden bunks in the parsonage looked hard. *The Place* was free but I'd pay good money for a real mattress. Silver had scoped out another hostel nearby in a converted garage. We went over and checked in. There were just four bunks. Superman was already there. Silver and I unloaded our gear. I got a hot shower, climbed into an upper bunk with a real mattress, sheets and blankets and slept very well looking forward to a zero in the best of all trail towns.

The Friendliest Trail Town

Damascus, Virginia is considered the prima donna of trail towns. Besides being the hub of five long hiking and biking trails, it is the home of Trail Days, an annual week-long festival for hikers, which is often spelled Trail Daze among those who have attended.

The festival was first held in 1987 to commemorate the 50th anniversary of the official completion of the Appalachian Trail. Each year the party grows in attendance and activities. There's a hiker's reunion, a talent show, hiking related vendors and exhibits, crafts, live music, dancing, and the ever popular hiker's parade through the middle of town. During Trail Days these quiet streets are flooded with free spirited hikers drawn like moths to a campfire. But the party wouldn't start for over a month and I would be long gone by then. This spring morning the streets were calm and quiet, just the way I like them.

When I'd arrived I'd called my sister and nieces who live in Boone, North Carolina, an hour's drive away. Martha sent word through the hostel owner that she had the day off and would come up and meet me by noon. I put in some time gathering supplies, picking up a mail drop and waited for the library to open.

Libraries were a great resource for thru-hikers. We'd get free internet access but only for a limited time. There were usually people waiting to take our place at the computer so librarians watched us with their timers, crossing their arms and tapping their toes if we ran over our allotted hour. It seemed barely enough time to get the news from home and send word of our progress. One email a week had to suffice to describe our exploits to the family and friends on my Trail Tales email list.

Of course some hikers carried cell phones but coverage was sketchy on the trail. People carrying these devices had to carry the extra weight of the phone and their chargers. It might not seem like much, but thru-hikers are obsessed with going light. Some continually mailed their chargers ahead from one town to the next. For me, it seemed blasphemous to carry such things into the wilderness, though I must say, access to a borrowed cell phone did come in handy from time to time. I just didn't want to carry one myself.

Some of my trail mates kept journals on an internet site, but knowing their words could be seen by anyone in the world, their parents and other members of their congregation, they chose their on-line words carefully. One hiker, whose name will not be mentioned, came across as a God-fearing Christian on the web, when in the shelter logs his comments were much more, shall we say, colorful.

After I'd run my errands, I sat on the wide front porch of the hostel soaking up the morning sun and waiting for Martha. Firefly came up to chat so he was there when her truck pulled up. Firefly gets a twinkle in his eye when he meets new people. He likes sizing them up. My sister often gets a scowl on her face, which made Firefly's twinkle even brighter. After introductions were made, with his initial first impressions intact, he excused himself.

Martha had brought David, her beau who worked on the AT trail crew. Both were former thru-hikers. As a thru-hiker with no car, I had a very narrow impression of the states as I walked through. Martha and David offered me a rare opportunity to broaden my experience, taking me to lunch in nearby Abingdon.

Abingdon is a quaint, historic town. Even without a sign, you just knew George Washington had slept there. I could see why Martha had raved about going there on weekends to see a play at the famous Barter Theatre, or just to mess around. During lunch I got a chance to get to know David. He's a dark haired, bearded, wiry fellow from Louisiana, a Cajun cook who had also put in hard labor on the AT trail crew.

After walking the trail in 2003, Martha had volunteered to work on the trail crew for two weeks. That's where she'd met David. When she got home, she wrote him a letter. Letter writing, now a dying art, is Martha's preferred means of communication. She's very good at it and got an immediate response from David. They teamed up to the delight of the whole family. They're great together. I was glad to see my sister so happy.

After lunch we went to a department store where I could replace my worn out umbrella and flip flops. I wore flip flops in camp to give my feet a break from my boots and they were good to wear in public showers or while doing laundry. They were nearly flat so they were easy to pack. But my feet had grown two sizes since I started hiking the AT so my old pair didn't fit.

While we were there a staff member was on the top of a tall ladder trying to change a light bulb. Another employee steadied the ladder and coached from the side. It was apparent that the fellow on the ladder was afraid of heights. Martha, who shared this malady, wondered why he, of all the employees, had to be the one on the ladder.

I asked Martha about how she managed her affliction as she walked the trail. There were some places that are totally exposed with steep drops on both sides. She said sometimes she had to sit down on a rock, focus her attention just ahead and talk herself into walking just ten steps to the next rock. There she'd sit again and talk herself into going just ten steps further. I admired her tenacity and determination.

When we got back to Damascus, we heard that my nieces were in town. Martha and David left and I went in search of my next set of visitors. I found them getting milkshakes at the diner. Emily and Bekah are the daughters of my sister, Sue. They're each other's best friends, blonde, beautiful, funny and wonderful to be around. Emily had been married a few years to a fellow named David. David's best man at their wedding was his brother, Nate. Bekah, who was Emily's maid of honor, fell in love with Nate. They were planning to wed the next month. That's right, two brothers marrying two sisters. I was determined to be at the wedding. But for now, they were here to see me. Emily brought her young son Elias and her new-born Faith. We sucked the last of our milkshakes through the straws and then headed back across the bridge to the hostel where I introduced them to Superman and Firefly. As we said good-bye out in the parking lot, Bekah commented on how good looking they were. It threw me off. I'd only thought of them as fellow hikers, but looking through her eyes, I had to admit, they weren't bad. It was a reminder that they were closer to her age than mine.

It was a beautiful day, visiting with family, holding the baby and hugging my own kin at the hiker's hostel. I was weaving two realities together into one richly textured cloth.

Silver was having his own family reunion. His wife, daughter and grandson were visiting from Michigan so he moved from our hostel to a B&B with them. He was totally absorbed in their company but took time to bring his favorite little boy and daughter to the hostel to introduce us. He would be slack packing with his daughter for the next few days while his wife took care of their grandson and shopped at the antique stores. Silver said this could be a very expensive way to hike the trail, but he loved having them there.

Cruise's family, who lived on a farm nearby, invited us all to a spaghetti dinner and bonfire. There was a buzz about the event and hikers pooled up in a parking lot waiting for a shuttle to the farm. I was craving salad but there wasn't a good grocery store in town, so I bought some canned peaches and pears at a dollar store to bring to the dinner. Other hikers brought liquid refreshments to be shared around the fire afterward.

Applesauce drove cars stuffed with hikers into the yard where we were greeted by George, the most bow-legged Boxer I'd ever seen in my life. The house overflowed with people. The family made us all feel welcome making more and more spaghetti as the need required. My giant bowl of canned fruit disappeared as well. I took a turn at the piano. Someone else strummed a guitar. We offered to help wash up but were instead shooed out toward the field behind the house where Cruise was lighting a huge bonfire.

Cruise had earned our utmost respect on the trail. He was young, competent, quiet and courteous. He'd walk with two walking sticks but seldom needed them for support. Instead he used them like chopsticks to clear the trail of branches. His cousin Applesauce wanted to hike the trail, too, so the family urged them to go together. Their family farm reminded me of my grandparents place in North Carolina with the farms of neighboring aunts, uncles and cousins nearby.

I've never been much of a late night party goer and once the bottles were passed around I could tell this could be a long one. But Applesauce had already offered to take a carload back into town for those that wanted to get an early start in the morning. I jumped in and bedded down in the hostel anxious to get back on the trail at dawn.

Mount Rogers

At dawn I swept my room, packed my gear and quietly crept out of the hostel while the others slept in. On the trail I caught up with Tank. We ended our day together in a shelter we shared with a weekend hiker and his dog. As we prepared our dinners, the weekender took out an interesting contraption, a backpacker's oven. I'd never heard of such a thing. It was light and small, about the size of my cook pot, but it had a hood that covered the pot with a dial on top that read, "Warm, Baked, Burnt". He mixed up some banana bread batter and poured it into the pot. By the time we'd finished eating dinner and washed our pots, the dessert was done. He shared it with us and his canine companion. A real treat! Just before dark, Zama and Lug arrived.

In the morning I started up my "Whisperlite" stove, waking my shelter mates with the roar. "Good morning. This is your captain speaking. Today we'll be cruising at an altitude of 5,700 feet."

After our customary oatmeal we were on our way toward Mount Rogers, the last big hurdle of the Southern Appalachians. We'd been warned not to mail home our warm   clothes until we'd crossed this peak. I'd asked my folks to include my jog bra in the next mail drop. My fleece jacket would cross it in the mail. Before leaving town we'd checked the forecast, so we expected thunderstorms to come in that night. Now was the time to get up and over Mount Rogers without delay.

At the approach to Mount Rogers where the trail neared a road, we found a bag of fruit hanging from a tree. There was Coconut Monkey and Wayfarer helping themselves to a second piece. They were slack packing and would be back in town that night where there were restaurants and stores. I was shocked. They were depriving fresh produce from thru-hikers with full backpacks that would be sleeping in shelters for the next week eating freeze dried cardboard. I gave them a look of disapproval which had no effect whatsoever. They went south while we went north, each with a banana, apple or orange in our hands.

We found out later that Silver was our trail angel and was as miffed as I'd been at those two. They obviously didn't have the guilt gene.

On the way up this heavily traveled trail I found a "bling-bling" as Firefly later dubbed it, a kid's bracelet with purple and silver beads on an elastic string. I picked it up for something special to wear to my up-coming Knee Party. Later I found a nice looking T-shirt by the side of the trail. I picked it up and shook it out. It looked to be about Tank's size. He'd been wearing the same T-shirt since he started in Georgia; that's thirty days and almost 500 miles of constant use sweating up and down mountains. It was rank, stained and had huge holes in it. I left this *fresh* T-shirt hanging on a branch by the trail with a note in the front pocket that read, "Tank, need a new shirt?"

We got to the top in good weather, but didn't linger. It was cloudy and felt like rain. Rain in the forecast could easily turn to snow on the summit. We headed down through rocky slopes and meadows where wild ponies roamed.

Mount Rogers is famous for its wild ponies. They look like Shetland ponies and are a huge attraction to visitors. I found a group of children chasing them around. I shared my apple with the kids and suggested they sit down, and wait for the pony to approach. I showed them how to hold a slice of apple in their flat open hands, turn their heads away, watch the ponies out of the corner of their eyes and try to be patient. We met with some success. Their father watched from a distance with an approving smile.

A little farther along I came across a pony that was not shy at all. I offered some almonds which it took without hesitation, but it wouldn't offer me a ride or even carry my pack. As I moved toward the shelter, I made up a little song:

I'm a little pony, short and stout.
My bangs are so long I can't see out.
If you have an apple hear my shout,
I'll kick up my heels and change my route.

That night Zama, Lug, Tank and I checked into the shelter just below the summit. As darkness fell, storm clouds moved in. We were all bedded down as the first sprinkles brought Firefly in to join us. He'd been one shelter behind for days. I'd left him messages along the way to hurry up. He brought news. While the rain poured down and he made his dinner, he told us of the night before.

He'd stayed in a shelter with the A-Team, otherwise known as Team Australia. They were a group of six twenty-somethings led by a thirty-something Australian fellow named Captain Kangaroo. The six of them were nearly inseparable and a bit rowdy. We tried to avoid them because they always filled up a shelter with little room for others.

He said they were perplexed about who was leaving the hearts in the trail. Each one had a different theory. Firefly had listened, but kept quiet. We smiled enjoying our little secret.

Lug had started it. He'd sometimes get ahead of Zama and draw a heart in the trail with his walking stick to direct her attention to a beautiful view or a tricky turn where it was easy to go the wrong way. We all had picked up on it by now and would draw hearts in the trail for each other just to show support. It was our Trail Family logo. After that we started playing with team names like Zama and the Lug Nuts, Team Tank, Silver and the Streaks, Fire and the Family Fly. None of them stuck.

We hiked together for the next few days. One afternoon, Firefly had been walking and talking just ahead of me. But when the conversation lapsed, he moved on. I found myself in a thick fog, in a barren wood of twisted, eerie looking trees. I expected wolves, witches or perhaps the headless horseman to come racing out at any moment.

A short time later, and with some relief, I dropped off the ridge and approached the shelter saying, "Honey, I'm home." Rounding the corner of the rock wall, I found Silver sitting at the picnic table with a broad grin on his face. We hadn't seen him for days. He'd figured out where we would be and had his wife drop him off nearby an hour earlier. Trimpi Shelter is built of stone and had a fireplace. We had a cozy evening, catching up and drying out our smelly boots, socks and rain gear by the fire.

I read in my trail guide that the Partnership Shelter was within the next day's hike. It was a newer building not far from a Ranger Station, the headquarters of the Mount Rogers Recreation Area. I was excited about getting to this shelter because it boasted of a shower and electricity. Not only that, but there was a phone at the Ranger Station where you could order pizza. I determined this would be the site of my long awaited Knee Party.

The next day I wore the bling-bling on my knee over my long johns and tied a white survey ribbon on it, too. My knee had carried me over Mount Rogers and felt just fine. It deserved a celebration. I quickened my pace. It was a sunny day and soon I'd get a much needed shower and a good meal.

We were at the front of the seasonal migration of thru-hikers which had its benefits and its drawbacks. When we arrived at the shelter, they had yet to turn on the water which was a terrible disappointment to me. But a menu from the pizza parlor hung on the wall. We made our selections and called in our order from the nearby Ranger Station. It was Sunday and the Station was closed so we couldn't get cold drinks from the pop machine just inside the door. There it sat, just out of reach.

When I found a faucet outside the building with running water, I got out some shampoo and washed my hair, then sat in the sun to let it dry. It wasn't a shower, but it felt good to get at least some of me clean.

When the pizza arrived we pounced on the food and toasted my knee with a liter of soda that came with the meal. I'd been low on food so had ordered a small pizza with meat and a large vegetarian calzone. I stowed the latter in my pack and ate portions of it over the next three days.

Using the phone outside the ranger station, I called my parents. They always seemed delighted to hear from me, asking where I was and how everyone was doing. Mom talked to Silver and Firefly, too.

After hiking with Firefly, I realized I shouldn't take this for granted. He was out here pretty much on his own without family support or even much contact. So it was no wonder that one day at a picnic shelter he looked up at Silver and blurted out, "I'd make a good son-in-law!"

Silver blinked, swallowed and said his two daughters were already taken. So Firefly suggested he and his wife have another one.

Team Australia

The weather was warming as we climbed up to Chestnut Ridge. There was an actual stone hut at the top, with windows and a door, not just a three sided shelter. It was very accommodating but the sun in the field outside had a stronger pull; besides it was only mid-day. Firefly found an odd contraption with wheels and turning it this way and that finally found a way to sit in it. We dug into our food bags and enjoyed a siesta lying on the grass, leaning against our packs and soaking up the sun and the incredible views from the summit. When we reluctantly departed an hour later, Tank stayed behind. I'd noticed his sluggish pace had slowed even more.

On the way down the ridge Zama and Lug fell back. Firefly, Silver and I continued on.

An hour later we came upon a group of Rotary Club members who were hosting guests from New Zealand. They peppered us with questions about the trail. Silver and I were suffering from brain melt in the heat. Firefly, from Alabama, sized up our condition and took it upon himself to answer on our behalf. How long is the trail? Where do you sleep at night? How much weight do you carry? Where do you get water? What do you eat? How do you keep in touch with your family? Firefly responded cheerfully with his usual dose of humor.

We walked with them down to their cars parked just off the trail. They opened the trunk and offered us cold sodas from an ice chest. We were very grateful as it was a hot day and we'd run out of water... again. We asked for two more sodas for Zama and Lug who we expected to come along any minute. As we entered the woods we drew a heart on the trail and left the sodas inside it. Lug told us later that Zama had been having a hard day with blisters, cramps, and then a bee sting, so the cold drinks were a godsend.

Knowing Team Australia was on our heels we spread out over the next few days so we wouldn't end up with twelve people in a shelter built for six. Firefly, who was running low on food, moved ahead, anxious to get to the next town. Zama and Lug stayed behind. Silver and I took a shelter in between and had a quiet evening to ourselves, until...

About 7:30 p.m. a fellow came up to the shelter, threw down his pack and greeted us with a hearty, "G'day mate!" He was soon joined by a buddy. The two of them made a lot of racket making dinner and setting up camp, but that was just the start.

Long after dark we heard voices calling from the trail below. The rest of the team had stopped to go swimming along the way. Captain Kangaroo called out to them and they called back. This continued again and again for a full half hour until the whole team had assembled at the shelter. Now there were eight of us there. One sat down and pulled off his shoes raising a cloud of toxic fumes so potent Silver exclaimed, "Good god man! Get those feet away from me!"

They rustled around making dinner, pulling out bags and stringing up hammocks with headlamps flashing wildly in the dark. When they'd finally finished with their dinner and camp chores, Silver and I thought we'd get some sleep, but no such luck. The Team demanded their bedtime story from Captain Kangaroo. He told them a scandalous version of Earl Shaffer's first thru-hike which drew raucous cheers and laughter from the crew. Silver and I put in our earplugs.

Over the next few days the A Team moved on and we caught up with Firefly. The three of us arrived at a shelter after a day of rain and met up with Messenger and Braveheart. Messenger's Dad had joined them for a few days on the trail. When we were introduced, he asked me if I was thru-hiking.

"Not yet," I answered.

Silver decided to hike another five miles ahead to the Interstate so he could get a hotel room and watch Nascar on TV. He invited us to come by in the morning for showers before he left.

We started out on that frosty morning eager for a hot shower and a good breakfast. I got the first shower and then put our clothes in the laundry while Firefly took the next turn. While our clothes were in the wash, we crossed the busy road for a much anticipated restaurant breakfast. Firefly and Silver ordered the 2x4 breakfast, 2 sausage, 2 bacon, 2 biscuits and 2 pancakes, while I got the special for half the price. Firefly said he was envious of my slower metabolism. He was having a hard time carrying enough food between re-supply stops. We went to the gas and sip across the street to see what kind of provisions they could offer. I got some cheese and canned biscuit dough recollecting a trick I'd learned as a girl scout.

That night I showed my shelter mates how to wrap the biscuit dough around a stick and toast it over the fire. When it was golden brown we put strips of cheese inside and had a tube-shaped grilled cheese sandwich. But what was a fun treat for young girl scouts seemed too tedious for hungry thru-hikers. It required too much patience while our bellies rumbled.

The following day I picked some wild onions, ramps, and brought them to the shelter as a tasty supplement to our bland diet. Zama politely added some to her soup but the others declined.

Along the trail the next day I came upon a clearing full of fiddlehead ferns. I wrote, "EAT" on the trail with my walking stick for Firefly who was coming up behind me. But it only confused him. Later he told me he'd thought I'd stopped to eat there and wondered why I'd made a note of it. When I explained he said, "Be sure to point out a hamburger tree or French fry flowers next time you see them."

Bland

My next mail drop was in Bland, Virginia. Zama and Lug had a package waiting in nearby Bastion. We reached the road crossing at the same time. They crossed the road and started hitch-hiking north. Silver and I needed a ride to the south, but instead of standing beside me, Silver stretched out on the ground leaning against his pack and let me stick my thumb out alone.

"This sure is taking a long time. Hitch-hiking is hard work," he complained.

Eventually a car pulled over and Silver and I jumped in. As it turned out, the same driver, on his return trip, picked up Zama and Lug, and took them to Bastion.

Silver didn't need to go into town, but told me he wanted to come get some real food. Later I learned about an incident ending in the death of two hikers in this area. I suspected Silver escorted me due to his protective instincts... and to get some real food.

The incident happened in 1981 when a local, Randall Lee Smith, took an interest in a woman hiker he met in a convenience store. His advances were thwarted by her male hiking partner. Smith followed the couple back to their camp and killed them both, burying their bodies near a shelter on the Appalachian Trail. Little did I know that the same man, after serving fifteen years in prison, was back in the area. Two years after I'd hiked the AT, he allegedly tried to kill two fishermen in the same area, shooting them both and later shooting himself.

Other than the occasional murders, Bland didn't seem very exciting. This would be a quick stop. Silver and I ordered burgers and fries. While waiting for the food I stepped into the restroom and locked the door. I wanted to get cleaned up and also check myself for ticks. Looking at myself in the full length mirror I was surprised at how skinny I looked. "This must be one of those trick mirrors," I thought, "like they have in fancy hotels." Then I reminded myself, "You're in a diner in Bland, Virginia. This is not a fancy hotel." After two months of hiking ten to twenty miles almost daily I really was thin for the first time in my life. I smiled until the dark reality sunk in. So that's what it takes.

After finishing our burgers, I left Silver in the diner diligently guarding my pack, while I went to pick up mail and a few provisions. When I returned I dove into a care package from my friend, Kelly, in Seattle. Silver leaned over the table to look inside. She'd sent me all my favorite treats: Cougar Mountain cookies, Thomas Kemper Root Beer, Kettle Chips, dark chocolate, candied ginger and other sundry surprises. We split the Root Beer and chips right there. I was struggling to fit the rest into my pack. Silver offered to carry the weighty gourmet cookies for me. What a guy.

While I'd been away, Silver had befriended the matronly waitress. As she cleared our table, he asked dreamily, "Do you have any lemon meringue pie?" He closed his eyes as his voice trailed off. "My wife makes the best lemon meringue pie."

Sadly, they did not, but before we left she had bagged up some hot apple fritters for Silver wrapped in tin foil. She said, "No extra charge." This was a real treat and I praised Silver's powers of persuasion. There's a term for when you charm someone into giving you tasty treats, named after a famous bear – Yogi.

Parting Ways

Firefly had flown ahead trying to get into Pearisburg, Virginia on fumes. He'd eaten every crumb of his trail food and wouldn't accept the charity of friends who offered to share. I thought about the story of Stone Soup where a community is tricked into sharing food with each other. It didn't work with Firefly.

When Silver and I arrived in town we came upon a reception committee. The family of another thru-hiker had brought a cooler of drinks and a huge basket of crackers and candy as it was Easter weekend. Silver got a hotel room so he could watch TV, while I got a ride across town to the hostel.

Firefly was already there when I arrived, but he was acting strange. He'd woken up at 4:00 a.m. that morning with hunger pains. For dinner he'd had nothing but a tomato and head of garlic he'd picked up at a roadside produce stand. So he'd watched the sunrise as he packed into town and spent twenty dollars on breakfast at McDonald's. You can buy a lot of breakfast with twenty dollars at McDonald's. He was so hyped up I couldn't exchange more than two words with him. He was buzzing around, playing with his new tent, making phone calls, in hyper speed. I thought he was on drugs. The next morning he came in looking like he'd been run over by a truck. He said he'd had three or four cups of McDonald's coffee the day before after having had none for weeks.

The hostel was a rough structure behind a church. A super Walmart was just a half mile away through a field. We all walked across that field at least once, coming back with armloads of food. I got a whole roasted chicken and a bag of salad veggies to share. Zama and Lug arrived at the hostel, walked to Walmart and bought a dozen eggs, bacon and bread for Easter breakfast. Silver decided the bed was too hard at the hotel but I think he just missed us. There was a big porch overlooking a forested valley and the distant ridges. The redbuds and dogwood trees were just starting to bloom and temperatures were mild. We pulled the mattresses outside and swept out the dusty loft. We slept on the porch watching the afternoon storms blow through and waiting for the evening stars.

At the end of each hiking day, when Lug arrived at a shelter and took off his pack, he'd lie back and sigh, "Joyous Rapture".

Each morning when Silver put his pack on, he'd accentuate the click of his buckle with the phrase, "Lock and Load."

Firefly had a phrase that warned of coming mischief, "Just for kicks and giggles."

But Tank was silent. One morning as he hobbled off down the trail, I watched him go, thinking he looks like he's in pain.

Most thru-hikers hobble like we're ninety years old when we first get up in the morning. It takes a while to get the blood flowing. But

Tank's step had slowed beyond his usual trudge and I was concerned. I mentioned it to the others who agreed.

Tank arrived at the hostel after dark. He looked exhausted. He said his feet had been bothering him. He couldn't walk more than five miles a day and that very slowly. It looked like he would have to get off the trail.

We met another hiker at this hostel. Feather was a lovely young woman from Atlanta. She'd walked the trail the year before but by the time she'd reached Pearisburg, she'd had the same ailments that Tank now had. She was diagnosed with plantar fasciitis, common ailment of long distance hikers. This year she'd come back to start again where she'd left off. She had anxiety about returning to the trail and an upset stomach had kept her at the hostel for a day or two before we arrived.

A middle aged fellow named Michael seemed to be a semi-permanent fixture at the hostel. He was extending his stay and doing some cleaning and repair in exchange. He drew the rest of us in to help. It was a beautiful spring day so we opened the windows and doors and swept clouds of dust and dirt outside. We washed the floors and windows and took towels to the laundry. The church offered this shelter for next to nothing. We were happy to pitch in.

We woke up on Easter Sunday to rattling noises and good smells from the kitchen. Zama and Lug were making what they called Breaky Pie, an egg, bacon and veggie dish that would stick to our ribs. The rest of us joined in the preparation making coffee, tea and toast. We set the picnic tables in the gazebo outside with lilac blooms in a jar. The hostel manager came by and smiled as we all sat round the table with our plates full.

Soon after, we would part ways. I didn't know at the time that this would be the last I would see of Lug and Zama on the trail. They were waiting for a package that wouldn't arrive for two days. Tank dropped off the trail so his feet could heal and I never saw him again. We kept in touch by asking other hikers who passed through, or sending emails when we got a chance. This coming together and then slipping away seemed a natural part of life on the trail.

Silver and Firefly went to different churches that morning looking for salvation and an invite to Easter dinner. The hostel manager offered to give Feather and I a ride to the trail which we gratefully accepted. So my trail family lost three members, Zama, Lug and Tank, but gained someone new, Feather. It was warm. The days were long. The trail was smooth. And we thought we saw the Easter bunny just ahead of us.

Messenger and Braveheart

Feather and I hiked up the trail from Pearisburg, Virginia, dodging snakes that frequented the ravine at the start. By mid-day we'd climbed to a bald ridge and came upon the first shelter. Feather wanted to go on, this was her first day on the trail, but I knew Team Australia was just ahead. They would take up the entire shelter, so we stayed back. And besides, Feather's stomach was still bothering her. She made a cup of peppermint tea and we settled in for the afternoon.

We were soon joined by Silver and Firefly (neither had benefited from a Sunday dinner). One member of the A-Team who had stayed behind to attend church caught up with us that night. Team Steve seemed a bit out of his element without the rest of his crew. We ate dinner and with plenty of light left, I went to write in my journal leaning back on a rock overlooking the town far below. The rest of the crew played cards or read until dark.

I laid my sleeping bag out in the meadow. Feather did the same. Then Firefly and Silver each pitched their newly acquired one man tents nearby. Only Team Steve remained in the shelter.

At midnight I awoke to the soft sounds of voices approaching. I opened one eye. In the darkness I saw the headlamps of hikers coming out of the woods and into the meadow. They paused at the trail sign and then turned toward the shelter. When they reached the shelter they found the gear of several hikers but only one sleeping inside. "I guess that's why they call him Team Steve."

Living outside we'd grown accustomed to the weather patterns, so I slept lightly in the wee hours. At 4:00 a.m. I woke to see lightning on the horizon. I woke Feather and we moved quickly and quietly into the shelter. Firefly and Silver soon followed not wanting to have to pack up a wet tent. So the night had started with one lonesome hiker in the shelter, but by dawn there were seven tucked in out of the rain.

The next morning we sorted everything out. Messenger and Braveheart had joined us. Team Steve hurried ahead to reunite with the A-Team. All along the way we found plastic Easter eggs filled with candy. I pulled out the Tootsie Rolls and left the rest behind.

Later Firefly and I walked together and I told him of the weird dreams I'd been having. Snakes. Lots and lots of snakes. He asked what I thought that might be about. I pondered for a moment.

"Maybe it's transformation. You know, snakes shed their skin. I'm transforming from a woman who'd been married for ten years to a woman on my own."

He nodded thoughtfully but said nothing.

Months later, after getting off the trail I thought about it again. Snakes. Lots and lots of snakes. On the trail I was surrounded by men. Lots and lots of men.

We hiked with Messenger and Braveheart for the next few days. They were big, strong college men who complained a lot, but had a good sense of humor. They'd been on the trail seventy days to my fifty. I knew this because they began each day by taking a photograph of someone showing the number of days since they'd started hiking. Feather and I posed for them one morning forming a seven and a zero with our hands. They said it took them two days just to get up the approach trail at Springer Mountain, Georgia, 8.9 miles. They don't like cold and rain, but complained about the heat rash they got when it was hot. They had flat insoles, plantar fasciitis, chaffing, etc. etc. etc.

I found them at the end of one warm day, sitting on a rock in the middle of a stream looking miserable. As I joined them I heard their usual list of grievances.

I asked, "Have you ever heard of Earnest Shackleton's expedition to Antarctica?" I told them how they sailed from England into the Weddell Sea in 1914 and then spent months stuck in the ice before their ship sank. Then they spent five more months camping on floating chunks of ice before they were able to use small open boats to get to solid ground on a tiny island. Then a few of them were able to sail across Drake's passage to Saint George's Island which was nearly impossible with the weather and monstrous waves, and when they arrived, a storm forced them to land on the far side of the island from the whaling station. So they had to climb over a glacier covered mountain range to get to the village. Still they had to wait for months for the weather to allow a boat passage to go and rescue the rest of the crew and they had to stay positive the whole time.

After I'd finished, Messenger said, "Well that makes me pretty depressed." I told them I was twice as old, half as big and was carrying more weight relative to my body size than they were and they should buck up!

I said, "Look there's just one more mile to the next shelter. I'll race you up the hill. But first you have to turn your heads so I can dunk my shirt in the stream." They obliged and said, "Tell us when we can look."

When I was half way up the hill I called, "You can look now."

They had asked Firefly how old I was.

"Thirty-five," he lied. But they were suspect. I'd dated myself with references in conversation. ("Where were you when Kennedy was shot?" "Kennedy who?")

One morning as I watched Messenger add nuts, raisins and M&M's until he could no longer see his oatmeal, he came right out and asked me.

"How old are you anyway?"

"How old is your mother?"

"Fifty-one," he said.

"I'm not that old." I laughed, shouldered my pack and headed off down the trail. It was fun to imagine that I'd turned the clock backward. I'd never been in better shape. I was thinner and weighed less than when I was in college twenty-five years before. There were no bills, no phones, no cars, no bosses out here. No stress, except the physical stresses and strains my body had grown accustomed to hiking now for almost three months. The weather was comfortable. The terrain was gentler. Daylight hours were longer so we had plenty of time to get where we were going. I was in heaven, felt great and apparently looked ten or twelve years younger.

Feather knew my age was the same as her mother. Feather spoke fondly of camping and hiking with her Dad, but had little to say about her Mom. From conversations with Firefly I'd gathered she was less fit, okay, plump, well, maybe even obese, while Feather was slim, active and practically danced down the trail, light as a... well, as a feather. One day, as we were walking, Feather voiced her disappointment in her Mother. "Why couldn't my Mother be more like you?" she asked.

"Feather, if I had been able to have children, my life would've been very different and I probably wouldn't be out here thru-hiking the Appalachian Trail."

Feather's stomach continued to bother her. We asked about changes in diet, maybe allergies. One day as I was hiking alone, another thought came to me.

When I was her age, I was leading a four day backpack for women and children east of Seattle, in the North Cascades. My friend, Tim, was our co-guide. I was married then and had just found out that I was eight weeks pregnant. My doctor and midwife had both said I was very healthy and could go ahead with my scheduled hike as long as I took my vitamins and rested each afternoon. We were only hiking about five miles a day and spending the afternoons swimming in lakes and resting at camp so the pace was relaxing.

At our highest camp I began to bleed, not much, but enough to raise concerns. The other women urged me to lie down and take it easy. Suddenly instead of me taking care of them, they were taking care of me. They did all the cooking and cleaning at camp while Tim took the kids out to play on the snow fields. That night we came up with a plan. In the morning I'd empty my pack, the rest of the group would divide the weight between them and we'd all hike out together.

But in the morning everything had changed. I had terrible cramps, acute abdominal pain. I couldn't get out of my sleeping bag. Hearing the others *talk* about breakfast was enough to make me nauseous. I wasn't going to be able to hike anywhere. Tim took charge. Jan would stay with me while the others hiked out with him. He would go get help. As they filed past my tent, one woman gave me a large crystal urging me to hold it on my belly. Another offered a vile of Rescue Remedy, a homeopathic cure all. Though I resisted taking anything by mouth, she put a couple of drops under my tongue and tucked the rest into my shirt pocket. Another woman of Asian ancestry, who had looked mystical to me as she'd hiked with a walking stick among the stone cliffs, simply lifted her hand at the door of my tent and said, "Peace be with you." I fell asleep.

A few hours later I woke up feeling fine. I stepped tentatively outside my tent. All seemed normal. I told myself that it must have been food poisoning. Some backpackers set up camp nearby and I went over to ask if they'd seen a ranger. A woman said, "No, but why?" When I told her about my symptoms she told me to go lie down, that it was a serious matter and when the helicopter comes they'd help us move our gear to the landing site.

Tim's plan was to hike the group out to the half-way point where they would spend the night. They could walk the rest of the way out on their own. Tim would continue hiking out to the trailhead, drive into town and get a helicopter back in to pick me up. This was Tim's first backpack since he'd been in a serious auto accident six months before. His car had been struck from the side which crushed his pelvic bone. He'd been in traction for six weeks. This hike would test his resilience.

At dusk, Jan and I prepared to spend another night on the mountain. Our neighbors came to check on us expressing their concern. As we talked we began to hear the steady clap, clap, clap of a distant helicopter approaching. We all leapt into action. Everyone busied themselves stuffing the sleeping bags, striking the tent, cramming gear into backpacks. The chopper hovered over us as we waved our arms, then circled round the snow field and set down. To get to it we'd have to cross a boulder bridge at the head of a waterfall and circle round an alpine lake. Our neighbors urged us to go ahead. While Jan and I started climbing over the rocks, they came close behind with our things loosely stuffed into our packs. The helicopter waited, looking like a giant mosquito, with the propeller still spinning.

There was a coffin-sized basket fixed to each side. The pilot said he was expecting to pick up a body. He wanted to take just me and my pack, but I talked him into taking Jan, too. We strapped our packs into the outside baskets. Jan climbed into the middle. Our neighbors now had to climb back around the lake and over the waterfall in the dark. I thanked them with a hug and gave them my flashlight before strapping myself in. There were no doors. We took off, set down, took off, set down and took off. The pilot explained he had to burn off some fuel in order to carry all our weight.

When we actually lifted up and flew over the lake and the trees and the 1,000 foot cliff to glide above the forest below, I could see tiny campfires in the darkness. One of them was the fire of the rest of our group looking up. It was beautiful and peaceful. My long hair was streaming out as we flew through the night sky.

It was just a few minutes floating in the dark sky before we landed. A circle of emergency vehicles waited with lights flashing as we set down in a field near Leavenworth. Men in uniform ran to my door. I was embarrassed. "Food poisoning," I told them, but they helped me into the back of an ambulance anyway, took my vitals and asked a battery of questions.

"I have no insurance," I told them. They made me promise to go to my doctor first thing in the morning. That would mean a long drive over the mountains that night. By then it was 10:00 p.m. Tim, Jan and I hadn't had dinner so went to a restaurant on the main street across from the park.

After being seated by a window, I went to the restroom to clean up. While washing my hands I started feeling really hot. I thought I was overdressed. We'd just gone from 4,000 feet to downtown Leavenworth in less than an hour. It was August. I went outside for some fresh air. At the park the sprinklers looked inviting. I lay down on the sidewalk trying to get cool and started vomiting into the gutter. That's when I realized that it wasn't food poisoning. A car was parking nearby and as the people stepped out I called out to them for help. I asked them to get my friends from the restaurant. One man stayed to lecture me about drinking too much.

That night I had emergency surgery which saved my life. In the morning, as I woke up in the hospital still groggy, I overheard the doctor tell Tim that if it had been ten minutes later I may not have made it.

The surgeon told me he'd never seen anything like it. An ectopic pregnancy, when the fetus doesn't make it to the uterus but starts growing in the fallopian tube, and the tube bursts, usually requires immediate surgery. The woman can bleed to death within a couple of hours. In my case, the tube had ruptured on the mountain that morning which explains the cramps and pain, but it patched itself until I was within two blocks of the clinic that night. I'd suddenly gone from leading a backpacking trip in the mountains, to lying in a hospital bed needing help to brush the tangles from my hair. I lost the baby, but not my life.

I thought about Feather and what little I knew of her. She'd spoken of recently breaking up with a boyfriend. I didn't want to pry, but this could be serious. That afternoon as we settled into a shelter, before the others arrived, she rubbed her sore stomach and fretted. I asked tentatively, "Is there any chance you could be pregnant?"

She thought for a moment and said definitively, "No."

The next day Firefly and I discussed Feather's ailments. Being acutely interested in his fellow trail mates, this lovely young trail mate in particular, he had observed that if Feather spent time writing in her journal, her stomach wouldn't hurt. He'd surmised it was nerves, anxiety. As the days wore on, he encouraged her to take some time at the shelter to sit alone and write.

Songs in the Key of Spring

I'd been working on more songs as I walked. Something about the rhythm of walking, and so much time to think without interruption, spurred the creative process. There was material for lyrics everywhere. It took me three attempts before I got a good song about Giardia, a gastrointestinal ailment you get from drinking untreated water.

Giardia, Giardia, We must be on our guardia,
And if you're not retardia, you can avoid giardia, giardia

❋

This was rejected by my trail family, not politically correct. Undaunted, I tried again.

It's a gastrointestinal malady, caused by a creature that you can't see.
It's caused by a dinoinflatulate, caused by something you drank Not by what you ate.

Rejected again. Not a very catchy chorus and I'd had to add that extra syllable in dinoflagellate. I persisted and finally came up with something at least acceptable.

Microscopic organism living in a mountain stream,
Lurking in your water bottle, life ain't always as it seems.
Pour it in a tiny cook pot, perched above a tiny flame,
Bring it to a rolling boil and those creatures you have tamed.
Add a pack of ramen noodles and a pack of tuna fish,
You can eat those mother duckers, isn't that a tasty dish.

I met my trail mates at a shelter for lunch and got their approval on the latest version. As we ate we watched a couple of hawks mating in a tree, tumbling from limb to limb. It didn't look like safe sex to me. I walked on rhyming and by nightfall I had a parody of the Beatles' song Yesterday.

Blistered feet. All my skin is falling off in sheets,
And I'm looking over stumps of meat. Oh, I have got some blistered feet.

Frost bite, comes from hiking when the world is white,
And the temps are in the teens at night. Oh, I believe I've got frost bite.

Why I had to go, I don't know, I'm in such pain.
Why'd I hit the trail in the snow, and hail and rain?

Yesterday, I was diagnosed with plantar fas -ciitis.

Now it looks as though I'm here to stay,
'Cause I can't hike another day.

I had already been serenading the troops with songs from other people like John Hartford:

Mouth to mouth resuscitation,
Good for the country, good for the Nation,
Nothing quickens your respiration
Like a little ole bit of that sweet sensation
Of mouth to mouth (gasp) resuscitation.

Or a parody I wrote with a friend while working in Alaska called, *The Gull from Ipanema.*

Gulls are birds they like the water,
They swing and swirl just like they oughta
And when they pass me, each time they pass me I'm awed.

They're so good at procreation,
They feed their young on regurgitation.
They eat bivalves and crustaceans and fish.

O, and I watch them so sadly.
O, people speak of them badly.
Nobody worships them madly.
So each day as I walk to the sea,
I look for the gull, not the eagle.

Flying high they'll mesmerize you.
Gleaming white they'll hypnotize you.
Just hope they don't fertilize you,
OOO, I just couldn't see, I just couldn't see, I just couldn't see.

But their favorite by far was a song the same friend had written on a cruise in Mexico where they saw those popular birds, the Blue Footed Boobies. It was a parody of the old swing tune, **Brush up on Shakespeare**, full of innuendo. He called it **Brush up on Boobies**.

I'd sung that song to Firefly as we walked toward the shelter one day. When we arrived, I mentioned Blue Footed Boobies to Zama. She excitedly launched into a detailed description of a Blue Footed Boobie Preserve she once visited in Baja. As she spoke, Firefly, who faced her from one side of a picnic table, maintained a serious and attentive look, while I sat on the other side, with my back toward her, silently laughing so hard tears streamed down my cheeks.

IPP... Immediate Pee Phenomenon

After my knees recovered from the steep ups and downs of the Smokies and the Blue Ridge Mountains, I found I was again able to squat with my pack on. I no longer had to find a small tree to hold on to for support. But I was noticing another problem. I called it IPP, the Immediate Pee Phenomenon.

At first I thought this must be what I'd heard about middle aged women, never passing up an opportunity to visit a restroom. When I led week-long hiking tours, we would gather for dinner and linger over coffee and dessert while I discussed the next day's details and answer any questions. Inevitably, a middle aged woman would ask, "Where are the restrooms and what kind of restrooms are they?" So I started to include that in my evening reports.

"There are flush toilets in the ranger station at the trailhead, lots of trees and bushes along the hiking route and an outhouse at the picnic area where we'll stop for lunch." When no restroom was available we encouraged people to find a stick and dig a little hole, fill it and cover it. I would sometimes elaborate suggesting that Big Leaf Maples provided good cover and excellent wiping material. I hate seeing used toilet paper out in the woods.

Now, here I was hiking almost daily for months on end and it seemed I could be having some similar problems. Only different. I didn't have to go frequently. But when I had to go, I had to go *immediately!*

For years I'd led groups of students on all day educational hikes. I was responsible for them. When you take kids outside in the spring, it's understood, you can expect mischief. I didn't want them to go wandering off, or climbing cliffs or trees or logs over streams the moment I was out of sight. Nor did I want to get caught with my pants down, literally. So I got good at holding it for six or eight hours.

Here on the Appalachian Trail, there were outhouses at most shelters, and few other opportunities to sit down in private. Within a week of starting on the AT I needed those privies only once a day, first thing each morning. I was hiking eight to ten hours a day, frequently drinking water. My body adapted. After my morning constitutional, I only had to pee for the rest of the day (no number two). But when the first inkling came to me, "Oh, I need to pee," I had about five seconds to find a bush to hide behind, unbuckle my belt and drop my drawers.

The position of my hip belt may have had something to do with it. The hip belt is the key to comfortable backpacking. The legs and gluteous maximus are the strongest muscles in the body, so cinching up the hip belt puts the weight of the pack on the hips and thighs, not the back or shoulders.

"Oh, gotta pee!" Five, scan for a bush. Four, race off the trail. Three, unbuckle the pack. Two, push down the pants. One, squat!

After relieving myself, I'd pull myself back together, re-buckle my belt and step back onto the trail. As I walked contemplating this phenomenon, I hypothesized that the belt was squeezing my bladder, constricting it so the abdominal muscles were atrophied and not performing as they normally would.

When Firefly came along I asked if he had any such experiences. To my surprise he answered in the affirmative and ideas bounced between us for a mile or two before he moved ahead.

So it wasn't just me. And it wasn't that I was a middle aged woman. I leave the rest to someone who knows more about anatomy or physiology than I. Perhaps some grad student working on a Masters can work out the exact condition and give it an important sounding Latin name. I just call it IPP.

Thirst

We were walking the narrow ridges that cut diagonally from Southwest to Northeast across western Virginia. The days were warmer and more humid. We sweated more profusely and needed more water, but it was hard to find. The shelters along the ridge tops had long blue blazed trails that led down steep slopes to the nearest spring. The valleys between ridges had muddy streams that were frequented by livestock.

I was struggling over the boulders of Dragon's Tooth when a lithe young man passed me with a quick greeting. I asked his name. "Wrong Way" he replied over his shoulder, "I'm dyslexic," and he was off.

After climbing over Dragon's Tooth and the ridge beyond, I found a cooler full of drinks where Wrong Way was finishing a soda. With several more hot miles to go I got a cold bottle of water and sat down for a short break.

A few miles later, I came upon Silver at a road crossing. He invited me to join him hitch-hiking to the Homeplace in Catawba that boasts the best All-You-Can-Eat on the trail. We caught a ride and were soon dropping our packs by the front desk. The hostess walked us by the waitress station where they had kegs of lemonade and sweet iced tea. It took all my will power to restrain from stooping right there and putting my mouth directly under the spigot.

They served family style platters of fried chicken, squash, corn, green beans, stewed apples and biscuits, just like grandma used to make. Minding our manners, Silver and I still caught stares from the Sunday after-church crowd as the two of us downed five pitchers of lemonade and iced tea and ate every crumb they brought to the table. At the last minute, I remembered Firefly and wrapped a couple of biscuits in a napkin with tiny plastic tubs of butter and jam.

We made our way back to the trail and caught up with Firefly at the famed McAffe Knob. These cliffs are the most photographed site on the trail. Firefly said we'd just missed his nude photo shoot with Messenger and Braveheart. They'd moved on while Firefly waited for us. We took a few pictures, too, of a more modest sort, and dangled our feet over the tops of the dogwood trees below. Silver took a picture of me sharing my biscuits with Firefly who seemed a little put out that, after we'd stuffed ourselves at the Homeplace, this was all we'd saved for him.

As the sun went down we made ourselves comfortable in the nearby shelter. Retiring to my sleeping bag just before dark, I opened the shelter log and read an entry left in January. Written in a scrawling hand it said, "Came up with my axe but nobody here. Better luck next time." I was horrified. Silver burst into uncontrollable laughter.

Appalachian Spring

Starting my hike on the first of March, I'd been just ahead of spring for the last two months. We looked over our shoulders and called to it, cheering it on, pleading for it to hurry and catch up. In April, we finally saw our first wild flowers, flaming azaleas, blooming redbuds and dogwood trees. Blue bells, lilies and lady slippers greeted us from the forest floor. It was intoxicating. But along with April's flowers came spring showers.

It became the norm to walk in drenching rain. I kept my little umbrella in a handy side pocket. When there was just a passing shower it conveniently covered both me and the top of my pack. It was in frequent use. In heavy rain, I used a poncho that covered my body and my pack and offered enough ventilation so I didn't get drenched underneath in sweat.

Silver and I were walking on a ridge one day when a lightning storm suddenly came up. At his suggestion I dropped my metal walking stick on the side of the trail as we rushed down slope to the scant cover of a rhododendron thicket.

As the lightning passed I asked Silver why we'd dropped our poles but kept our packs with us? We had metal fuel bottles, cook pots and his pack had a metal frame. He looked at me and shrugged.

"And you call yourself an electrician?" After that I made sure to park my pack under one boulder while I searched out another.

We got into Troutville and checked into a hotel. Feather and I shared a room while the guys piled in together across the hall. I offered to take all the laundry to the truck stop nearby and wash it while I ate dinner there. They were anxious to take me up on my offer. But at the laundry I realized I didn't have much cash so I stuffed the washers full. The clothes came out only slightly better than when they went in. When I dumped the clothes out on the bed in their room, they smelled to high heaven.

It was stormy the next morning and I stayed inside sending emails and making multiple trips to the breakfast buffet. I watched Silver leave with his big, blue poncho whipped by the wind, but I lingered. Firefly and Feather left, too. And then Braveheart and Messenger checked out. I finally, reluctantly, left the hotel and walked around town to get my mail drop and supplies.

Walking down the rain slicked street I saw a large, beautiful, orange snake on the asphalt ahead. I couldn't tell if it was alive or dead.

Cautiously, I poked it with my stick. It sluggishly curled. I stepped aside giving it a wide berth. Copperheads were common in those parts.

The snakes were coming out as the days warmed. I came upon king snakes and black snakes. Firefly almost stepped on one before I grabbed his arm. Another climbed a tree next to us and slid out on a limb at eye level which gave me the heeby jeebies. A very clever black snake curled up at my approach and did its best rattlesnake impression, wiggling its tail in the dry leaves to mimic the sound. Though black snakes aren't poisonous their strike can hurt. It was intimidating. I kept my distance.

Somehow, while doing the laundry, I'd lost a stuff sack that belonged to Braveheart. I felt awful about it, so I went in search of a replacement. At the outfitters, I looked over the new stuff sacks and balked at the prices. When a salesman asked if I needed help, I told him of my plight. He led me to a box of freebies in the back, used, returned or otherwise rejected that looked to me like a treasure trove. I found a stuff sack the right size and left the store beaming. But how would I get it to Braveheart? I wasn't sure where he was, but had a hunch that he had yet to leave town. So I hit the trail.

At the first shelter, which is where I thought Braveheart would spend the night, I left the stuff sack and a note. Then I walked back up the spur trail to the AT and started to head on. Just then I heard footsteps and turned around to find none other than Braveheart himself. I greeted him with the news of what awaited him at the shelter. He wasn't planning to stay there. I ran back to retrieve it. He would have missed it had we not met. Ah, but that's how things seem to work on the AT. Magic.

That night Braveheart, Messenger and I shared a shelter but Silver, Firefly and Feather had moved on to the next. The day after, Braveheart and Messenger caught a ride at a road crossing to go to church with a friend and, hopefully, be invited to Sunday dinner. I walked on alone. My trail family was just six miles ahead. I thought I might catch up with them by hiking late that day, but when I came upon the next shelter it was such a palace I had to stay the night.

The Bryant Ridge shelter holds up to twenty hikers. It has different levels and a wonderful porch overlooking the confluence of two streams. I was all alone, so I happily took a sponge bath, washed out my quick-dry clothes in the stream and hung them from my bear line on the porch. I enjoyed my dinner in the late afternoon sun and leaned back on a bench listening to bird songs. The worst thing about this shelter was trying to decide the best place to sleep. There were so many delightful options. In the end, I slept on the porch serenaded by the cadence of moving water.

In the morning I woke early, fully refreshed and ready to charge up the trail. The weather was perfect and the trail was inviting. I do my best hiking on a gradual uphill grade. As I passed day hikers, I asked if they'd seen my friends and described what they'd be wearing, which was pretty much the same everyday.

"They're just ahead," I was told, again and again, "Just a few miles ahead." I was closing in on them.

It was just after noon, at the top of a ridge when I came upon Firefly laid back on the grass. I walked up singing, "Ain't no mountain high enough."

It was a warm day and I was wearing shorts and my jog bra. Firefly looked up and said, "You're naked." I laughed and put on a shirt. It had felt good to feel the breeze on my skin, until I stopped on the crest and started to cool down.

After a rest, we both took off to join the others. We walked on together over four mountains that day. As we walked they told me that Wrong Way had been hiking with them. He'd slowed down a little, from twenty-five miles a day to just twenty, in order to partake of their company. He'd gone ahead promising to hitch to a convenience store and bring back ice cream to share at the next shelter which was just a mile from the road.

Meanwhile, I was starting to feel the extra six miles I'd put in that morning. As we neared the big James River, my legs were giving out. I kept seeing flat places by the trail and suggesting we make camp here, or here, or here. "This looks like a good spot," I'd say. But they'd just laugh. I longed to get horizontal, but they reminded me there would be ice cream at the next shelter.

When we started across the long bridge over the James River we found a couple of young guys in wet shorts trying to look nonchalant.

Firefly asked, "Whatcha doing?"

"Nothing much."

"Are you guys jumping off the bridge?"

They looked at each other but kept their mouths shut.

Firefly continued, "Cause if you are, would you mind if I joined you?"

It was a long way down, but it was a hot day and the guys emerged with hoots and hollers and big grins on their faces.

I was dead tired by then. Firefly urged me to jump in saying it would refresh me, but I didn't think I had the energy to swim to shore.

I lay down on the bridge and gave Feather my camera. She took a picture over the rail, three men, three shadows and three reflections on the water the moment before they splashed in. Looking at those pictures later, I realized how thin Firefly was, half-starved on the trail. He needed that ice cream more than any of us.

I crossed the bridge twirling my walking stick hoping it would propel me the last mile to John's Hollow Shelter. We were almost there. I limped in last. They were all sitting around a picnic table with Wrong Way gorging on cook pots full of cereal with milk and ice cream. I dropped my pack, lay flat for a few minutes and then fished out my "Vitamin I" before joining them at the table. No one cooked dinner. Who needs dinner when you have ice cream?

That was my longest day on the trail, 26.6 miles. It was much harder than the day I walked 26.5 into Damascus, as there were many more ups and downs. I made a note of it in the shelter log. Other hikers had walked farther, but for me it was a milestone. I could feel it in my aching legs.

In the morning I got up and dunked my hair in the stream. I filled my cook pot and water bottle and then stepped away from the stream to wash my hair. When you drink water from the streams where you camp, you try to keep pollutants like shampoo at a distance. I was rinsing my hair when two men walked into camp. By their mannerisms I suspected they were gay. My trail mates had left, but I explained my need for "a new do". They sympathized wholeheartedly.

That night our shelter was near a road. Wrong Way and Silver hitched into town and shared a hotel room. The next morning Silver came back alone. He said Wrong Way caught a bus home. He was bored and missed his girlfriend in New York. It sounded like a case of the Virginia Blues.

About 500 miles of the trail is in Virginia; that's almost a quarter of the entire trail. Some thru-hikers get frustrated and feel like they'll never get out of Virginia.

Cedar Moe had to get off the trail because of an infected spider bite. Tank had foot ailments. Braveheart eventually dropped out with plantar fasciitis. We heard of others getting off with shin splints and bad blisters. By this time, we'd hiked almost 800 miles. It was taking its toll. Firefly and I determined that most folks could walk eighteen to twenty-two miles a day, at least in Virginia with its more gentle slopes and ridge walking, but if you tried to do more, you're likely to run into trouble.

Silver had complained of sore knees, aching back, tired feet and neck pain. He wondered if he should keep going. Firefly asked if I was planning to leave the trail. I assured him I had no such intentions. But you never know what lay ahead. The trail has its surprises.

That night when we arrived at a shelter, I found a nice flat spot in the leaves under the trees. My last view of the tree tops were bare branches, but when I opened my eyes in the morning, they had all leafed out overnight. It was finally spring.

Waynesboro, Virginia

Firefly was feeling talkative so he was slowing down as we approached Waynesboro. He'd gone to seminary school but dropped out. Still he seemed fascinated about the Bible and spoke of the people that wrote it and the different views of theologians and historians about their perspectives and motivations. He was not a religious zealot but spoke as a historian, fascinated with a specific period, series of events and the different characters involved. I could count on Firefly for stimulating conversation on multiple subjects. On this particular day we also discussed homosexuals, transsexuals, metrosexuals, feminism, paganism and pantheism.

Feather and Silver had moved ahead. When they reached the highway, they hitched a ride into town. First stop, Dairy Queen, where Silver asked for a thru-hiker's special. The puzzled teen across the counter didn't know what he meant. He instructed.

"You start with a chocolate shake. Add a banana and mix in some peanut butter." which she did. "Top it off with whipped cream and chocolate syrup." He raved about it. It was high calorie, high protein and high sugar content, perfect for thru-hikers. Word spread and all weekend they got multiple orders for this new concoction.

Firefly and I reached the highway and stopped at the visitor center where we asked for a ride from the "Trail Angel Network".

Waynesboro is famous for the volunteers who are on call to give rides to thru-hikers. Some take their jobs very seriously and consider themselves tour guides as well, expounding upon the attractions and services available in downtown Waynesboro. We would get such a ride, but it took awhile for them to arrive.

In the meantime, we studied a 3-D exhibit of the Appalachian Trail in the lobby. We could trace our route and imagine what might come next. Firefly noted how the Shenandoah River paralleled the trail and told me how some raft the river instead of hiking that section. He'd worked as a river rafting guide for a while so was tempted, but couldn't work out the logistics.

A woman and her young son joined us looking at the display. We entered into conversation. The boy was amazed that we'd walked over 800 miles of the trail so far, over two months of living outside and hiking over mountains carrying everything we'd need in our packs. I said, "One day you could hike this trail, too." His eyes widened. I could see the wheels turning, just as they had for me many years before.

When Ed and Francis arrived, we piled into the backseat of their car and rode the four and a half miles into town. Our guides showed us the movie theatre, the hardware store, the Baptist Church, which was all great, but we needed to get to the post office before it closed for the weekend. We made it there, thanked our chauffeurs and ran inside with just moments to spare.

Silver was meeting his wife and taking more time off the trail. Feather, Firefly and I planned to check into a hotel for the night. Feather was the first one there so she checked in and we soon followed. We all got showers, put on our cleanest clothes and headed out to the All-You-Can-Eat restaurant.

We had to stand in a long line to pay before we could be seated. It was hard to wait in the tedious Friday night line with the overweight locals ahead, while we scrawny, half-starved thru-hikers drooled impatiently behind them. In our minds we were leaping over fragile old ladies, knocking down football champs, pushing off little kids trying to get to the food at the buffet. In reality, we waited, not exactly patiently, but still.

Once we were finally seated there was just a half wall with some plastic plants separating us from the All-You-Can-Eat nirvana. So close yet so far away. We wanted a conveyor belt that ran down the middle of our table with constant helpings of hot, tasty meats, pastas and sauces, fresh veggies, fruit pies, cakes, brownies and ice cream with sprinkles. Perhaps it was the soothing elevator Muzak but we somehow managed to conduct ourselves in a civilized manner. We filled our plates to overflowing, drank gallons of iced tea and returned to the buffet again and again.

A few booths away was Team Australia, a bit noisier than our well-mannered group. Some of them came over to socialize. After they'd gone, Firefly noted that the ratio of male to female on the trail was five to one, but he was fortunate enough to be hiking with two lovely ladies. He thought that might have something to do with the friendliness of the A-Team.

I knew he was speaking of Feather who was half my age, a fast hiker and a beautiful young woman with wisps of curly blonde hair. While our clothes were in the laundry, Feather wore the most enticing silk slips over her polypropylene leggings which added to her allure. Her baby blue hiking shorts were slit up the side. She had learned to get in or out of her leggings while standing right in front of you carrying on a conversation without revealing a thing, a trick she'd learned as a girl in ballet class. This mesmerized her mostly male shelter mates.

Both Firefly and Feather had suitors off the trail but neither felt strongly attached. It was in Waynesboro that both of them broke off these ties with emotional phone calls that cast a shadow over our stay.

After dinner at the hotel I tried to fix my sleeping pad which had sprung a leak… or six. I filled the bathtub, blew up the inflatable sleeping pad and pushed it underwater. The idea was to find the leak by spotting the air bubbles under water and then patching the leaks. I was having a hard time getting the pad to stay under and called for help. It took all three of us to wrestle that air mattress into submission, or submersion to be precise. Laughing uncontrollably didn't help much.

We spent the day doing laundry, buying fuel and groceries and filling up on town food. That night we moved to sleep in the park behind the YMCA which was free to thru-hikers. I made my bed beneath some willow trees by a pond. As I wrote a letter in the fading light I saw Firefly and Feather sitting together on a bench talking with their little tents set up nearby. Another hiker came in late and laid out his sleeping bag on a picnic table. In the morning his alarm went off, over and over and over again with no effect on him, but waking everyone else. Later I found out it was Chronic who we'd met just before we got to Damascus. We would be hearing more of his alarm clock in the days ahead.

Shenandoah

Our chauffeur came by after church and gave us a ride back to the trail. We were about to enter Shenandoah National Park. As Firefly and

I hiked along we spotted a black bear. It smelled us and high-tailed it through the sparse woods. Moments later, we saw a cub no bigger than a bag of bagels. It looked so cute and cuddly. But since it was calling its mother back, "Maw! Maw! Maw!" we kept moving.

That night we settled into a stone shelter by a stream. The park provides bear poles where campers are to hang up food at night. There are many types of contraptions that keep food safe from wildlife. This one was a tall metal pole, maybe twelve feet high, with a horizontal hoop around the top with hooks to hold the food bags. The challenge was to get our food bags up there using a long, heavy metal pole they'd provided. It took a lot of heft to lift the pole with our newly filled food bags all the way up to the hoop and then secure it to a hook. It was a team effort and turned into the evening's entertainment.

Chronic arrived just before dark, cooked his meal, hung his food and took an upper bunk centrally located in the shelter. None of us were particularly enamored with Chronic, but we weren't rude. The same wasn't true for our new shelter mate. In the morning his alarm went off, over and over and over again. It didn't wake Chronic but it woke all the rest of us so we started preparing for the days hike.

Throughout the day we leapfrogged with Chronic. At one point I caught up with Firefly at an overlook on Skyline Drive. Chronic had been speaking with him but left when he saw me approaching. Firefly laughed as I walked up. He said it was driving Chronic crazy that he was a big, studly young man but couldn't seem to shake a small, middle aged woman. I'd be happy to be left behind by Chronic so as never to hear his insistent alarm clock again. I came to the woods to get away from those things.

That afternoon as we paralleled Skyline Drive, weaving from one side to the other, we enjoyed the views and the forest in turns and I developed a blister. I told Firefly to go ahead while I doctored it up. Blisters were a common occurrence and we all had our ways of dealing with them. One view we shared in common was that when you feel one developing, you stop and tend to it immediately.

Sitting on a rock, a little off the trail, I got out my first-aid kit and found a safety pin and band-aid, but I was out of alcohol wipes. So I poked the budding blister, drained it, and covered it with the Band-aid. I put my sock and boot back on and started off again.

It wasn't long before it started to ache and then throb and then got down right painful. I began to hobble leaning heavily on my stick. I consulted my trail guide. It was four more miles to the next shelter. Leaning against a boulder I asked my blister, "What's it going to take?

Music? Candy? What's it going to take to get me to that shelter?" The blister answered, "Just take it slow."

It was the first of May. There was plenty of daylight. No need to hurry. I crept along trying not to put weight on my heel. Mile after mile I plodded wincing in pain and finally made it up to the High Top shelter where Firefly sat at the picnic table snacking. I sat opposite him, closed my eyes and lay back on the bench with a great sigh of relief.

When I opened my eyes again, Firefly had been to the spring and filled both our water bottles. I thanked him. Feather and Silver arrived and then two locals who brought wonderful food that they shared with us, fresh fish, eggs and produce from the family garden. We sat around the fire and talked. They were painting a house not far away and decided to camp here for a night instead of driving a long way home again. They told us about a short cut to Skyline Drive, just a mile and a half to where they'd parked their car. I took note thinking if this blister wasn't better in the morning I may have to bail.

The next day we all took a good look at my blister that had blackened overnight. I knew it was infected and I couldn't put my feet into boots in this condition. I had to get off the trail and deal with it.

If I were to get an ailment that would take me off the trail, this was great timing. I'd planned to meet my sister, Martha, the next day so we could attend our niece's wedding in Tennessee. I'd just get off a day early. I tied my boots to the top of my pack and wore my flip flops, slowly walking out with the locals on the shortcut. Silver, Firefly and Feather planned to walk twenty miles that day and meet me for dinner at the historic Big Meadows Lodge.

Once I reached the road, I hitched a ride with a kind park ranger to Big Meadows. There was a snack bar near the road that was famous for its blueberry milkshakes. Further back from the road was a campground, and the nearby lodge was built in the 1930s by the Civilian Conservation Corp. I claimed a campsite but had no way to indicate that it was taken. I didn't have a camper or a tent. So I hung my bear line between two trees, got a shower and washed my clothes in the sink, then hung them on the line to dry. I scrubbed my poncho on the picnic table. It doubled as a ground cloth and had been adorned with pine pitch. I hobbled up to the snack bar for lunch and called my sister to finalize our plans. Back at the campsite I lay down on the bench and managed a mid-afternoon nap. I felt alone in an alien landscape with RV's and paved roads, flush toilets and showers. I was anxious for my friends to arrive.

Late in the day I walked up to the Big Meadows Lodge and fell in love with the place. Its big stone walls were framed by Chestnut beams. The wood floors were well worn and homey. Passing through the lobby I entered a room full of windows that looked out over the mountain ridges outside. A fireplace large enough to stand in was in one corner. A round antique table sat in the middle of the room with a jigsaw puzzle on it. But what welcomed me with open arms was a long line of rocking chairs. I made myself at home.

Eventually my trail mates arrived eager to partake of the many food options in the fine dining room. We were seated by the window. When a waiter appeared he set a tray on a stand by our table and served us a plate of crackers and cheese and a small loaf of bread to share. When he turned his attention to the next table, Silver looked at our table, then back at the tray and helped himself to another plate of crackers and cheese and second loaf of bread. When the waiter turned around, he hesitated for a moment, then smiled in our direction.

We ate well that night and enjoyed the sunset from the rocking chairs in the lodge. When darkness fell we headed back to the campground where we all shared my campsite. In the morning everyone got showers and washed clothes before heading back to the lodge for breakfast. The waiter was familiar with us now. He served everyone coffee except for my hot chocolate. I was just complaining that they would all get free refills while I would not when the waiter brought a second hot chocolate for me! Now he was getting the idea. We got large helpings of eggs and hash browns, flapjacks, bacon and fruit.

Fired up for another day of hiking, Firefly and Silver shouldered their packs and vowed to meet us at lunchtime at the Skyland Lodge just nine miles away. Feather had a blister problem, too, so we stayed together and hitched up to Skyland. We'd heard you could eat your way through Shenandoah National Park and now we were doing just that.

There are mostly tourists driving on Skyline Drive and tourists don't like to pick up hitch-hikers so it took a long time for us to get a ride. When Feather and I arrived in the parking lot at Skyland we saw Firefly obviously under the influence. The coffee at breakfast definitely affected his behavior. Sitting down to lunch at the lodge, he told us about meeting a woman day hiker on the trail who asked, "Is it hard to find water out there?"

He answered, "It's harder to find FOOD!" (hint, hint, hint).

"How do you filter your water?" she asked.

"Through my beard," he replied.

He had me in stitches until Silver arrived looking half dead. His feet had been bothering him. He was getting off the trail soon to see his daughter run a marathon in Cincinnati and stay with his family through Mother's Day. His hiking the trail had been hard on his family and his business so he'd been considering getting off at Harper's Ferry, West Virginia. He'd save the northern half of the trail for next year. I thought that would be wise considering the pain he'd been in lately. But I told him I'd miss him. We'd hiked more or less together since our third day on the trail. He left it up in the air.

My plan was to take this week off, get treatment for my blister, attend my niece's wedding and visit the family, while eating as much as I could. Then I'd get a ride back to the trail in Harper's Ferry where I could meet up with Firefly and Feather again. I'd skip about 120 trail miles but I could come back and finish that in the fall.

After lunch I checked into a cabin and offered the shower to my trail mates. Firefly took me up on it. He was still cranked up on caffeine and came leaping out of the shower and flew onto the bed wearing only his shorts. A few minutes later he and Feather were about to leave when my sister arrived. We shared some butterscotch candy she'd brought and then sent them on their way promising to meet at Harper's Ferry in a week.

Off Trail

Martha had worked on some trail construction projects nearby. She took me for a tour. I was impressed when she showed me some huge rocks she'd moved herself. She's smaller than I and was then over fifty years old so I figured for this feat she'd used her brain more than her brawn. She kept her secrets to herself.

We dined again at the Big Meadows Lodge and then went downstairs to the Taproom Lounge to hear live acoustic music. I sang along and wrote post cards to friends. We dodged deer all the way back to Skyland. They seemed to be licking the white line in the middle of the road, an unfortunate attraction.

Martha and I got an early start the next morning. She drove me all the way back to Boone, North Carolina, passing through many small towns I'd walked through weeks before, reversing all my efforts. It felt weird to be going south so fast after months of walking north. We picked up a thru-hiker hitching near Boone and gave him a lift to a local diner. He told us that over 100 thru-hikers had started in Georgia on April first. That blew my mind. I'd heard rumors of a big crowd coming up behind us on the trail, but I never dreamed it was that big. I couldn't imagine trying to share shelters with that many hikers around.

In Boone, we went to the thrift shop and bought all the plastic flowers they had. Our assignment for the outdoor wedding was to decorate the Porta-Potty. I went to the hospital emergency room where they treated my blister. They lanced it, cleaned it, bandaged it and gave me a prescription for antibiotics. They told me to stay off of it, elevate it and wrap it in a hot compress for the next few days. Just what I had in mind.

Now that my blister was taken care of, Martha took me to an All-You-Can-Eat buffet to take care of the rest of me. The first plate was heaping with vegetables. The second was brimming with fruit. I polished it off with an ice cream sundae and chocolate chip cookies. I slept well in Martha's cabin at the edge of town.

In the morning we headed for the wedding in Rock Island, Tennessee. I traveled with a hot water bottle wrapped around my heel in a towel. We stopped for first and second breakfast, gas and snacks. On the long drive I was able to quiz Martha about the northern half of the trail making notes in my trail guide. I was ahead of schedule and needed to coordinate logistics and mail drops for the next leg.

My plan was to get to Hanover, New Hampshire at the end of June where I'd get off-trail for the summer. There's a train station nearby that would provide transportation back to North Carolina to visit the folks and from there I could fly back to Seattle for my summer job leading hikes in Olympic National Park and the Columbia River Gorge. I'd return to the trail in Maine and hike South through New England in the fall finishing near the same train station for an easy ride South. I'd fill in the 120 miles I was now skipping in the Shenandoah and be back with my family for Thanksgiving.

The shift from trail family to birth family was sudden but sweet. I'd been walking an average of 18.6 miles a day in Virginia. Then suddenly I was off-trail hobbling around in flip flops not walking much at all. There was a lot of food available any time of day and cold fizzy drinks on ice. I got to wear cotton clothes, read books, or listen to music. They told us they'd reserved "cabins" for us in a state park. As it turned out, the cabins were modern homes that slept ten in double beds, with two baths, a full kitchen, a gas fireplace and cable TV. The wedding party rented ten of these "cabins" so it was like renting a neighborhood. I went from one cabin to the next visiting extended family and grazing.

The only thing these cabins didn't have was cell phone reception. A phone might ring, and you might be able to tell who was calling, but you'd have to go up to the tennis courts nearby for any hope of a conversation. At any given time there could be a half dozen people at the courts waving their phones up in the air. We arrived in the late afternoon, kissed the babies, hugged the old folks and were getting ready for the Cinco de Mayo party when my sister, Sue, stopped by.

Sue, the mother of the bride, told us Bekah, the bride, had been in a panic all week. She recommended that when we saw her, we should tell her how beautiful she looked. A few minutes later Bekah came in dressed in sweat pants and a T-shirt. Her long blonde hair looked like it hadn't been washed or combed in a week. I told her she looked beautiful. She smiled, glowed a little and gave me a hug. But after she heard the same thing from everyone else in the house she became suspect.

"Did my Mother tell you to say that?"

That night we celebrated with festive Mexican food and a slide show of the happy couple throughout their adventurous young lives. While we visited with both families I was introduced to Chad, a friend of the groom, who had thru-hiked the AT a few years before. He'd seen the AT sticker on the back of Martha's truck and asked "Who's the hiker?" When I told him it was Martha's truck and she'd thru-hiked, too, he was delighted. He hadn't expected to meet two middle aged women thru-hikers in the same family. He told me he'd helped to build a new shelter just North of Harper's Ferry. I told him I'd look for it at the end of the week.

Mom made bouquets for the wedding party while Martha and I went off to decorate the Porta-Potty. The wedding would be in a field under a huge oak tree. The guests sat on bales of hay or on quilts laid out in the tall grass. We "planted" the plastic flowers all around the Porta-Potty. My now retired hiking boots served as a vase. A rainbow colored wind sock flew from a fishing pole above it making it easy to spot among the willows. Mom brought by a bucket of real irises that we put inside the john. We stood back and admired our work. It was the nicest Porta-Potty I'd ever seen.

Sue had brought me a size four skirt and it fit me perfectly. I was thrilled. I joined my aunts and uncles, cousins and friends to witness the ceremony and celebrate the wedding of Bekah and Nate.

Up in the front stood Bekah's sister, Emily, with her husband, David, Nate's brother. On the trail I'd been practicing singing "I Am My Own Grandpa". It was one big happy family and a perfect spring day for a wedding. The wedding party was lovely. My four year old grand niece stole the show when she arrived dressed in white with fairy wings to distribute flower petals riding in a little red wagon.

The reception afterward featured two huge cakes, one white and formal and the other playful, pink, blue and lopsided as if it were catered by Dr. Seuss. Mom, who was not known for her cooking, used to say, "Just because it's not pretty doesn't mean it won't taste good." Truer words were never spoken. I had multiple helpings.

We spent another day visiting and cleaning up, and then my parents drove me back to the trail. My heel had healed and after eating my fill for a week I was ready to hike. We arrived in Harper's Ferry and found the outfitters store. I needed new hiking footwear, but this time I wanted to steer away from boots. Instead I went with the recommendation of other hikers and got lightweight hiking shoes. I wouldn't have a chance to break them in first, so I chose the most comfortable pair. The salesman, Garlic Man, a veteran thru-hiker, encouraged me to walk around, go up and down the stairs to make sure. They felt great. Thankfully, Dad picked up the tab. I asked them to leave me in town where I could wait for Firefly and Feather. We hugged goodbye and they started their long drive back to North Carolina.

Harper's Ferry is a town with a rich history best known as the site of John Brown's Raid. He was an abolitionist who attempted to take over the Federal arsenal in 1859. Colonel Robert E. Lee led a crushing defeat. John Brown was hanged sixteen months later which, along with other events, sparked the Civil War.

Now half the town is an historic park. The houses on the main street have been preserved looking much like they did 150 years before. I walked along reading placards and dates on a street of historic homes, delighting in the architecture and aesthetics. It seemed not much had changed in 150 years. The trail's white blazes lead by the lawns of the National Park Service Headquarters. From there, down a narrow trail, was a viewpoint of the confluence of the Potomac and the Shenandoah rivers where they say Thomas Jefferson admired the view in the 1850s. It's still an inspirational scene.

I found the office of the Appalachian Trail Conservancy in an old building on the main street. Stepping up on the porch, I opened the screen door and went inside. The receptionist asked if I was a thru-hiker. I checked in. There was a message from Feather saying she and

Firefly would be there the next day. I looked around at the post cards, guide books and hiker's box. There were computers available so I checked emails. In the bathroom I saw a sign I'd heard Martha talk about. It read, "Just because you live in the woods, doesn't mean you should act like an animal."

I thought about my fellow thru-hikers and the developing trail culture. Some hikers wore skirts they found at thrift shops to get better ventilation where it's needed. Big brawny men in polka dot skirts, packs and hiking boots may appear a tad bit unusual at a grocery store in town. Some bought new insoles. They were supposed to be heated before putting them into their boots for the first time to assure a good fit. Hikers used the microwaves at gas station snack counters. One hiker decided to see how long he could go without taking a shower. None of the shop owners wanted his business. Later, as I was hiking, I wrote a song about them.

The staff asked me to pose out front by the AT sign and put my picture in this year's scrapbook, NOBO number forty-three. I found out later that 1,150 hikers started from Georgia in 2006 intending to hike to Maine. About half of them had dropped out by the time they reached Harper's Ferry which is roughly half-way.

I left the office and headed back down the street toward the hostel outside of town. It was closing time at the outfitters and Garlic Man was heading out. He offered me a ride to the hostel where he was living.

At the hostel I asked about a work exchange. The hostel keeper gave me half price if I'd clean the bathroom, which I would have done anyway. It was a pig sty. After settling into the women's bunk room which was empty except for me, I met the other occupants who had gathered in the common area. One named Eveready was an insurance salesman from Nashville. He was a white haired Southern gentleman, fit and healthy looking, just about to start hiking for a month. He'd been taking time off to hike the trail one month at a time for years.

In the morning, I found a box of chocolate cake mix in the kitchen cupboard but there were no eggs. Just as Eveready was heading out to get breakfast at a nearby diner, I asked if he'd bring back some eggs. He was happy to oblige. I made two cakes and served one up hot for the hikers at the hostel. Eveready had already left so he missed out. I saved one cake for Firefly and Feather. Later that day I met them at the Appalachian Trail Conservancy office and offered the cake. We cut it into nine squares. Feather and I each got one piece while Firefly got seven. They ran errands and stopped for a beer but I was anxious to get back on the trail.

I crossed the Potomac on a pedestrian bridge and entered Maryland, my sixth state. Across the river there's a long, flat, section of the AT that leads out of town on the C&O Canal tow path. The C&O linked the waters of the Chesapeake Bay to the Ohio River, a major trade route. I read that barges used to be towed up the river by mules that plodded up the tow path. This 185 mile-long path that follows the Potomac out of Washington, D.C. was slated for highway development until a protest march was led by Supreme Court Justice William O. Douglas, who was himself an Appalachian Trail 2,000 miler. The public called for the tow path to be spared. Now it's preserved as a National Historical Park accessible to hikers and cyclists, but closed to motorized traffic along its full length. I made a mental note to come back to walk or bike that route someday.

For me it was effortless and somewhat mindless walking. I missed my turn, walked an extra mile or two and had to double back. Climbing up the rugged trail I tried to move fast to make up for the lost daylight. I didn't arrive at the Ed Garvey Shelter until near dark. This was the shelter that Chad, the wedding guest, had told me about. It was beautiful with a loft that actually had a door and windows like a real house. Firefly and Feather were there and said they'd been wondering about me. We were eating dinner at the picnic table out front when Firefly felt something on his leg. He brushed it off and then did a double take. We'd been dining with a black widow spider.

Feather asked me if I had anything for nettle stings. She had stepped off the canal road and dropped her drawers without noticing the type of greenery around her. In my experience the best remedy for a nettle sting is Dock, a plantain which usually grows near nettles, but it should be applied as soon as possible. At this point there wasn't much I could do. However, it offered inspiration for a new song with a catchy chorus which I wrote while walking the next day.

Be careful where you squat,
You'll be sorry if you're not.
Better look before you drop your drawers
When you can't use a pot.
Be careful where you squat.

Sally hiked with Jane
From Georgia up to Maine
But I heard her cry on the 4th of July
When she squatted down in pain
Stinging nettles she explained.

Maryland

There's a four state Challenge for thru-hikers to walk from Virginia, through West Virginia, Maryland and into Pennsylvania within twenty-four hours. The total is about forty-three miles. Hikers start hours before dawn with one foot in Virginia, lunge across the Shenandoah River, skip through Harper's Ferry, West Virginia and race across the twenty-nine miles of trail in Maryland to collapse across the Pennsylvania border in the wee hours of the following morning. What do they get for such a feat? Satisfaction. We took it at our usual pace stopping to enjoy the parks and shelters along the way.

At Gathland State Park there were interesting stone structures, arches and pillars, some worn down through the years and grown over with vines and vegetation, but others still standing tall. One very impressive monument, surrounded by a well-kept lawn, honored war correspondents.

Ten miles further at Washington Monument State Park there was a brick tower built in 1827 to honor George Washington. I spent a few minutes there soaking up the view and the afternoon sun. I didn't know if Firefly and Feather had passed while I was there but we'd planned to meet at a nearby roadside pub for dinner that night. So when I got to a parking lot I asked a woman getting into her car if I could get a lift.

The Harleys and Indians were parked side by side out front as if on display. Inside, burly tattooed guys played pool with girls in low cut shirts, tight pants and jean jackets. I walked to the less populated end of the room, took a seat at the bar and ordered a tall iced glass of cranberry juice. As I studied the menu a large fellow in a denim shirt with the sleeves ripped off sidled over and planted his big, raw elbow on the bar next to me.

"Are you hiking the Appalachian Trail?

"Yep."

"Well," I could see he was just starting up as if he were kicking his motorcycle into gear,"I'm a Ridge Runner," he explained, "and I know this section of trail like the back of my hand."

I had my doubts but played along. He talked on while his buddies observed from the pool tables, snickering behind their beers. I concluded that this was a regular game for them, like Kick the Can or Pin the Tail on the Donkey. Maybe they called it Hook the Hiker-chick.

Walking roughly twenty miles a day over challenging terrain builds more than muscle and I wasn't going to let some beer-gutted biker dude intimidate me, even if he was easily twice my size with a couple a dozen friends backing him up.

I stood my ground, or at least stayed on my stool, and met his gaze with a smile. I'd studied animal behavior in college. With some predators I knew I shouldn't make eye contact but this was different. I kept my cool and hoped Firefly and Feather would show up soon.

They arrived a few minutes later. Feather looked at me and asked with her eyes, "Are you alright?" while Firefly smiled mischievously as if to say, "Oh, this will be good."

I introduced them to the "Ridge Runner" and told them he was an AT expert. They nodded, yeah right. We ordered dinner and the biker dude went back to his pack.

I once worked at a zoo. When I first started I went on an orientation tour for new employees. It was different from anywhere else I'd worked going far beyond a tour of the copy machine, restrooms and employee lounge. This was a combination of animal behavior and emergency procedures.

At the bear den they told us, "If someone falls into the bear enclosure, throw a garbage can lid in. While the bears are sniffing the lid, drop this rope ladder down for the person to climb out."

Over by the wolf enclosure they said, "If someone gets on the wrong side of this fence, call them over and get them as close to you as possible. Then get a crowd to stand next to you by the fence. If your 'pack' is bigger than their pack, they'll leave you alone." With Firefly and Feather joining my pack, I didn't look quite so vulnerable. I was no longer prey.

Firefly and Feather

The next day we crossed the Mason Dixon line and entered Pennsylvania. I read that the word "Dixie" is not derived from *Dixon* as many people think. Before the Civil War, a Louisiana bank printed ten dollar bills where the word *dix* appeared, French for ten. The bills were distributed so widely that soon the South became known as "Dixie".

Once we crossed the line from South to North we were supposed to start pronouncing *Appalachian* the way Northerners do, that is to make a long *a* sound in the middle of the word and follow that with a soft *shun*. Growing up in the South, however, I'd always used the correct pronunciation, keeping all the *a*'s the same and finishing with a decisive *chin*.

Firefly and Feather both came from the South as well. Firefly hailed from Alabama while Feather came from Georgia. Needless to say we spoke the same language. We'd been traveling together for about a month, except for the week I'd taken off the trail for my niece's wedding. During that same week Silver had been off the trail, leaving these two youngsters unchaperoned.

It was spring. Birds were singing, flowers blooming, bees were buzzing, so it should have been no surprise when one rainy afternoon I came upon the two of them sitting close together on a bench in a park pavilion. Firefly had his arm around her shoulders until he heard my footsteps. His quick shuffling away from her confirmed what I should have already known. They were becoming sweethearts.

It caught me by surprise and so did my emotions. I sat with them for a few minutes and then quickly set off under my umbrella. Firefly followed running to catch up and calling my name. He asked if I was upset. I hadn't really sorted out my feelings but yes, I was upset. I felt like they'd been keeping secrets. Messenger had asked me back in Harper's Ferry if Firefly and Feather were *together*. I said they were together but not *together*.

"That's not what I heard," he'd said.

Now I felt like an idiot. Of course they'd fall for each other. They're both beautiful, adorable, intelligent people, the same age, from the same part of the country, hiking the trail together. It made perfect sense. But I felt hurt just the same. I'd been hiking with Firefly for six weeks before we met Feather. Now she had snuggled right in next to him and I was feeling left out, jealous, awkward. I'd never thought of Firefly as a sweetheart so I didn't know how to classify my feelings. I liked Feather and I wanted to be happy for them. But at the same time I felt the balance of our trail family shift. They would be a couple and I would be the odd one out.

He tried to reassure me, but I just needed some time alone. I took a deep breath and walked on in the rain.

It had been nice walking with Silver and Firefly. I was able to enjoy the company of men without any obligation or sexual undercurrents. I was safer with them than traveling alone, and my heart was safe, too... or so I thought. But I was a big girl. I'd get over it. Firefly and Feather were both kind and beautiful people and of course, I would give them my blessing. But it would be different. I felt like a third wheel.

Eveready

In Pennsylvania, the days were warm and the terrain was gentle. Volunteer shelter keepers seemed to be in a competition to provide the nicest trail accommodations. We met a fellow in the middle of the day polishing the shelter floor. We stopped to compliment him on his work. He told us a shelter up ahead used to have hanging baskets of flowers but they made him take them down. They were a little too domestic. There also seemed to be twin shelters at many stops, two identical shelters side by side. We had moved through different regions where place names used the words "knob" or "gap", but Pennsylvania seemed to have the "runs", Tumbling Run Shelter, Birch Run, Tom's Run.

I had just finished the bottle of antibiotics I'd been taking for my infected blister. The next day I crossed through a hay field. The owner was cutting a path through the middle for the hikers. Fresh cut hay used to set off my allergies but this field seemed to have no effect, until that night I started to itch. It began with the hottest, sweatiest parts of my body, my feet and my back. The next day it spread from there up my legs, around my sides and down to my hips. I couldn't figure it out. I'd never had an allergic reaction like this before, swollen eyes or runny nose maybe, but not a rash that was covering my whole body. It was like I'd rolled around in poison ivy, though I knew what it looked like and had been careful to avoid it.

The next afternoon I walked toward Caledonia State Park. The itching had become so bad that at one point I just sat down right on the trail, leaned against a rock and closed my eyes. I was in agony. I didn't care if I ever stood up again.

"Well that's not a very positive attitude." A voice in my head piped up. I talked myself into getting back on my feet. Leaning heavily on my walking stick, I pushed myself to a standing position, but the pain in my feet was like wearing shoes made of stinging nettles. I looked down at my feet and willed them to move forward, first one foot and then the other.

Slowly I made my way into the park where I found Firefly and Feather drinking sodas at a picnic table. Feather offered me her drink saying she'd bought it for me. I was too distraught at the time to catch her fib. I asked if they had any aspirin and they dug around until they found some. The combination of the aspirin, caffeine and sugar relieved my pain and lifted my spirits.

I was able to walk on. Our old friend Salsa met us at the Quarry Gap Shelter, a delightful Garden of Eden with twin shelters connected by a covered porch with a skylight. The ground was covered with white gravel and framed on one side by a trickling stream lined with flagstones. Rhododendrons bordered the clearing making it look like a small private park.

We made dinner, but my stove was acting up again, so Feather heated extra water for me. My rash was still bothering me so she suggested I take some Benadryl. I carried some in my first-aid kit. After a few minutes, it helped take the edge off the itching.

On one side of the clearing was a wooden tent platform where Feather went with a magazine to smoke. Firefly went over, and though there was no music, he began to do his fluid dance behind her. I'd never seen anyone move like that. Michael Jackson had nothing on him. Salsa and I watched in amazement, but every time Feather turned to see, he'd stop and innocently look up into the sky. I had to admit they were cute.

The next day I walked on. The weather had grown cloudy and chill. The sky was spitting rain and tree branches shivered. My rash was spreading, itching, driving me crazy. At a shelter by the trail, I sat in a corner out of the wind, hugged my bare knees to my chest and covered up with my poncho. The cold wind and dark day dampened my spirits. My rash plagued me and as it was a Saturday and I was miles from any town, the chances of seeing a doctor were next to nil. I felt defeated.

Then Feather came along and urged me to charge ahead to Pine Grove Furnace State Park. There was a hostel there, a general store, a phone, a road, maybe even a way to get to a doctor. I pried myself up out of the shelter and let her pull me along.

We arrived at the store at about 3:00 p.m. The first person I saw was Eveready, the section-hiker I'd met at the hostel in Harper's Ferry. He greeted me warmly.

"How are you?" he asked. The words spilled out of his mouth without a thought.

"I have a medical emergency." I lifted the end of my shorts to show him the rash that had crept down over my hips.

Maybe it was because he was an insurance salesman, and I had used the word "emergency", but I could see his inner "sirens" go off. His blue eyes flashed. He immediately sprang into action.

"There's a doctor at the hostel on vacation with his family. I'll introduce you." He led me over to the hostel at the old Iron Master's Mansion next door. Up on the porch several people were enjoying the rainy day sitting in rocking chairs. Eveready introduced me to the doctor who took a look at my back and asked a few questions. When I mentioned I'd been taking an antibiotic for an infected blister he determined that was the cause of the rash. I was allergic to sulfa drugs. News to me.

He gave me a prescription and my first dose of Allegra D right then and there. He said it would last about twelve hours. I thanked him and went back to the store.

By then, Eveready had found a ride for me to go into town with a local fellow named Fred. He said there was a pharmacy there that was open on Saturdays. As I turned to follow Fred outside, I caught a glimpse of the store keeper across the room waving his arms as if trying to get my attention but I was in a hurry. The nearest drug store was fifteen miles away in Mount Holly and would close at 4:00 p.m. There was no time to lose.

As we left the State Park in Fred's old truck, he explained that he had Alzheimer's. He talked the whole way telling dirty jokes and lies. He told me the best thing about having Alzheimer's is you get to go to bed with a different woman every night. He'd laugh and then asked, "Now, where is it we're going?"

"The drug store," I said.

"I hope they have one in Mount Holly."

Then he'd repeat the same dirty jokes, tell me about his family and ask, "Where are we going again?"

"To the pharmacy," I'd say.

"I hope they have one in Mount Holly."

When we pulled into town I saw the drug store across the street. I jumped out saying they were about to close and I'd have to run in while he parked. A few minutes later I was at the counter inside waiting for my prescription when Fred came up to me and asked, "Are you the one I'm taking back to the State Park?"

"Yes," I said, "that would be me."

On the drive back I noticed a lot of little fishing cabins. It had started to rain. I knew the hostel was full and it was seven miles to the next shelter. So I asked Fred if he knew anyone with a cabin near the Park that might allow us to spend the night on their porch. Fred thought for a minute then said, "I have a cabin!"

"Is it near the Park?" I asked.

"It's *in* the Park." he said. "No one ever goes there," he added distractedly. "It doesn't have running water." I assured him that wouldn't bother us at all.

When we got back to the store, Firefly jumped into the back of the truck and went with us to see Fred's cabin which was just a mile away. Fred kept repeating, "No one ever goes there."

When we arrived, there were three cars parked outside the cabin and inside the lights were on with music playing. I followed Fred to the door while Firefly looked around the yard outside. Fred opened the door to a homey scene with three men preparing dinner and talking. One looked up and said, "Dad! What are you doing here?"

Fred uttered again as if in a dream, "No one ever comes here."

His son responded, "Well, we're here tonight, Dad."

Fred said nothing more and I could see the son looked concerned so I stepped in and introduced myself. The son introduced his friends. We made our exit and Fred took us back the way we'd come.

I wondered later what Fred's son... and wife would think of Fred showing up at his old fishing cabin with a younger woman. It could make another good story for his repertoire of dirty jokes, though he probably wouldn't remember it.

Back at the store, Salsa had accepted the Half Gallon Challenge. Upon reaching Pine Grove Furnace State Park thru-hikers were challenged to eat a half gallon of ice cream in one sitting to mark the half-way point of the trail. It was no big deal to Salsa who said he used to do that at home all the time. I got a burger and wondered where I would spend the night. I really didn't feel like walking seven more miles to the next shelter in the rain and growing darkness.

Once again Eveready came to my rescue. He said there was a bed for me at the hostel.

"I thought the hostel was full," I said. He said the women's bunk rooms were full, but he'd talked the owner into letting me take a bunk in the men's dorm. I was incredibly grateful. Eveready had earned his trail name.

There wasn't enough room for Firefly, Feather and Salsa at the hostel but before they moved on we all got a tour of this historic mansion. We'd read that there had been an iron furnace here that made weapons used in the Revolutionary War. The Iron Master's mansion had later been a stop on the Underground Railroad. I wondered if runaway slaves had walked the same trail I had just walked that day. The hostel manager showed us the secret door that led to a large underground room where the slaves had been hidden.

Later I took another entrance to the basement to do my laundry.

It felt good to get a hot shower and slip into clean clothes. The doctor's family moved from the porch to the kitchen and made a pancake dinner for everyone with a wide array of condiments on top.

It was such a relief to stop itching, get cleaned up, eat a stack of pancakes with good company in a warm, dry, building that I didn't mind the loud snoring in the men's dorm. In the morning Eveready and I started hiking together.

We walked sixteen miles to the shelter where we'd planned to spend the night but when we arrived, there was a spot already taken. The occupant wasn't there at the moment, but we noticed he had some odd hiking gear, an old cotton sleeping bag, heavy cans of stew and denim jeans. Eveready and I looked at each other. We had a bad feeling about this. We whispered our concerns to each other and made a plan.

We sat outside at the picnic table, ate a snack bar and waited for the fellow to return. It wasn't long before he came from the outhouse nearby. He was dressed in dirty street clothes and old worn loafers. We greeted him and chatted, then asked, "How long are you planning to be out here?"

"A couple of weeks," he said, and then under his breath, "or until they catch me."

It was another four miles into Boiling Springs. We could still make it before dark.

Thoroughbreds

The trail passes right through Boiling Springs, a lovely little Pennsylvania town with a lake in the middle. The trail follows the shoreline. Stately old homes lined the streets on both sides of the water. One of these was a B&B where we aimed to stay for the night. There was no hostel in town and the campsite outside of town wasn't open until Memorial Day, still two weeks away. The B&B was a step up from our usual accommodations but we thought we could split the cost of a twin room and enjoy the luxury for one night.

We stepped up to the door and rang the bell. When the owner appeared I felt like Dorothy at the gates of the Emerald City.

"Go away!" Though he didn't use those exact words, the sentiment was obvious. We would have left gladly, but we'd walked twenty miles that day, it was nearly dark, about to rain and this was our only overnight option. Just like Dorothy and her friends, we pleaded.

The owner told us to walk around back, climb the fire escape and leave our packs outside. We followed his instructions though we hated to leave our packs out in the rain. We took what we needed out of them and tucked my tarp around them before crawling through an upstairs window into a laundry room.

The owner met us there and ordered us to wash our clothes and take baths before we sat on the furniture. We had just done our laundry at the Iron Master's Hostel the night before but didn't want to argue, so I washed my sleeping bag. We went out to an Italian restaurant for dinner, strolled around the lake and then came back up the fire escape and climbed through the window to our luxury accommodations. In the morning, we packed our gear and then enjoyed a delicious breakfast in an upstairs parlor quarantined from the other guests in the downstairs dining room.

Stopping at the Post Office I got a wonderful care package from a friend with plenty of gourmet chocolate. We briefly stopped by the Appalachian Trail Conference regional office where we got some information then moved quickly out of town.

I was leading the way until mid-morning when Eveready complained of a shin splint coming on. He said he was breaking all his hiking rules, going too far, too fast, too soon. He considered thru-hikers "thoroughbreds" and wasn't up to hiking at my pace, at least not on his first few days on the trail. I offered him the lead and we hiked on at a kinder, gentler pace.

My stove had been acting up again and I hadn't been able to fix it. Eveready had given it a try at the B&B with no luck, so he invited me to dine with him that night. He had put a lot of time into planning his three week hike. He'd worked out menus at home, cooked special meals with tasty sauces and then dried them. As we walked, he told me what the menu options were and allowed me to choose. Cajun sounded good.

"And what sort of music shall I arrange?" he asked.

"Ziedico, of course."

"And we'll have a white linen table cloth, candelabra and silver place settings."

Pause.

"With Cajun food? How about a red checked spread and a kerosene lamp?" He smiled approvingly. Studies have shown that people who walk through natural settings, as opposed to manmade surroundings, gain creativity and imagination.

When we reached Darlington shelter, we met Magic Touch who, true to his name, was able to fix my stove. So I ended up cooking my same old pasta for dinner but with a very tasty Cajun sauce. Magic Touch worked on the AT trail crew and was just taking the night off. We told him about the odd fellow we'd met at the previous shelter and he said he'd have someone check it out.

The next day we hiked at a slower pace into Duncannon where we planned to meet Firefly and Feather at the Doyle Hotel. Eveready decided to spend the night, take a day off the trail and give his shins a rest. I was just stopping for a good meal.

When we arrived there was a message from Firefly and Feather. They'd been there the night before and were out running errands. They'd be back soon.

Eveready and I chose a table in the restaurant. There were neither white linen table cloths, nor a red checkered spread. Just long wooden tables with room for eight, much like the picnic tables at the shelters, making hikers feel right at home.

The Doyle Hotel, though a bit run down, was a very hiker-friendly establishment. It is one of the original Anheuser-Busch hotels and must have been grand in its day. It had stood for over a century, but perhaps would not be standing much longer.

I ordered a Sunday dinner with pot roast, mashed potatoes and gravy, peas and a house salad on the side. Other hikers joined us as we ate. I took my time savoring every bite. As I used a biscuit to wipe my plate clean a man across the table smiled saying he didn't think a small woman like me could finish the whole thing. There was never a doubt in my mind. I dabbed the corners of my mouth with a napkin and ordered peach pie a la mode for dessert.

I eventually reunited with Firefly and Feather who informed me that Silver Streak was back on the trail. He'd spent the night at the hotel and left earlier promising to meet us at the shelter. Eveready and I would part company here. I took his picture outside the hotel, thanked him for all his help and hugged him good-bye. Firefly, Feather and I shouldered our packs and moved on. As we started walking, Firefly noted a resemblance between Eveready and Silver Streak.

"They're both handsome men, about six feet tall, slightly older, with sparkling blue eyes. They're both courteous and helpful and liked to laugh." He looked at me sideways and smiled.

"Both happily married," I added. We crossed the long bridge over the Susquehanna River under stormy skies.

Mysterious Disappearances

The next day we came upon the beautiful Peter's Mountain shelter which could sleep twelve hikers. It was spacious enough for a table inside the shelter and even had a loft. We stopped for a snack.

Within sight of this large, new shelter was a very small, old shelter built by none other than Earl Shaffer, the first thru-hiker. We went to investigate. Earl was a native of Pennsylvania and a hardy individual. He'd first hiked the AT in 1948 when the trail was much more rugged than it is today. This tiny shelter must have seemed extravagant to him. Our party of four wouldn't stay in either of them as it was only mid-day.

That afternoon friends of Feather met us at a road crossing with cold drinks and treats. They'd hiked the trail with Feather the year before and arranged to pick up Firefly and Feather and take them to Trail Days in Damascus, Virginia, 691 trail miles behind us.

A friend had emailed an article to me from the New York Times. It described Trail Days, a three day event, which had been attended by 20,000 to 25,000 people the year before. (The population of Damascus is 1,094.) It was described as "the backpacker's Mardi Gras." Anyone who has ever hiked the trail was invited and the younger hikers were especially inclined to attend.

There would be a town-wide yard sale, a pageant, a tarp raising contest and Appalachian Trail Jeopardy. Gear merchants move into town and set up booths where they'd try to sell stuff to hikers who, in turn, would try to get it for free. The Whittling Club would show off their skill. There's a hiker's talent show. And then, last but certainly not least, is the thru-hikers parade. It's tradition for on-lookers to soak them with squirt guns, hoses and water balloons.

The Times article said this year's festival would feature 150 vendors, five musical performances, and more than forty other events. A makeshift campground would sprout a colorful array of 2,000 tents and tarps snuggled closely together. What wasn't mentioned were the interesting cigarettes and jars of homemade moonshine that would flow freely throughout. It would be a huge party for thru-hikers, not to be missed, at least if you liked to party. Firefly assured us they'd get back to this spot in a few days and hurry to catch up. With their youth and ability, we had no doubt that they would.

This left Silver and me to hike on without them. When we arrived at the shelter that night, there we were with the other old timers, Dreamer, Spiritual Pilgrim and others. We missed the light-hearted spark of the twenty-somethings. The conversation around camp that night was about how many "Vitamin I" each had taken for what ailments. Silver and I felt like empty nesters, but we carried on.

Pennsylvania on the Rocks

In Pennsylvania the trail is paved with sharp, pointy rocks like broken dishes stuck in the mud, pointy ends up. In some places we climbed piles of loose rocks or jumped up and over boulders the size of parked cars. It took concentration. I was constantly looking at the ground. My eyes signaled my brain. My brain passed messages to my feet, "Step there, step there, step there, step there," all day long. If I wasn't paying attention, chances are within a few feet, I'd trip and fall. There were no soft landings. Despite the rocks and the rainy weather we made good distance each day though it was agonizing to our feet.

After another long and painful day, ending with a steep descent to make sure our knees as well as our feet ached, we entered Port Clinton, Pennsylvania, a small historic town. I was ahead of Silver, so I walked into town with Dreamer. Food was our primary focus so we headed for the only restaurant in town, dropped our packs in the entry and stepped into the dining room. The wait staff hurried over and told us to take our packs to the front porch. We did though it made us nervous to leave our packs outside right next to the parking lot. We returned to the dining room to wait for a table. I longed to sit down and put my feet up, but we were informed that we were not allowed in the dining room. We'd have to eat in the bar, so we went back outside and carried our packs around the side of the building to the bar.

It was Friday night and the place was packed. After twenty-four miles of walking on pointy rocks, a bar stool was not the most comfortable perch. Sitting between the smokers made it more unpleasant. We waited fifteen or twenty minutes before they even served us a glass of water, but when they finally brought us a burger, it was huge!

By the time Silver and Spiritual Pilgrim arrived it was after dark. Dreamer's wife came to meet him and they got a room upstairs. I left the others to finish their dinners and went to find a spot at the town pavilion where our guidebook said thru-hikers could sleep for free.

The long, low building was in a park just a few blocks away. I was more than ready to get off my aching feet. By the dim glow of a distant street light I moved cautiously into the open structure among the trees. It was dark and dirty. At least the shelters usually provided a broom. Putting down my pack I checked the place out as best I could in the tiny beacon of my headlamp. I claimed a spot near the corner, laid out my tarp, my sleeping pad and my bag and crawled in. Getting horizontal was bliss. While falling asleep I heard other hikers quietly come and settle into their respective corners. Or, I thought they were hikers. They could have been homeless people. Same thing. I was too tired to care. Rain pounded on the roof all night.

In the morning, I packed up and headed for breakfast at a roadside café. While waiting for a seat, I studied a series of pictures on the wall of a bear trying to get to a bird feeder that was strung on a wire between two trees. The bear looked like a trapeze artist and it reminded me to be sure to hang up my food.

After breakfast I went to the post office. They had all the packages for thru-hikers under a table out front. I saw one for Firefly and asked if I could put a note on it. The clerk was downright rude. I was getting a bad impression of Port Clinton.

I took my mail drop outside and was sorting through it when other locals passed greeting me warmly. One fellow stopped in his car and offered me a ride to the grocery store a few miles away. I gratefully accepted. My provisions were low and the only place in town that sold food offered only candy and nuts. The man waited while I shopped and then offered the use of his office computer to send emails. That seemed a bit above and beyond. Going to a public shopping area with a stranger was one thing. But going to a private office on a weekend seemed risky, so I thanked him, but declined. He dropped me off at the trailhead on the edge of town.

It was a beautiful Saturday and I met a lot of day hikers as I approached the famed Pinnacles, a rocky outcropping with spectacular views of the surrounding region. Sitting among the locals, I was asked if I was a thru-hiker. When I answered "Yes," I was given a whole roll of Oreo cookies. My Port Clinton impressions improved.

That night Silver and I ended up in the Eckville Shelter, the only AT shelter that I'd seen with electricity and a nearby flush toilet. It was a shed behind an old farmhouse. The owner was paid by the National Park Service to keep the shelter open. There was even a shower house but I was disappointed to find that the solar water heater hadn't seen enough sun that day to be warm.

The next twenty-five mile day brought us into Palmerton, Pennsylvania. Just before dark, Silver and I hitched a ride three miles into town with an older couple. The driver, Earl, told us his brother had hiked the trail fifteen years before. He gave us his phone number and offered to give us a ride back to the trail in the morning. It had been a long day. Our feet ached, and we were looking forward to the fine hospitality for which Palmerton was known. Earl dropped us off right in front of the police station where they throw hikers in jail.

Free showers, a warm room and a soft bunk sounded good to us, but the door was locked. We knocked and rang the bell to no avail. It was 8:30 on a Sunday night and not much was happening. We circled the building but found no one. So we went to the diner across the street and ate a good home style dinner. It was getting late now. I felt like I was about to drop. We returned to the police station but still found it empty. The hostel would close at 10:00 p.m. So it's true what they say, "You can't find a cop when you need one."

Then Silver spotted a police car at the Chinese restaurant a block down the street. He went in pursuit while I stood waiting. As I watched Silver disappear into the restaurant I heard a commotion behind me. Some teens were coming down the street in my direction. They wore all black. Streetlights reflected off metal studs and chains. They had a malicious air. The hair on the back of my neck stood up. These guys were potential trouble. A year before, had I been in this position I might have been looking for a place to run. But that was then. I had walked twenty-five miles on sharp rocks that day. I was tired. I was dirty. I was irritable, and I was in no mood to be messed with. I turned to face them and visualized my walking stick, lightening fast, hacking them to shreds before they could utter the word, "Dude."

The teens headed up a side street as Silver returned with a cop. We all went inside. The policeman filled out some forms while Silver and I made jokes about carrying concealed weapons and outstanding warrants. I'm sure he'd heard it all before. He registered us and showed us around. I got the first shower, washed out some clothes and hung them on a rack near the furnace. I came back into a large bunkroom where Silver and another hiker were talking. Climbing into a bunk on the other side of the room I fell into a deep and grateful sleep.

In the morning I spent time in the diner across the street having breakfast, drinking tea and writing a letter as the morning sun streamed in. It was luxurious. But Silver was antsy to get going. With more than enough food, I mailed a five pound bounce box up ahead so I wouldn't have to carry the extra weight. Then we called Earl and got a ride back to the trail.

We were met with a wall of loose rock three hundred feet high known as Lehigh Gap. We cinched our hip belts tighter. I climbed carefully as strong gusts of wind tried to throw me off balance. Silver followed trying to stay to one side in case I launched a stone from above. We breathed a little easier once we reached the top and had a look around at the town below, the factory by the river, and then the trail ahead.

There was something disturbing about it. Not a tree or shrub grew here, a lifeless wasted landscape. We walked on speculating. A fire perhaps? But there was no sign of charred remains. Logging? But there were no stumps. Then I remembered reading about it months before. The rusted old factory by the river was a former zinc smelting plant and the emissions had poisoned this hillside. We were walking through a superfund site.

That night I came to the shelter and who was there to meet me but Captain Kangaroo and Team Australia. They had been to Trail Days and were just returning. Silver was on his way. This meant there would be eight of us in a shelter designed for six. They made room for Silver sleeping like sardines shoulder to shoulder across the back. Because I was the shortest, it was decided that I'd sleep across the entrance of the shelter and people could still step around me if they had to come and go in the night.

As darkness fell we had all bedded down when a fellow came out of the woods with four dogs straining at their leads. One out in front was a Pitbull that barked and snarled lunging at the end of its lead. The others of mixed breeds joined in. Suddenly, we were all wide awake, sitting up in our sleeping bags, with me being their first line of defense.

The man, finding he had a captive audience, launched into a long tirade about diminished uranium and political conspiracies. Meanwhile, the dogs continued their wild barking in a competition to see which one could be the most intimidating. They were all doing an excellent job but the Pitbull was getting my vote as it was just a few feet from my sleeping bag.

Thinking I must look odd to them, a giant blue slug with a human head, I slowly got out of my sleeping bag. Sitting in shorts at the shelter entrance, I tried to calm the dogs with soft, soothing tones, "Good dog. Nice doggie." In a minute or two they'd calmed down though their owner was still ranting away with no sign of letting up. He was obviously brilliant, reciting studies done by distinguished scientists at prominent universities, but he talked like a raging mad man. This went on and on as the dogs laid down and my shelter mates and I grew weary. The man barely breathed, taking no pauses in his discourse. Finally, he turned abruptly, yanking all his dogs to their feet, and walked back into the dark woods still raging.

In the shelter, we were stunned. We stared into the woods where the man had disappeared. Eventually, Silver broke the silence.

"It's all Scout's fault."

The next twenty mile day brought us to the Delaware Water Gap, a place of significant beauty and history. Though this day was much like the last, with morning showers and miles of bouldering and dancing on pointy rocks, I enjoyed the walk up Mount Minsi where I paused to look north across the river. A mountain stood out like a tall, lopsided layer cake with streams of broken rock spiraling up its sides. As I looked at it in the distance and admired its majestic beauty I thought, "They're going to make us climb that one, too."

From there the trail eased along woodland roads. I met a growing horde of day hikers in the last few miles. Stepping from the trail into quiet lanes I found a lovely little town with quaint shops. Though my feet were tender and sore, the weather had improved and I was in good spirits.

My old friend, Al, had promised me a trail angel at this stop. Across the river lay New Jersey, his home turf, and he'd asked his old college buddy to take me in as I passed through. I was looking forward to eating real food, getting cleaned up and sleeping on an actual bed.

I came upon the Church of the Mountain hostel and was greeted by Jolly Green Giant who I hadn't seen for weeks. He and his hiking partner, Fat Camp, had totally embraced trail culture, growing long hair and beards, and wearing pink poodle thrift shop skirts. I admired their spirit. They're young and strong with nothing to prove to anyone. There was just one thing that bothered me about Jolly, and it cost him at least one hug. He hadn't bathed for over a month. He reeked.

I used the phone at the hostel to call my trail angel, Bruce. I got an answering machine and left a message. Then I called my friend, Al, who told me Bruce teaches school so he won't be able to come get me until later and he's an hour's drive from there. But Al assured me, "He'll be there." I got his work phone and his wife's cell phone number, too. I called them all and left messages at each number. Then I waited.

By this time I thought Silver would have arrived. I went out to the street and sat down on the curb watching the town folk go about their business. An antique shop in an old house next door was getting ready to host a gala event stringing up rows of tiny white lights and setting tables with candles and flowers on the wide porch. The atmosphere was charming. Watching the festivities take shape enhanced my good mood.

Then Silver came stomping out of the woods, grumbling and scowling like an old bear who couldn't reach the food bag. He barely said hello and stormed right past me, and the hostel, without so much as a nod to the hikers standing outside. I went back to my pack at the hostel, got my fanny pack and followed Silver into town. I hadn't seen where he went, but knew he'd be looking for food. After ducking in and out of a few cafés, I found him in an Italian restaurant looking glum in a booth at the back. I sat down with him and looked over the menu. He was uncharacteristically silent. When the waitress came, Silver could hardly put a sentence together.

After a big plate of pasta and a salad, he asked about pie. After the pie, he ordered a shake. He was considering getting a burger, but decided to hold off. He told me he needed a rest. His back was bothering him. The rocks had worn him down, but he had new shoes and a knee brace coming in his next mail drop and only a few more days of hiking through these dang, blasted rocks. We both planned to take a zero day. As he paid his tab and headed for the hotel next door, I gave him the number of my trail angel, and then strolled up the hill to the hostel.

Other hikers at the hostel said they'd seen Firefly "flying down the trail" but they had not seen Feather. If Firefly could catch up, I was sure it would lift Silver's spirits. I found out later that Feather's feet gave out again, just as they had the year before when she'd hiked 700 miles. She struggled along, but finally had to get off the trail. Those Pennsylvania rocks were taking their toll.

I got a shower and hung out with the others, but all I really wanted to do was get horizontal. The Church of the Mountains has a hostel in the basement with an overflow lean-to at the edge of the parking lot out back. Since Trail Days had ended, twenty-somethings were back on the trail in full force. I didn't want to take up a bunk in the hostel, so as darkness fell, I laid my sleeping bag out in the lean-to and got comfortable reading by the light of my headlamp. It would be okay if my trail angel didn't show up, I thought, but Al's words rang in my head, "Oh, he'll be there. You can count on it."

Sure enough, about an hour after dark, just as I was about to nod off I heard a booming voice with a Jersey accent just like Al's calling across the parking lot.

"Is Scout here? Which one of you is Scout?"

Bruce and Al met in college. They'd had many wild adventures together and had great stories to tell. As we drove under the cliffs of Mount Kittatinny on the Jersey side of the Delaware Water Gap, Bruce reminisced about sleeping in a bivouac hung from the rock cliff above us. The hour long drive passed quickly as I learned more about my host, a large man who raced Mini Coopers, something totally outside my range of experience. At the house, he introduced me to his wife, Wendy, and their two teenage daughters. Wendy offered me a pair of flannel pajamas which was a thrill, and soon I was nestled into their guest room falling fast asleep.

In the morning the whole family was up early grabbing breakfast and lunch. Wendy and Bruce were both teachers where their girls went to school. They had a busy day ahead. I stayed home to clean up my clothes and equipment, send emails and explore their refrigerator. I was under the constant surveillance of three cats and a goldfish. The cats promised not to tell as long as I shared some ice cream with them. The goldfish however, offered no such assurance.

I did laundry and hung it out on the line, scoured the burnt oatmeal off my cook pot, scrubbed the bird poop off of my poncho (aka: ground cloth) and tried again to patch my leaky sleeping pad. After sending emails, I sat down at their piano. It had been months since I'd played. It took a while for my fingers to find their place, but playing a few songs felt good deep down. I had played piano and banjo before I left but on the trail, my only instrument was my voice.

Bruce came to get me in the late afternoon. They had plans to attend school functions that night. Their girls were in sporting events. It was a typical American family with very busy lives. Between events, Bruce took me to the hardware store to get stove fuel and a few other supplies. Back at the house he asked if there was anything else I needed. I'd lost my bandanna on the trail the day before. Anyone who has ever been camping knows how useful a bandanna can be. He produced a half dozen and told me to take my pick. I chose his red bandanna with white stars and carried it for the rest of the trail.

Bruce drove me back to the hostel at the Delaware Water Gap and gave me a big bear hug goodbye. He raced off to his frantic life and I settled back into the slow and steady pace of the trail.

On the phone, Silver informed me that he'd spent his "zero" day at a chiropractor getting x-rays and trying to fix his old knee injury. I hoped that the new knee brace in his mail drop would help.

Fond Farewell

To enter my eighth state, New Jersey, we crossed the Delaware River and Interstate 80 on a bridge and wove through parking lots where day hikers and back packers prepared for their outings. There was a visitor center, restrooms and picnic tables, bustling with activity. We trudged through it all and started up the trail. The climb up Mount Kittatinny wasn't as bad as it had appeared from across the river on Mount Minsi. The trail followed old road beds, so the grade wasn't steep. Unfortunately, the Pennsylvania rocks didn't end at the state line. We were told they'd go on for another fifty miles or so.

On our way up, we met long lines of inner city high school students from Newark who were on their way down. They'd spent a few nights out in the wilds of New Jersey with Outward Bound leaders, a requirement before they could graduate. They looked exhausted, dragging their sleeping bags and kicking their gear down the trail. Large cook pots strapped to their packs banged with each step. Their shoe laces were untied and gym shorts hung low and loose. All I could do was smile.

We passed Sunfish Pond and later the Mohican Outdoor Center and finally ended our day at Camp Ken-Etiwa-Pec. It was before Memorial Day and no one was around. We walked by an empty house and empty workshops to a row of empty cabins along the lakeshore. These cabins had four walls, not just three, and even a screened door. Inside were squeaky metal cots with plastic covered mattresses. Pure luxury! We sat outside at a picnic table to make our dinners. The breeze from across the lake kept the bugs off. My stove was acting up again. Silver boiled extra water for my pasta. Dinner was an unusually quiet occasion as we looked out over the lake.

That night, as we climbed into our sleeping bags and the old cots squeaked, Silver talked about getting off the trail. He'd been in a lot of pain. At fifty-three his old injuries were coming back to haunt him. His feet, ankles, knees, back and neck had all been complaining. Without Firefly, Feather, Lug and Zama there was little comic relief.

As darkness fell I asked him what he'd gained from his hike. He said he thought the experience had changed him. He'd learned he didn't need so much stuff. When he got home, he thought he'd try to stay in shape by getting around on his bike more.

I didn't know what to say. I knew this was a big let down for him, not being able to finish the trail in one year. But if he were in such constant pain, the joy must have gone out of the endeavor.

"I've enjoyed hiking with you," I said, "and I appreciate how you looked out for me on so many occasions." I paused and said, "I'll miss you."

Across the cabin, his bunk squeaked. He rolled over and went to sleep, but apparently not very well. When we woke up the next morning, he said he'd felt his knee pop in the night, not a good sign.

While hiking that day he stumbled and came down hard on his knees among the rocks. He cried out in pain and I went back to check on him. He said he was okay and kept on walking. Later, he fell twice more and by noon he'd decided he'd had enough. He would get off the trail. He'd given it a gallant effort. I admired him for knowing when to quit. He had just passed his personal half way mark (1,100 miles) and planned to finish the trail the next year.

We met for lunch at a pub where the trail crosses US 206 at Culver's Gap. We ordered burgers. I went to the rest room to wash up and take advantage of a mirror to check for ticks. I pulled four off before re-joining Silver at the bar. He introduced me to three Ridge Runners who had sat down beside him. Ridge Runners are paid to hike the AT and offer assistance to those in need. They would give Silver a ride to the next town where he could get a motel room and make arrangements for his trip home. One last dose of trail magic.

Secret Shelter

As soon as I stepped back on the trail, I felt more vulnerable. I'd lost a layer of protection. People had asked for months if I was hiking alone. I could answer truthfully, "I'm not alone. I have a family of friends traveling with me." But now Silver was gone. I hadn't seen Firefly or Feather since they left for Trail Days ten days before. So I decided to keep Silver's departure to myself. I climbed up to Sunrise Mountain and sat in a lonely stone pavilion where a cool breeze kept the bugs at bay. It was a solitary place with a forlorn feeling that suited my mood. I ate snacks and wrote for a couple of hours before moving on.

The next shelter was a sad, dumpy structure. The shelter log mentioned snakes in the rafters so I laid my bag outside on the picnic table under the trees. I had the place to myself. Knowing the shelter was within a mile of the nearest road, I hoped it would stay that way.

The next day, I noticed the rocks had disappeared from the trail. Silver had almost made it. The trail had dropped in elevation and now flowed through wooded hills much easier on my feet. Though the rocks were gone, there were more soggy spots and a few board walks. I noticed sweet little orange salamanders. Or were they newts? Whatever they were, they were all over the place. I had to watch my step to avoid squashing them. It slowed me down, doing dance steps down the trail, but brought joy just witnessing this burst of amphibious activity! I made up a chant, "Beware of the newt that could not avoid the boot."

I traveled on and in the afternoon came upon the turn off to the Secret Shelter. I'd read about it in my trail guide and heard it mentioned by other hikers. It was on private property and only open to thru-hikers. I was curious and needed water so thought I'd check it out.

It was paradise, a pastoral setting with a few solid, but rustic looking buildings. One had a mouse baffle hanging from the porch made of a can hung from a string. They were common in shelters on the trail. There was another welcome site, an outdoor shower on one side and a clothesline on the other.

The door was open so, like Goldilocks, I went in. It was a lovely shelter with electric lights, a commercial size stainless steel sink and a sleeping loft with a fan! Though it was still early afternoon, I decided to stop for the day. I showered, did some laundry and hung it out to dry while I explored the farm and met the caretakers, two boisterous donkeys. I even got an afternoon nap on the porch. Only one other hiker came up for water and then left, so again, I had the place to myself.

The only problem was that my stove had been acting up. Now, no one was around to boil water for me. I checked my guide book. It was just two miles to a diner in the next town and rumor had it they had good milkshakes. So I thought, "If I can't get my stove working, I'll just stroll in and get dinner there." But lo and behold, my stove worked just fine and I ate dinner on the porch watching the donkeys mow the tall grass nearby.

I'd finished my dinner, washed my cook pot, taken my clothes from the line and was getting into a good paperback on the porch when I heard a car. This was not just any car. This was a shiny red Porsche. I thought, "This must be the owner."

Jim Murray was a soft spoken man who thru-hiked in 1989. He lived nearby and just came over to check on things. I told him how I'd just lost my hiking partner, how coming across his place with the donkeys had cheered me up, and how I'd been fantasizing about a milkshake in town. He offered me a ride... in his Porsche!

As we rode into town, I offered to buy him a shake, but he declined and waited in the car while I ran inside.

On the way back, between draws on my straw, I asked what he did for a living. He said he was a photographer. I asked if he'd hike the Appalachian Trail again but he had set his sights on other trails. The Camino Santiago was calling to him now.

Returning to the farm, Jim showed me the other shelter which was his own cabin. He unlocked the door and we stepped inside. It was clean and Spartan, a rug on the floor, an old overstuffed chair, a plain wooden table and a sleeping loft. This was his retreat. Black and white photos adorned the walls, some framed, some pinned to the rough wood panels. He showed me the best photo from his thru-hike. He set it up with a timer which showed him sitting alone atop Katahdin, his thin form, head back, arms outstretched, fingers reaching wide as if embracing the entire world and all the heavens, too. It captured the feeling of achievement, of victory, of a passionate quest, in timeless black and white.

After he'd gone, I climbed the hill behind the shelter and enjoyed the view from the top. The sun set while the donkey's followed me around and honked at each other half hidden in the hay. I had started the day on a picnic table outside a shelter full of snakes and ended it in this pastoral paradise. I climbed into the loft and read by an electric light, then slept well with a cool breeze from the fan. The next day I hated to leave but Unionville lured me in with the smell of bacon.

To Build a Fire

Later that day, I crossed the New York State line, my ninth state. A line of white paint marked the spot on top of a boulder with *NJ* on one side and *NY* on the other. I continued to weave along the New York and New Jersey border. It was Memorial Day weekend and the temperatures soared. I'd been hiking in sixty-five degree weather and suddenly it was eighty-five degrees and humid. I was hot and dehydrated, "sweating like a whore in church", as Silver had said just a few days before. I'd entered the lowlands, hiking through swamps, on boardwalks and through mud. Cows stared at me blankly from behind barbed wire fences. Mosquitoes swarmed. I swatted at them constantly with my bandanna using my arm like a windshield wiper.

I walked through the Walkill National Wildlife Refuge with its long boardwalks over marshy wetlands. Tourists and birdwatchers parked along the dirt roads and crowded the boardwalks with baby strollers and leashed dogs. It was nice to see so many people out enjoying the area. Though there were many puddles and swamps, I couldn't find any water to drink.

When I reached the road crossing into Vernon, New Jersey, I stuck out my thumb and got a ride into town. I left my pack at the church hostel and went over to the Burger King across the street.

"Are you a thru-hiker?" asked the clerk.

I looked up. "How did you know?"

"The Zip-lock bag. All the thru-hikers keep their money in a Zip-lock bag."

I sat down with a big chef's salad and drank about a gallon of iced tea, free re-fills, before returning to the hostel for a nap on the lawn under a shade tree.

Half awake I could hear voices and smell burgers grilling nearby. It was like a blissful dream and I almost sleep-walked into the neighbor's yard and invited myself to dinner. Instead I drooled at the smell of their barbeque and envied their companionship.

I waited until 6:30 p.m. to get back on the trail. I was met with an 800 foot climb. All that iced tea then sweated out of my pores. I hiked to the next shelter in the twilight as the temperatures cooled slightly. There was a couple in the shelter with their tent set up to protect them from bugs. I lay down on top of my sleeping bag on the picnic table and used my poncho as a blanket. We didn't say more than hello.

I was out again at 5:30 a.m. trying to beat the heat. I hiked to the Wawayanda State Park office where I got water from a hose and made breakfast by the parking lot as the staff slogged in to work. The morning was foggy but the sun burned through as I hiked. In the heat of the day I sought refuge at an air-conditioned road side ice cream parlor. I got two sodas and a milkshake while I waited for the afternoon to cool. Late in the day I hiked on, but the next shelter was in a swampy, lowland, mosquito heaven.

The bugs were eating me up! It was too hot and humid to get into a sleeping bag and I didn't have a tent or a screen so there was no escape.

I was sharing a shelter with a fellow I'd met at the Delaware Water Gap named Mark (who, when he wrote it, turned the R backwards). Another fellow, a big red haired section-hiker, was enjoying telling us all the different diseases that we could get from ticks and mosquitoes and how they would manifest in our bodies. Far too much information.

Even though it was hot, we decided to build a fire hoping the smoke would keep the bugs away. We all gathered wood. Mark sat by the fire ring getting it ready to light. I retreated to the relative cover of my poncho in the shelter. As I watched and waited, it became clear that Mark didn't know how to build a fire.

It seemed incredible to me that anyone would set out to thru-hike the Appalachian Trail, or any extended hike, without that basic skill. I'd heard Mark say back at the hostel last week that he was a nuclear physicist or something. Though no doubt brilliant in some fields, he was definitely lacking in this one. As I was being eaten alive, I grew impatient. Finally, I threw off my poncho exposing my bare arms and legs and stepped in. I tore a page from my journal, broke small sticks and stacked them over the crumpled paper, put some slightly larger sticks in a teepee formation over it and lit it. I explained to Mark that you have to start with the small stuff and work your way up to the larger wood. If you wanted to make smoke to get rid of the bugs, you'd gradually add wet leaves.

As the smoke engulfed the shelter and I got some relief from the bugs, I thought about when I'd learned to build a fire.

My Great Aunt Gladys, a science teacher for thirty years, wouldn't let us light a single candle in the old family homestead until we could recite the three things that fire needs, oxygen, fuel and a spark. These lessons were reinforced on countless family campouts and Girl Scout trips. After camping on the rainy side of Washington State for decades, I was pretty good at starting a fire in the rain as well. I felt like I'd known how to start a fire since I was big enough to strike a match... though I still struggled with cigarette lighters.

Then I started thinking about those without my kind of outdoor upbringing. When I led hiking tours as my summer job, my clients from large cities would study me for a minute and conclude, "You're outdoorsy, aren't you."

I took my outdoor skills for granted. Hiking, camping, sleeping on the ground, were no big deal to me. I not only knew how to make a fire, I knew how to cook over a fire, and had even worked one summer putting forest fires out.

But perhaps Mark grew up in a city. Perhaps he never was a Boy Scout or went on family campouts, in which case he was pretty much out of his element on a thru-hike. That would make his experience much more challenging. I felt bad about my impatient behavior. It was all getting to me, the bugs, the heat, the humidity and the loss of my trail family.

Paying It Forward

The next day I walked into Harriman State Park, New York. Again, it was hot and muggy, and again, I was out of water. I knew I had a big climb ahead so I sat by the road at the park entrance hoping I could get help from a passing motorist. I remembered my sister writing to me about getting dehydrated while hiking in this area. She'd become lightheaded and had to sit down. I'd sent her some Emergen-C powder that she mixed into her last bit of water and after a while, she recovered. I learned later that drinking too much water when you're sweating can drain your body of electrolytes. So Gatorade, Emergen-C, or something like it, was better than pure water. Either way I was out and needed to rehydrate before going forward.

A van came along on its way out of the park. As I raised my hand it stopped. They were kind enough to give me a liter of bottled water. I carried on through the park over the leafy forest floor as the trail rose and fell until I got to the "Lemon Squeezer".

The Appalachian Trail builders occasionally throw in some interesting features. There's the "Guillotine" in Virginia where the trail passes under a large rock suspended between two boulders. And this was another natural formation that the trail could easily go around, but instead goes through, "Just for kicks and giggles," as Firefly would say.

The Lemon Squeezer is a very narrow passage about 100 feet long between rock faces. I could see from the entrance that swarms of bugs lay in wait for an ambush. I put my bandanna over my face and ran through as fast as I could, getting bitten all over my exposed legs and arms. The ordeal made me irritable. And soon I was out of water *again*. I pushed on thinking I would get some relief up ahead where I could swim in the lake.

The trail led up a rise to the back of the Fingerboard Shelter where I found a hand written sign on a piece of cardboard duct-taped to a walking stick by the trail. I thought I was hallucinating. The sign read, "Cold Beer". Though I wasn't interested in beer, the word "cold" was intriguing. I went to investigate.

Inside the shelter I found two hikers. One, talking on a cell phone, walked outside as I entered. The other, a thin young man dressed in olive drab asked, "How are you?"

My mood got the better of me.

"I'm exhausted and dehydrated, but otherwise, I'm fine. Is there anything besides beer?"

The hiker jumped up and emptied his pack. He pulled out a jar of peanut butter, Snickers bars, packets of Kool-aid and a large bottle of cold water.

"Fresh from the spring," he said, "Take whatever you want."

I studied him as I took the water and Kool-aid and began to mix the two. He studied me back and silently pushed a Snickers bar in my direction. I asked if the guy on the phone was a friend of his. He shook his head.

As I gulped the cold spring water, it slowly dawned on me that the cold beer hadn't just been left here in a cooler, but that *he* was the trail angel that had brought it in. Quite a haul. As I drank the Kool-aid, he told me he'd walked the trail the year before, from Maine to Georgia. He used the trail name O. D. Green (which stood for olive drab, his favorite color). I was beginning to get the picture. He said he'd received a lot of trail magic on his hike and it was his turn to "pay it forward".

I thanked him and said I was looking forward to going swimming in the lake below, but he had bad news, the swimming area was closed. I was crushed.

Just then a silver patterned snake curled around the rocks of the chimney, getting our attention. It slithered across the fireplace mantle and entered a thin crack between the rocks. As it disappeared a mouse jumped out of the same crack with a newborn baby mouse in its mouth. It leapt onto the bunk where O.D. sat, dropped the baby and ran back up to the mantle. Too late. The mouse mother came back to retrieve her young and ran around the shelter in a panic. We were fascinated. This was like watching Animal Planet. We figured it was a rattlesnake. These stone shelters were known for them.

O.D. offered me a beer, but I said I'd prefer a soda and asked if there was a pop machine in the park.

"Yes, what kind would you like?" I looked at him sideways.

"Grape, I guess." He suggested I take the half mile blue blaze trail down to the lake and find a private place to jump in for a swim. He'd come by with a soda in about an hour. That sounded good to me.

After my swim, I waited by the road trying to get comfortable on a rounded rock perch. Soon O.D. came by in a little blue car. We went to the Ranger Station where he bought us two sodas. We sat at a nearby picnic table and talked for an hour or so before he mentioned that he worked at a pasta place that had All-You-Can-Eat on Tuesday nights. (Was it Tuesday?) And he'd take me there if I was interested.

Though I ate pasta almost every night on the trail, I was enjoying his company and agreed to go, but took advantage of a nearby restroom to freshen up first.

In the dim light of the restroom I checked for ticks. Deer ticks, the kind that carry Lyme disease, are very small. I started inspecting a suspicious looking little spot on my side. I pulled out the tweezers from my Swiss Army knife and pinched it and tugged, but it was stubborn. I pinched and pulled and twisted until I figured it wasn't a tick at all.

I was nearing Lyme, New York, where ticks are as numerous as stars in the sky. I'd known someone years before who had Lyme disease and I'd seen her suffer which made me extra cautious. The tick check took awhile but women are known for keeping their dates waiting, though probably not for these exact reasons.

O.D. had worked in the pasta restaurant for years so when we arrived all the staff came over to talk. We had salads and then went into another room where the chef was standing behind a long counter full of different kinds of meats and vegetables. We chose the ones we wanted and he threw them into a sauté pan. Then we chose which kind of pasta and finally which kind of sauce, some of which he lit on fire. It was incredible to watch how he kept eight or ten dishes going at once. I got a huge plate of food and went back for more. We had an enjoyable evening swapping stories from our trail experiences. The owner gave us a complimentary dessert.

Leaving the restaurant we opened the door onto a downpour. O. D. turned to me. "I can take you back to the trail in the dark and the rain and the rattlesnakes, or," he said, "I have a couch."

He lived in a charming little Cape Cod style cottage that was completely furnished with free stuff, tastefully arranged. He told me the landlord planned to demolish this cottage in the fall and build a large new duplex, so he got the place for cheap, but only for the summer. There was a huge sectional couch, a comfy chair and a 1950's style lamp tree where the lamp shades were colored Nalgene bottles with the bottoms cut out. He had a shelf of natural history books where we studied pictures of snakes, and there were several framed photographs of scenic places on the trail. He'd even framed a piece of bark with a white blaze on it that he'd cut off of a fallen tree. I felt right at home.

O.D. said he'd been depressed. His girlfriend, who'd been a long time pal, had broken up with him. He was hoping they'd eventually become friends again. But in the meantime, he thought he'd go do something for other people instead of moping around alone.

O. D. seemed a little flustered having an unexpected house guest. I got out my sleeping bag. He brought in a little fan, set it on the coffee table and turned it on. I had the best night's sleep I'd had in weeks. In the morning we woke up early and he took me back to the trail, a stone's throw from the shelter where we'd met the day before. I gave him a hug, thanked him and started walking. At the next road crossing there was a Snickers bar tacked to a tree with a note that read, "Scout, drink more water!"

Bear Mountain

As I walked through Harriman State Park in the misty morning hours, I passed the William Brien Memorial Shelter, all made out of stone, and thought "That must be a palace for rattlesnakes." Mark was there getting ready to go. We exchanged greetings and then I climbed the next hill. It was pure joy, walking through the woods after a good night's sleep. My mood had improved remarkably. I noticed the mountain laurel blooming. Lovely.

It sneaks up on you, these more occupied areas. You see more people on the trails. Instead of backpacks they carry small day packs or sometimes nothing at all. As we'd pass, I'd catch a whiff of shampoo, deodorant, scented soap or cologne. I hated to think how I smelled.

The trails are wider, more beaten down and then there's actual pavement, a road, picnic tables, plaques. I was within shouting distance of New York City, but still a world away.

Climbing up on Bear Mountain's stone summit I saw more snakes disappearing between the cracks just ahead of my feet. I watched my step. There were beautiful, wide open views at the top. A stone observation tower sat on the windy crest. A paved road made it easy for tourists to reach the summit, but the few that had made the drive that day lingered near the tower at the edge of the parking lot. I explored the boulder field. A wind-whipped Bonsai tree leaned out over the edge. The breeze felt good as I stood absorbing the silence and the views of the Hudson River Valley below. I read the inspirational plaque about Joseph Bartha, the Trail Chairman of the New York-New Jersey Trail, a champion of trail preservation.

My trail guide told me there were plans to build a New York State prison here a century ago, but Mary Harriman, widow of the railroad magnate Edward Harriman, gave 10,000 acres of land for a park on the condition that there would be no prison here. The Sing Sing prison was later built twenty miles South which is where they got the phrase "sent up the river."

I thought of my friend Al, who used to captain the Schooner *Clearwater* singing with Pete Seeger and a boatload of sailors and environmental educators working to clean up the Hudson River. He'd come from the *Clearwater* to the *Adventuress*, a 101 foot tall ship in Puget Sound, which is where I met him. I was a volunteer educator on the ship and helped on winter work days. After a long day of work in the cold, damp weather, the volunteers would stay overnight sharing a hearty dinner, singing for hours afterward and sleeping in the main cabin with fourteen bunks. There was a great sense of camaraderie.

I loved singing with Al. He's like a cross between his two idols, Pete Seeger and Bruce Springsteen, both of whom came from Al's old stomping grounds, right around here. Al and I would play banjo and guitar. My favorite song Al would sing, **the Sloop Sally B**, told a story of two ships in a race up the Hudson River and referred to places near here, Tappan Zee and Haverstraw Bay. From this perch on Bear Mountain, I could imagine the two sloops sailing in close quarters around the bend.

Bear Mountain is the AT's highest point in New York State, but within a mile the trail drops to the lowest point on the entire trail in the Trailside Nature Center. Between the two was a popular lodge and picnic area. Renovations were underway which meant a lot of orange cones and plastic fencing which marred the appearance of the historic building.

The Bear Mountain and Palisades area was the birthplace of the Appalachian Trail. The first sections were completed here in the 1920s. Modifications would be made to the trail later in the season but on this day it was clear. I was looking around for the snack bar when I came across Mark who gave me directions, then went looking for the post office. The snack bar was a bit disappointing, offering no hot food. But they did have bags of chips, granola bars and drinks. I got all of the above, taking a short break on a bench to watch all the people go by.

At the Trailside Nature Center, I was greeted by a statue of Walt Whitman who seemed to be striding out for a walk himself. At the lowest point, 124 feet above sea level, I stopped in front of the black bear enclosure. Watching these bears surrounded by concrete with trees painted on the walls made me sad, but I read the animals here are part of a rehabilitation program. They wouldn't have been able to survive in the wild. While they're here, over a half million people see them each year, mostly school kids from New York City. These children may never get another experience of wild animals which made me even sadder. So this really was a low point.

I walked to nearby Fort Montgomery, stopped by the post office and picked up my bounce box. Just outside I greeted an Australian thru-hiker, Glenn, whom I'd met on the trail. He seemed to be a loner, quiet, not always staying in the shelters. We spoke for a minute. He recommended a deli on the next corner. I took my bounce box and spent a luxurious afternoon in an air-conditioned deli working on a huge sausage and pepper sandwich, downing a large bottle of juice and organizing my food stash.

I'd sent a five pound box of extra rations from Palmerton, Pennsylvania and it turned out to be just what I needed at just the right time. There was no real grocery store in Fort Montgomery so the box full of trail staples provided enough for my next week of hiking. The thought of trail food for another week made my stomach turn and the deli sandwich was so good, I ordered another, a vegetarian sandwich, to take with me. The heat subsided, the day leaned toward evening and I walked back to the Bear Mountain Bridge. As I crossed the Hudson River a strong breeze cooled me for the climb ahead.

Enlightenment

After crossing the mighty Hudson River on the Bear Mountain Bridge I climbed up along a ridge and walked through a lovely forest. It was just another five miles to the Friary where I planned to spend the night. The trail is very near the West Point Military Academy at this point, but I would be benefiting from a different sort of brotherhood, the monks at the Graymoor Spiritual Life Center. The brothers allow thru-hikers to sleep on their baseball field. Next to it, there's a picnic shelter with a sink and showers. I arrived just before sunset.

There were other hikers with tents set up around the outfield. I noticed the Australian hiker, Glenn, and sat down on a bench to chat while he set up his tent nearby. I left my pack with him and went to get a shower before dark. There was no hot water, which I guessed was part of the spiritual discipline. Once I got over the shock, it was refreshing. I checked out the picnic shelter as a possible overnight spot in case of rain. It could accommodate several hikers sleeping on the tables. Ideally, I'd like to be out on first base where there was a little breeze to keep the bugs away. I returned to my pack looking forward to my deli sandwich dinner.

Glenn was impressed that I'd packed out that enormous sandwich but declined when I offered to share it with him. He had cooked up his usual trail dinner and we ate sitting on the bench near second base. We talked quietly as he pointed out each tent and described the occupants, most of whom I didn't know. He said he was hiking alone and didn't have or want a trail name. Other hikers had tried to pin one on him. The one he liked the best was Tea Man, but mostly, he went by Glenn.

He sounded Australian, but said he grew up nearby. He'd moved to Tasmania over a decade ago and loved it. His mother's terminal illness had lured him back. After her death, he started hiking, but planned to move back to Australia when he was done. He was different from the other hikers, tall and gentle, more mature, more at peace. Walking the trail seemed to help him through his grief.

I threw my sleeping bag on top of a picnic table near first base and slept well enough with a light breeze. In the morning I went to the shelter to make breakfast. A monk came by to check on everything and brought some homemade banana bread for all the hikers. I would have loved to eat the whole loaf myself, but exercising great restraint, I stuck with my usual oatmeal with a slice of the sweet bread on the side.

The morning was foggy. I was introspective. As I walked through the forest, the trail climbed up on an old roadway supported by rock walls. There was no mention of it in my trail guide which left me to speculate on its construction and use. These walkways looked like they were built centuries ago in a simpler time, but were still functional though a bit overgrown. I could imagine horse drawn wagons loaded with produce or hay, making their way between farms and town.

It was shady, but still hot and muggy. The fog had burned off and the sun was bearing down on me just above the canopy. My hand swung continually holding my red bandanna, swishing black flies and mosquitoes from my face, arms and legs. Gradually as I walked, a thought occurred to me. I could leave the trail early. Why not?

I was planning to leave sometime in mid-June, return to the Northwest for my summer job leading hikes, and come back to finish the trail around the first of September. It was now June 1st. After twenty-eight years of living on Puget Sound, this heat and humidity of a New York summer made me miserable. My trail family had disbanded. I was sharing the trail with ticks, flies, snakes and mosquitoes. As I walked on I let the idea roll around in my head.

Crossing a quiet dirt road I caught up with Glenn who was taking a break. There was a lovely, old stone hut with a water faucet at shoulder height. I wet my head under the cold tap and then filled my water bottle. We sat together and ate some almonds. I shared my idea of leaving the trail. He urged against it.

"If you leave now, you won't come back to finish."

That thought had never occurred to me.

I hiked on by an old stone building almost completely grown over. The roof was gone, but the walls with the rows of arched windows made me think this had once been a church. Though I wondered why no one was trying to preserve these historic structures I was also enchanted to discover them myself, hidden in the woods, like lost archeological ruins.

I walked on and eventually arrived at Clarence Fahnestock State Park by Canopus Lake. Dark clouds were gathering so I decided to settle in before the approaching storm. In the campground I found a fellow thru-hiker named Red B, a smallish man with red hair who had hiked the trail before. I'd met him in Erwin, Tennessee at Miss Janet's. He was set up in a site with his tent and his dachshund, Low Profile, or L.P. for short. He invited me to share his campsite. I didn't have a tent so hoped the storm would blow over before dark. Then I could set up my tarp. But the storm blew in with such force both of us took cover in a nearby restroom entryway.

With every terrifying rumble of thunder and corresponding crack of lightning we clung to the concrete building around us. Rain pounded on the roof with a deafening roar. We had to shout to hear each other. The lights flashed off and on a few times before they gave up altogether. Giant puddles formed outside the doorway. Other campers came in and out but didn't seem to mind us taking shelter in the restroom. After all, they were snug in their RV's. Red B and I made dinner with our camp stoves and spent the evening sitting on the floor. By the time darkness fell, the storm had abated, though it continued to rain. Red B went back to his tent with L.P. and I laid my tarp out on the floor, then my sleeping pad and then my bag, but it still felt a bit creepy sleeping on a dirty restroom floor.

Using my headlamp, I consulted my guide book. It was a two day hike to a train station where I could catch a train from the AT directly into New York City. It would be culture shock. But from there, it would be easy to catch a train to North Carolina. I could celebrate my birthday with Dad whose birthday is the day before mine, and then fly to Washington State. The wheels were turning. I formed a plan.

The next morning, I ate breakfast with Red B and L.P. at their campsite before we packed up for the day's hike. Red B led the way with his four legged friend following close behind. I watched that little dog scramble over boulders and logs. He even climbed trees that leaned against other trees until he was ten feet off the ground. His legs were all muscle and he had a brave heart.

Red B recounted how he had found L.P. on the trail as a puppy three years before. The terrified pup had been attacked by wild animals and was half dead. Red B wrapped him in his arms and carried him into the next town where a veterinarian patched him up. Back on the trail Red B carried L.P. on top of his pack, putting him down to walk the gentle sections of trail until the dog grew stronger. Since then that dog had put over 2,000 trail miles under his four little legs.

Red B told me how he and L.P. had hiked with Juliangelo and her husky, Thoreau. When they got to a town, they'd get a motel room, turn on the TV and leave the dogs watching the Nature Channel while they went out to eat. The tales of the dachshund and the husky entertained me as we walked.

After twelve miles L.P. was tiring. We had turned off the trail at a road crossing for lunch at a pizzeria. L.P. suddenly gave out and refused to take another step. He rolled over on his back and waited. Red B picked him up and hoisted him to ride on top of his pack.

Red B had heard how loud my stove was when I made breakfast that morning. I'd told him how my trail family had complained and how finicky my Whisperlite had been. When we got to the pizzeria and the convenience store in Stormville, he found a couple of soda cans in the trash and in ten minutes, he'd made me a new alcohol stove. It was small and light and simple, no moving parts, nothing to break down. He gave it to me as an early birthday present.

We split a pizza and gave L.P. a piece. Then I used the phone to call my good friend, Kelly, in Seattle. Kelly's parents lived in Manhattan and had said they'd host me when I got to New York. I told Kelly of my plan to take a train from the trail to the city and hoped I could spend the night with her folks. I wanted to get cleaned up before I boarded a train for North Carolina. She called them and in a few minutes she called me back.

"They're not in the city," she said. "They spend the weekends at their house in the Catskills. They'd come get you, but today is not a good day. Their beloved cat, Audrey, is sick, maybe dying, and they're with her at the vet's."

She told me if I could get to Kingston, they'd come get me and I could spend the weekend with them in the Catskills. I could ride into the city with them on Monday to catch a train. My original plan had seemed a little too good to be true.

So I went into a convenience store to look for a road map. I asked the attendant how far it was to Kingston and what roads were the best. It wasn't a straight shot. He asked a delivery guy and then another customer got involved. I took notes on some scrap paper. The clerk got me some cardboard from the recycle bin out back and let me use his big black marker to make a sign. Red B gave me a hug and wished me luck. Then he and L.P. got back on the trail and I took a deep breath, nodded toward heaven and hit the road.

New York's Finest

People who learned I was going to hike the Appalachian Trail without a partner frequently asked, "But what about the bears? Aren't you scared?"

In my experience the most dangerous animal out there walks on two legs. Now I was stepping off the trail and into a much scarier place, just outside New York City, full of those two legged creatures armed with speeding vehicles and who knows what else. But I believe that most people are good hearted, even in New York, and I hoped to find those people on this next leg of my journey.

The delivery guy gave me a ride to the main road a few miles away. I stuck out my thumb, held up my sign and crossed my fingers. The first driver took me a few more miles up the road while asking, "Are you crazy?" He dropped me off at a good intersection, pointed me in the right direction and wished me luck.

The next driver took me a long way up the Taconic Parkway. He was a professor from Vermont with a long drive ahead and was happy to have the company. We studied the map and he dropped me off where I could catch a ride across the Hudson.

From there I caught another ride with a guy who was very concerned and told me this was too dangerous. He took me across the river and back south on the other side, but not quite all the way. Finally, a van with two women took me the last leg of my trip and dropped me off at a grocery store in Kingston. So five rides and two hours later, I made it to Kingston safely. I said a little prayer of thanks and called Suzen and Brian.

While I was waiting, I found a restroom and did my best to get presentable. Fortunately, I'd met them before when they'd visited Kelly in Seattle so I didn't worry too much about first impressions. I took a damp paper towel to wipe off the first layer of sweat and dirt on my face, arms and under my shirt. Then I switched to a slightly cleaner shirt. With the heat and humidity I smelled like curdled milk.

They arrived about 6:00 with plans to go out to one of their favorite restaurants in nearby Woodstock. It was in an old home with an orchard outside. Suzen runs her own cooking school in Manhattan and she has very high standards. When I looked at the menu I almost cried. I fought to keep my composure, but this was almost too much. It was just the kind of meal we would fantasize about on the trail.

As we walked, Firefly and I would pretend to order a meal at a high end restaurant like this. I'd tell Firefly, "I'll have the organic field greens with gorgonzola, glazed pecans, thinly sliced pears and raspberry vinaigrette. Then I'll have the New York steak, medium rare, with Demi-glaze, twice-baked potato and a few sprigs of asparagus on the side." But here it was for real. I pinched myself and then ordered just that.

Back at their magnificent Catskills home, Suzen took me upstairs and encouraged me to take a long, hot soak in a deep tub full of bubbles. It was heaven to sit in that tub and soak. How long had it been since I'd enjoyed a bubble bath? I emerged feeling much fresher, put on her clean T-shirt and sweat pants and looked around.

This was their office with a solid wall of Brian's books about geology, statistics and history. He said he'd been working on developing a computer model which would help predict earthquakes. He has a brilliant mind and photographic memory. I'd done very little reading on the trail, just walking, a little socializing at the shelters and then sleep. Life had been limited to the bare basics for the past few months. I crawled in between flannel sheets with the windows open to hear the sound of rain coming down and the rushing stream outside. Sleeping on the couch in a study never felt so good.

In the morning they introduced me to their cats, Audrey and Clint. Clint, a big, grey tabby, went into hiding directly after breakfast. Audrey, a fluffy white creature, was friendlier.

"Is this the cat that was so sick yesterday?" I asked. She looked fine to me. Suzen and Brian were also amazed. The day before, she seemed at death's door. The vet had offered to put her down, but Suzen insisted on taking her home to die in her own bed, surrounded by those she loved. Apparently, that had been a good decision. Audrey had fully recovered.

Suzen and Brian went to the gym and then to the farmer's market, leaving me to fend for myself in their gourmet kitchen. I started my laundry and then got excited making a huge breakfast. Crusty home baked breads, exotic cheeses, eggs, ham and cocoa. I ate at a large island in the middle of the sun-filled kitchen with windows that went from the granite countertops to the high ceilings.

After breakfast I went on a self-guided tour. The kitchen opened onto an Italian-style dining room that would sit a dozen people. The living room had a gas fireplace, leather sofas and chairs, and a wall with floor to ceiling bookshelves. Large windows framed the backyard and the stream. The dark wood, leather furniture, tile floors, artwork and rugs had an air of casual elegance. I had landed in a palace and made myself at home.

As I settled back for more tea and toast in the kitchen, I read the paper. The headlines were ghastly. People had been shot, stabbed and beaten up by other people. There were wars, scandal and political corruption. I had to put it down. I'd been out of reach of the media for three months. My experience of people on the trail was far removed from these headlines. To suddenly be re-introduced to mainstream media was disturbing.

Not long ago on the phone, my mother had told me about a conversation at one of her lady's luncheons. My sister, Tortoise, had just started her Southbound thru-hike from Maine and Mom had bragged that she now had two daughters hiking the Appalachian Trail. A friend had asked if she wasn't worried about her daughters hiking the Appalachian Trail alone.

She pointed out that just that week, in our home town in North Carolina, a high school student held a teacher at gun point and the whole class hostage for an hour until police rescued them, a distraught man had driven his pickup recklessly through a crowd of people on campus because his girlfriend had broken up with him, and a young woman had been brutally murdered walking home on one of the main streets in town. She thought her daughters were probably safer out in the woods.

I thought so too, but I also wondered what the media does to our culture by filling our heads with these awful occurrences. Sure, it sells papers, but doesn't it also promote that kind of behavior? Or would reading about it so routinely make us more callous?

In my experience, a lot of people are kind and generous. Even if I didn't like everyone I'd met, very few were intentionally vicious. Was

I naïve? Was I experiencing some of the best of human-kind on the trail? I'd been hiking with people of all backgrounds from inner city to small town country, privileged and poor, young and old, church goers and nature worshippers, Republicans and Democrats, and we all got along pretty well. Perhaps hiking the trail puts us in an environment where we are all more vulnerable, where we benefit from being more cooperative and less competitive. Most of the people we met in towns and road crossings along the way offered kindness and support. It was the seed of a new song but that one wouldn't be written for months.

When my hosts returned they made a wonderful breakfast and included me. I love second breakfast. We had sausage and crepes filled with fresh berries, whipped cream and drizzly sweet sauce on top, with fresh squeezed orange juice on the side. I was in ecstasy.

Later Brian went upstairs to his office while Suzen and I took a walk around the neighborhood. The quiet roads through the forest were adorned with old farmhouses, stone fences and rustic barns. We met the neighbor's rescue cow, Bluebell. Suzen pointed out the home of some local artists.

She told me she and Brian were planning to fly to Texas next week to visit the grandkids, but she was concerned about leaving Audrey home alone so soon after her close brush with death. She'd like to have a house sitter, but she couldn't find anyone that was available. After a moment's pause, I offered my services. Her eyebrow lifted. She'd talk to Brian and let me know.

That afternoon, I hung out with Suzen in the kitchen. She made four different kinds of bread and a gourmet dinner while conversing with me the whole time. Brian made a batch of chocolate chip cookies. Oven timers were going off all over the place. It was amazing. I was in awe.

Suzen's a short woman with a mop of thick curls. She's from Brooklyn and worked hard to achieve her success. Like a stereotypical New Yorker, she's not shy about sharing her opinion and doesn't mince her words. She and Brian, both highly intelligent, shocked me with their use of colorful language. Growing up as a Southern girl from a *good* family, this was new to me. I found it fascinating and entertaining as well.

Suzen's cousin was invited to join us for dinner. I set the table, lit the candles. Wine was poured, bread was broken. Even the Brussels sprouts tasted good. The house was filled with the smell of fresh baked bread and the mirth of lively conversation over a delicious meal with Brian's warm cookies for dessert.

The conversation turned to Kelly's love life. As the three of them debated the merits of Kelly's new boyfriend, I just smiled. What a contrast from two nights before, eating the same old trail food and sleeping on a restroom floor.

In the Lap of Luxury

The black flies were relentless. I had to keep moving or I'd be eaten alive. But I enjoyed exploring the neighborhood between thunderstorms.

Suzen and Brian agreed to let me housesit for them and left for a week in Texas. Suzen had been concerned that I wouldn't have a car.

"How far is it to town?"

"About two miles."

"I think I can make it."

"But there's a hill."

Before they left she insisted on taking me to the grocery store where she bought a cart full of food for me. Even a thru-hiker would have a hard time eating it all. Then her cousin invited me over for dinner. So I did the best I could, eating heartily and often.

Suzen insisted that I sleep in their bed "to make the cats more comfortable". Indeed, Audrey stood nose to nose with me in bed and let me know, in no uncertain terms, that it was time for her 5:30 a.m. feeding. Afterward, she went back to sleep with her head on my shoulder. Clint let me give him lots of rubs as I fixed breakfast and then hid the rest of the day.

The tiled shower in the master bath was as big as a shelter on the trail. There were two showerheads the size of dinner plates. Next to that was a deep Jacuzzi tub by a window looking out into the forest. I took a shower, then a bath, then tried to find the holes in my still leaking sleeping pad by submersing it in the tub and looking for bubbles.

After my daily walks, I typed up my memoirs from the trail and checked emails. At night I watched DVD movies or read. Their big, cushy bed had stacks of books on each side. I leaned back on piles of pillows and fell asleep to the sound of the stream outside.

Being there for a week and needing to walk each day I got to meet some of the neighbors. One morning I was walking by the farm next door. The Border collie was barking from the front walk. It took a few minutes for me to coax the dog down to where I could make friends and give it a scratch behind the ears.

Then an elderly gentleman came out. I introduced myself. We chatted for a few minutes before I asked about the curious stones that sat on each side of his steps. I ended up getting a full tour of his museum out back.

Hal had been collecting arrowheads in this area since the 1930s. He gave me a chipped one that he said was between 3,000 and 5,000 years old. He introduced me to his wife, Dorothy, his dog, Daisy and his cow, Bluebell (we'd met), and invited me to stop by anytime. I waved each time I passed their place and during the week they invited me to stop for tea and muffins, and later gave me a large fish he'd caught to take home for dinner. More food.

Hal had told me about some good horse trails nearby and mentioned another neighbor who had hiked the AT. I met Dot one day on another walk when she was out working in her yard. She invited me in for iced tea and shared her trail stories and photos. She'd started walking in Georgia, but she'd taken a fall and hurt her knee. By then she was so close to home in New York, that she called her husband who took her to the doctor. She'd missed her husband and daughter and decided not to return to the trail, so she never finished her thru-hike. I thought I detected a hint of regret in her voice, but maybe that was just me.

I'm sure it would be difficult to leave your family behind, and the lure of a home so close to the trail would be hard to resist. Now that her daughter was grown, I asked if she'd consider going back to finish the trail. She assured me that she'd given up that ambition years ago. She urged me to keep in touch.

Following Hal's instructions I walked up into the hills around the Ashokan Reservoir and down the other side into Woodstock. I got a little lost at times but stopped to ask for course corrections and met other neighbors as I went. I walked five or six miles a day over gentle hills without a pack, then went back to the house for more good food, hot showers and a cushy bed. Life was good. Really, really good.

The next weekend Suzen and Brian returned with stories of their trip to Texas and the grandkids. There were more fabulous meals and then we packed up for the city. Clint hid and had us all looking under the furniture and through the closets. Clearly, we all preferred the Catskills to New York City.

South Bound Train

Back in the city, Suzen's staff was preparing for a group of forty coming in for a cooking class that evening, so Brian and I went out to eat. We got some great burgers in a place with dark paneling and tall windows that looked like Woody Allen could walk in at any moment. It felt late by the time we got back to the loft. The group was just leaving. Suzen wrapped a loaf of fresh baked bread for me to take in the morning. I'd catch an early train from Penn Station. As I began to fade they gave me detailed directions on how to use the subway and which line to take to what stop. It was all new to me.

They offered me an alarm clock, "You'll have to get up early to catch your train." I declined. I would be sleeping in compared to my usual start at dawn. I slept fitfully on a couch dreaming of the city that never sleeps.

In the morning, I helped myself to some fruit in the kitchen, hugged my sleepy-eyed hosts good-bye and headed out into New York City. Dressed in hiking clothes with a backpack on my shoulder and a loaf of French bread under one arm, I found my way to the subway. I've never been a city girl, so for me, this was a real adventure. I took pictures of street signs and buildings as the city started buzzing around me.

I caught the subway, found my way into the train station, bought a ticket and got instructions on where to wait and how to board when they called the number of my train. Then I sat down to watch people while breaking bread, a communion with the global community. There were people dressed in long robes, starched suits, black leather and colorful silk. Vacationing families hurried by with a suitcase in one hand and a child in the other. Musicians played with cases open, glittering with change. Focused business men strode straight ahead with a newspaper sticking out of a shoulder bag. Dark haired tattooed youths with multiple piercings hung out in corners. Workmen in overalls pushed loaded hand trucks. People came and went, some rushing, some slow. It was like the currents and eddies in a stream. I stared, fascinated at the hub of one of the largest cities in the world.

The train ride to North Carolina was long, made longer by damage done by heavy rain storms in Pennsylvania. I heard that the Delaware Water Gap had flooded two weeks after I'd passed through. The pasta place where I'd dined with Silver had water up to the tables. Thru-hikers had to stay in town until the water dropped enough to get across the pedestrian bridge. By late afternoon I'd made it to North Carolina and was happy to step off of the train and into the arms of my waiting parents. My mother gave me a sandwich for the thirty minute ride home.

Home Again, Home Again

It was great to be in my home town again. I was born and raised in Chapel Hill, North Carolina, but since I'd moved to Washington State, my folks had sold the house where my siblings and I grew up. They lived in Europe, came back and bought another house, sold that one, traveled around the world for a year, came back and bought another house, lived in Japan for a year, and finally settled in the neighboring town of Carrboro. Chapel Hill and Carrboro rub elbows so it's hard to tell where one stops and the other starts.

Growing up, Chapel Hill was considered the coolest, most progressive town around. Home of the University of North Carolina, a prestigious college, it hosted intellectuals and artists from around the world.

Carrboro was literally on the "other side of the tracks". It was home to an old cotton mill with run-down shanties where poor families lived. But since I left thirty years before, real estate in Chapel Hill had become too expensive for the University students and staff, so they started buying the shanties across the tracks and fixing them up. The old mill became a boutique shopping mall and now there was a gourmet natural foods store next to it. Street musicians performing under the large oak trees outside draw crowds. Families picnic on the lawn. People sit with their lattes at the outdoor tables working on their laptops while sparrows pick up the crumbs, singing for their supper. It's the hub of the community surrounded by pubs, eateries and historic downtown shops.

My parents had bought a dull brown rambler in a quiet neighborhood about a mile away. Over the years they'd painted and landscaped and built a fence and a deck and a sunroom and remodeled the kitchen and the bathroom until one day their postman said that they'd have to move. My Dad asked why. "Because you've done about as much as you can to this place."

That's about the time they bought a vacation house in the mountains where they'd go to escape the summer heat. It was a run-down place. The previous owners had parked their motorcycles in the living room. But my folks had cleaned it up nicely and enjoyed sharing it with family and friends.

Just after picking me up my folks were going to head for the hills as they did every weekend, but I asked to stay behind. I just wanted to be in one place for a while. So I had the house to myself. On Saturday I walked about a mile to the farmer's market with twenty dollars in my pocket. It was bustling with people crowding in around the produce and flower stalls. There were musicians and crafts and friends gathering in little knots everywhere. The atmosphere was so buoyant I felt like I was walking on a cloud. I didn't really need anything as there was plenty of food at the house, but I wanted to support the market and soak in the community atmosphere. And I needed a walk.

The moment I saw it, I knew I had to have it. A coconut pie! Oh, how I yearned. I'd been craving coconut on the trail and now here I was, face to face with the object of my desires in its most perfect manifestation. How fortuitous to have the house to myself for the weekend. I could eat the whole thing and no one would know. I bought it and started walking home salivating.

About half way home I realized that Monday was Dad's birthday. I didn't have a gift for him yet. What could I get? He loves pecan pie! I could buy a pie for Dad, too! So I turned around and headed back to the market.

When I got to the pie lady, I pulled out my cash and realized I didn't have enough for a whole pie. I only had enough for a tiny one person pie. So I bought Dad his very own little pecan pie and started walking back to the house. My large coconut pie looked huge next to Dad's tiny little pecan pie. He'd done so much for me, been so supportive. Guilt began to weigh heavily on me. By the time I got home, I'd decided to put these pies in the fridge, get some more cash and walk straight back to the market.

My birthday is the day after Dad's, so we had a double birthday party. My sister Sue and her husband and my niece came over for dinner, bearing gifts. Mom cooked up a nice dinner of pesto pasta. She invited me to go first through the buffet line in the kitchen. I looked at the pot of pasta and then back at the others.

"So what are the rest of you going to eat?" Showing great restraint, I assured myself there was plenty of birthday pie for dessert.

Sue always dresses well, wears make-up and does her hair and nails just so, unlike her sisters. So it was no surprise when she gave me a gift bag of peppermint foot cream, a pumice rock and other tools for a pedicure. Though the thought was nice, my feet were in tough shape. I told her I'd save it for later.

"These calluses were hard earned and I need them to finish the trail." With that I slipped off a shoe. My niece, sitting closest to me, jumped back in horror.

A thru-hiker's feet go through constant resurfacing as the top layers peel away and are replaced with a fresh layer of skin. Blisters add another layer of complexity requiring cleaning, popping and some kind of covering. And then there's just plain dirt which collects in your shoes and socks and works its way into the cracks of your feet and between your toes. I'd spent many evenings at the shelters with my fellow thru-hikers peeling away layers of skin, popping and treating blisters, or whenever possible, getting into a hot shower and spending several minutes scrubbing my feet until they were clean. We paid a lot of attention to our feet. So to me, my feet, now clean and without blisters, looked pretty good, even if they did have layers of calluses and peeling skin.

I tried not to eat my folks out of house and home during my stay. I'd go for a walk and end up at the natural food store, buying a quart-size smoothie and drinking it on the way home. My metabolism was still burning up the calories as fast as I could consume them.

Summer in the Northwest

After a couple of weeks in the hot and humid South, I flew back to Washington State to start my summer job. There is no place I'd rather be in the summer than in the Pacific Northwest. The clouds part and the sun comes out. You discover that Mount Baker, Mount Rainier and Mount Olympus really do exist. It's cool in the morning and then warms up for some lovely afternoons. The waters of Puget Sound call you to bring your kayak out and play among the islands. The surrounding mountains lure you onto the trails.

I was first hired for my summer job leading hikes in Olympic National Park in 1996. A few years later, I developed a new tour of the Columbia River Gorge region. During that week-long tour we'd visit Mount Hood, Mount Adams and Mount Saint Helens, too. I had run these hiking tours for over a decade. I looked forward to hiking to my favorite places and staying in the scenic lodges, eating my fill of good food and earning my only income of the year.

Flying into Sea-Tac, I could see many of these iconic peaks before sinking below the cloud cover of Puget Sound. I stayed at Kelly's house in Seattle, sharing stories over a good dinner. I got the clothes and equipment that I'd stored in her basement and rented a fifteen passenger van. Early on Sunday morning, I met my friend and co-guide, Terry, at a grocery store and together we stocked the coolers and stuffed the vans with food and equipment. We met our group at a downtown hotel. After a quick orientation, we headed out to the Olympic Peninsula.

It's a long drive on the first day of each tour to shed the cloak of urban sprawl. We'd drive south from Seattle through Tacoma to Olympia straining for glimpses of Mount Rainier over the acres of warehouses and shopping malls. Then we'd exit I-5, wave to the State Capitol building, sweep the southern tip of Puget Sound and head west toward the big trees.

I always felt a since of relief when the gray concrete jungle disappeared in the rear view mirror and we cruised into the forest of tall evergreens. The bigger the trees the more alive I felt. There is a green tunnel on the approach to Lake Quinault where the trees are so tall and so lush on each side of the highway that I feel about as big as a mouse scurrying through. That's when I know I've arrived.

We turned toward the lodge and pulled over at the interpretive trail to stretch our legs. We led the group around the half mile loop trail pointing out edible berries, an osprey nest and stopping to admire the largest tree, a Douglas fir as tall as a skyscraper. Then one guide would take the luggage van to the lodge to get the group checked in, while the other walked the group along a three mile trail that would end at the lodge. For me it was like coming home.

I started each morning of the tour by asking a trivia question. Our guests had twenty-four hours to come up with an answer. Anyone with the correct answer would win a prize, a post card, pencil or chocolate slug sucker. How much rainfall does the Quinault Rainforest get in an average year? What was the name of the dog that traveled with Lewis and Clark? What do chocolate, a tiger and an avalanche have in common? They're all subalpine lilies.

To set the tone for the day I'd share a reading or a poem. Some I'd memorized and had left in shelter logs on the AT. Lug especially seemed to enjoy them. *To Know the Dark* by Wendell Berry, *Where Many Rivers Meet* by David Whyte, *Lost* by David Wagoner. My favorite poem, and Lug's, too, was Mary Oliver's *Sleeping in the Forest.*

I thought the earth
remembered me, she
took me back so tenderly, arranging
her dark skirts, her pockets
full of lichens and seeds. I slept
as never before, a stone
on the riverbed, nothing
between me and the white fire of stars
but my thoughts and they floated
light as moths against the branches
of the perfect trees. All night
I heard the small kingdoms breathing
around me, the insects and the birds
who do their work in darkness. All night
I rose and fell, as if in water, grappling
with a luminous doom. By morning
I had vanished at least a dozen times
into something better.

We'd walk five to ten miles most days, in the rainforest, by lakes, rivers or waterfalls, on beaches by tide pools and sea stacks, or sometimes in subalpine meadows full of familiar wildflowers with breathtaking views of snowcapped peaks. Someone inevitably would break out in song, *"The hills are alive with the sound of music"*. We'd see deer, sometimes elk, marmots, mountain goats or bear. Mostly we were charmed by birds, chickadees and juncos, iridescent blue black Stellar's jays, circling red tail hawks, swooping Harriers and soaring eagles.

On our hikes I sang songs I'd written on the trail about blistered feet, frost bite or Giardia which drew some laughs and prompted more songs from the group. Our groups were made up of great travelers from all over the country who shared stories of their trips around the world. Over the years working as a trail guide I'd been amazed by many of the people that traveled with us. That summer was no exception.

One fellow was an astronomer and took us to the beach one night to tell us about the stars overhead. Another had been working in Washington D.C. for social justice issues since the Civil Rights era when he was just a teen. One man, traveling with his son and daughter, shared my banjo to lead a sing-along around the picnic tables after dinner.

A caring and experienced nurse, traveling with her hiking girlfriends, sat next to me at dinner one night. She expressed concern about me going back to the trail to hike alone. I told her about all the kindness and trail magic I'd received on my northbound hike. I expected no less from my hike going south. I was trying to convince her, as well as myself.

By September most Northbound thru-hikers were completing their hikes if they hadn't already. Southbound thru-hikers would be much farther south. I knew starting south from Maine in September would mean I'd be on a solo hike, much different than the experience I'd had hiking north in the spring with my trail family and so many others.

I was planning to get back on the trail near its northern terminus in Maine. I didn't want to start at Katahdin itself as I'd heard it's very rugged and I'd had a cushy summer of day hiking. I thought I'd start in Monson, just before the Hundred Mile Wilderness, as a kind of warm up.

While I'd been busy leading hiking tours, which is a twenty-four/seven sort of work schedule, Dad had been studying maps and schedules. He made my travel arrangements, bought my plane ticket and booked a hotel near the airport.

From the airport in Maine, he suggested I take a bus as far as it would go and then hitchhike the rest of the way to Caratunk where I'd met my sister Martha a few years before. It was a tiny town but a straight shot on the highway. It was just a three day hike from there to Monson, the perfect distance for a shake down hike.

There wasn't much time between my last tour and my flight to Maine and I had several details to manage. I switched to an alcohol stove as my trail mates had suggested months before. They wanted me to ditch the noisy "Whisperlite" so they could sleep in while I made breakfast. I'd be hiking alone on this leg so noise wouldn't be an issue. I made the switch because it's so simple. I wouldn't have to worry about technical problems or broken parts. Several times on the way north when my "Whisperlite" had failed me, I'd had to rely on my trail mates to boil water for my dinner. I would not have their stoves for back-up this time. I'd tried the little stove that Red B had made out of aluminum cans but opted for a slightly bigger store-bought model that was sturdier and could use more fuel and thus heat more water and cook more food. It fit neatly inside my cook pot cushioned by waterproof socks.

My previous experience in Maine warned that I would be fording rivers and streams, so I got a new pair of Keens sandals and tried them out on a walk around Green Lake in Seattle. Though some people hiked in sandals, these immediately gave me blisters so I stayed with the trail shoes I'd bought in Harper's Ferry. Though they wouldn't keep my feet dry, I hadn't had a single blister since I'd been wearing them.

I stocked up on food and quickly sorted out my gear for the hike south. I cleaned and stored the tour equipment and put away my nice restaurant dinner clothes. Finally, I dropped my car off with some friends on Whidbey Island with a few things left inside. They had guests coming and going and I was running late. I meant to ask them to take my stuff out of the car and stash it in a closet for me but these details were lost in the rush to catch the ferry. Walking on the ferry with my pack, I waved goodbye to the Island and then turned to face my future. On the mainland I caught a bus into Seattle where I spent the night at Kelly's. In the morning she dropped me off at the airport with a big hug for luck. I was headed to Maine.

Transition to the Trail

August 30, 2006. I'd been in constant motion. After my last hiking tour in the Columbia River Gorge, I drove from Portland to Seattle, turned in my rental van and picked up my car. I drove to Whidbey Island to leave my car with friends who then took me to the ferry. From the ferry I caught the bus to Seattle and spent the night at Kelly's house. She took me to the airport in the morning. So in the last two days I'd traveled by van, car, ferry, bus, and plane. I was in New York City and I still had another flight, a bus and more car travel before I'd reach my destination. Then I'd travel for almost 1,000 trail miles on foot.

But for now I was still. My flight was late. Hurricane season in the south results in rain in the north. A storm of humanity inside these glass corridors. A constant drizzle in the darkness outside.

Airport terminals are restless places. This one at JFK seemed even more so than most. Everywhere there's Muzak, TVs and travelers with their wheeled luggage, elevators, escalators, conveyor belts full of people, kids screaming, languages from all over the world being spoken, whispered, shouted.

A finely dressed, well groomed gentleman eyed me in my hiking clothes as I waited for my backpack on the carousel at baggage claim. I realized we're all stereotypes. It's fascinating to watch people, every color, size and shape, all manner of dress and mood, tired, excited, relaxed, anxious. I sat on the floor by the elevator on the verge of too much stimulation. I retreated into a book. I'd read most of it on the plane. There was still more to read and another flight on which to do it.

A friend gave me the book before I left. It was one of those books you'd find on the self-help shelf. It provided a formula, you enter a few dates and facts about yourself and it spits out your future, like reading your horoscope. It lists your key characteristics, gifts and challenges. I studied it on the flight across country and much of it rang true. I'd been in "tour guide" mode all summer, gregarious, knowledgeable and responsible for the group. Now I was setting out on my own. Reading turned my focus inward.

The book encouraged me to work with the dualistic emotions I'm feeling, strong yet vulnerable, independent yet dependent, wanting to finish my commitment to the trail while longing for a place to put down roots. There were journaling exercises that would help me find a balance. I took notes to carry with me instead of the whole book.

The friends I saw over the summer seemed to think my hike would provide an opportunity for contemplation. What else is there to do if you're just walking all day? What else is there to think about? But I was so caught up with what I encountered around me everyday, the natural surroundings, the people I met, the antics of my trail family that I didn't spend a lot of time in contemplation. I also think the endorphins kept my spirits up most of the time. I'd read that endorphins, released with exercise, also minimize pain. I'd had no back pain though I'd slept on wooden shelter floors for months. I'd grown stronger and felt better than I ever had before. In my experience, it's when you're upset or depressed that you ask yourself difficult questions and spend a lot of time searching for answers. So far, walking the trail had been the happiest time of my life. It felt like the most natural thing in the world.

Though I was aware that I was floating in a sort of in-between time, between married and single life, between homes, between jobs, I didn't have to figure it all out right now. I could put it off until I finished the trail. I didn't have to work out relationship issues. I didn't have to find a job or please the boss or get along with co-workers. I wasn't struggling to make ends meet. I was living in the present. Life was simple. Life really was good.

It had been hard to leave the Pacific Northwest. Late summer is the best time to be there. So much of the year is grey and damp, but August and September are warm, dry and sunny. The mountains, lakes, islands and waters of Puget Sound are hard to resist. But then I started to think about seeing moose and hearing loons in Maine and got a little excited about being back on the trail.

I knew my hike south would be vastly different from my hike north, as I would be alone. I was a little anxious about that. I'd started alone back in March, but there were so many other thru-hikers heading north at that time of year, it was easy to link up with people I liked. Going south in the fall would be more of a solitary experience. The southbound thru-hikers would be far ahead of me and the northbound thru-hikers would be, for the most part, done. I might meet a few stragglers in passing but that's it. So I had some anxiety, but also felt confident. More dualistic emotions. In any case I'd start walking the next day and that night I'd be sleeping by the trail.

My sister Martha, aka Tortoise, had started her second thru-hike in June. This time she was a SOBO walking from Maine to Georgia. Most southbound thru-hikers wait for the snow to melt on Katahdin and try to dodge the black fly season, too. A southbound hike is more difficult to complete because you get started late in the season in Maine. Winter can sneak up on you and make it difficult to complete the trail when you reach the higher elevations of North Carolina and Tennessee. My parents told me Martha was past Cheshire, Massachusetts now and headed for the Delaware Water Gap. I would be literally following in her footsteps, both of us heading south. I bought a card at an airport gift shop to let her know I was on her trail.

Flippity Flop

I got just five hours of sleep between getting in late on my flight from New York City to Portland, Maine and catching the bus to Waterville the next morning. I was closing in on the final leg of my cross-country journey. Dad had made my travel arrangements while I was still leading hiking tours. It was no easy task. If I were to start from Katahdin, I'd either have to know someone who could drive me to Baxter State Park, which is out in the middle of nowhere, or hire a driver which could be expensive. So I thought I'd start from some place that I could reach, or get close to, with public transit. Thus the first leg of my southbound hike would be going north.

An AT thru-hike that goes north for a section and south to finish (or vice versa) is called a Flip Flop. I thought I'd call mine a Flippity Flop. I would start at Caratunk, Maine, about 150 miles from Katahdin and go north. Once I summited Katahdin, I'd find a ride back to Caratunk to head south hiking back to New York State where I left the trail in June.

I'd skipped 120 miles in Shenandoah National Park when I got off the trail with an infected blister in May. I'd attended my nieces wedding and then rejoined my trail family in Harpers Ferry a week later. So I still had to go back to finish that section which I would save for last. It was confusing when I tried to explain it to others, but at least, I thought, I could keep track.

What I was planning paled in comparison to the complexity of Silver Streak's hike. He had left the trail several times to check on his business and be with his family. Then he'd rejoined us when he came back to the trail, so his thru-hike was like playing hopscotch. I'd heard that after he got off the trail in May he'd recovered and had come back to fill in the sections he'd missed, though I had no idea where he was at the moment.

Through emails over the course of the summer I'd followed the adventures of my trail family. Feather had painful foot problems and struggled through Pennsylvania's rocks before she had to stop hiking. Firefly had gone on to finish. A 2,000 mile hike wasn't long enough for him so he added a quick jaunt up and back on the International Trail from Vermont to Ontario. Zama and Lug had sent pictures of their hike including finishing on Katahdin in August. Cedar Moe had recovered from a spider bite infection in Tennessee and finished the trail with them. I heard that Tank had to step off the trail with foot problems but recovered and was able to finish the trail as well. So our trail family had a good success rate. I hoped the same would be true for me.

When I arrived in Waterville, I would have to hitch a ride to Caratunk, but it would be a straight shot up the highway. While on the bus, I took out a spiral notebook and a ballpoint pen and wrote CARATUNK in large, thick letters. Once I got off the bus I stood by the road and held up my sign.

Within minutes a middle-aged man pulled over in a VW van and offered me a ride. He said he didn't usually pick-up hitch-hikers but he couldn't believe someone was actually going to the tiny town of Caratunk. He was on his way to his son's wedding. Apparently there's a community of river rafters, which included the bride and groom, who live and work in that area. He thought I might be attending. I guess I looked the part. He had cases of bottled water, juice and soda in the back, provisions for the reception. He told me to help myself.

Starting in Caratunk would give me a chance to practice using my new stove and make sure I had everything I needed. I'd already realized that I didn't have a spoon, my only utensil besides a pocket knife, so I held on to a plastic one I got at the airport. If I thought of anything else I'd forgotten, it was just a two or three day hike to Monson where I could re-supply. If I didn't hurry, I'd be in Monson for the Friday night jam session at the general store, if they were still on.

I felt a few butterflies as I started out for the trail. My mental check list was not as good as a written one. Besides my spoon I'd forgotten stove fuel. Consulting my trail guide, I found I could get some from a store and campground just outside of Caratunk. I was dropped off there. The small store was circled by tent sites and RVs. Inside the shelves were stocked with just about anything a thru-hiker would need. After buying the fuel and a snack, I headed for the trail just a mile away. This was the only part of the trail that would be familiar. The maples were already starting to turn color. I had followed spring north from

Georgia to New York. Now I'd be leading fall south. The geese flying overhead told me not to dawdle.

"Moose scat," I thought, "I must be in Maine." I smelled them, saw the droppings and the tracks. I knew they were out there, but had yet to see one. As I crossed a beaver dam, I noticed many trees felled leaving pointed stumps. Master engineers.

I was alone, hadn't seen a single soul since I set out. On my first day back on the trail I got started at 2:00 p.m. and didn't get as far as I would've hoped. It was getting dark. I wasn't near a shelter. Studying the sky I hoped the clouds building to the west weren't going to dump on me. I tucked myself under the trees with my tarp over the branches above me and hoped for the best.

As I got settled into my sleeping bag my mind flooded with thoughts and feelings, torn between the past and the future, East and West, contemplating what direction my life would take when I got done. Then a voice came through clearly reminding me of the present. I was walking the Appalachian Trail, eight hundred miles to go, but on my first day, less than ten. The clouds parted and offered a glimpse of the moon between the branches. I closed my eyes and slept.

In the morning I ate a banana and carried the peel a ways, but when I stopped for water I tossed it. Banana peelings are among the most unaerodynamic objects on earth. They never go as far as you'd like. I felt bad about it hanging in that bush for all to see.

"A fine example I am," I thought. So back I went to fetch it and carried it to the next outhouse three miles away.

Climbing Moxie Bald I was surrounded by fluffy green mist of Caribou moss, tastefully adorned with the tear-shaped leaves of Kinnickinick turning a brilliant red. Midget spruce trees struggled to stand against the wind and weather on the stony summit. I looked out over the cairn-covered rocks and saw for miles, forests, ponds, and was that Katahdin in the distance?

After five miles and a 1,630 foot climb I arrived at the next shelter and stopped for water and a snack. Reading the shelter log, I found Martha's Tortoise logo. The date was July first and her note, "In for the night." She was two months ahead of me. I flipped through the pages and found notes left by Yahtzee, Spiritual Pilgrim and Messenger just before completing their northbound hikes. It warmed my heart to reunite with friends this way, but clouds were gathering and temperatures dropped. With miles to go before dark I got moving.

That night I stayed in Horseshoe Shelter with four others. A brother and sister were already in their sleeping bags when I arrived at 6:00 p.m. The brother said he'd lived in Seattle for twelve years but had moved to Rangley, Maine to vaguely "start a new life". His sister was soon snoring. The other two were thru-hikers heading north, Donkey Love and Hot Springs. They'd started from Georgia on April third and provided good company. We were just ten miles from Monson.

I'd passed a lot of hikers, college groups, section hikers and a couple starting a SOBO leg of a Flip Flop. Butterfly and Light were engaged, so their AT hike was a "shake down" for the rest of their lives together. I wished them luck.

It got me thinking about my recent divorce. My mind clouded with painful memories. I had told his mother that David is like a lighthouse. When he smiles in your direction, all the world is a sunny day. But when he turns, you're left in complete darkness and it's a long time before you see that brilliant beam again.

I tried to put it out of my mind.

Coming back to the present I realized my backpack was pulling on my shoulders. I had to lean slightly forward to balance the load. Was this a metaphor? The backpack is baggage from my past. I had to lean forward, into the future to counteract the tug. I also realized the pack was heavier than it should be. I didn't pack enough food for two days. I'd packed enough for a week. And I found some duplication of equipment. When I reached Monson, I'd mail some things home and lighten my load. I would keep only the essentials. I would retain past experiences, lessons learned, but rid myself of excess baggage. In the meantime, I adjusted my attitude, and my hip belt to redistribute the load.

On September 2nd I reached Monson, Maine. I hitched into town and walked up to the General Store to get some lunch. Sitting outside at a picnic table, gorging on a huge burger and fries, was none other than Silver Streak! He saw me coming and got up to give me a hug. I couldn't believe it!

We hadn't seen each other for months, but he wasn't at all surprised to see me. He'd heard I was getting back on the trail and heading for Monson so he'd arranged to be here, too, though he was heading south. We ate lunch together as he told me about what happened after I'd seen him last.

His body had fallen apart on our hike north and on Memorial Day weekend he got off the trail and flew home. When he arrived his family was all out of town at a reunion so there was no one to call for a ride from the airport. But his house was just twenty miles away so he figured he'd walk. He grinned as he told me he stopped at Dairy Queen and then Jack in the Box and then McDonald's and then Burger King. When he reached the house the doors were locked and he had no key. So he pitched his tent in the backyard and got water out of the spigot.

After lunch Silver went off for a nap at the hostel while I went to the post office and then stopped in at the General Store. I greeted Tim, the owner, and asked if there was still a jam session on Friday nights. He assured me there was. I inquired about an extra banjo. He said he'd scare one up for me. I went to the hostel to check-in and sort through my mail. Silver was just waking up. We went out to the barbeque place for dinner with some other hikers and then headed for the General Store.

The jam session was well underway when we arrived with more folks coming in. There were a half dozen musicians sitting in a circle at the front of the store playing the *Roseville Fair*, one of my favorites. I picked up the extra banjo and they kindly made room for me in the corner. There was another banjo player on one side of me and a guitar player on the other. More musicians arrived until there were a dozen of us. Tim was among the guitar players, while others played harmonica, mandolin, accordion and even saxophone. Hikers and locals of all ages filed in together. Besides the musicians, there were another twenty or so standing between the frozen food and the bread aisle singing along. *Tennessee Stud, This Land is Your Land, Will the Circle Be Unbroken,* everybody knew the words.

I'd played in a lot of jam sessions like this over the years. The songs were like old friends. You only need to know some basic chords to jump in. It made me feel like a part of the Monson community, at least for a few hours.

Silver stood among the crowd looking like he might jump out of his skin. We'd hiked together for months. He'd heard me sing silly songs on the trail but he'd never seen me play banjo. Then he left. I tried not to take offense. Soon he returned with a camera and took a couple of pictures. Later, he told me he'd called his wife from the pay phone outside and held the receiver up to the window so she could hear. He was tickled pink.

By 10:00 I began to fade. Knowing I'd have to get an early start in the morning I started to get up, but Tim asked if I had one last request before I left. I asked them to play *Roseville Fair* again and they let me sing lead. That was a highlight of my trail experience.

Walking back to the hostel Silver talked about what an exciting event that was for him. It occurred to me that making music with friends is not part of most people's lives. Everywhere you look people are plugged in, on the phone, listening to music, wearing ear buds. But how many play an instrument or just sit around and sing, harmonizing with others? How many of us just like to have fun making music?

I'm jealous of people who grew up in musical families. My people don't sing except quietly in church. I started singing in choirs when I was a kid, in church and in elementary school, where I learned to harmonize and sing different parts. I took piano lessons in third grade, and later taught myself to play the banjo. In high school I was shy and sang softly. In college I began to sing in coffee shops with my best friend Susie. Over the years I'd gained confidence. As an outdoor educator, I led sing-alongs in parks and on ships wherever I worked. I sang every time I got a chance and the groups always seemed to enjoy singing along.

My favorite singing buddy, Al, grew up in New Jersey and worked on the tall ship *Clearwater*. Legendary folk musician Peter Seeger was associated with the *Clearwater* and Al had played along with his mentor on several occasions. I learned from Al, who learned from Pete, that participation is a lot more fun than performance. Al taught me how to sing songs that everyone could join in, at least on the chorus, call and response songs, and songs with catchy lines that change only slightly from verse to verse. Al brought tremendous energy to his playing and singing. We led many rambunctious sing-alongs together.

Shaw's hostel in Monson, Maine was known for its big breakfasts and thru-hikers are known for eating. But Tim at the General Store had invited me to breakfast there. I took him up on it. When I'd been there with my sister three years before, they served breakfast at the store from a little grill on the side. I was surprised to find that the grill was closed.

Tim was making breakfast for me on a hot plate in the back while I waited near the check out counter way up in the front. Meanwhile, customers came in and Tim would stride quickly to the front to ring them up, then rush back, the length of the building, to the hot plate in the back. I was thinking I should have stayed at Shaw's, but the smell of bacon was emanating from behind the shelves. Other thru-hikers came in to re-supply and asked what I was doing there. When I told them they raised their eyebrows, "He didn't invite us for breakfast. He must like you." I smiled but felt a bit embarrassed.

I had a tasty breakfast with Tim in between him checking out customers and then headed for the hostel to get my pack and hit the trail.

After stacks of pancakes, eggs and bacon, my fellow thru-hikers shouldered their packs. I gave Silver a hug and said, "Don't forget to take your Gingko Biloba," to which he used to reply, "I can never remember why I'm taking that stuff." But that morning, as he headed down the road he called back over his shoulder, "I stopped taking that stuff! It doesn't work! And neither does that glucosamine! I'm still a lame-brained cripple."

That was the last time I saw my trail mate. He was the first of my trail family that I'd met in Georgia and the last I'd see, on the trail in Maine.

The Hundred Mile Wilderness

A young couple from Australia offered to give me a lift to the trailhead in their pickup along with Cash, Twist, Life Saver, King Pen, Radley, Donkey Love and Hot Springs. That made eight of us starting north at once. I wondered if all of us would end up at the same shelter. Donkey and Hot Springs passed me a couple of times. I ate lunch with the others at Little Wilson Falls, a beautiful spot where the water poured over shelves of flat stone. I stayed ahead of them all afternoon thinking I might make it to the shelter at nineteen miles. But no. I gave out at the fifteen mile shelter. Hot Springs and Donkey kept going. The rest of us plus Wild Bill ended up crowding in together. It got dark at 8:00 p.m. and we all turned in. Someone set their alarm for 5:00 a.m. to get over the biggest climb in the Hundred Mile Wilderness, Chairback Mountain. They're all aiming to summit Katahdin on the eighth, four days away. They'd made arrangements for friends and family to meet them there. If I kept up with them I might possibly get a ride to a good place to start my southbound hike.

Silver said the trail in Maine isn't pretty, but I begged to differ. There were spectacular views from the summits and we'd passed some beautiful waterfalls. The forest was thick with flora and fauna. I heard birds and saw the tracks and scat of dozens of other animals sharing the trail with us.

I forded Big Wilson which was only knee deep for me. That's where my sister Martha nearly drowned three years before. These river crossings are tricky. There aren't any bridges, they just get washed away. There are dams upstream and you never know when they will release the water, so the depth and velocity can change quickly. Whenever I came to a crossing I'd pick up an extra walking stick from the ground and search for the best way across. My shoes were wet much of the time as I walked through Maine, but thankfully my river crossings went smoothly.

Was I pushing it? "Too far, too fast, too soon," as Eveready had said. I had a stomach ache all day. My hip belt cinched up tight made it worse. Every now and then I had to stop, take off my pack and find a place to lay down flat. I'd start feeling better, but then I'd pick up my pack and go again and it would get worse. I went up and over Chairback Mountain. A lot of climbing up steep rocks, jagged, irregular stairs, up and down and up again. My stomach ache got worse in the afternoon. I started getting sharp pains in my abdomen and felt like retching a couple of times. I'd step off the trail and double over but nothing came up. I walked with that awful taste in my mouth, but was afraid to eat anything thinking it would make me heave. I didn't drink much water either as it was tainted with iodine pills. Just the tea-colored look of it made me nauseous.

Meanwhile, all the twenty year olds were passing me, stopping and re-passing me as they hurried on to a BBQ some trail angels were providing up ahead. They'd left a sign on the trail saying meet at the road crossing at 11:00 or 3:00 and they'd pick up hikers and take them to the BBQ seven miles away. There was no way I was going to make it. I was so slow. Besides, I wasn't much interested in food.

During that last hour before the road crossing, Hot Springs and Donkey Love came by. They could see I was sick and asked if they could help. I appreciated their concern, but there was nothing they could do.

I thought the boys that went to the BBQ might be getting a ride back as I arrived, but it was 5:00 and raining when I got to the road. They would either stay at the trail angel's house for the night, or they'd returned to the trail earlier and were heading for the next shelter. There was a parked truck, but no one was in it. Some trail angels had left snacks in a bag hanging from a tree. I helped myself to a soda which I hoped would settle my stomach.

I sat by the gravel road, on a big rock in the rain, covered up in my poncho, drinking a soda two days into the Hundred Mile Wilderness. The next shelter was miles away. I was never going to make it there before dark. The nice Australian couple came by and tried to use their cell phone on my behalf, but there was no signal. They were sweet and sympathetic but couldn't help, so they went on.

The soda helped my stomach feel better. I started thinking about putting my tarp up nearby and climbing into my sleeping bag. I had just put on my pack when a truck came down the road. I flagged it down and asked for a ride into town. They were kind enough to make room for me and my gear in the cab.

Dave and Julie had been out trout fishing. The rain had turned them homeward. They said they'd take me to Millinocket. I had no idea how far it was. The ride took us along about a half hour of dirt road and another half hour of paved. I kept wondering how I'd get back to the trail, but I was glad to be getting out of the rain with darkness coming on. They gave me a bottle of cold water and talked about fishing and moose encounters and hunting and their kids. When we got to town, I used their cell phone and called the hostel listed in my trail guide. Yes, they had a room and I got directions. The couple dropped me off and the good Samaritans went on their way.

It was just before dark when I arrived. I circled the building looking for the door. Out front a claw foot tub full of flowers suggested a hot bath inside. I found the office door around to the side and met Don and Joanne sitting at a small table on the glassed-in porch. They were having soup. It smelled good. I told them I'd been sick and needed to come off the trail. They took me in and Don showed me to a small, private room upstairs under the eaves. He asked if there was anything he could do for me. I asked for directions to a café where I might get a bowl of soup. He invited me to join them for some salmon chowder. That sounded really good to me.

They pulled another chair up to the table and brought out crackers, ginger-ale and another bowl of Alaskan Wild Salmon chowder. Don pointed to the photos on the wall of his fishing trip to Alaska. So my host had wrangled this fish for their supper. It was a Northwest favorite and Don and Joanne made me feel right at home.

As it turned out they were the ones that had helped Firefly when he'd burned his back and shoulder the year before. I was happy to report that Firefly had finished the trail and was doing well.

Don introduced me to some other hikers staying at the hostel. After dinner, he took some to the store to buy a bottle of wine to celebrate the completion of their hike that day with the climb up Katahdin. I felt like a salmon swimming against the current.

After a hot shower, I climbed into bed feeling much better and started wondering what had made my stomach so upset. I was eating the same kind of trail food I'd eaten on my northbound hike. Maybe my stomach was protesting the trail food after a summer of eating so well in park lodges and restaurants. Maybe it was the iodine tablets in my water. I'd used Aquamira drops on the hike north with iodine for an emergency back-up. I made a mental note to get some Aquamira before I left town. I needed a few other things, too, stove fuel and rain pants, so maybe I'd stay in town for a day and eat more real food before going back to the trail.

And how will I get back to the trail? I was sure the hostel owners would have some ideas. I would figure that out tomorrow. I leaned back in bed to read a National Geographic with the soft sound of steady rain on the roof.

A little while later, opportunity knocked. Literally. Two hikers at the lodge knocked at my door and offered to take me to Katahdin. One had reserved a lean-to at Baxter State Park. The other had a rented car. The weather forecast was good, which was also rare at this time of year, and they said there was plenty of room for me.

This was nothing short of miraculous.

Baxter State Park has lots of restrictions for thru-hikers and the folks that come to meet them. Most thru-hikers cannot commit to being in a certain place at a certain time so they don't have reservations. There's a designated shelter for them but we wouldn't be considered thru-hikers if we arrived by car. So to be with a hiker who had reserved a shelter would alleviate those concerns.

To have transportation to the park many miles from town was another precious commodity. If I went with them I could summit Katahdin and hike south from there.

There was just one thing. If I hiked from Katahdin south back to the long gravel road where I got off when I got sick, I'd either have to keep hiking over Chairback Mountain, and on to Monson, and Caratunk, hiking a week over the same ground I'd already traveled, or find a ride out on that remote road and hitch to Caratunk which seemed unlikely. I told them I'd sleep on it.

Climbing the Big K

The morning shone bright and promising. I woke up energized and ready to head for Katahdin. I still didn't know how things would play out after our summit, but I couldn't pass up this opportunity. After breakfast I shopped for my trail necessities and later climbed into the car with Bob, from Alabama, and Chase, from Virginia.

Bob was sixty-two. He'd hiked the trail the year before but failed to summit Katahdin. His knees had given out. He was back to finish the job. Chase was fifty-two and he'd hiked the whole trail in sections.

Both had a comforting Southern drawl. They'd met at the hostel and everything had fallen into place. I was lucky that they included me in their plans.

Chase had reserved the lean-to by Katahdin Stream near the trailhead for two nights. Bob had been car camping so he had an ice chest in the trunk. He grilled Brauts for our dinner. My stomach had obviously recovered. Afterward Chase shared some tea and I brought out some chocolate for dessert.

I was jazzed about the climb the next day. The hike up Katahdin was about five miles – not far, but it was a rugged 3,757 feet up. There was a three dimensional model at the ranger station so my fingers could do the walking and tell my knees what to expect. The climb would begin with a steep grade, level off on the Tablelands, and then climb a bit higher to the summit. We'd start at first light.

As I snuggled down in my sleeping bag that night, I was amazed at my good fortune. These were truly trail angels, loudly snoring angels, but angels none the less.

Bob slept fitfully, but was up before light quietly packing his gear. He set out with a headlamp at 5:30 saying he needed a head start. Chase and I packed and left at 6:00. It was just getting light. The morning was cool and I took off, but my stomach started hurting, so I slowed down a bit. We all moved at our own pace. I caught up with Bob at about 7:30 and went ahead. It got steeper. It took both hands and feet following the white blazes over the bus-sized boulders. Gusts of wind threatened to knock me off balance but I climbed steadily on. When I made it to a shelf, I looked over my shoulder and waited until I saw Chase coming up in the distance. I scanned the region as the sun stretched the shadow of the mountain over miles of forests and ponds. Climbing on I arrived at the Tablelands, a flat stony field among wind swept grasses. Nearing the summit, the sun warmed me and I paused to soak it all in. Magical.

I met a young man, Brian, on his way down. He was just starting his thru-hike south. It was September fifth, late for a SOBO, but he was agile and fit and would make good time.

When I got to the top I had a look around. There was the battered Katahdin sign I had seen in so many photographs with thru-hikers in various poses of celebration. To one side was an enormous cairn, the rocky summit, and all the world stretched out below. There were the gentle Tablelands to one side, and to the other the Knife Edge, leading northeast, beckoning, daring me.

No one else was there. I couldn't see anyone coming from below. I had the place to myself. I felt deeply grateful for the opportunity to be there, to hike the trail, and for all the support I'd been given along the way. I took out small gifts from trail angels, family and friends and arranged them on the Katahdin sign. There was a red bandanna from Al's friend, Bruce, who had taken me home in New Jersey, the now slightly dented walking stick my mother had loaned me, the "bling-bling" I'd found on the trail in Virginia that reminded me of my trail family, and the two small stones from Whidbey Island given to me by my good friends back in Washington. I took a picture and said a little prayer of thanks.

I sat down and ate a pb&j while I watched Chase come up between the cairns. When he arrived, we took pictures of each other. I'd been puzzling over the Knife Edge, one of the options for the hike down from the summit. Al had urged me to take that route. But while standing on the summit and eyeballing the narrow ledge with steep drops of thousands of feet on either side, I had reservations. Maybe I would do it if it were my last day on the trail, if I had finished my thru-hike with this climb up Katahdin. But since I had over 800 miles yet to hike, I decided not to risk it.

Others arrived, and then Bob came up and the three of us sat down to toast our accomplishments with some Katahdin spring water and Girl Scout cookies my mother had sent. They were a bit stale but it was all I had to celebrate being on Katahdin. My trail name was Scout, and my mother had been my Girl Scout leader, so for me at least, it was something significant. For anyone attempting to thru-hike the AT, a climb to Katahdin's summit is something to celebrate.

A group of four thru-hikers arrived. Two carried full packs. One had a camcorder and a six pack. The other pulled out a little banjo. Unbelievable! He'd carried it all the way from Springer Mountain, Georgia! He sat down at the sign and played a flawless Cripple Creek in the classic old time style. I was thrilled!

His hiking buddies showed considerably less enthusiasm, rolling their eyes and groaning playfully. They told me someone had given him that banjo the night before they started their hike. They'd taught him how to play that one song and every night since, when they reached their shelter, they'd have to hear him practice that one song, over and over. Every night. For six months.

The banjo player, Lunchbox, was kind enough to let me take a turn. I told him I'd written a few songs while hiking the AT. I began to play the one about Robert Redford's movie while the camcorder operator scrambled to record the song and setting.

Oh Miss Janet asked a question of the hikers gathered round.
We discussed it over breakfast and then everyone left town.
But the question lingered with me as I hiked along for days.
I began to see my trail mates in distinctly different ways.

If Robert Redford made a movie of the Appalachian Trail,
Who would you want to play your part?
Who would you want to prevail?
Johnny Depp or Leonardo or Matthew McConaughy,
Sandra Bullock, Katie Hudson oh, or Angelina Jolie.

When the question came upon me I responded in a pinch,
Keira Knightly in the morning, in the evening Judi Dench.
Can you see them wearing backpacks,
Can you see them climbing stiles,
Can you see them popping blisters after miles and miles and miles.

If Robert Redford made a movie of the Appalachian Trail
Who would you want to play your part,
Who would you want to prevail?
Kevin Costner or George Clooney or perhaps Orlando Bloom,
Oprah Winfrey, Queen Latifa, love to see them in costume.

And of course there'd be some drama
And of course there'd be romance.
Kathy Bates would run the hostel with an element of chance.
But if someone were to ask me I would tell them proud and true
Let the hikers tell their stories 'cause the rising stars are you!

Applause erupted from the group that had gathered. I bowed and surrendered the banjo back to Lunchbox.

What goes up must come down and soon that applied to us. Bob again took the lead. We stopped at Thoreau Springs and filled our water bottles. I wanted to save one bottle for my sister, Tortoise, a taste of the trail. Every spring from Georgia to Maine has a slightly different taste. I'd never liked drinking plain tap water but had really grown to appreciate the taste of cool spring water from a mountain top.

From there, we decided to take the Abol Trail down thinking it might be less steep than the Hunt Trail that we'd come up. As it turned out the Abol Trail was just a 3,000 foot rock slide. I took the lead and

Chase came along with Bob. We stopped a few times to rest. I had to wait for my knees to stop shaking. Once I had to find a flat place to lie down to rest my legs and almost went to sleep in the sun before the boys arrived.

When Chase and Bob caught up, Bob gave me the keys to his car. He told me to go ahead and see if I could catch a ride back to the campground. I'd bring the car back to the trailhead for him and Chase which would save them a two mile walk. When I reached the end of the trail I caught a ride with the ranger who was just heading that way. I had the car back at the trailhead when Bob and Chase arrived.

We enjoyed a nice dinner at the lean-to in good spirits while Bob iced his knees and took some Vitamin I for dessert. Bob had done what he'd come to do and now was thinking about helping me accomplish my goal. He hatched a plan for the next day.

Chase and I would hike south eleven miles to the edge of the park at Abol Bridge. Meanwhile, Bob would drive out of the park and around to meet us. There was a campground and a small store there with plenty of vehicle and foot traffic. Then Bob would take me up the remote gravel road where I got off when I got sick. He'd drop me off to continue my hike north through the Hundred Mile Wilderness. When I reached Abol Bridge, it would be much easier for me to find a ride back out to paved roads and then hitch over to Caratunk to start hiking south to New York. It was a convoluted plan but sounded feasible. Again, the Universe had come to my aid in the form of Bob, the angel.

There are certain dates that are now cemented in my mind. I started the Appalachian Trail on March first. On April first, we woke up from a night of thunderstorms and tornadoes to do a 26 mile day into Damascus, Virginia. On May first, I was in Shenendoah National Park with an infected blister. On June first, I was getting off the trail in Stormville, New York. On September first, I returned to the trail in Caratunk and now on September fifth, I had summited Katahdin. Even though it wasn't the end of my thru-hike, it was at least a noteworthy highlight. But I still had 800 miles and seven states to go.

Riding with Angels

In the morning we separated. Chase and I headed south on foot while Bob drove out of the park. We had a good day of hiking with light packs on a smooth and easy trail. It was heaven. Bob was waiting at Abol Bridge with cold sodas. I had a burger at the store, my last chance for "real food" that week. We said goodbye to Chase who would continue walking south. Then, Bob drove me to the long gravel road by the Katahdin Iron Works.

We had to stop to check in by the gate. I went into the ranger station to pay the entrance fee. Inside I noticed a phone and at the last second, made a quick call to Dad. I told him about summiting Katahdin and my convoluted plans. I also asked him to call Kelly, my friend in Seattle, and ask her to send me her Thermarest.

"A what?" he asked.

"A Ther-ma-rest," I said slowly and clearly.

"Am I supposed to know what that means?" he asked.

"It's an air mattress. Mine doesn't hold air anymore. I'm sure Kelly's got one I could borrow. Ask her to send it to Caratunk. I'll be there in a week."

My Thermarest had too many holes now to patch it. It wouldn't hold air for more than an hour at a time. Besides an inch of comfort between me and the plywood floor of the shelters, it also added warmth. I'd been waking up several times each night, cold and uncomfortable, roll off of it and blow it back up.

Kelly had told me that I could call her for any gear I needed. She lived just a stone's throw from the REI flagship store, the Seattle Mecca for outdoor equipment. She told me she could get just about anything I might need and send it in overnight mail.

Or ... she could just go down to her basement where she stored her own vast collection of outdoor gear.

After the call I jumped back into the car and Bob took me all the way to the trailhead near Gulf Hagas. I gave Bob a big hug, thanked him profusely and said goodbye. His email would be added to my list for trail tales as I continued my hike. I shouldered my pack, grabbed my walking stick and headed... north.

I was thinking of the scarecrow in the Wizard of Oz when Dorothy asks for directions. "Some people go this way," he points, "but then others go this way," as he flips his arms around.

I'd gone north five miles yesterday to summit the "Big K", hiked south for eleven miles this morning from Katahdin Stream to Abol Bridge, and now would head north for six miles that afternoon planning to stop at the Carl Newhall lean-to. This was the flippitiest part of my flip flop. It was confusing. I looked forward to arriving in Caratunk next week where I could start hiking south and keep hiking south all the way back to New York.

I'd been here three years before when I came to meet Tortoise. I reminisced as I passed the day hikers heading back to their cars.

That night I shared a shelter with Longknife, a SOBO, and Sandman, Irish and Phil, all NOBO's about to finish their AT thru-hike. They were nice enough but I chose to leave the men to snore together in the shelter while I picked a spot near a brook under the trees. As darkness fell I turned on my headlamp and wrote in my journal;

"It's quieter on the trail this time of year. I'm concerned about getting through the White Mountains. I haven't read much about what lies ahead and feel a little unprepared so I'll start getting ready tonight." Mostly I lived day to day, but for major challenges, it would be wise to plan ahead. I studied my trail guide until I couldn't keep my eyes open.

Northbound in the Hundred Mile Wilderness

The next day I'd planned an easy hike to East Brook Lean-to so I took my time getting started. I waited to hear the birds call to let me know it's really time to wake up. Their chorus began before dawn. There were plenty of chipmunks, too, to compete with the birds. At first light I *pishted*, calling the birds closer. From my sleeping bag I could see the branches above me fill with tiny Kinglets chattering away.

The plan was to hike eleven miles up and over White Cap. There's a steep climb in the first mile or two. Then the trail continues up and down the rest of the way. It was either eleven or nineteen miles to get to a shelter. Between the two were areas where no camping is allowed, so I decided to take my time. I still had a sensitive stomach. The next few days would flatten out and I was planning to do a couple of twenty mile days to get within fifteen miles of Abol Bridge. That would be on a Sunday so maybe I could catch a ride with people leaving the campground. The post office in Caratunk opened Monday morning at 7:30 so I could get the Thermarest and still make the canoe ferry across the Kennebec River at 9:00. From there I'll be ready to go on to Stratton two days south. It felt good to have a plan.

That day, walking casually, I passed the rounds of bent grass that indicated where moose had spent the night. I kept hoping to see one… at a safe distance. Getting too close in rutting season could be hazardous so I was careful what I asked for. I climbed over Gulf Hagas Mountain and then Hay Mountain. From there I could see White Cap just ahead. At 3,654, it is the highest in the Hundred Mile Wilderness. "Then it would be all down hill," I told myself. I was surrounded by bunchberry, bead lily, small hemlocks, spruce and fir. Bracken and blackberries crown the summits. Below, there were trees so thick, no daylight could get in and only moss grew beneath them. It was very quiet on the trail. I passed two SOBO's but they didn't say much.

Stopping at a viewpoint on the northwest side of White Cap, I heard several tweeters in the thick, stunted evergreens around me. I *pishted* and out came the Chickadees, and another something harder to see. Perhaps it was a Golden Crowned Kinglet. Without binoculars it's hard to get a good look. So I sat very still among the branches and tried to call them closer. *Pisssssht, pisssssht, pisssssht.* I don't even know if our West Coast birds are the same species that I would find here. Then I remembered a bird list I got at Baxter State Park. I pulled it out to help me try to identify what I could only glimpse.

I thought of friends in the Northwest who are much better at this than I and tried to channel their expertise. Spending time with them this summer had inspired me to try to identify the birds along the trail this fall. Kelly sent me several pages of raptors copied from her bird book. But the little songbirds among the trees are tricky. I contented myself with listening to their chatter and being in their cheerful presence.

Walking on I came upon a message scratched in the peat on the trail, "U can see it!" with an arrow pointing to a huge rock in the distance. There "it" was, Katahdin, the tallest peak in Maine, looking mean and menacing. I'm glad I'd already climbed it or this view would be intimidating. In the Northwest, the tallest peaks are volcanic cones with a certain symmetry about them. Katahdin spreads out like a big bully, all boulders and cliffs. I could see the rock slide we came down. It felt odd to have skipped out in the middle of the Hundred Mile Wilderness, climbed Katahdin, and then jumped back in where I'd left off. It reminded me of when I skipped a grade in high school and graduated with a bunch of people I didn't know. Most of my trail family had "graduated" and climbed Katahdin, at different times. I'm the last one, and I'm not done with the trail. So it's like getting a diploma and going through the ceremony with a full load of summer school courses yet to complete.

I *pishted* again and got a new cast of characters. A small yellow headed bird, a touch of blue with the yellow, black and white bars on the wings, and a little round body. And another slightly longer and leaner fellow with pale yellowish green head, like porcelain, with black and white bars on the wings. I had no idea what these little tweeters might be, but I took notes in case I found a bird book somewhere. I caught a glimpse of a Tufted Titmouse. That one I remembered from watching birds at the feeder where I grew up in North Carolina. My mother taught me my first birds. Her mother taught her. My great grandmother used to sit by a window in the old log homestead with her spectacles and her bird book watching the feeder just outside. She knew them all.

A Big Rack

I decided to pass the shelter after eleven miles and go "cowboy camping" instead. It would shorten a twenty mile hike the next day. I stopped by Mountain View Pond at sunset and found three canoes pulled up with one end resting on a board lashed between two trees. I threw my poncho out on the peat below them with my sleeping bag on that, a nice, soft bed. If it started to rain I could tie my tarp over the canoes to make a shelter.

I had stopped at a shelter earlier that day. While having a snack and water break I read the register. Flipping back to the first of August, I found Lug and Zama, and another entry from Tortoise. Then I read a recent one from Sandman saying he still didn't have cell phone reception so he couldn't call his wife to "tell her he hadn't run into something with a big rack like a moose or a female." Yet another good reason to avoid the shelters.

I made my dinner and ate by the pond, savoring the soft breeze that would keep the bugs at bay. The setting sun cast a blaze of last light as it torched the treetops in a brilliant blaze. I'd washed my pot and hung my food and was nestled into my sleeping bag as darkness fell. I was just lying still, listening to the evening sounds across the water when I heard something big entering the pond not far away.

I listened as it moved into deeper water. The splash of the water masked the sound of the zipper on my sleeping bag as I cautiously peeled back my covers. Then there was silence and I froze, until I heard another great gush of water spilling down into the pond. It sounded as if someone had waded in and was now taking a bath using a bucket to pour water over their head. I slowly and quietly edged toward the water waiting for the splashing to cover the sound of my approach.

A bare hint of moon was casting shadows among the trees and shedding an eerie light on the pond. When I reached an opening in the brush, I could see an enormous animal about thirty yards away, standing in the water with its head below the surface. Suddenly, he lifted his magnificent head, with a full rack of antlers, and sent water cascading down in sheets. My first actual moose sighting in Maine!

His jaws worked on a big mouthful of moss from the bottom of the pond. After a minute, he belched and then dipped his huge head for another bite. Moments later he lifted it again with a rush. This rhythmic gush of sound and silence in the moonlight was exhilarating. I watched stone still as long as I could. In my thin sleeping shirt, I was getting chilled. When I began to shiver I thought it best to move carefully and quietly back to my bed. I knew if the moose charged, the canoes would offer feeble shelter so I took great pains to keep quiet. It took several minutes, but eventually I was snuggled into my bag, though I didn't dare pull up the zipper. Besides the noise it would make, it might also impede a quick exit, if necessary.

As I lay there, I realized that a thru-hiker, sweating daily over many mountainous miles with no chance of a shower for days at a time, has a strong and distinctive smell. As dogs love to roll in foul smelling things to cover their own scent I wondered if I smelled foul enough to not smell human, or if my thru-hiker aroma made my human scent ten times more potent and easier to detect.

The warmth slowly returned to my body as I laid in my sleeping bag listening to the moose gorge on his boggy buffet. I was about to drift off to sleep when I heard the moose exit the dining room and with a last great snort in my direction, he was gone.

Then a thought occurred to me and I almost laughed out loud. Poor Sandman was missing out on both the large rack and the female.

Coyotes sang at dawn. I awoke at 5:30 and had just enough drinking water to make a stout ten grain breakfast. But I couldn't eat it all. As soon as it began to cool it turned my stomach and I fed the rest to the fishes. A squirrel on a tree trunk scolded me from a few feet away telling me I was in his territory. I looked him in the eye. "I understand that. You live here with your friends, moose and coyote. I'm just passing through. Don't worry, I'll be leaving shortly." I took one last look around the pond, gave thanks for this lovely spot and my magical moose encounter and moved on. I had eighteen miles to go.

The weather had been as promised, partly cloudy with perfect temperatures for hiking. After climbing little Boardman Mountain that morning, the trail had been nearly level. Trails often followed old forest roads, some of the easiest AT hiking I can remember. I met a nice young fellow at the last shelter, Cooper Brook Falls, with a swimming hole out front. "Crake" hailed from Devon, England. I'd traveled there twenty years before and mentioned Satish Kumar who had offered me a place to stay while I was there. Crake had just read Satish's book, *No Destination*. He invited me to visit his place on the shore if I should find myself "back in the old country." I'd love to go back and walk the trails along the cliffs of North Devon. I put that on my list of someday adventures.

Later, I met Chase on his way south. He told me of a very nice sandy beach up ahead where he'd camped the night before. He recommended it as a place to take a private swim. I came upon the spot that afternoon. It was indeed inviting. I had wanted to take a swim in the pond the night before, and again at the shelter at mid-day, and then at this lovely beach, but as a woman hiking alone I dared not be too lax about skinny dipping. If I were with a man, or even another woman I would feel less vulnerable. I put my pack out of sight of the trail and slipped in still wearing my underwear and shirt. Cautiously, I took a quick dip not knowing who might pop out on the beach or when. I faced the shore and tried to stay quiet. It was not fun or relaxing but felt good to think a thin layer of dirt and sweat might be washed off.

I felt more comfortable sitting with my back against a warm rock to dry in the sun with my clothes close at hand. It was a bit frustrating to think a man could just strip and dive in to enjoy a relaxing swim as Firefly had done many times on our hike north, but it was a different matter for me. I had to accept it as a part of being a woman hiking the AT alone. After an hour or so, I moved on toward the next lake to cut the distance I would need to hike the next day.

Within a mile of the lake, I saw something large walking toward me through the brush. It was dark and big and broke sticks loudly as it came. I quickly scanned the area nearby for a place I could get off the trail in a hurry. A few steps more and the large animal turned out to be a young man, wearing a black shirt, with dark hair, stretching his arms over his head. He looked tired, his pack heavy. We passed with few words.

As I walked my mind wandered into the cloudy future. When I got off the trail I could do some substitute teaching and move into my house in Anacortes that I'm renting out now. I began to think of what I could do with the yard and put wainscoting in the hall. Clearly the fall weather made me think of nesting in a warm home of my own, but that was still months away.

I finished the day on the shores of Pemadumcook Lake. Lovely. Familiar. It could easily be the San Juan Islands back in Washington State, with evergreen trees and tiny islands across the expanse of blue water. I imagined a ferry boat chugging by. I had to remind myself this was a fresh water lake. Katahdin beckoned in the distance, getting closer. The almost mythical power of it pulls mightily.

But NOBOs are pulled more by the lure of humongous burgers at the nearby White House Landing. The private camp offered a bunkhouse or private room, showers, a camp store with basic re-supply and all you can eat breakfast. Shelter logs are full of reports of the big burgers which draw hungry thru-hikers like a magnet. It's a bit pricey by trail standards but there aren't many other opportunities to get "real" food in the 100 Mile Wilderness. Most young male thru-hikers have raging appetites and struggle to carry enough food for the distance, so White House Landing gave them a chance to chow down on their way to Katahdin and replenish their supplies. Hikers sound an air horn at the shore to call for a ride to the camp across the lake. Thru-hikers hurry to get there before dark.

I set up camp just a half mile beyond the Potaywadjo Spring Lean-to where I found Bravefoot alone. After a quick visit, I moved on. Perhaps Sandman joined him. I preferred the lakeshore except for the tiny pale green bugs that flocked to me, my food bag and cook pot. The temperatures dropped with the sun and soon they were too cold to be a nuisance. I ate by the water to take in the view. A big cloud climbed Katahdin at dusk and clung to the top. Skies were clear over the lake. I hoped it would stay that way as I had not even tied up my tarp.

I'd been enjoying the colors and patterns of the leaves on the trail. At this campsite I also noticed the bright chartreuse green of mosses and bold golden and burgundy colored fungi. There was still plenty of light on the shoreline, but looking over my shoulder into the trees, I realized it was getting dark. I hurried to clean my cook pot and hang my food bag. Darkness gathered first in the dense woods where I'd laid out my sleeping bag. I turned from the lake before dark in order to find it. At this time of year I'd go to bed at 7:30 and wake at 5:30. As the days grew shorter I tried to make the most of the daylight.

Lying in my bag under the thick canopy of trees, I recalled coming to Maine with my family as a kid. It captivated me then as it did now.

I thought if I ever left North Carolina, I would like to live in Maine. But as fate had it, I moved to western Washington instead, which looks a lot like Maine, only the winters are much milder. Despite the steep trails and the multitude of stream crossings, I loved hiking in Maine.

Mosquitoes pestered me all night. Thank goodness I had a small mosquito net hood which was just enough to cover my face between my sleeping bag and my hat. It was given to me at a dinner party when I got off the trail last June. I didn't think I'd need it, but accepted it anyway. I'd put it in my first-aid bag and forgot about it. But it came in handy that night. I listened to those mosquitoes whining all night inches from my face but at least they couldn't bite me.

In the morning I couldn't stand the thought of more oatmeal so I ate peanut butter on a snack bar and got an early start for the twenty mile day I'd planned. There were lots of rocks and roots and a steep mountain to climb but I was lost in thought while writing a new song. It was based on a sign in the restroom at the Appalachian Trail Conservancy office in Harper's Ferry, West Virginia. The sign read, "Just because you live in the woods, doesn't mean you should all act like animals."

The words of that sign became my chorus and I wrote verses about my trail mates Tank, Jolly Green Giant, Superman, Juliangelo and her dog Thoreau.

(Chorus first, last and in between each verse.)

Just because you live in the woods,
Doesn't mean you should act like an animal.
Just because you live in the woods,
Doesn't mean you should...

Tom the Tank started the first of March with a clean, white T-shirt,
He said, "Hold the starch."
But he wore that shirt each and every day
T'll it disintegrated off of him and rotted away.

Jolly Green was a Giant in the woods.
He hiked the trail just as fast as he could.
He passed up every shower along the way. When he came in my
Direction you could hear me say...

Juliangelo an artist on the trail,

Brought her dog with a waggle of his tail.
The two of them made quite the scene
When they settled down to dinner they would lick the bowl clean.

Superman flew down the trail
With his X-ray vision through day or night he'd sail.
But his wild behavior really slows him down
'Cause he parties for three days and nights whenever he's in town.

Besides working on my own songs, I stopped on bridges and at road crossings and sang old swing tunes. "Fly me to the moon and let me sing among the stars, let me see what spring is like on Jupiter and Mars." I sang my way up a steep peak and nearing the top I heard voices, other people's voices. I could see people up ahead through the branches. As I broke cover a feisty young lady demanded, "Who goes there?!"

I asked her right back, "Who are you?" She introduced herself as Frederica. She asked, "Are you on the Appalachian Trail?"

"I'm on the trail. Are you on the trail?"

She rolled her eyes and said, no, she wasn't hiking the trail.

"But you're sitting on the trail," I pointed out.

I'd come to a rock where several adults, and a few children, were enjoying the view. Frederica pointed out her house about 1,000 feet down by the lake below and explained that she lived at Camp Nahmakantal. "You may have heard of it."

"I may have heard of you," I replied. She was taken aback.

Her mother asked, "A feisty seven year-old?"

"Who likes to swim," I added.

"That's true." Frederica nodded.

Word of such encounters got written up in shelter logs as are wildlife sightings and reports of trail magic ahead. This would qualify as all three.

As the group smiled and brought out snacks from their day packs Frederica's mother asked about my thru-hike. I eyed the sky and gave a quick response. I moved briskly on hoping to dodge the dark clouds that were gathering overhead. I didn't want to be on top of an exposed peak if a storm was brewing. I hoped Frederica and her group would head down soon.

Minutes later, as I made my way down through the trees, rain began to fall. I pulled my poncho on over my head and pack. Thunder rolled, followed by a quick stab of lightning. I felt safer in the woods until I realized that I was approaching the lakeshore. Which is more dangerous in a storm, an exposed mountain top or a body of water?

Just then a flash of lightning and thunder crashed simultaneously, so loud and so close I jumped four feet off the trail! When I recovered I picked up my pace. Water came down in buckets and the trail soon became a trough. My shoes got soaked which passed the wetness on to my socks and pant legs. My poncho covered most of me and my pack but I was still wet inside and out.

Crake came by in a panic. "The last crack of lightning was not one meter away from me!" He sprinted on and was soon out of sight.

I knew I was miles from the next shelter. Rain poured down for an hour or so, and then lightened up to a mere sprinkles as I plodded on and on in my wet clothes. I'd decided not to stop for lunch in order to keep warm, but promised myself a hot meal as soon as I reached the shelter. When it stopped raining my quick-dry pants began to live up to their name and by the time I found the shelter in mid-afternoon they were nearly dry. It was indeed a welcome sight though it was a slightly run-down place on the banks of Rainbow Stream.

Crake was there planning his next few days of hiking, and an older man, Fuzzy, had his damp things laid out. During a break between showers Crake moved on. I tried to get acquainted with Fuzzy but he was hard of hearing and it was a struggle to make conversation over the sound of rain on the metal roof. Soon he put in ear phones and listened to his radio.

I put on warm layers and zipped into my sleeping bag. Sitting up, cozy and warm, I cooked and ate a hot pasta dinner and then relaxed into a paperback I'd found at the shelter the day before. Crake had told me it was left by the Librarian, a woman who hikes the trail leaving books in shelters.

I relaxed reading with a cup of tea and a chocolate bar while rain came and went all afternoon. It felt sinfully luxurious.

The next day I still had trouble stomaching trail food. I made a note in my journal.

> "I'm sitting in a spot of sun by the trail eating a peanut butter and jelly and cold tea. I don't think I can stomach oatmeal anymore. Might have to switch to cold cereal and powdered milk. I'll have to take a break from the peanut butter, too. Cheese and crackers this week."

I was following Fuzzy who I'd shared a shelter with and didn't really like. He seemed grumpy, so when I saw him just ahead on the trail, I stopped for a break. The first thing he'd asked me at the shelter was how fast I'd hiked to Monson. I dodged the question. It's not a race. Then he complained that he couldn't get good radio reception. He seemed bored. Then he got up before dawn and started making breakfast and packing and was none too quiet about it. So I thought it best to let some distance fall between us.

It had been a beautiful morning, bright and breezy. Maine was gorgeous with glorious views across the ponds. I kept thinking I was going over the last big hurdle in the 100 Mile but the next day there would be another and another. But the hike this morning was easy, at least as far as elevation gain was concerned. The trail was soupier than usual after the downpour the day before. It was a fun challenge to leap over the mud trenches and find words to describe it. It's been a rock-hopping, log-straddling, balance-beaming, mud-diving good time.

I had just fifteen miles to go to finish the 100 Mile Wilderness and reach Abol Bridge. The mud in the trail had some fine tracks, coyote, squirrel, and moose! I'd heard loons almost every night and coyotes at dawn. I'd come across a covey of grouse with the male strutting his fancy collar. And just a few miles short of the end of my hike I was examining some tracks in the mud when out of the corner of my eye I saw a stump move. When I looked up, the "stump" had sprouted a large nose and four feet! She looked at me and grunted, then trotted off into the brush. Then the "stump" behind her lifted its head and grew a fine set of antlers! He snorted at me. I backed up and looked for a tree to climb, but he just trotted after her. I walked on smiling and thinking "I need glasses".

I made it to Abol Bridge by early afternoon and went straight to the store for a burger. From there it was easy to catch a ride back toward Caratunk. There was a former thru-hiker who had camped there with his wife who was offering Fuzzy a ride to Millinocket, so they cheerily squeezed me in, too. They took me the first thirty miles and left me at a convenience store at the edge of town, a good place to find my next ride. I stood outside checking out the clientele. A fellow went into the store and on his way out offered me a ride just ten miles down the road. I hesitated, not wanting to get stuck in a remote spot with no traffic. But after we started, he decided to take me all the way to Dover Foxcroft, an extra thirty minutes out of his way.

There, I stood at a corner for twenty minutes with a lot of cars passing by staring at me. A man in a red jeep drove by and in a few minutes came back for me. He took me the rest of the way to Caratunk, about forty-five minutes out of his way. He said it was a beautiful Sunday afternoon and he had nothing better to do.

I made it from Abol Bridge to Caratunk in a few hours. Afterwards, I looked at a road map and saw that this was not a straight shot on well traveled roads. I hadn't realized at the time how convoluted and remote my route was that day. I consider that trail magic even though I was far from the trail. It was another instance of being well aware of my vulnerability but also believing in the good nature of most people and trusting that my angels would look out for me.

My last ride dropped me off at the Northern Outfitters campground just past Caratunk. I checked in and got a "cabin tent" to myself, a shower and towel. I did laundry and had a fine dinner with a big green salad. After struggling to hold down my trail food I was grateful for the variety of choices. I'd overdosed on oatmeal and was getting pretty tired of peanuts and peanut butter, too. I normally love pesto, but I'd eaten a lot of it on the trail. My stomach was still sensitive so I was eating with caution. That night I dined on delicious chicken parmesan, no resemblance to trail food whatsoever.

I sent a few emails and then headed for my tent. The campground was no resemblance to the quiet shelters on the trail. It was lively with car stereos blasting, bonfires, beer drinkers and it was a Sunday night in mid-September. I thought I could handle it by putting in ear plugs, but just as I climbed into my sleeping bag, another SUV arrived at the camp site next door with the music cranked up loud. There was no way I'd get to sleep. I considered reporting it at the front desk, but thought I'd try a more personal approach first. I got out of my bag, put on some clothes and walked into the light of their fire.

"Hello, I'm your neighbor." Nothing more needed to be said. They jumped up offering to turn down the music. I thanked them and went back to bed. I must have looked pretty cranky, and congratulated myself on my new intimidating physique... five foot three, 120 pounds, able to leap tall buildings in a single bound... in my dreams.

Crossing the Kennebec

I got a late start. It's hard to leave a hot shower and good food. I called my folks. They always sounded so excited to hear my voice. I asked them to send my winter clothes to Andover.

"No, not Hanover. Andover, like the two words **and** and **over.** It's in Maine. If you send them to Hanover, New Hampshire, I'll get them just *after* crossing the Whites."

I had to admit it was confusing. I told them I'd get to Andover in a week.

I picked up my mail in Caratunk and found not only the package I had bumped up to myself, and the Thermarest from Kelly, but also a box from my folks. It was supposed to go to Stratton. The only thing I'd asked them to send to me in Caratunk was my address list. So I bumped it up to Andover. A bump box costs nothing to send on if it's unopened. I sent my disposable camera to my folks in North Carolina. I didn't have much time, so I repacked and then went to catch the canoe ferry across the Kennebec.

I walked over to Steve Longley's camp store and stocked up on trail snacks and stove fuel. Out on the front porch there is a scale. Wearing my pack I stepped up to find I weighed 145 pounds. "Small but mighty," I thought. After the last of the hikers stepped outside, Steve locked the door. The other hikers started north while Steve and I headed down to the river.

Steve Longley ran a camp and guide service just outside Caratunk for many years. He was hired by the Appalachian Trail Conservancy to offer a canoe ferry since a hiker drowned trying to cross the Kennebec in 1985. The river is wide and if it were to rise suddenly due to water released from an upstream dam, the chances of getting across safely quickly diminish. Steve had painted a white blaze on the bottom of his canoe. It's considered part of the official trail. The canoe ferry runs during peak hiking season and on a certain schedule. I was happy to cross a river without getting my shoes wet.

Steve offered me a post card of him and his canoe. He said he usually asked his passengers to paddle but this beautiful Maine morning he urged me to relax and enjoy the ride. Crossing in a canoe was luxurious. Once we reached the far side, I climbed out, shouldered my pack and watched Steve start back across the river with a couple of NOBOs.

I turned toward the woods. This was the end of my flippity flop and the start of my southbound hike. I would continue south for another 600 miles into New York before leaving the trail again.

On the trail I'd passed a lot of NOBO's. As I walked through a pleasant wood that morning a hiker approached from the south. It took me a minute, then it came to me. "Slip and Slide!" It had been months since I'd seen him. He'd been a quieter member of Team Australia but was now hiking alone. We paused for a quick reunion. He told me Superman was just a day or two behind. I hadn't seen him in almost five months. After a minute, we went off in opposite directions.

I had an easy day of it but with my late start I hiked only fourteen miles instead of the twenty-one I had planned. As I resigned to stopping one shelter sooner I slowed my pace. It was a warm, sunny day but as I watched flocks of geese fly south in their long and noisy migration, I was reminded that summer would soon come to an end. Maine is a beautiful state and I would have lingered but I had yet to cross the challenging White Mountains of New Hampshire and winter was nipping at my heels.

At about 4:30 I arrived at Arnold Point (named after Benedict) on West Carry Pond. A couple of women hikers with wet hair were just shouldering their packs. They recommended the beach and the water. I checked my trail guide. I was less than a mile from the shelter and there was plenty of light left. I left the trail and found a private spot along the shore. Slipping out of my pack, I unlaced my shoes and took off my socks. Looking and listening around me I felt the warm sand under my feet. The sun bathed the beach in afternoon light. I couldn't resist. Quickly I took off my pants, removed my shirt and walked into the pond. I splashed water under my arms, across my chest and around my neck. I gasped short breaths as the chill water hit my warm skin. Wading in deeper I washed my legs and back and then rushed back out to dry on the sun soaked beach with my back against a warm rock. I read a chapter from a paperback and snacked on almonds for almost an hour. As the sun dipped behind the trees in the west, I reluctantly dressed and headed for the next shelter.

It was a dingy old place with a lot of half burned logs sticking far outside the fire ring. The lovely lake was just a hundred yards away but the shelter seemed grim.

My shelter mate for the evening, a man in his early fifties, arrived just before dark. It seemed like most of the men I met on the trail at this time of year were older, retired. The young men have presumably gone back to school. He was all business and shocked me when he asked, "What's a loon? Is it a bird-like animal?"

I didn't think anyone would be allowed across the state line without knowing about loons. Since entering Maine I'd heard their haunting call every night. I described loons to him, and right on cue they started calling out from the pond as if to introduce themselves.

He planned on finishing his AT hike and then switch to a bicycle and ride back home to Maryland. He told me about his plans as we had dinner and shared a fire made of the half burned logs.

Bigelows

The next day I hiked along easily until I came to a dirt road at about 9:30. I'd heard about the awesome trail magic a crew had set up just off this Forest Service road. Rumor had it that they offered freshly grilled burgers and served up a feast of other treats to thru-hikers. I came upon the site and walked by hoping to attract their attention and be invited in. No one noticed me, so I walked by again. Hint, hint, hint? Finally, I just walked straight into their camp.

There was a line of plastic chairs, several coolers, boxes of food and a big rental truck they were loading. They were leaving that day, but were still serving ham and cheese sandwiches, chips, drinks and candy bars. Amazing!

Walking Home, class of 2000, and his friends Janice and Potato Man, class of 2002, gave me a pin shaped like a potato with the word "Maine" on it. Each year since they'd hiked the trail they'd spent their annual summer vacation, and quite a bit of their own money, parked here doling out this incredible feast to thru-hikers. They gave me two sandwiches, chips, milk, tea, and then offered a candy bar, a cookie, pop tarts and a bottle of peach lemonade to go. If I had been an hour later I would have missed this entirely. Instead, they were trying to unload before they headed out so I feasted on their generosity. This was a welcome treat for my stomach that was rejecting trail food, and good fuel to take on my next challenge, the Bigelows.

It was a long steady climb up Bigelow Mountain. When I reached the top, I saw other nearby peaks and thought, "Okay, that's where I have to go next, but I hope I don't have to go there!" But of course that's just where the trail led me. I took a nap up on Mount Bigelow with a bandana across my face. The sun was warm. The Gray Jays frolicked in the updrafts. I heard one buzz me while I had my eyes closed. But I couldn't rest long. I had a lot more climbing to do yet.

Mount Avery was wicked steep from that side, like climbing waterfalls or going up six flights of stairs only to turn the corner and climb up six more and six more and six more and so on and on until I was shouting inwardly, because I had no extra breath, "Enough already!"

I made it to the top of Mount Avery and took a little break, ate some crackers and cheese and then pressed on. I checked my guide book and my watch.

"Just three more miles to the shelter." But looking up and around I thought, "Odd how the sun looks so low at 4:00 p.m."

The south side of Avery was just as steep, but not so far. Still it took me longer than expected, so I ended up at the shelter as darkness fell. It was Horns Pond Lean-to and I was mightily disappointed. It was small, with just three narrow benches around the inside of the shelter, barely enough room for a small person to sleep. I heard voices. I'd passed a caretaker's tent but no one was there. I'd almost unpacked everything but had a nagging feeling that this couldn't be right.

By then it was almost completely dark so I pulled out my headlamp and looked around the small clearing. I noticed a nearby kiosk and walked over for a look. There was a diagram of the site indicating that this small shelter was for day-use only. There were two larger lean-tos nearby. So I quickly repacked and found the caretaker talking with a woman thru-hiker named Square Peg who had settled into one of the lean-tos for the night. I said hello noticing that the woman had a book open next to her. I was tired and since they were in conversation, I went to occupy the other lean-to.

Rob, the caretaker, came to welcome me as I boiled water and pulled out my sleeping bag. His laugh was just like a friend I knew in North Carolina, and his silhouette in the darkening sky was like his, too. If it weren't for his Maine accent, I would've thought it was the same guy. Though he was friendly and offered good company I was exhausted, needed rest and politely excused myself for the night. I read a chapter in my book while enjoying a cup of hot cocoa and a ham and cheese sandwich from the trail angels.

At over 3,000 feet the night was getting cold. I dressed in long johns, socks, hat and two shirts with my fleece vest as a pillow in case I needed it for warmth. I did. But I slept reasonably well.

I woke at dawn though my watch said 4:30. I knew that was at least an hour slow. My watch battery was failing. My sister Tortoise hiked without a watch, but I found it helpful. I could better gauge the speed of my travel, and thus where I was and how far I'd have to go to the next shelter.

I packed and headed out stopping by the composting toilets which were the most well-kept and odorless of any I'd used yet. There were posters and intriguing reading material inside which would be nice once it got light enough to read.

I walked down the trail with just four miles to Stratton, determined to have a good breakfast there. The pop tart I ate was definitely inadequate. I could see an imaginary fuel meter in my mind that swung way over with a handful of almonds, or pot of oatmeal, but with a pop-tart, it barely moved off empty.

I got to the road crossing and stuck out my thumb. After being passed by several trucks and a few cars, a jeep came up from town and pulled over across the road. Two hikers jumped out. The driver waved me over and offered me a ride back into town. Don owned the Stratton Motel and said I could use the internet and free phone as long as I wasn't staying at some other hostel. I went by the post office and got my mail, just one box, thank goodness. Then I went to get breakfast at the diner down the street. Other hikers occupied different booths. I greeted a couple of locals by the door then went to sit alone in the back. As I ate I studied my trail guide. If I didn't waste too much time here in town, I could get back on the trail and do ten more miles to Sugarloaf Mountain Hut. I gave myself until noon, just a couple of hours. As I was leaving the diner, other hikers were paying their tabs at the register. One looked up in surprise, "Scout! Is that you?"

It was Superman! We hugged and went across the street to a picnic table in the morning sun. I told him I'd written a song and one verse was about him. I sang it for him and his new hiking partner, a robust young woman. The verse described him as being fleet of foot but slowed by his wild behavior in trail towns. She laughed and said I'd nailed him.

He told me his mom in Chicago had heard my former husband, the stand-up comic, on the Bob and Tom radio show which has a following of millions throughout the Midwest. He'd been saying I'd stolen all his money and other derogatory remarks concerning our so called private lives. My worst fears had been realized. I tried not to think about it. What could I do about it from here anyway? I didn't want it to ruin my hike.

I got a few things in town, including a ride back to the trail with the other hikers. Superman and I parted with a hug then I went south while he went north.

Sugarloaf

I started from Stratton an hour later than I'd hoped, so I hiked hard all afternoon. My goal was Sugarloaf Mountain Hut on the summit of the second highest peak in Maine. I knew there was some climbing ahead and hoped the Coke I drank just before leaving town would give me the kick I'd need, but it fizzled after the first five miles. That's when I downed the bottle of iced tea. In late afternoon I crossed the

Carabassett River jumping from boulder to boulder and looked up… straight up. Dark clouds were moving in, the sky was thickening and I had to climb 1,350 feet in less than a mile to reach the summit.

I was already losing daylight. I began climbing steadily up and up and up, using both hands and feet. There wasn't time to take a break. Now and then I'd glance down a 1,000 foot drop and think, "If I lose my footing here, I would fall to the rocks below. My bones would be smashed to pieces, the ravens would peck my eyes out, the autumn leaves would cover my body and no one would know where I lay." I prayed frantically as I climbed that my footing would remain true, that the rain would hold off and the light would last until I reached the summit house on top. That may have been when I developed my mantra, "Strength, Health, Safety, Vigor," which I repeated inwardly and sometimes whispered out loud when faced with a particularly challenging stretch.

With my heart pounding and my knees shaking I reached the top and breathed a sigh of relief. It was 7:00 p.m. I looked around in the twilight. I was in a cloud and could only see my immediate surroundings. As I left the cover of stunted spruce and fir and stepped out onto the rocky summit, the trail disappeared completely. I had no idea which way to turn.

Then, for an instant, the clouds parted as I happened to be looking to my left. Not 100 yards away stood a great grey octagonal structure and I made a beeline for it. I circled the outside of the weathered building looking for a way in. It had many tall windows reflecting the darkening sky. There were no lights, no sound, no sign of life. The summit conditions were hard on plant and animal life and had definitely taken a toll on this weathered hut. It was almost dark and I still had not found an entrance. Thoughts of sleeping beneath the porch were beginning to develop when I discovered an open door and took a few steps inside.

Once I closed the door behind me it was completely dark. Did I hear voices? With one hand brushing the wall, I followed the sounds and entered a vast room. I saw little lights flashing on an upper floor like fireflies dancing in the dark. I called, "Hello?" and instantly, all the lights turned toward me.

Three older men welcomed me. They used their headlamps to guide me up the stairs to the cozy upper level where they were making dinner and had their bedding spread out on benches. I noticed a wood stove but it wasn't in use. We introduced ourselves and since they had fully occupied that level, I pulled out my headlamp and went down the stairs to find a place to sleep on the spacious lower level.

I unpacked my gear on a picnic table and soon was making dinner. One of the fellows came down to visit while I ate. He'd grown up in New Hampshire, not far away, and told me about all the edible plants that grew around there. He told me how to make tea with this one, use that one for wine and that one for healing burns. He told me not to be afraid of the notorious Mahoosuc Notch, reputedly the roughest mile on the trail. He thought I'd make it through in a couple of hours.

They went off to bed as the first raindrops pattered on the roof and trailed down the dark windows. The wind picked up and howled all night. I was glad to be inside. The men snored and snorted in their sleep, but I enjoyed a comfortable evening catching up on my journal and reading, praising this roof and four walls. Or was it eight?

We woke up in a cloud. Not only was visibility poor outside the hut, but I had slept on a very dusty, dirty floor, something I hadn't realized when I arrived in the dark, so my eyes were puffed up from allergies. They felt like they were full of gravel. I wiped them with a damp cloth but couldn't spare anymore water. The guys cheerily packed and headed out sharing their plans to walk to the next shelter eleven miles away. But I lingered behind. I would normally be packed and ready to go by this time. I had planned to hike twenty miles with plenty of ups and downs. But with yesterday's climb and my puffy eyes, I thought I might take it easy, give myself a break.

For the last few nights I'd arrived at the shelter just before dark. It's cold in the evenings so not conducive to reading or writing. But here I found myself in a closed-in hut with a wood stove. I went out and gathered a little wood. Inside, I made a fire in the stove and had another cup of tea while I wrote in my journal.

I had to admit the news of David's nationwide radio rants had bothered me. I decided to try a writing exercise to process my conflicting feelings. I wrote exactly what I was feeling, my own private rant on paper. Then I went back and underlined the words that were the most emotionally charged. Then on a clean page I listed the underlined words and phrases on the left and their opposite on the right. It started with "bothers me" across from "puts me at ease" and "David tells millions" across from "private conversation".

After making the list I was better able to get a balanced perspective on the situation. I wrote, "David didn't want the divorce. He felt hurt and rejected. I pray for balance in my relations with David. I hope to gain understanding and perspective. I know that on some level there is still some sort of love and admiration for each other. I pray that we can focus on those positive elements as we untangle our lives from each other. I hope if we cannot be friends, then, at least not be enemies, and eventually find peace in our hearts." It helped to write it, even if emotionally I couldn't yet fully embrace it. Processing it in my journal allowed me to let it go and get my mind back on what I was doing.

I got my act together, packed up and headed out of the hut into the cloud outside. The next shelter to the south was the Poplar Ridge shelter just eleven miles away so I could take my time. I eased over Lone Mountain and Poplar Mountain. When I arrived at the shelter there were already ten people there. I looked around for a place to hang my tarp. It looked like it might rain so I chose a little nest beneath the close branches of stout subalpine trees. I cooked and ate dinner at the shelter but people weren't very friendly. No one spoke to me. I just ate, cleaned my pot, hung my food and went back to my tarp to read until dark. It didn't rain and I slept well while the men in the shelter snored all night. My bed of fir needles was softer than the wooden floor of a shelter, so I awoke refreshed, ready to walk on.

Sketches

I had ambitions of doing a twenty mile day but I didn't realize how much climbing I would have to do. First I climbed the steep slope of Saddleback Junior. Then I hiked on over the Horn, which was a long, bald ridge and beautiful, even though it was fogged in. Finally, I started down and down and down. I had lunch on a little overlook above the first pond.

For the next four hours I walked between ponds, which meant mud. I had tried to be quick and make good time, but who can walk fast dodging mud holes, roots and rocks? Each time I got to a relatively flat, easy stretch, I breathed a sigh of relief, but it never lasted more than ten or twelve steps. At one mud hole, I was jumping from log to stump to whatever, and the wood I had balanced on rolled as I stepped off of it, so my whole foot went into a mud hole. Ugggh!

By 4:00 p.m. I'd decided I was too tired to make it to the twenty mile shelter. I settled for a campsite at the sixteen mile point. I arrived at Swift River Pond Campground at 4:15 and it felt great to have a few hours of daylight and plenty of water to get cleaned up before bed.

There was a tent pitched on the high end of the campground where a giant man that looked like a Viking sat quiet and alone. I greeted him and introduced myself. He said his name was "Sketches" and he hailed from Durham, North Carolina, not far from my home town. He was sketching as I came over. I told him I'd go set up my camp and come back to visit.

I found a place near the pond to hang my tarp, lay out my bag and cook dinner. With a cup of cocoa in hand, I went back up to talk with Sketches. He showed me his sketches and said he only goes ten miles a day. I could see why. His drawings were elaborate and must have taken a lot of time. But he obviously enjoyed doing it and the results showed talent and patience. He may look like a giant, but he was a soft-hearted giant.

While we talked, a couple arrived, Peacemaker and Timber. They'd met Sketches before and I introduced myself. They set up their tent between ours and then went out in one of the canoes left by the pond. A second, somewhat bedraggled canoe was also waiting on the shore. I invited Sketches to join me and he accepted. I stepped into the bow and turned to face Sketches as he shoved us away from the shore and settled into the stern. With his great size and weight there was very little freeboard left. It was so tippy I didn't dare turn around to face forward. We paddled around the pond facing each other and laughing. I asked, "Why do you think the water is so dark? Is it the tannin from the evergreens, or the peat bog?"

He answered without hesitation, "I think it's the moose. They walk around in the mud and they don't wipe their feet when they get into the pond."

Sketches was mesmerized by the diamonds of water caught in the leaves of the pond lilies, the beauty of small things.

The next morning, I woke up and started my ritual of breaking camp when a fiery red jewel grabbed my full attention. There was a most glorious sunrise across the pond. I had to stop and find a clear view. The radiant orb climbed through the trees from limb to limb. It rose changing from deep red to brilliant orange. As it launched free of the trees, it was swallowed by clouds and could have easily been mistaken for a full moon. What a magical way to start the day.

I was only going twelve miles that day so I took my time. Most of the trail was low, which meant more mud. At one spot I stepped onto a board and just off to one side I saw a perfect bear track. It was a fore paw about five inches wide at the ball of the foot. There had been a report of a bear about a mile south of our campsite, so I had hung my food bag high on a line with Sketches. It was bear hunting season so I strapped my red wind breaker to the top of my pack and wore a red shirt. Still it gave me an uneasy feeling when I heard gun fire in the distance.

Peacemaker and Timber and later Sketches walked by as I was sitting by Sabbath Pond writing down the words of a new song. Sketches stopped to listen. This one was a parody.

I can see by your outfit that you are a thru-hiker,
You can see by my outfit that I am the same.
We can see by our outfits that we are all thru-hikers,
We live in the woods and we use silly names.

When I left Seattle I folded my cotton shirts,
And stored them away with my favorite blue jeans.
Now I wear synthetics that dry with my body heat,
They weigh next to nothing but the cost is extreme.

I can see by your outfit that you are a thru-hiker,
You can see by my outfit that I'm a thru-hiker, too.
Where the boys can wear skirts and the girls wear bandannas
And it seems everybody wears cute plastic shoes.

Now the fashion this year is to have an umbrella
A hiking umbrella keeps you dry in the rain.
So I got an umbrella but the wind blew it inside out
It was torn by the branches but nothing ventured, nothing gained.

I can see by your outfit that you are a thru-hiker,
You can see by my outfit I'm a thru-hiker, too.
My pack's held together by a network of dental floss
And I see you have duct tape on both of your shoes.

So let's sing to those guys in their high corporate offices
That make piles of money selling us our new gear.
When they raise a glass and lean back in their easy chairs
Let's hope that they're toasting all of us way out here.

I can see by your outfit that you are a thru-hiker.
You can see by my outfit that I am the same.
We can see by our outfits that we are all thru-hikers,
So good luck and God willing, I'll see you in Maine.

Sketches moved on and after I finished writing I followed. I passed them later as they sat on the beach of another pond having lunch. It was a good walk. At one point I came out at a very beautiful road crossing with an overlook at ME 17. A wide valley dropped below me and the rugged Bemis Mountains rose beyond. I figured that's where I'd be going next and I'd best be getting on with it.

I remembered meeting a SOBO last March just south of Hot Springs, North Carolina called Bemis, who hiked with South Paw. They'd been on the trail for eight months and still weren't through. They had stopped to do work for stay at hostels and got odd jobs along the way to pay for their trip. They had camped one winter night on Mount Rogers in Virginia, waking to find themselves surrounded by several feet of snow. They waded through it to the closest hostel and stayed there until the snow melted weeks later. I thought of him that day as I walked through the woods approaching his namesake.

The climb was a stiff one but I was growing used to that after three weeks in Maine. I got to the balds along the stony top and came upon Shrek. We talked for a minute and he said, "You must have started with Stinky and Orangutan." I recalled my second day on the trail when I'd met those two. He said they weren't far behind him and neither was the shelter.

I hiked along the beautiful rocky top maze following cairns this way and blazes that for another mile. Then I came upon a group of college students out for the weekend. I asked if they'd be staying in the shelter. They said, no, they would camp outside of it. So I walked on and found the shelter fully occupied with thru-hikers playing music with tiny electronic gadgets. They were a noisy bunch. I asked about Stinky and Orangutan and they said they were about ten miles ahead. Somehow I had missed them.

I asked their names. One said Cheeze Wiz. I told him, "I met someone who was looking for you, and Tatoo and Pigeon. His name is Hike Zilla. He gave me a ride to the trail back in Stratton." They were excited to hear it and looked forward to seeing him.

I went off to set up my tarp away from the noisy hikers at the shelter. The college students quietly camped nearby. Then just before sunset, the rowdy thru-hikers packed up and left, all six of them. I thought that was rude, to have occupied the shelter until dark never having mentioned that they'd be leaving. Now it stood empty. Ah well, I figured I could move into it if it started to rain. Otherwise, I'd stay under my tarp.

It was a quiet night. The college group talked and laughed which was comforting from where I lay about 100 feet away. I'd camped under my tarp three nights in a row. The next day's hike would be a tough one but afterward I hoped to sleep inside.

Mahoosuc Notch

Having breakfast at the General Store the cook seemed calm, cool and collected though she had several customers at the counter and thru-hikers in the booths. I sat at the counter last night but my feet couldn't reach the floor. Perched on a stool with one foot tucked under, I wasn't very comfortable, especially after seventeen miles and four mountains. While eating, I read the local paper. An eleven year old local girl had bagged the biggest bear. I thought about all the eleven year old girls who take ballet or gymnastics. But Maine is different.

I had pushed hard to make it to the hostel the night before. I'd been so looking forward to a hot shower and my food bag carried nothing of interest. I climbed with my new mantra in my head, "Safety, Health, Strength, Vigor!" praying hard to stay on course. It took eleven hours to go seventeen miles. I can't go fast in Maine. Twenty mile days will have to wait for gentler terrain. As I peaked on my last steep climb of the day I began thinking, "I'm going to make it (huff, puff) before dark." But at 5:00 p.m., I came upon a beautiful pond with a campsite that was so appealing. I had two more miles to the road and thought, "I could camp here and save hostel money."

But the thought of what I had left to eat pushed me on to the road. I got there at 5:45 and the first truck that came by gave me a ride... in the back. I really needed a shower. I'd hoped to go further to a place called the cabins, but my ride wasn't going that far, so I settled for the Andover Roadhouse.

There were a couple of hikers on the porch, one with a little guitar and one with a cigarette. There were packs and walking sticks here and there. The owner was just getting back from a mountain bike ride. She was a heavy woman but wore skin tight Spandex. More power to her. She showed me around. Hikers were flopped on couches in couples watching movies. One was at the computer, others in the kitchen. We climbed two flights of stairs to the bunkroom, $20 a bed with linens and towels. A private room was $50. I took a bunk.

All the twenty year olds made me feel like I was in a college dorm. They're all NOBOs. No one introduced themselves or asked my name. Maybe it's the time of year or the fact that I was a minority, a SOBO,

Flip Flopper. I haven't put myself out there much lately either. I used to go around introducing myself to everyone as I settled in for the night. But all these NOBOs are in well established groups or couples. We would meet just once and then head off in opposite directions, so we generally stuck to ourselves.

In March there were so many hikers heading north that it took just three days to link up with Silver Streak and another week or so to find Firefly. Then we hooked up with Zama and Lug and Tank and had our trail family well formed by the third week. Not so going south in September. I knew it would be a more solitary experience. And more so the farther I'd go. The NOBOs fly by, heading for Katahdin. As summer leaned into fall, fewer and fewer hikers were on the trail, occasional day hikers and section hikers, but no one to link up with for any length of time.

It changed the dynamic. I had to be completely self-motivated. I wasn't doing this for anyone but me. It was a completely selfish act. No one urged me to do it. So it was all me out here. There's no one to look forward to meeting at the shelter at the end of the day. I find I'm more careful on the dangerous spots because I know no one will miss me if I fall. I can feel down at times, wishing I could just go home and sleep in a comfortable bed, soak in a tub, eat real food, or most of all to be with friends and family, be a part of a community, find a good job and do good work. But I knew I had to finish this first.

I started psyching myself up for Mahoosuc Notch, the toughest mile on the trail, just twenty miles away. After that I'd hit the White Mountains of New Hampshire, above treeline, cold, rugged and exposed and it would be late September. Then the terrain would get easier through Vermont, Massachusetts and Connecticut before I got back to New York State again. It would get easier as far as terrain goes, but then there's the weather. The geese flying south and honking overhead kept reminding me, move along, just keep moving.

At Full Goose Shelter it was foggy and cold so I was still in my sleeping bag at 9:00 a.m. I was giving myself an easy ten mile day after a tough twelve miles I'd done the day before going over steep Old Speck Mountain and then Mahoosuc Notch followed by Fulling Mountain.

I had psyched myself up for my hike through the Notch. So many hikers had shared different stories of going through, I had no idea what to expect, or how much time it would take. I had blasted out of Andover mid-day after getting re-supplied, calling home and checking the weather forecast. Mom said there were two hurricanes off the coast down south that might be bringing up rain. I checked online at the hostel and found a 30% chance on Tuesday, the day I expected to go through the Notch and a 50% chance on Wednesday.

My parents had sent my warm clothes to Andover and with the fresh food I was packing from town, I was carrying a heavy load, but I was happy to have it. The nights had grown cold and I'd go miles out of my way to get *real* food.

I got a ride to the trailhead at about 1:00 and went eight miles up and over Bald Plate, gorgeous. I kept thinking I'd like to spend more time in these beautiful places. I'd have to come back to Maine. Bald Plate was steep and rocky at the top. I could see for miles, the colors of the forest, the distant lakes and river below. Cairns marked the way and ravens called warning me not to fall.

I sank back into the forest and hurried on to the Bald Plate shelter where I found two sociable NOBOs, Crescent City and a fellow from Vermont. They told me of their hike through the Notch that day saying it was fun and it had been the hardest day they'd had on the whole AT. The one mile section of trail through Machoosuc Notch had taken them two and a half hours to get through. That made me a bit anxious. So I determined to get up early and take advantage of all the daylight I could get.

I got up at 5:00 and started packing and making breakfast. I had packed out a calzone from the general store and had eaten it for lunch, dinner and now breakfast but I still had more for that day's lunch. I apologized to my shelter mates for making so much noise. They were very understanding. It's difficult to break camp quietly and I wanted to take extra pains to make sure everything was tucked inside my pack, nothing in the side pockets or tied on with straps.

I started hiking at 6:30 and made good time. Nearing the top of Old Speck I met a NOBO named Boulder. I introduced myself. He said we'd met. He asked the day I'd started. I replied, "March first." It was the same for him. He remembered my sister bringing a chocolate cake and he'd had some. So here we were, seven and a half months later, meeting again.

Later I passed a father and son who had just come through the Notch, Minnow and Fish. The father, a white haired man with a long beard, looked tired coming up a really steep slope. The son voiced his discontent of the entire AT experience. He referred to Mahoosuc Notch as the "Hell Mile" which he said took them two days to get through. The son apparently didn't want to hike the AT but because his family didn't want his father to hike it alone, he'd been forced to go along. He was obviously miserable, and with his complaining, his father was miserable, too.

Minnesota Smith also passed me. I remembered him taking every hiker's picture as we left the Fontana Hilton just before we entered the Smokies in March.

When I got to Speck shelter no one else was around. I sat on a bench by the pond and ate lunch. There was a towel hanging on a nearby branch. How nice, I thought, to have a towel after a swim. For most hikers, a T-shirt had to suffice. But a swim would have to wait for another day. I was still hyped up about going through the Notch. I didn't stay long. It was a lovely day so far, and I wanted to take advantage of it. I hiked around the pond toward the Notch.

It was hard to tell exactly where it started. I began climbing at about 1:00 and I stopped around 3:15. The Notch is a narrow canyon with high stone cliffs on one side and a steep forested slope on the other. The canyon was filled with boulders and the trail went right through it. There were rock faces the trail climbed over and tunnels the trail crawled through. There was the continuous sound of running water. I could imagine all the hiking sticks and gear that had been lost between the cracks, never to be retrieved. My extra heavy pack was a challenge. When I reached a rock wall I could not climb, I had to heave my pack up over my head. A rock face is much easier to climb without the extra thirty pounds on my back. When I wasn't climbing over boulders, I had to drag it behind me as I slithered under and between the rocks.

I think the trail is marked better for NOBOs than SOBOs through the Notch. I went up at one point, struggling up a rock face with my heavy pack, only to realize I should have gone down and through a tunnel. I had to retrace my steps. Despite wearing ace bandages for support, my knees started shaking, so I stopped to rest and have some peanut butter and crackers.

I remembered a story my sister had told of going through the Notch. She's small and carried a full pack. At one point she stepped between two boulders and down but her pack, wedged between the rocks, held her in mid air. At another spot a large German hiker who had passed her came back to find her face to face with a rock wall she couldn't climb. He reached down and pulled her up, pack and all saying, "I thought you might have trouble with this." I had no such help.

I thought I heard some hiking sticks clicking on the stones up ahead. I listened intently but didn't hear anything else for a few minutes. I thought it might be another hiker going in the same direction and getting farther away. Then I heard the sound again. I called out, "Hello?" as I put my pack back on.

A woman's voice responded, "Hello?" I waited, hearing only the click of her sticks. "Where's the trail?" she called.

"I was hoping you could tell me!"

After another minute or two, she appeared from behind a rock wall. She was a woman, much like myself, only perhaps a little older. She was going north. I was going south. We'd both thought we were alone in the Notch. We stopped to talk for a moment. Her name was Possum. She said I was almost done. I told her I'd been in there for two hours. I called it a "torture chamber" and later wished I'd been more encouraging. She was just starting at 3:00 and soon after I'd finished, it began to rain. I had prayed all the way through and talked to myself repeating my mantra "Safety, Strength, Health and Vigor". Then I prayed for her as well. The Notch was hard enough for a fifty year old woman, but doing it alone in the rain with darkness coming on would make it that much more challenging.

After clearing the Notch, I started up Fulling Mountain, as steep as all the Maine Mountains, as if it were flat. I had finally adjusted to Maine. There were the rocks and bogs, as I'd seen before, and boards to walk on to preserve the fragile alpine environment. I was grateful that they were flat and solid (which was not always the case) so I could keep my feet dry as the rest of me was getting wet in the rain. Fog had rolled in so there was no visibility. It was getting cold and near dark. I was still just in a short sleeved shirt and shorts so I kept moving as fast as I could. Only a short distance away was the shelter where I could get warm and dry in my sleeping bag.

Then the boards I'd been walking on skipped a section. I tried to step around the side of the mud hole, slipped and went down on one knee in the bog. It was a soft and sloppy landing. When I stood again, my shoe and sock were soaked in mud. Mud clung to my leg up to my knee. I'd made it all the way through the Notch without falling, but got taken down by a mud hole instead. Maine!

I heard many voices as I approached the shelter and prayed there would be a dry spot for me. Outward Bound had a group of teenagers that were tenting nearby but using the shelter to cook and eat out of the rain. There were a couple of thru-hikers, Prana and Beardo, who were tenting and two section-hikers, too. But the shelter was large and there was room for us all, at least for dinner.

After I cleaned the mud off of my leg using the water pouring off of the metal roof. I made an unappetizing, but almost effortless, meal of instant potatoes and cheese. I bundled up in my bag while we all ate and talked together. One of the Outward Bound kids came over to take pictures of us with his disposable camera. We told him he needed a trail name. He asked about ours. When I told him mine was Scout, he said, "Better than nothing." I laughed and said I should change mine to Better-than-Nothing. We named him Cameraman. He approved and left for the tents.

After dinner all that was left in the shelter with me were the two section-hikers Dick and Dave. They used to be brothers in law, but after a divorce they were no longer related. They didn't let that stop them from continuing their outings together. One was a gourmet cook and gave me tips on preparing trail food before leaving home. He'd become proficient with a food dehydrator which was inspiring. He gave me some chocolate chip cookies! Later the Outward Bound group gave me some leftover mac and cheese with chili! I applied myself to helping them clean out their cook pot.

Dick and Dave were talkers, humorous and good company. It was wonderful to be warm, dry and well fed after the challenges of the day, while the rain poured down and darkness fell with a thud. We swapped stories. I told them what I'd heard about my ex-husband making false statements about me to millions of radio listeners in the Midwest. "And I can't do anything about it," I said.

They looked at each other and paused. One was a lawyer and said I actually could do something about it if I chose to. He gave me a few examples of how people could sue for slander. It was the last thing I wanted to get involved in at the time.

Along about 8:30 p.m. we were almost asleep when we heard more hikers coming out of the darkness. We aimed our headlamps out of the shelter. It had been dark for hours with non-stop rain when another Outward Bound group arrived. It's their policy not to occupy shelters, but instead pitch tents and string up tarps nearby.

We peered out from our warm sleeping bags in the dry shelter to see the group leader instruct the kids to sit on a rock wall along side the shelter in the pouring rain, their ponchos and rain coats dripping wet, with long faces and heads bowed. Hardly anyone spoke. One girl looked as if she might cry. I wondered if this kind of experience would completely turn them against wilderness outings, or somehow assure them that after this, they could accomplish anything. Their leader went to look for tent sites and assistance from the group that had already bedded down for the night. In a few minutes they moved to a nearby site to string up a tarp and pitch their tents. Another leader came back to the shelter to make a big pot of food for their dinner. Soon all was quiet.

In the morning Dick and Dave gave me crackers and more chocolate before they left the shelter. The Outward Bound group left early to go through Mahoosuc Notch. I made some oatmeal and enjoyed it in my sleeping bag, getting off to a slow start. It wasn't until I left the shelter and headed off in the direction the Outward Bound group had come the night before that I appreciated their challenge. Some of the trail was so steep, ladders were needed to get up the cliffs. Doing that in the dark and rain would certainly be tough. They say Maine is between a rock and a hard place. I think they'd agree.

New Hampshire – Not for the Weak of Heart

I woke up at Gentian Pond shelter, a lovely log cabin perched above a waterfall at the head of the White Mountains, my first shelter in New Hampshire. I was low on both fuel and water so no oatmeal today. I'd eat a cold breakfast of peanut butter and crackers, fig Newtons, apricots, almonds and chocolate. Yesterday I came from Full Goose Shelter, climbed up and over Goose Eye Mountain and then over Mount Carlo, passing Carlo Col shelter. Some NOBOs had told me they'd just come from Gentian Pond shelter and it was a rocky rutted trail. They compared it to Mahoosuc Notch and said it took them eight hours to go six miles. I was planning to do the same six miles in less than five. But their packs looked heavier and they looked older. I hoped I was in better shape, but I quickened my pace just the same. Just after seeing them I came upon a Mahoosuc Notch-type climb up and over a tumble of rocks. I got up my gumption and hauled myself and my pack up and over. Then I hurried up the usual steep and rocky slopes. I passed a small sign on a tree, the Maine - New Hampshire State line; ten states down, four and a half to go. I hurried on into the state known among most thru-hikers as the most rugged. I was advised not to expect to do more than ten to twelve miles a day in the White Mountains.

At a trail intersection I chose a trail that seemed suddenly easier, no steep rocky slopes, just soft leaves. I should've known better. I flew along for fifteen minutes before I looked up and saw a blue blaze. Yikes! Wrong way. So I hurried back the way I'd come. I probably went a mile out of my way, which makes two extra miles round trip.

So I scurried even faster over Mount Success and prayed I'd get to the shelter before the rain and darkness fell. Some more NOBOs I met said it had taken them two hours to get there from the shelter. It was then 5:00 p.m. There were more steep rocky slopes, up and down, but I was used to them by now. I was giving thanks for all my friends and family one by one and almost done when I saw the first tent platform at the edge of camp. It was 6:15. Though it was nearly dark the threatening rain had held off. I'd made it!

The shelter was a sweet little three sided cabin with a loft inside. I met Polar Bear there and soon Dogwood came up. I went for water. Gentian Pond was lovely with moose tracks on the shore. Polar Bear tried fishing, but got nary a bite. Dogwood and I ate dinner while Polar Bear zipped into his bag in the loft. As darkness fell, so did the rain and I was grateful to be snug inside the shelter.

Dogwood enjoyed talking. He lit some incense and gave me a stick for later. With our headlamps we studied his maps of the White Mountains.

"You'll need to get your own," he said. "There are lots of confusing trails there and not many white blazes to mark the AT. The Lake of the Clouds and Madison Huts are closed for the season now, but you should try to take advantage of the rest."

He was helpful and courteous, but farted loudly in the wee hours of the morning. It's a good thing these shelters are open on one side.

Taken for a Ride

I got started around 8:30 for my ten mile hike to Gorham, New Hampshire. There was a bitter cold wind so I layered up with a short sleeved shirt, a long sleeved shirt and my windbreaker. But once I built up momentum I shed the windbreaker. It was the autumn equinox and the chill lingered even though the sun was out. Leaves were falling in flaming colors across the black soil of the bogs and mud holes. I still wore long sleeves, gloves and my buff, a stretchy cloth scarf around my neck. Stopping for water, I got chilled. The trail was easier that morning, but I was sure that would change.

I had high expectations going into Gorham. My first stop was the post office where they gave me four packages! I kept two and bumped the others to post offices further along.

Then I walked another mile to the Hiker's Paradise. I chose it out of the guide book because it said there were tubs and little cottages that sounded quaint and quiet. But when I arrived I found it to be a tired old place run by tired old people. They had rooms for $38 or I could get a bunk upstairs for $17.50. I paid for a bunk and went upstairs.

I had passed about a dozen NOBOs on the trail that day. This place must have had a lot of use lately, but it hadn't been cleaned. The dishes in the drying rack still had food on them. The kitchen counters and table hadn't been wiped. The floors were gritty and the bathroom really needed a good scrub. It felt grungy and made me feel grungy, too. How can you feel clean if you bathe in a dirty shower? No way would I use the tub. But I was the only one there so I chose a small room at the end of the hall. I sorted out my clothes and took my laundry downstairs. The old woman hobbled me out to the little room full of clutter and cleaning supplies. She watched me closely as I put my clothes in the coin-op washer. She told me I had to finish by 9:00 p.m. That was long past my bedtime.

I walked down the street to find some dinner. She'd suggested the KFC and mentioned Mr. Pizza, but I wanted something more wholesome. After walking in pristine wilderness for days, walking by a busy highway cluttered with urban sprawl was an assault on the senses. I was tired and hungry and it seemed like I was walking a long way so I finally settled on a Pizza Hut. The crying toddlers and hard rock Muzak didn't enhance my dining experience. I got a salad and pasta with meatballs and lots of cheese. It was all very mediocre but I packed up the leftovers and walked back to the hostel. By then it was getting dark and chilling down. Frost was expected. People had covered their shrubs for the night.

I moved my clothes from the washer to the dryer and climbed the stairs to the bunkhouse. In the grungy kitchen, I wiped off the table and opened my mail drops. The one from Kelly had treats! I ate some Cougar Mountain cookies and drank some cocoa while I sorted the rest of my stuff. Mom had thrown in some extra things in her mail drop that I didn't need so I filled another box to send ahead the next day. I got my laundry, left my stuff on the kitchen table and got into my sleeping bag to read. Electric lights were a big bonus.

After awhile I heard someone come in, create a lot of noise in the bathroom and then go back up to the front. I got up, collected my things from the kitchen and then met the new arrival, a nice fellow named Skip. He took his gear into a room at the opposite end of the building. His end turned out to be quieter.

Opposite my wall was the apartment for the elderly folks who ran the place. Being hard of hearing they were talking loudly with the TV cranked up, too. I put in my earplugs and managed to fall asleep. In the night, I heard trains go by and then Skip got up. I didn't sleep well.

At 7:00 a.m. I got up and tried to decide what to do. I heated my leftover pasta and made some Bisquick biscuits I'd found in the cupboard there. I had cocoa and tea and studied my trail guide.

When Skip got up we tuned the radio to the weather channel. It was supposed to rain on Saturday and Sunday but today would be clear. So I decided to hike up to Imp Shelter, just eight miles. Then, hopefully, get an early start and get over to Carter Notch Hut Saturday before the rain started, six or seven miles. Then, on Sunday, I might make it to Pinkham Notch, if weather permitted.

I told Mom on the phone I was going to play Red Light, Green Light with the Whites. If the weather was good, I'd make a dash for the next hut. If the weather was bad, I'd stay put. Snow and ice were reported on Mount Washington the day before. I had some steep slopes ahead and I didn't want to do them with ice or in the rain if I could help it. It was already getting pretty cold at night, and the wind chill made the days chilly, too.

So I rushed to get ready to go. I stopped at the post office to send a bump box to Salisbury, Connecticut. I stopped by the outfitters to get a battery for my head lamp and top off my fuel bottle. On the way out of town I couldn't resist getting a chai tea latte.

At the edge of town I stood for a long time hitching for a ride. I'd reached the end of the sidewalk and there was no shoulder for pedestrians. Finally, a gold minivan came from the opposite direction, spun around and pulled over on my side of the street. A man asked if I was heading for the Appalachian Trail and offered me a lift. It was just a few miles. As I climbed in I noticed a child's car seat in the back. The man wore a wedding ring, sunglasses and baseball cap, an average looking guy. He talked about the risk of picking up hitchhikers. Of course, the risk goes both ways, I said, but I'd been very fortunate and met a lot of nice people. When we arrived at the trailhead, I was stepping out with my pack, reaching back for my walking stick when he said, "Hey, you look really good. Do you want to have sex with me?"

Shocked, I couldn't believe what I was hearing. I laughed nervously and said, "No, thanks, but I appreciate the ride." I got out of the car and headed for the trailhead. He rolled the car window down and said, "How about a quick flash?"

I turned, aghast and said, "Sorry, no."

I couldn't believe him. What nerve! Worried that he might follow I lit both burners and hiked into the woods and up the steep trail as fast as I could. Funny how my instincts told me it was safer to be on the trail than near the road. I was grateful that I'd always made it a practice to hold my pack on my lap whenever accepting a ride from a stranger. I realized how lucky I'd been that he didn't ask for sex until I'd stepped out of the car. Looking frequently over my shoulder, I blazed ahead.

Recently, in a trail magazine, I'd read that after a month or so, most female hikers are in better shape moving over rough terrain than the average American male. I clung to that tidbit and hoped it was true. Before long, I'd reached the Rattle River Shelter a couple of miles from the road. In the shelter log I wrote a warning for women hikers in big letters about the man in the gold mini-van. Then I hiked on, putting more miles between myself and Gorham.

With all the people I'd met, all the rides, the food and drinks, the kindness and encouragement from strangers, this was a complete shock and really disturbing. I wondered if I had done anything to invite this behavior from a strange man.

Hiking on mountain trails all day, day after day, carrying a pack, women thru-hikers tend to shed the bra. I know I did. But when I approached a town I'd put an extra layer over my lightweight hiking shirt for modesty. Not all women did.

A busty female thru-hiker I'd met back in Stratton shared a story of being harassed in a bar one night in town. I asked what she was wearing. She defiantly said, "What I have on now." I just looked at her and shook my head. I told her, "You were lucky it wasn't worse."

Being on the trail among fellow hikers is one thing, but women hikers should be aware of our appearance when we go into a town. We have to remember we're representing all women thru-hikers when we meet people along the way. Women dressed like her may have given my driver a false impression.

The ironic thing was that the day before, I'd been writing a song in my head about the kindness of strangers. I felt like this incident was a warning. The song goes like this:

Well my mamma once told me, "Girl, think again.
Before you get in a car with any strange men.
They could rob you, they could rape you,
They could leave you for dead."
And I had to consider each word that she said,

But I've been blessed by the kindness of strangers,
Who have instantly become my friends.
They offered food, drink and shelter,
And a ride to the trail,
And "Good Luck!" as we started again.

Well the media tells us that there's evil out there,
And you just cannot trust anyone, anywhere,
There are shootings and stabbings all over the place,
But the trail has been blessed by amazing grace.

I've been blessed by the kindness of strangers,
Who have instantly become my friends.
They offered food, drink and shelter
And a ride to the trail,
And "Be Safe!" as we started again.

Well you know that I've walked over 2,000 miles,
I've climbed over mountains and I've crept over stiles.
Then I come to a roadside and I see we've been blessed,
With cold drinks and some snacks in a loaded ice chest.

And I've been blessed by the kindness of strangers,
Who have instantly become my friends.
They offered food, drink and shelter
And a ride to the trail,
And "Take Care!" as we started again.

Meeting "God" in the Whites

The trail up to Imp Shelter was much like the trails in Maine with steep, rocky slopes, and like Maine, the views were spectacular. When I arrived at the camp, I found a couple of tent sites, an outhouse and a log cabin like shelter with a man sitting in the middle of it on a little log chair which also served as a step up to the loft. Dave introduced himself. He was a local carpenter who enjoyed coming up here on the weekends to soak up the quiet. We chatted a bit as I fixed my dinner and ate, but I left him in silence and climbed into the loft to write in my journal. He sat still as a statue until well after dark before finally slipping into his sleeping bag for the night.

I slept soundly all night, snug in my bag until just before dawn. Suddenly I was awakened by the roaring of an angry bear! It was 5:30 a.m. and still pitch dark. Dave seemed to be sleeping soundly. Since he was on the ground floor near the open side of the shelter I called softly to warn him. After calling his name a few times he woke up. I told him there was an animal growling in the woods. He immediately shouted in a sleepy voice, "Go on! Get out of here!" But I told him the animal wasn't near the shelter. The roars seemed to be coming from near the outhouse where Dave had hung his food bag from a tree. Dave asked me, "Where did you hang your food bag?"

"Mine's right here over my head." I was in the habit of hanging my food bag inside the shelter to keep mice out. But this was New Hampshire. Though I couldn't see Dave's reaction in the dark, I kinda knew it wasn't good. We listened and heard it roar again but it seemed to be moving away.

Neither of us went back to sleep but got up and readied for an early departure. Dave was heading down the mountain that day and gave me his map of the Whites. I would need it, he said.

I set out in a dense fog and drippy forest. I was hoping it wouldn't rain until I reached the first hut in Carter Notch but there were intermittent showers all morning. I grew more and more damp as I walked. In the first hour, I walked up North Carter, elevation 4,505 feet, the steepest trail of the day. As the morning progressed I hiked over Middle Carter, 4,600 feet and then South Carter Peak at 4,458 feet. I still had to hike over Mount Hight at 4,675 feet and then Carter Dome at 4,832 feet in just the first four miles. I stopped for a snack and stepped off the trail to pee behind the stubby subalpine trees. I hadn't seen anyone all day so I didn't go far. Just as I was re-fastening my pack belt another hiker came up. He took one look and smiled knowingly.

He was a local, "Bagging the fours," he said, which is a favorite pastime among New Hampshire hikers. They go about tagging the summits of New Hampshire's 48 mountains over 4,000 feet and this was his third time around. We were both headed for Carter Dome so I followed him up the steep slope. Just before leaving treeline he stopped to put on rain gear. I stepped past him but when I reached the summit the wind and rain were intense. There were cairns and a trail intersection with no trail signs. So I waited some long, cold, wet moments for him to come up and eventually he did.

When we were both on the summit he pointed me in the right direction and then took off the opposite way himself. A little later I came upon a trail sign and discovered he had made a wrong turn. I looked over my shoulder but there was no sign of him. I was headed the right way so I carried on. He caught up with me soon after and we came to Carter Dome together. Then we wished each other well and parted on separate trails.

I felt like he was sent by my guardian angel to point me in the right direction. Otherwise, I may have tried different directions getting colder and wetter by the minute. With the cold wind and intermittent rain, hypothermia was haunting me.

I had finished summiting the Carters and was on my way down toward the hut on a trail that seemed to be made for giants. Each large step was from one huge, wet rock down to the next in steep progression. Every step was a stretch. I leaned on my stick to protect my knees. At least I was in the cover of the trees that cut the wind somewhat if not the rain.

As I was carefully making my way down this treacherous passage, I saw a little girl in a yellow slicker climbing up the slope below me. She seemed to be all alone, but climbed confidently upward. When she reached the same giant step on which I stood, she looked up and smiled. She addressed me with her best manners.

"Good morning, how are you?"

"Fine, thank you," I replied, "and you?"

"Very well, thank you."

With that she continued toward the summit as I stared after her, opened mouthed. When I turned around I saw an elderly gentleman coming up from below, wearing a kilt. Interesting people you find here in the Whites.

The fellow greeted me warmly and asked if I was a member of the President's Club. I'd never heard of the President's Club. I said, "No, I'm a thru-hiker." He smiled and passed as I stared after him following the child ahead.

Moving on down the steep mountain side I looked forward to getting to the warmth and comfort of my first hut. But I continued to meet hikers coming up toward the summit. Each one I met asked, "Are you a member of the President's Club?" "Are you a member of the President's Club?"

"No," I'd say, "I'm a thru-hiker." And they'd smile and climb on toward the stormy summit. A most curious day.

Finally, the trail leveled out at a little pond, just as picturesque as it could be as the fog swept around it like in a Japanese painting. It was a welcome sight, especially when I noticed the sign saying ".1 to Carter Hut".

The word *hut* is misleading. Some of the huts are more like a lodge, big enough to house thirty people in bunkrooms or cabins, with a dining hall and good food cooked by the staff. I was looking forward to the step up from a three walled shelter to a four walled hut, real food, and companionship. I walked around the pond and up a rocky rise to a little stone house with a few wooden cabins on the hillside behind it. I opened the door and stepped inside with a sigh of relief. It was warm and dry, but not exactly welcoming.

A man and two women were at a table talking. I gathered that they were with the hikers I'd passed, members of the President's Club, I presumed. A younger woman sat alone at a table reading a paperback; a tray of mugs and thermoses of tea and coffee sat by her side. I stepped up to her in my dripping poncho and wet hair and smiled. I introduced myself, told her I was a thru-hiker and asked to stay the night. She glanced up from her book blankly and told me... "No."

No?

I couldn't believe my ears. The word bounced around in my head. No?

How could you say no to a cold, wet thru-hiker who has weathered the summits of all the Carters this morning after waking to the roar of an angry bear?

No?

How could you turn away this small, middle-aged woman hiking alone in New Hampshire in late September? Where else could I stay? I don't even carry a tent! You'd have this shivering, wet hiker string up my little tarp under a short stubby subalpine tree somewhere out in the wind and the rain and lay on a bed of rocks? Have you no mercy?

All this ran through my head in an instant. She went on to explain.

"We have a large group here tonight and don't have any room for thru-hikers."

There are eight hiker's huts throughout the White Mountains, owned and operated by the Appalachian Mountain Club. The AMC was established in 1876, long before the Appalachian Trail was conceived. It's here that the typical AT thru-hiker suffers an incredible blow to the celebrity status enjoyed on most of the rest of the trail. Space in the huts is usually reserved in advance and guests pay an impressive sum to stay the night with a couple of hearty meals. Hut staff, "croo" as they're called, are skilled at upkeep and maintenance of these remote facilities far from grocery stores, electric lines, running water or sewers. They cook, clean and host hundreds of people each year. Some croo give talks on natural history, lead children's activities or guide hikes. They're a resourceful, talented and hard working group. But by September, some are probably suffering from burn out.

Thru-hikers are not expected to reserve space in a hut. We're hiking for months on end. Weather, injury, trail conditions or any number of other unforeseen variables force us to adjust our plans day by day. However, each AMC hut offers space for four thru-hikers a day in exchange for an hour or two of work. Often, thru-hikers are directed to wait until the other guests are fed before we're invited to eat what's left. We must wait for the paying guests to go to bed. Then we can roll out our sleeping bags on the dining room tables. So thru-hikers are the last to bed and the first to rise in the morning. After breakfast thru-hikers may be asked to clean up the kitchen or dining room. This gives them a late start on a day of challenging hiking. So it's understandable that thru-hikers and hut croo are sometimes at odds.

So why don't thru-hikers sleep somewhere else? In the White Mountains there are few other options. The Whites are home to the largest alpine plant community in the eastern United States, a fragile ecosystem within a designated Forest Protection Area. Hikers are restricted to walk on "scree walls", i.e., stay on the rocks, and camp sites are highly restricted.

New Hampsters, as they've come to be known, are rugged folks, crossing this challenging terrain in all seasons by ski, board, or boot. I learned later that Galehead Hut, which had been recently built, had to be wheelchair accessible to meet new Federal standards because it was on U.S. Forest Service land. Ramps were dutifully installed even though no one ever expected they'd be used by wheelchair-bound guests. But once a local group of athletic paraplegics learned of it, they considered it a challenge and determined to pay the hut a visit. With lots of help from friends, ropes and come-alongs, they made their way up the rugged slopes from the parking lot miles below. The trip was exhausting for all involved but was enough to prove their point. Never underestimate the people of the White Mountains.

I stared at the unyielding hut hostess in disbelief. I cringed at the thought of having to go back outside to try to find a place to make a shelter in the cold, wind and rain. I'd packed light knowing I could get food at the huts along the way. Suddenly, it seemed I would get neither food nor shelter. I began to beg.

"I can sleep on the table." I pleaded. "I can help with the chores." But the croo lady held steadfast.

Just then a voice from the other table broke in.

"We may have a vacant bunk in our cabin tonight. I'm pretty sure we'll have a no-show."

The man had a shock of shining white hair, soft blue eyes and an angelic countenance.

"If it's alright with you," he added with a nod toward the croo member. She looked reluctant but gave in. "Whatever," she seemed to say. I was so grateful and thanked him with all my heart. The croo lady said I could have leftovers after dinner, if there were any.

I approached the white haired man and introduced myself by my trail name. He said his name was Andy. He told me which cabin he was staying in, but said I'd have to wait until 3:00 p.m. to find out if there actually was a bunk available. He said for my work exchange he'd like for me to tell the group a little about my thru-hike before dinner. I thought I could handle that.

So I put my pack down in a corner, hung my poncho up on a drying rack, and sat against the back wall as far from the croo lady as possible. I spent an hour or so reading, writing and snacking. Gradually the other hikers returned from their summit of Carter Dome. The little girl I'd met first sat with me and we read children's books that were stacked in the corner. She'd come with her grandmother who was, as you might have guessed, a member of the President's Club.

Three o'clock came and went and Andy came over to tell me it was okay to go claim a bunk in their cabin. Despite being inside for a few hours, I'd sat away from the woodstove so I was still a bit chilled and damp. I excused myself from my young companion. Her grandmother thanked me for reading with her. I went up to the cabin with my gear, threw my sleeping bag onto an unoccupied upper bunk and soon was fast asleep in my warm cocoon.

I must have slept very soundly for when I awoke, another bunk was occupied with a sleeping hiker and another pack sat beside it. It was dusk. I checked my watch and found it was just forty-five minutes before dinner. I smoothed my hair and clothes and walked down to the stone hut. The windows were fogged up and the room inside was buzzing with people milling about. When I entered out of the cold drizzle, I was enveloped in warmth with cheery people sipping wine and nibbling appetizers. Clearly this was no ordinary night on the trail. I had a few chips and said hello to Andy, the grandmother and her little granddaughter. Shortly the croo rang a bell and asked everyone to step outside for a few minutes so they could set the tables for dinner. Andy nodded to me with a look indicating this was my time to "entertain the troops".

No one wanted to leave the cozy hut and stand in the cold drizzle but once outside we circled up and I introduced myself. I told them how shocked I was to encounter a little girl that day merrily hiking the steep trail to Carter Dome's stormy summit all alone, and soon after meeting an elderly man climbing the mountain in a kilt. They laughed and listened, smiling.

I told them I was a thru-hiker and it was my parent's fault for packing me and my siblings into a station wagon every summer driving around to forty-five states visiting National Parks and wilderness areas. It was no wonder I'd become a nature lover and developed a career leading hikes in the Pacific Northwest. But I'd always wanted to return to the state of my birth and hike the Appalachian Trail and this year I got that chance. I spoke of my Flip Flop and how different it was to hike north with a "trail family" vs hiking south alone. I spoke of the extraordinary trail magic I'd been so fortunate to receive, including this exceptional evening at Carter Hut. By then the croo had set the table for dinner and called us all back in.

As they all filed back inside, Andy took me aside to say he was impressed at my ability to handle an impromptu presentation to a group that had been drinking wine for half an hour. He said, "After your thru-hike, if you want to settle in this area and need a job, you should give me a call."

"Who are you?" I asked.

"I'm Andy Falender." My blank expression told him that the name meant nothing to me. As he held the door open he added, "I'm the Executive Director of the Appalachian Mountain Club."

My mouth dropped open. That's like saying you're God in these parts. He ushered me inside and invited me to sit with them as their guest at dinner.

Dumbfounded, I entered the room crowded with happy people. With a glimpse at the croo lady who seemed none too pleased, I took a seat on the bench. A man about my age sat across from me and introduced himself as Chris, the manager of both the Dodge Lodge at Pinkham Notch and the new Highland's Center. He told me this was the annual meeting of the President's Club, a group of people who had each contributed $1,000 or more to the AMC. He pointed out a former State Representative, the Chairwoman of the Board and other distinguished members.

We ate well, soup, salad, bread and lasagna. I'd thought I'd be lucky to get leftovers. Everyone was so friendly and treated me as one of the group. I enjoyed their company. Andy invited me to stay for the after dinner discussion about their plans to acquire and protect more land and extend the hut system into areas around the Hundred Mile Wilderness in Maine.

Later Andy spoke about their Maine Woods project, showing maps taped to the wall and flattened out on the tables. I was impressed. They aimed to acquire contiguous parcels of land, restore some classic camps and make trails for year-round travel moving from camp to camp. It included trails for cross-country skiing and hiking and canoeing across lakes. They would be partnering with The Nature Conservancy to purchase and protect large swaths of adjoining lands for connectivity. This is good policy for wildlife habitat protection as well as low impact outdoor recreation.

Then he asked me to speak about hiking through the Hundred Mile Wilderness. I was surprised to be asked to speak again and stammered at first. I told them about looking for moose and finally encountering them but mistaking them for stumps. And that it was like a pilgrimage for thru-hikers approaching Katahdin after six months of hiking.

After the presentation most people were heading off for their bunks but a few were milling about. They asked of my plans for the next day. I asked them for a weather forecast. Wet and windy on the summits, they said, with possible lightning storms. I sighed. I had hoped to hike across the Wildcat Mountains to Pinkham Notch.

Their group would be hiking out on a lower elevation trail. They suggested I come along and catch a ride with someone to Pinkham Notch to wait out the storm. I went up to the cabin and found another hiker had come in and been given a bunk but no dinner. I considered myself extremely lucky and slept very well as the wind roared and the rain beat against the windows.

In the morning, Andy approached me at breakfast. He gave me his email and quietly encouraged me to report to him how I was treated as I stopped at the huts on my way through the Whites. I felt a bit sheepish, like he was enlisting me as a spy, but I appreciated his concern for thru-hikers.

I sat with Chris at breakfast. He'd worked on a hut croo years before and had hiked the Whites for decades. I asked for his advice on getting through the Presidential Range. The Lake of the Clouds Hut would be closed for the season, he said, but I could stay in the Dungeon.

Andy overhead the word *Dungeon* and seemed alarmed, "That's only for emergencies," he said.

"Well," I said, "It would be an emergency if I had to sleep outside on Mount Washington at this time of year." He conceded.

The Dungeon is a small, unheated room under the Lake of the Clouds Hut. It has a few bunks and is little used but it's there if one needs it. I would need it.

After breakfast everyone was packing. The AMC staff had extra food to pack out. The hut was closing for the winter and they didn't want to haul out the extra weight. When I came in the door their eyes lit up. They gave me pounds of cheese and bread. I took as much as I could carry.

I walked down the trail with Chris who offered me a ride to Pinkham Notch. When we arrived, I checked in at the Dodge Lodge, a lovely place. Eating a sandwich in the deli I studied my thru-hikers guide book making plans for the next few days. Some of the President's Club joined me. They seemed understandably reluctant to leave for their "normal" lives.

After lunch I went to the outfitters shop. My poncho wouldn't cut it with the wind in the Whites. I bought a new red rain coat taking a big gulp at the expense, but I'd been shown so much generosity lately, it seemed to even out. I got a good map while I was there, one that was coated to be somewhat water resistant.

At the checkout I spoke with Lindsey, the clerk, and asked if I could leave my pack with her after checking out the next day. I told her I'd planned to hike north nine miles over the Wildcat Mountains back toward Carter Dome to hike the section I'd just skipped, then turn back south to return to Pinkham Notch. I planned to take the Gondola down the mountain which would save my knees and should be much more fun. Then if all was going well, I'd grab my pack and hike five more miles south to the Osgood Campground for the night. From there I'd be in a good position to climb over Mount Madison and Mount Washington on Tuesday and Wednesday when the weather is supposed to be clear. Lindsey offered to loan me a day pack to carry some essentials across the Wildcats. We'd trade packs in the morning.

I went to my room which would hold four but there was just me that night. The rooms were so clean and comfortable, with cozy quilts on the beds, I wanted to stay longer, but had to go when the weather allowed.

After a hot shower down the hall, I washed out a few clothes, hung them up to dry in my room and then spent the rest of the afternoon in the library. It was a wonderful room at the quiet end of the hall with a big stone hearth and tall windows letting in the wavering light, but not the storm outside. I sat pondering the many maps of the surrounding peaks and checking my guide book strategizing about the best plan for getting through the Presidential Range with so many treeless summits. Mount Washington, in particular, is known for clocking the highest surface wind speeds on earth… until the monitor broke. It could snow there any day of the year and the weather can change in an instant.

I wanted to stay at the huts when I could but I knew some were closed for the season. This was the most exposed portion of the trail and to be doing this alone so late in the season made me anxious. I tried to take in all the advice I'd been given and come up with a good plan.

Then a thru-hiker came in. He was heading north so he had just covered the territory I was about to enter. He sat down with me for half an hour and told me what to expect and how much ground I could reasonably cover in a day. The occasional flash of lightning outside accentuated the importance of careful planning. With his help, and the advice Chris had offered at breakfast, I came up with a plan and felt somewhat reassured.

Red Light, Green Light

At dawn I ate a quick breakfast at the lodge and stopped at the counter to trade packs with Lindsey. I pulled my water bottle, some snacks, my first-aid bag and extra layers from my backpack and threw them into her small day pack. Then I left my backpack with her and hurried for the trailhead. It was a steep climb up to Wildcat Ridge but much easier without all my gear. My knees were glad I wouldn't be coming down this slope. I hiked to the top in about an hour. It was pleasant hiking along the ridge. I reached Carter Dome, gave thanks for all the trail angels I'd met at Carter Hut, and turned around keeping up a good pace.

I was looking forward to riding the gondola. Hearing a funny little bell in the woods made me smile and told me I was getting close. The little cars sat up to four people but again, I was by myself. I kept thinking of my sister, Martha, and her fear of heights.

As my car left the ground I felt like I'd leapt off the top of a mountain, but was suspended in mid air, which is pretty much what was happening. The car stopped for a moment and then jerked into a gliding swing as I began to drop slowly and effortlessly down the mountain. For my knees it was pure joy. The views were incredible. There was Mount Washington, Mount Adams and Mount Madison. I could see my whole route for the next day laid out before me. And the colors were spectacular, crimson, gold and green, in the forest below!

I arrived at the bottom, checked my watch, walked to the deli and ordered a pizza. I bought a post card with a picture of the gondola and wrote to my folks while I ate. There was no post office box but the sales clerk said she'd mail it for me. Then I walked a short ways up the road, returning to Pinkham Notch.

Ted, a staff person, was surprised to see me back so soon. He said I looked good. People kept telling me I looked too good to be a thru-hiker. I felt pretty good. I'd had a good night's rest, hot showers and lots of good food. I swapped Lindsey's day pack for my backpack and headed for the trail.

It was a beautiful afternoon. I kept hearing the cog railroad on Mount Washington blowing its whistle miles away. A group of eight or ten Amish boys passed me coming down the trail speaking their particular dialect. I made a wrong turn at a trail intersection but got a weird feeling so turned back. Soon after, I met a NOBO who got me going in the right direction. When I arrived at the campground I had plenty of daylight with which to find a good site and string up my tarp. I made dinner, and as the temperatures dropped, I settled in for the night. That's when I realized I'd left my long-johns in Lindsey's day pack five miles away.

Up at first light, I packed my gear and started climbing at 7:30. I broke treeline about an hour later. Approaching the top of Mount Madison, the first peak in the ten mile ridge of the Presidential Range, the wind was so strong I couldn't stand upright. I'd planned to cross Mount Madison, Mount Adams, Mount Jefferson, Mount Clay and Mount Washington that day but I couldn't get past the first peak.

I tried hiding behind the five foot stone cairns, waiting for a lull and then dashing to the next cairn. Desperately lunging from cairn to cairn, I got up the steep slope and then sought refuge from the wind between large rocks on the leeside of the summit. Sitting still, I started to chill down so I added layers while I watched the weather.

The clouds both ahead and behind me were racing by, some light and fluffy, some dark and ominous. I waited and watched and prayed for a sign. The ceiling of clouds was just over my head. For a few minutes I thought I could continue, it was only a mile or so to Madison Spring Hut. The hut was closed for the season, but at least there was water and perhaps the building would offer some protection from the wind. But as I approached the summit the wind knocked me back and I could make no progress except on all fours.

I retreated again to my leeside refuge and saw, at last, another hiker crossing the ridge below me. He moved with certainty and confidence and I thought maybe we could go on together. But by the time I had struggled over to the trail again, I had decided to go down. The cloud ceiling was dropping and the wind never ceased. I knew if I followed the trail over the summit I would be in the damp clouds, colder and wetter than I already was, and I was wearing all my layers. I was kicking myself for leaving my long-johns behind.

I spoke to the man saying I couldn't stand up in this wind so I had decided to retreat, but he chose to forge on ahead.

Once back in the cover of the trees, I stopped to have lunch and see if the clouds would lift or the wind die down. I'd hiked up almost 3,000 feet and hated to lose what I'd gained. I pulled out my paperback and read for a while. An hour later the man returned saying he wasn't able to make it either. He said he weighed 210 pounds plus the weight of his pack and the wind was blowing him over. My pack and I together weighed less than 150.

He said the weather was supposed to be better the next day. We hiked down together. He couldn't take tomorrow off of work so would be returning to Pinkham Notch. He was good company. When we parted I asked him to deliver a note to Lindsey for me asking her to mail my long-johns to Hanover.

I spent another night at Osgood Campground. As darkness fell I was reading in my sleeping bag when a hiker came by looking for a spot. I said hello and he answered with a German accent and set up his tent nearby.

For Most This Amazing Day

On the AT they say, "Don't believe the hype." But when the hype is about the White Mountains, you can believe it. It's all true. And here is something else that's true. I am a very lucky girl.

I started early from my campsite, a little after 7:00 a.m. By 5:30 p.m. I was having tea and cookies outside the Dungeon at Lake of the Clouds Hut. It was not an extremely nice room, but I had it all to myself and had made it as comfortable as possible. After dinner I sat outside watching a glorious sunset with the hulking summit of Mount Washington looming over my shoulder, giving thanks, in the words of e. e. cummings, "for most this amazing day".

This was one of the most challenging days I'd hiked on the AT so far, though it was only about ten miles. For a while, I thought I'd go another three miles to Mizpah Hut which is open, serves food and has a warm wood stove inside, but my feet and legs were tired of the difficult terrain. I thought I'd sleep well at the Dungeon after all that I'd done that day. The weather forecast promised another day of clear weather, sun, partly cloudy, with temperatures in the 40's. I could stop in at Mizpah Hut for lunch.

That morning, I'd started at 2,550 feet at Osgood Campground and climbed the same 2,800 feet I'd climbed the day before. This time, I'd prayed the wind would be calmer and the skies clearer, and sure nuf!

Just as I reached treeline, I was passed by the big German fellow that had pitched his tent near me the night before. He went on ahead, but stopped frequently to take pictures, so I was able to keep him in sight as we crossed Mount Madison (5,363 feet) and then Mount Adams (5,450 feet). It was psychologically comforting, knowing I wasn't up there alone. The peaks were intimidating and the weather unpredictable. But so far the day was clear and bright, and after I eventually lost sight of the German I started seeing other hikers coming toward me from the opposite direction.

I began to relax and enjoy my surroundings. I stopped a few times to rest and snack and adjust my layers of clothing. Climbing, I'd sweated inside my new rain jacket. Then, on the ridge, the cool wind hit me. Regulating body temperatures can be critical, so I tried to stay one step ahead.

I met other German-sounding people and locals who seemed to be having a lot of fun as if they didn't understand the life or death situation we were in. Then I checked my attitude. But rounding Mount Jefferson (5,400 feet) and approaching Mount Clay (5,050 feet), the clouds started banking up against Mount Washington (6,288 feet) and I grew anxious again.

I began saying silent prayers, "Please let the clouds part and allow me to pass." As I walked my prayers became more specific. "Please allow me to make it safely to Lake of the Clouds Hut." I had one eye on the trail and one on the sky. "Please let me make it safely to Lake of the Clouds Hut and be well fed and warm before sundown."

As I approached the summit of Mount Washington, with its very bad reputation for wind and weather, the sun came out and the clouds parted. The trail crossed the tracks of the old cog railroad and the comical little train chugged by spewing dirty smoke. You can climb Mount Washington as I had, or you can drive, or take this cute, smutty little train. It's a thru-hiker tradition to moon the train, but I completely forgot about that. I was focused on reaching the snack bar at the top.

I ordered a big bowl of chili, a pile of chips and a muffin for the next morning and went to sit down by a window. I ate among tables of obese tourists. Then my eyes fell upon a slim man at the next table. He looked like a hiker.

He came over and asked if I was a thru-hiker. Jeff said he was playing hooky from work in Portland, Maine (which seemed about a month away for me). After finishing my chili, Jeff offered me some organic, homegrown tomatoes and carrots. I couldn't believe it! I was sitting on a most unforgiving mountaintop whipped by wind and weather all year round and here I was eating fresh, organic, homegrown garden produce!

Jeff had lived in western Washington years before. We kept trying to figure out if we knew people in common, six degrees of separation and all that, but we never found a match. I enjoyed his company but needed to get going to reach my destination before dark. After using the flush toilets (what a thrill), I filled my water bottle, zipped up my layers and headed back outside.

I'd just started down the trail toward Lake of the Clouds Hut about a mile away, when I heard hiking sticks striking the rocks behind me. I turned to find that Jeff was following me and catching up fast. He said he'd altered his course to hike with me to the hut. We walked and talked as the sun sank in the west and warmed the mountainside. At the trail intersection we sat and talked some more. With less than an hour of daylight left, he took the trail back toward his car on the road below, while I walked the last 100 yards to the Dungeon.

A Night in the Dungeon

The Lake of the Clouds hut sits on a rocky shelf by a small lake. Built of rocks and timbers, it promises comforting shelter in the stark landscape near the summit of the infamous Mount Washington. The main floor of the hut was sealed up tight but I walked around, standing on tiptoes, peeking in the windows to try to get a feel for the place. From what I could tell, the main floor looked warm and inviting. I could imagine hikers finding comfort and companionship there along with good food and a bunk for the night.

On the lower side of the building, opposite of the main entrance, I came upon a large, iron, vault-like door. "Ah, ha!" I thought, "The Dungeon!"

I pulled open the heavy metal door and peered cautiously inside. When my eyes adjusted to the dim light, I could see it was a solitary stone cell with a small window at the top of one wall. Bunks had been built against two other walls. On a small shelf below the window I placed a candle and stick of incense and lit them both to get rid of the musty smell and cheer the place up a bit. I got my stove going and heated water for tea. There were worn foam sleeping pads on each bunk. Piling them all on one bunk, and throwing my sleeping bag on top, reminded me of the Princess and the Pea. With all the dirt I'd slept on and the sweat and grime caked on my skin, I felt sure no one would mistake me for a princess.

When the water boiled, I made a cup of tea, grabbed my box of cookies and went outside. I sat down on some scrap lumber and leaned against the wall to watch the sunset from this 6,000 foot perch soaking up the last warmth of the day. I felt deeply satisfied to have crossed the Presidential Range, a huge psychological as well as physical challenge for me. My belly was happy with the hot chili and chips I'd eaten at the summit. And the incredible sunset with the cookies and tea polished off this extraordinary day. It had been a treat to make a new friend and be given homegrown produce from Jeff. As I sipped my tea I thought about other friends and family so far away.

Once the sun disappeared over the horizon, I was just getting up to go back into my cell when I thought I heard footsteps. I walked around the corner and looked into the Dungeon but saw nothing, so I circled the building calling, "Hello? Hello?"

It appeared that the building was still vacant and there were no other hikers in sight. As I returned to the door of the Dungeon it occurred to me that someone, or something, could have slipped inside while I was out, so I cautiously peered in.

Empty. So I stepped inside and closed the heavy door behind me. Temperatures dropped sharply after sunset so I snuggled into my sleeping bag wearing almost all my layers. I read by the light of my headlamp wearing my gloves and hat as my breath rose in clouds in the air. Reading by headlamp was a bit of a luxury. It was important to save the battery in case of emergencies, which this clearly was not. But when sleeping alone in a Dungeon at 6,000 feet, in late September, I felt like a little extravagance was in order.

As I read, I began to hear noises on the other side of the stone walls around me, little scufflings here, thumps and bumps there. I glanced around the room and at the handle on the big, metal door. As long as whatever it was stayed on the other side of the wall, I didn't mind having house mates. This place probably served as a shelter for a lot of animals, not just humans. In my mind's eye, I imagined mice, marmots and bears crawling under the house for the night. But I was happy to have this room to myself.

At dawn I lay in my cocoon making clouds with my breath thinking about the day to come. Eventually and reluctantly I exited my sleeping bag and opened the door to a world of white. A thick fog enveloped the mountain top. Taking my time, I made oatmeal and packed my gear. By 8:00 the fog was breaking up. It was a mystical experience leaving the hut moving through the fog along a trail I could barely see.

As the fog gradually lifted I was able to get glimpses, first of the miniature forest of stunted evergreens and windswept heather around me, and then of the stunning views that occasionally presented themselves. Dropping in elevation, I eased into the shelter of the forest.

I put in another fifteen miles that day, stopping at Mizpah Hut for two bowls of excellent soup. I added crackers and cheese from my pack.

The fog had turned to drizzle so stopping for an indoor lunch gave me a chance to dry out and warm up a little. Croo member Emily answered my questions about the trail ahead.

I reached the next road crossing at 4:00 p.m. and longed to hitch a ride to the Highlands Center, the new AMC lodge that Andy had told me about. It was just three miles from there and tempted me with hot showers, good food and a warm bed.

But I knew I needed to get into position for the next big hurdle, Franconia Ridge, two days away, and I needed to get there when the weather was good. If I stayed on course, I'd hit it on Saturday, which was the only day that week with no rain in the forecast. So I crossed the road and kept going toward Ethan Pond Shelter.

I pushed hard to get up the hill. The pond was lovely, but the shelter looked dismal. A couple arrived and we dined together by the water. They tented nearby while I had the shelter to myself. The rain came in around midnight and the drip, drip, drip off the eaves made me grateful for the roof over my head, as shabby as it seemed.

I hiked all day on Friday in the wind and rain, stopping to dry out at Zealand Falls Hut where I got some fresh baked bread, cheese and lemonade. Gates and Neil, members of the croo, were working on the oven and hydroelectric system. They had packed in parts for the repair up eight rugged miles from the nearest road. I admired how they worked calmly together. Trouble shooting. Resourceful. It was a different way of life.

Once I'd dried out a little, I took a deep breath and went back out into the weather. I had seven more miles to get to Galehead Hut for the night. The wind and rain picked up and blew through the trees around me. As I climbed Zealand Peak, I emerged from the cover of the trees and was suddenly exposed to the full force of the torrent. I was getting soaked through and cold. I hiked as fast as I could to ward off hypothermia. Climbing kept me warm, but the trail began to follow a level ridge. The trail had become dangerous because it was too easy. That was a first. I began repeating my mantra, "Safety, Strength, Health and Vigor", at first just in my mind, and then out loud.

At another exposed place, I passed a hiker in shorts! He seemed to be enjoying himself. I told myself, "See, there's nothing to worry about. You'll be fine." But soon I was back to chanting my mantra.

I got to the final peak where the wind howled. I would have to go right up on the summit to read the sign at a trail intersection. I hated the thought of leaving the moderate shelter of the trees but stepped quickly out onto the peak, into the gale, to read the sign and quickly popped back down behind some rocks. Once I'd left the summit and started down the path, I had doubts about being on the right trail. I ducked in between two boulders and pulled out my map. It was soaked and disintegrating rapidly.

I thought I was going down the right trail so I continued but still had a nagging feeling that I was on the wrong path. I didn't want to get lost when I was soaked through, so I turned around and went back up toward the summit cursing the whole way. Just before I reached the top I saw a white blaze marking the AT. Once reassured, I turned around to go back down, down, down.

In places the trail was like a waterfall. I kept repeating my mantra praying that I'd make it to the hut. It was about a 1,000 foot drop in less than a mile but it seemed to take forever. Finally, I came upon a sign saying I was entering a Forest Recovery Area which is always posted a quarter mile from the huts. Yes! I walked on briskly. How glad I was to see that hut! I walked up on the porch, opened the door and felt safe.

I met Chicklet, a member of the croo, who welcomed me in and told me I could change in the restroom and sleep on the table that night. But I overheard that they had at least a dozen cancellations so there would be a spare bunk.

I changed into some dry clothes and asked where I could hang my wet ones. She looked flustered but said I could use the hooks in one of the bunkrooms. A puddle had formed beneath my pack on the bench in the hall. They gave me a roasting pan to catch the drips. I hung my clothes, helped myself to some hot chocolate, ate some leftover pancakes and almonds, and then crawled into a spare bunk wrapping myself in wool blankets.

When I went back for a second cup of cocoa, I also filled my water bottle with hot water and stuck it between my feet under the covers. Then I read for the rest of the afternoon shivering in my bunk.

The huts are a safe haven in these mountains but the only source of heat in this one (besides our own bodies) was the cook stove in the kitchen which is only open to the croo. People hung out in the common room wearing down parkas, draped in sleeping bags and wool blankets.

The croo asked me, as my work exchange, to give a talk about thru-hiking to the other guests after dinner. I was happy to get off so easy. I ate my fill of leftover chicken pot pie with the croo in the kitchen. The room was warm. The meal was great. I got two servings, plus lentil soup and dessert, but there was no place to sit down and take the weight off my tender feet.

After the meal, I sat at a table in the dining room wrapped in my sleeping bag and brought out my map of the whole Appalachian Trail. Eight or ten guests gathered round and I showed them my guide book and talked about my gear. They asked questions but as the temperatures dropped both inside and out, most people seemed anxious to retire to the warmth of their bunks.

I asked a few locals about the miles I would cover the next day. I checked my trail guide to see what kind of accommodations I might find in town that night. There were no hostels, only hotels. That might be expensive on a Saturday night, but I was too tired to worry about that now.

Soon I was ready to retire myself. I used my best manners and asked the croo, if I might sleep in a spare bunk, since there were so many available, instead of on a table. They reluctantly agreed. The worst part was that my still damp clothes wouldn't be dry in the morning unless I put them on and slept in them. Uggg! And I'd finally gotten warm!

In the morning I listened carefully to the radio for the weather forecast. It would be clear and cold. Clouds would come in the evening and more rain was predicted for Sunday. Hiking the Whites this late in the year can be serious if you misjudge the weather. But that day the light turned green!

A Very Lucky Girl

When I woke up I could see my breath in the bunkroom. I carefully read the thermometer on the porch. It was thirty degrees outside. I had come down a waterfall on the trail the day before. In freezing temperatures that waterfall would be ice. I waited until it warmed to thirty-three before heading out. As the temperatures climbed, so did I.

It was clear with no rain. That was the green light I'd been hoping for to cross Franconia Ridge, two miles of exposed trail above treeline. Another hiker, John, who'd been staying at the hut, was going the same direction. He was "bagging the four's" and left early to summit Mount Galehead. I caught up with him later and we leapfrogged all morning. I realized I was passing him on the uphill climbs and he was passing me on the down, an indication that my strength and aerobic condition were excellent, but my knees were wearing out. It had been a challenging week for my body. My feet were sore. But I hoped to make it through the last of the White Mountains and sleep in a warm bed that night.

Mount Lafayette looked ominous, far away and high above at noon. I was searching for a place to eat that was in the sun and out of the wind. Nothing level fit that description, so I leaned against some boulders on a steep slope to snack. I longed to take the weight off my legs. They were tired and shaky. Most of the trails around there were nearly vertical.

John caught up with me there and stopped for a minute but expressed some concern that he wouldn't make it out before dark so he moved on. It got me wondering if he knew something that I should know. I consulted my trail guide, calculated the hours of daylight and the miles ahead and thought I could make it. After a few almonds, cheese and a snack bar, I started hiking again and kept up a good pace.

I pushed on and was soon charging up Lafayette's frosty north flank. Ice crystals clung to every little spruce tree and each cairn I passed. Then I was climbing up above treeline. Almost at the top I came upon three women day-hikers having lunch and I stopped to chat. One waved a banana at me as she talked. I warned her not to wave food in front of a thru-hiker and she gave me the banana. Real food! She even offered to pack the peel out for me.

John was about forty yards ahead as we came to the top of Mount Lafayette (5,200 feet) where I stopped to take some pictures. Climbing to the summit there were dozens of other hikers and I lost sight of John. I followed the ridge for the next two miles and must have seen a hundred people. There were teens, grandparents, everyone and their dog was on the ridge. It was like a party, everyone smiling and laughing. Where did all these people come from? I heard a lot of French spoken, people from nearby Quebec perhaps. There were people from Boston and "the Cape". Others came from Maine and there were even some locals. It was a bright, sunny day and the views were spectacular from the now snowy peaks around Mount Washington to the colorful forest of Franconia Notch far below us.

I saw a picturesque lodge on a shelf just below the ridgeline and concluded that must be Greenleaf Hut though there were no green leaves around. I met a group of women who were backpacking to Greenleaf, but most people seemed to be on day hikes. I thought there must be a lot of trails to the ridge that were shorter and easier than the way I'd come. I saw Lindsey, from Pinkham Notch, hiking with her boyfriend. We stopped to chat for a few minutes before moving on in opposite directions.

I enjoyed people watching; it was like going to a circus, until I realized I was losing precious time. There were streams of hikers coming from the other direction. I had to step aside to let them pass. I started becoming less courteous in order to make it down before dark. A group of young teens came by and I stepped in behind them and barreled through.

At the end of the ridge I turned to descend through the trees and realized the crowds were taking another trail. Very few were staying on the AT. I swept past Mount Liberty and came by Liberty Spring campsite which was very full. That's when it occurred to me. It's a beautiful Saturday, peak leaf peeking season in the Whites, and if it's this crowded up here, imagine how crowded it will be in town tonight. The rooms in nearby hotels are probably booked solid. If I can find a room it will certainly be very expensive and there are no hostels in the area.

I tried to think of the best case scenario. If I could find a ride from the trailhead to the Highlands Center, that would be ideal. They have an inexpensive bunkhouse for hikers, and shared rooms that don't cost much more. I'd read about a trailhead shuttle that takes hikers to and from Pinkham Notch and the Highlands Center run by the AMC. I hoped to reach the trailhead in time to catch the last shuttle of the day.

I passed lots more people as I started to hear the road, welcome sounds after a week in the woods with more rain in the forecast. I came upon a couple with two dogs who were enjoying the water in the creek, a Newfoundland and a black Lab, both water loving breeds. The Lab was lying down in the water. I felt the same way, ready for a bath. I crossed the creek on rocks and soon came to the trailhead parking lot. There I found a kiosk with a schedule for the Intermountain Shuttle. The last shuttle had left an hour earlier.

I was downhearted, but only for an instant. Just then, I heard an engine start. Turning I saw Lindsey waving at me. She asked if I needed a ride. I told her I would love to get a ride to the Highlands Center. With a nod to her boyfriend, I was in! I had no idea that it was a forty-five minute drive.

Lindsey and her boyfriend were wonderful. She said she'd been given my note and mailed my long johns to Hanover. They told tales of working for the AMC as hut croo and remembered other thru-hikers they'd met. They obviously loved the White Mountains.

The drive from Franconia Ridge through Crawford Notch was stunning. Cliffs 3,000 feet high soared above us as a river rushed alongside. In the last light of day, the autumn leaves shimmered their red, gold and green. I could see why all of humanity was outside that day.

It was near dark and starting to rain when we arrived at the Highland Center, a beautiful modern lodge with an aura of rustic elegance, a hiker's haven. Lindsey and her beau walked me inside to say hello to friends and introduced me to the staff at the front desk. I gave them a hug and thanked them for the ride. Before I was properly checked-in the woman at the counter gave me a meal card so I wouldn't miss dinner. I left my pack behind the counter, smoothed down my hair and walked into the crowded dining room.

They serve family style and I was seated with two older couples. One fellow wore a name badge that said "Warren, AMC Ambassador". He explained that he'd been a volunteer naturalist and information officer in the huts for about seventy years and now worked here at the Highlands Center. He and his wife had celebrated sixty-five years of marriage at this lodge two years before.

The other couple lived near Hanover, New Hampshire and offered to host me when I got there. They were great dinner companions. I ate as much as the four of them put together. Now all I needed was a shower, a bed and maybe a laundry.

When I went back to the front desk to get checked-in, I was told the bunkhouse was full. So I asked for a shared room, but the only one left had two men in it and they had a policy about not mixing genders. I told them I had no car, no tent, and now it was dark and raining outside. I asked for suggestions.

Josh, a friend of Lindsey's who worked behind the counter, had an idea. Many of their summer staff had gone back to college. He was sure there was an empty room in the staff dorm. They went to the linen closet and got a set of flannel sheets, a pillow, a towel and a comforter and Josh escorted me to a vacant room in the staff housing complex next door. I threw down my pack and linens on the bunk and then Josh showed me the way to the women's bathroom and computer room. He said if I stayed another night they'd put me in the lodge proper, but for one night, I had access to email.

I made my bed and then went for a long, hot shower. I was really tired and wanted so much to get horizontal, but I needed to wash my clothes so they could dry overnight. I thought I'd have to wash them in the sink but as I was getting out of the shower, another woman on staff showed me the laundry room. What luck! But I didn't have the right change. All I needed were two quarters so I knocked on a door where I heard several voices. When I asked for quarters, a man fished them out of his pocket refusing my offer of five dimes. "I hate change", he said. So I got my clothes started.

Back in my room I emptied my pack. My poncho was soaked, my pack was wet. Everything was soggy. I strung my bear line back and forth between the posts of the bunk bed and the curtain rod above the window, turned on the heat and strung it all up to dry. Laying down on the bunk I was too tired to write. I kept looking at my watch struggling to stay awake for another half hour. When my clothes were done I hung them up, too.

At last I climbed in between flannel sheets under a down comforter. Heaven. I put in ear plugs, though I probably didn't need them. I was exhausted. All the sounds of this waking life were already distant. I fell asleep like a leaf falling to the forest floor on a soft, thick cushion of mulch melting into the earth. My last thoughts before fading away... "I am a very lucky girl." I'd made it through the worst of the Whites. But mountains are just one kind of challenge and I was soon to find out about another.

Phone Home

I was up before dawn. The staff was either already at work preparing breakfast in the lodge or sleeping. I was sore and my feet tender but another hot shower loosened my stiff muscles and warmed my achy body. It felt great to be warm and washed and dressed in clean, dry clothes. Sitting down at the computer desk I wrote a long email letter to the folks back home about my adventures in the Whites and all the incredible experiences I'd had with the President's Club, climbing Mount Washington, sleeping in the Dungeon, moving through the huts, all the people on Franconia Ridge, and the good folks here at the Highland Center.

When I was done writing, I began reading several emails sent by family and friends. Eventually I came to one sent by my sister. Sue wrote to say she'd found a lump in her breast and the doctor had said it was cancer. I wanted to call her immediately but it was too early so I went down to the dining hall.

Breakfast was served buffet style. I was eating alone at the end of a long table. Across the aisle from me sat a middle-aged couple with two older women. The man's voice was deep and clear. It kept wafting across the aisle cutting through the chatter around the room. They were talking about thru-hiking. Their friend's son was thru-hiking but he was much farther south. While I ate, I was studying my thru-hikers handbook and he noticed it. When I cleared my table, their party was doing the same. He and his wife started chatting with me. They had a hard time believing I was a thru-hiker. "You look too fresh," they said.

I responded, "Besides the good food, they have showers, a laundry and soft cushy beds here."

We ended up standing by the front desk together and the fellow generously offered to pay my bill for the next night. He was a corporate executive and he and his wife had brought his mom and aunt up for the weekend.

After breakfast I climbed the stairs looking for a book in the library. I found an older woman in a rocker in front of a window at the top of the lodge. She had a book in her hand, but she wasn't reading. I came up beside her and said she had the best view in the house. As it turned out she was the man's mother, a delightful woman. She and her sister used to hike the White Mountains in tennis shoes. She made me feel like a wimp.

Exploring further I found a phone in the basement next to the vending machines and pool table. I tried to call my sister but didn't get an answer, so I called my folks. Mom said they'd found a large mass and wanted to start Sue on chemo to reduce the size before surgery. I asked how Sue was holding up. My sister is usually stoic, putting on a happy face, but mom said when she told them, she couldn't help but cry a little.

I tried to call Sue again, but could only leave a message, sending her strength and prayers.

Sue's a few years older than I. She's a polished professional woman, well dressed and charming. She was one of the most popular girls in school.

In comparison, I was awkward, a sloppy dresser and enjoyed playing outside and getting dirty. I was always known as Sue's little sister.

It wasn't until I moved to Washington State where I didn't know anyone that I felt like I'd become my own person. Since then, even though we don't see much of each other, we have come to love each other and respect our differences. She admired me for hiking the trail. She told me I was doing something really brave and daring, though it felt totally natural to me. I'm sure she'd prefer a week at a spa resort or vacation at the beach with her family.

I called my best friend, Kelly, in Seattle and tried to leave a message but fell apart on the phone.

It was stormy outside and I was glad to be inside and get a break from the weather. Through the staff, I was able to hook up with a couple who would give hikers a ride back to the trail the next morning. They were even willing to stop by a grocer on the way so we could stock-up on supplies. With those logistics covered, all I could think about was Sue.

How devastating this must be for her. She seemed to be the woman who has everything. She's smart, competent and beautiful with a wonderful husband, two gorgeous daughters and grandkids. She and her husband have a big house in a nice neighborhood. They have impressive jobs with fat paychecks. She's well loved and respected. But what good is all of that if you don't have your health?

Mom said Sue had another doctor's appointment in a few days and her daughters were coming to hold her hand. Mom would take care of her great grand kids. This is the first time cancer has appeared in our extended family, so it's quite a shock. The more I thought about it throughout the day, the more I cried.

I started thinking I should be there, too. If I kept hiking it would take me six more weeks to finish. By then it would be November. I could spend some time with her, cook for her, help take care of her.

Later in the day they checked me into a "shared room" which I had to myself. I left my pack in the corner but felt shut in. About an hour before dinner I knew I'd be dining family style, so I tried to compose myself by going out for a walk. It was almost dark, spitting rain and gusting wind, but the cold air felt refreshing after a day inside. I went to the gallery next door with a showing of stunning black and white photos of the White Mountains, early settlers and the train station that used to occupy this valley. I was able to pull myself together and returned to the lodge prepared to be sociable.

As I entered the dining room the family that I'd met at breakfast waved me over to sit with them. Not long into the conversation, Steve told me of three women he'd met hiking that day who had asked him to take their picture. They said they usually had another woman hiking with them, but Kim couldn't make it. They wanted to spell out her name, each taking the shape of a letter. He said one of the women started to cry and he thought that Kim might be seriously ill.

He told me his aunt, who was sitting across the table from him, was a breast cancer survivor and that his sister had died of cancer. I noticed his mother started to cry. I told them I'd just heard that day that my sister had breast cancer. They were very kind and urged me to finish my hike and then spend whatever quality time I could with her. He said it was fate that we crossed paths that day.

His sister had lung cancer and the doctors had given her six months to live, but she stretched that to three years. Her children got three more years with her. They got three more camping trips, even if they just hiked a mile from the road.

He emphasized quality time. It didn't even occur to me that Sue could die. I just thought she'd be really sick for a while or missing a breast, lose her hair, but I hadn't really thought through the significance of this news. Tears crept into my eyes a few times at the table.

The conversation went to other topics. Steve and Fran have two daughters. One's name is Bekah and she's a naturalist. I told them I worked as a naturalist and have a niece named Bekah who lived in Granby, Colorado. Fran has a family home on nearby Grand Lake. I told them I was there for July 4th once and saw the fireworks over the lake. They have family that went to the University of North Carolina. My dad was a faculty member there. Now my sister and her husband worked for the University. They were thrilled with all these commonalities.

After dinner I checked the weather. I'd need at least three clear days to get out of the Whites but won't get them until three days from now. It would be expensive to stay here for three more days. I tried again to call Sue but got no answer.

At 4:00 a.m. I woke up thinking about Sue, thinking about the weather, thinking about my route. Then I remembered an email I'd received from my friend Al. He'd said he had a college buddy, Pat, who lived near here in North Woodstock and if I needed a place to stay, I should call him. But I didn't have a pen at the time, and didn't think I'd need it, so hadn't written the number down. I thought I might be able to sneak back over to the staff dorm and get on the computer to retrieve the number. So I got up and took a hot shower, my last for a few days. As the water poured over my head, I let the tears flow with it.

I packed and then crept quietly into the staff dorm but someone else was using the computer. So I came back over to the lodge. It was still dark and a while before breakfast, so I sat by a single lamp in the corner of the lounge and read a magazine about the Appalachian Trail.

As the dim light of morning eased in through the windows the lodge began to come to life. Smells of breakfast wafted from the kitchen and staff occupied the front desk. Steve came downstairs and greeted me, but he was in "transition mode" getting ready to catch a plane to his next corporate event. He gave me a hug and I thanked him for his kindness.

His family came down and we all went in for breakfast together. They were a bit rushed, but he took out his camera and took a couple of pictures of me over the breakfast table. I asked him to email the photo to my sister and gave him her address. I didn't know when I'd see a computer again. I posed smiling, holding a mug of hot cocoa. But when I saw the photo later it showed my wind burned cheeks and tousled hair. At least I had a smile.

I caught a ride to the trailhead with a Canadian couple. We stopped at a store to buy trail food but they didn't have much to offer. I was used to making do so I bought raisins, nuts and peanut butter crackers and we were off.

I still had not talked to Sue and felt conflicted about getting back on the trail. I was also a bit concerned about the weather. The driver let us out at the Flume visitor center near the same trailhead I'd left two days before. There was a pay phone outside. I tried calling Al to get Pat's phone number. I wasn't able to reach him so I left a message. My voice broke when I mentioned my sister's cancer.

Then I met a couple from Durham, North Carolina. They offered me a ride into North Woodstock. From a phone booth in town I called again and this time I got Al. I asked him to call his friend Pat and let him know I'd be at a diner across the street.

As I crossed the street two guys parked their cars in front of the diner. As they got out, one of them pointed at me and asked, "Are you a thru-hiker?"

"Yes."

"Let me buy you breakfast."

I always appreciate a hot meal so I gratefully accepted. Charley and Callum were hilarious. They were in their twenty's. Charley had hiked the AT when he was eighteen. They were good company and lifted my spirits and I got another good meal of real food.

After breakfast I went back to the phone booth across the street. Al had not been able to reach his friend, Pat. He wasn't at work or at home. But he had emailed his buddies from the area and gave me the phone numbers of a half dozen other friends I could call along the trail between New Hampshire and New York. It warmed my heart to feel Al's long arms of support wrap around me from 3,000 miles away. I thanked him and told him I'd go to the coffee shop and try calling Pat one more time a little later.

At the coffee shop, I found a computer and was able to check my email. There it was, an email from Sue. It said, "No more tears."

She had started to do research which made me feel better. It was good to know she was engaged in her own healing. She urged me to get back on the trail and finish what I'd started. She said her treatments would take months and she would welcome my help when I was done with my hike. With that assurance I shouldered my pack and headed out the door. A woman came out right behind me and offered me a ride back to the trail. I couldn't believe my string of good luck.

I hiked in just three miles to the last of the huts at Lonesome Lake. When I arrived, Lynn gave me a chore to clean the bunkroom thoroughly for winter. I spent a couple of hours on it until it was too dark to see. It was more than she'd expected but it felt good to work for my stay after getting what I considered a "free pass" through the other huts.

It was a croo member's birthday and friends had packed in a canoe! After dinner they pulled out a fiddle and a flute, an odd combination but the music was merry. I flipped the pages of the hut log back several months and found entries from Firefly, Messenger, Lug and Zama and my sister, Tortoise. I slept on the table though they offered me a bunk. The hut was warm but the bunkhouses were not. It felt good to be back on the trail and now I was motivated to finish without delay.

Friend or Foe?

I left Lonesome Lake and climbed over Mount Kinsman and down the steep south side. Mount Wolf doesn't rise above treeline so it was hard to tell when I'd reached the summit. All afternoon the trail went up and down, up and down. It was thirteen miles to Highway 112 and I told myself if I got there and still had good energy, I'd climb the 2,000 feet to the next shelter and be in good position to climb Mount Moosilauke first thing in the morning.

At least that was the plan. But I didn't move well all day. I was tripping and slipping and generally getting more cranky as I went along. When I was crossing Eliza Brook at about the half way point, stepping from stone to stone, one rock rolled beneath my foot. I ended up going down on one knee in the stream. Then in slow motion, pushed by the current, I had to put the other knee down before I could regain my balance. I was wet up to my waist. It was too cold to stop by the stream for lunch as I'd planned. I had to keep going in order to dry out.

Later in the day I was feeling achy and wondered if I was coming down with something. I got a stone bruise on one foot and though I'd worn ace bandages on both knees, by late afternoon my ankles were hurting. I was tired. So, when I got to the road, I walked a half mile to a concession stand and used the phone to call one of Al's friends who lived nearby.

Liz came right down to get me. As it turned out, she'd never met Al, but she'd heard of him through her husband's cousin Alfred who lived in Nova Scotia. Still she seemed thrilled to have company. She and Jim have a sturdy lodge-like house. I got a guest room with flannel sheets on a big log bed. The first thing she did was run a bubble bath for me in their huge Jacuzzi tub.

I had a nice long soak that washed all my aches and pains away. The smell of cookies baking lured me from the tub. Following my nose I went downstairs and got to know Liz while she heated up some leftovers. She's a gourmet cook and caterer so her leftovers were fabulous. Liz told me she went to cooking school in New York City and then came back here to try to apply her trade. It's very rural but there is a big company in town and she started taking over baskets of sandwiches, chips and cookies at lunchtime to sell to the staff. The upper management found out about it and asked her to meet with them upstairs. She thought she was in big trouble but as it turned out, they wanted her to cater their lunches, too. It kept her plenty busy.

She told me when she comes from the store with her many bags of groceries she has to back the car right up to the front door to unload. If she parked at the garage and walked the bags into the house, before she could get back for a second load, the local bears would be in her backseat helping themselves.

Jim came home from work, greeted me and plopped down in his recliner. His Chocolate Lab, Daisy, jumped into his lap and everyone was happy. We watched the news. I was especially interested in the weather. Soon dinner was on the table and we sat down to eat. We had warm chocolate chip cookies for dessert.

They invited me to use their internet and long distance phone service. I called my folks for an update on Sue. They reported she was in good hands and had lots of support. They also said my brother was moving from Port Townsend, Washington back to North Carolina and was staying with them until he could find a house nearby.

When I checked my emails I found one from Jeff, the gardener I'd met on Mount Washington the week before. He said he'd come down for a business meeting and was staying at his sister's house nearby. He asked if I wanted to get together for a walk. The weather on the summits was still nasty so I called and we planned to get together the next afternoon. He said he'd already gone to the trailhead and left me a bag of homegrown tomatoes hanging from a tree in case he missed me.

Liz and Jim were worried that Jeff would turn out to be a serial killer and asked what I knew about him. I told them all I knew, which didn't take long, and gave them his email address and phone number. I told them if I didn't come back, to pass the information on to the authorities, which didn't make them feel any better. He seemed like a nice enough fellow to me, an organic gardener, for goodness sake.

The next day Liz and Jim were gone when Jeff arrived so they didn't get to meet him. I asked his intentions before we left the house. He said he hoped we'd at least be friends. That seemed okay though I thought geography would probably intervene.

We went to the trailhead and retrieved the bag of garden tomatoes and then walked a short ways to a waterfall. I wanted to give my knees and ankles a break so we didn't go far. We talked about family and friends. He's a professional mediator but is with a woman who apparently loves conflict. He'd been thinking about leaving her. Though he seemed like a kind man and I enjoyed his company, the more I heard about his relationship with her, the less I wanted to become involved. I'd met so many good people while hiking alone and had grown used to making those connections and then letting them go. He took me back to the house and gave me some garden produce for Liz. Then he drove back home to Portland, Maine.

We had pizza for dinner. Liz had been babysitting her three year old grandson and was too tired to cook. That was fine with us. We sat around the living room talking for awhile and then got ready for bed. The phone rang and I heard Jim say, "North Carolina?"

It was Sue. She'd been to the doctors with her husband and daughters and gave me the latest news. The biopsy they'd performed on her lymph nodes came back negative, good news. But they wanted to run a bunch more tests and start her on chemo in two weeks. She seemed upbeat and talkative.

Her daughters had come up with a few reasons why her cancer was a bad idea. Emily said she didn't look good in pink. Bekah said she's pregnant and can't run triathlons. Sue said she'd picked out three wigs, one of each color. So they're supporting each other with their usual good humor. What a great family.

Bright and early the next morning, Liz packed up some chocolate chip cookies for me as I said goodbye. She thought she'd start taking in more thru-hikers. I warned her that they'd eat her out of house and home. I hopped in the truck with Jim and Daisy who gave me a lift to the trailhead and wished me luck.

Moosilauke

I'd been frustrated in the Whites. I'd had to wait for good weather to cross the peaks so had to take two zeroes and two nearoes (nearly zero miles in a day), but I knew my knees appreciated the rest. The kindness and generosity of the people I'd met more than made up for the brutal terrain.

At 4,802 feet in elevation Mount Moosilauke was the last of the 4's I'd cross in New Hampshire. From the trailhead, it was a steep climb but I was fueled with a good rest, terrific food and really wonderful hospitality. My mom had called that morning just before I left and talked to Jim for a good five minutes. She wanted to thank my hosts personally for taking care of me. Finally, she asked to speak to me to make sure I'd spoken to Sue and then recapped everything Sue had said. As soon as I got off the phone, we were on our way. It was good to feel included though I was far from my family.

It was cold but I didn't feel it as I climbed 2,500 feet toward the summit. A cloud sat on the top and a light wind blew. Moisture collected on my hair and frosted up. No white blazes were visible. Everything looked white. As I reached the top there was a sign where two trails intersected, but it was covered in four inches of ice and impossible to read. I had to knock the ice off with my walking stick in order to determine my direction. I was getting chilled in the cold wind, so I didn't want to linger, but I made sure I was going the right way before I proceeded.

On the far side of the summit, I met a hiker coming from the other direction who smiled when he saw me.

"You look frosty," he said smiling as we passed.

I looked up and saw ice crystals dangling from my bangs. National Geographic images of polar explorers came to mind. I soon thawed out as I reached the cover of the trees and began to descend. The weather grew mild and the trail did, too. Half way down the mountain I was able to walk normally. It was a weird sensation. I could actually put twenty steps together that didn't involve dancing around mud holes or climbing up or down a rock face! I could walk for hours without using my hands... much. And my mileage was increasing rapidly!

I stopped for lunch on a bed of golden leaves in the sun. Studying my trail guide I became delusional. I thought, wouldn't it be nice to get to the Hexacuba Shelter, a geodesic dome, for the night? But I would have to hike a twenty mile day and there wasn't enough daylight to do that. Still, I hiked at a good clip for a while and loved the trail.

I got to a road crossing and met a man who asked if I was thru-hiking the Appalachian Trail. I heard him say what I used to say myself, and have heard so many times from others.

"I've always wanted to do that."

But I could tell he never would. I was struck that I was finally doing it. I would've hated for that to be me in a few years knowing that I'd waited too long.

I put in eighteen miles, the best mileage since I'd left Maine, and settled into the Ore Hill Shelter by myself. I hoped to be able to log seventeen or eighteen miles in the next two days so I could get into Hanover on Saturday. If I could get there before noon, I could get my packages, but that seemed too much to ask. It was dark by 6:00 p.m. now and cold, too. I tucked into my bag early and fell into a satisfying sleep.

After a nineteen mile day, I got no sleep at the Trapper John Shelter. The full moon brought out all the night life. Owls called and coyotes howled and in the shelter the pitter patter of little feet kept me up all night. A squirrel jumped onto my food bag and got it swinging. I aimed my light at it and it dropped off. I took down the food bag to use as a pillow, but the mice bothered me so much I hung it back up, closer to me this time.

This shelter must have been a cabin at one time. The remains of a fireplace stood out front and rows of rocks indicated a foundation. I wished I'd had more of an inclination to build a fire when I'd arrived. It would have made this place more cheery. But it was getting dark, I was near a road, and I didn't want to attract attention.

I recalled the day before. I went over some small mountains. Mount Cube was a huge granite dome with shoulders of crystals. I picked up a small one and saved it. There were views of miles and miles of rolling, tree covered hills. Hills!

On my way down, I was worrying about my packages at the Post Office in Hanover. I'd never make it there before they closed on Saturday. When I came across some hikers with a cell phone I asked if I could make a call. The post office number was in my trail guide. But we got no reception. We were in a valley. Later that day I had just passed the Fire Warden's Cabin on a summit when I came upon another couple with two Great Danes. They had a cell phone I could borrow and this time I was able to reach the post office. The clerk said she could leave the packages in the lobby for me. They have a display about the AT there and my packages would be under that table. I was much relieved and thanked the hikers for the use of their phone.

Late in the day, I was crossing a field with a few late season wildflowers hanging on. I started singing "Heaven, I'm in heaven." When I saw a sign that said "free water" pointing across the road, I paused. I had last filled my bottles at a questionable source so I was happy for the opportunity to get a refill with something better.

I walked up to a large farmhouse and found a man whacking down weeds by an old stone wall. I said hello, and he greeted me most pleasantly, saying his name was Bob. I asked to fill my water bottles and he shook my hand, but wouldn't let it go. He brought me into the house and introduced his wife, Francis, who was reading on the couch.

She nodded hello and went back to her book. Apparently, this was not an unusual occurrence at their house.

He poured me some orange juice, served crackers and cheese and then took down a book where he kept records of all the thru-hikers that stopped by. He informed me that a couple of SOBOs were just a few hours ahead of me, Laluz and Duct Tape. I remembered meeting them in the Hundred Mile Wilderness, but I thought his trail name was Butterfly. He thought they were the last of the thru-hikers this season, but I guess that would be me.

I looked around the comfortable kitchen and saw a picture of the Dalai Lama on a bookshelf. I asked if he was Buddhist and he said, "In a past life." He said his son worked for the Dalai Lama. "Now that would look good on a resume," I thought.

Small birds flitted to a shrub outside the window and his eyes lit up. "Tufted titmouse," he said with delight and reached for another book where he kept track of the birds that stopped by. Hikers were just another species migrating through.

I filled my water bottles at the sink and before I left and I asked to use the phone. I called ahead to Hanover where Win and Marilyn had offered to host me. They'd been on one of my hiking tours in Olympic National Park the previous summer and urged me to call when I got to town. Win seemed pleased to hear from me and eager to offer their home as a hostel. I thanked Bob for his water, juice and crackers and headed back out to the trail.

It had been a beautiful day and I was able to make good time. The terrain grew gentler, yet there were still some swampy areas and smooth rock faces to negotiate. The views were of colorful forests, scarlet, yellow, orange and green over rolling hills. I was excited. I could actually walk again, not just climb and scramble and hop and slide.

I had worn boots when I started the trail in March knowing I'd be hiking through snow in the Southern Appalachians. But though my boots were well worn in, once I started hiking over fifteen miles a day, which was in the first week on the trail, I started getting blisters, blisters on top of blisters, on top of blisters. When one blister got infected, I pitched the boots.

When I went back to the trail after my niece's wedding, I started wearing low cut hiking shoes. They came recommended highly by Feather. From day one, they felt great. I never got a single blister. I'd worn them for 1,420 miles from Harper's Ferry, West Virginia to Stormville, New York. I'd worn them a couple hundred more miles leading hikes in Olympic National Park and the Columbia River Gorge. I'd worn them for 440 more miles from Maine through rugged New Hampshire. I figured they'd logged at least 2,000 miles and they were starting to break down. If I kept wearing broken down shoes, I'd have broken down feet. Thankfully, I had new shoes mailed to me in Hanover.

As I walked, I wrote another song. This one is called Phone Home.

Torn between the trail and the folks back home,
They want you to finish and they want you to phone.
So give them a call from wherever you may roam,
When you're torn between the trail and the folks back home.
Bekah's getting married to her boyfriend, Nate,
They want you to come so don't be late,
Just put it on your calendar and hold the date,
'Cause Bekah's getting married to her boyfriend.

Emily and David had a baby boy.
He's a tiny little fella, looks just like a toy,
They brought the whole family a whole lot of joy,
When Emily and David had a baby...

Your brother's moving home again from way out west.
He's staying with us, now he's our house guest.
He's working on his own place and doing his best.
'Cause your brother's moved home from way out west.

Your sister Sue found a lump in her breast.
She's going to the doctor to get some tests.
We're praying real hard and we're hoping for the best,
'Cause your sister Sue found a lump in her breast.

Later I added this verse.

You're finishing the trail and you're heading home.
Your feet are happy, no more to roam.
They're throwing you a party, they told you on the phone,
'Cause you're finishing the trail and you're heading home.

Whites to Greens

I arrived in Hanover on a warm and sunny afternoon to the cheering of crowds. They were at a soccer game at Dartmouth College, but it was still nice to hear. I felt like cheering. As I came out of the woods within sight of the game, I sat down on a log and removed the ace bandages I'd worn on both knees through most of the White Mountains. But now I was leaving the rugged White Mountains of New Hampshire and entering the verdant rolling hills of Vermont. And I certainly wouldn't need the extra support as I strolled through town.

I found a phone at the nearby food co-op and called Win and Marilyn Hunter. As I waited for them to arrive, I enjoyed the hustle and bustle of people at the market, buying flowers, produce and wonderful smelling baked goods. It was a beautiful fall day. Everyone seemed in good spirits which certainly applied to me. Arriving in Hanover was like crossing the finish line after a marathon of getting through the White Mountains. I could relax and enjoy a day of rest.

The Hunters arrived and took me to the retirement community where they lived and showed me around. There was a library that was open twenty-four hours a day. There were two restaurants and a coffee shop. One restaurant was staffed by high school students working as interns in a job training program. They had a fitness center with yoga and Pilates classes, a movie theatre and a community garden out back. They were active seniors and frequently took the ski bus for a day in the mountains. As we neared their apartment, they pointed out the laundry and recycling center across the hall.

They had a nice two bedroom apartment. One bedroom was used as an office. They'd brought in a rollaway bed for me which was surprisingly comfortable. They'd picked up my packages at the post office earlier that day. I was especially grateful as it was Columbus Day weekend and the post office would be closed on Monday. Among the care packages were my new shoes! I tore open the box and put one new shoe on. Then I rushed out on their deck to take a picture of my feet propped up on the rail wearing one old shoe and one new shoe for contrast. I told them the old shoes should go across the hall into the box of hazardous waste. They looked terrible and smelled worse.

I got a hot shower and weighed myself on the bathroom scales, 119.5. Then I ate and ate and ate Win's good stir fry dinner. The salmon, asparagus and spinach were worth their weight in gold. After dinner they showed me some beautiful images of our hiking tour in Olympic National Park. Win had a nice camera and a good eye. He really captured Lake Crescent which is my favorite place on earth. Win and Marilyn had maps of the White Mountains on their wall and reminisced about all the hikes and ski vacations they'd taken there. They had hiked the Himalayas, too. We swapped stories until we couldn't keep our eyes open which was about 9:00.

In the morning I went through my care packages. Kelly had sent another great box full of Seattle's best, Tim's Chips, gourmet chocolate bars and Cougar Mountain Cookies which I shared with my hosts. Zama had sent a package of good trail food, organic oatmeal with dried blueberries, cranberries and nuts, homemade cookies, multi-grain crackers and peanut butter. Mom and Dad sent one of the packages I'd boxed up myself, but for some odd reason they'd removed the vitamins and chai tea mix. That was okay. I had plenty of supplies and could send some ahead to Harper's Ferry.

One package that hadn't come was the long-johns Lindsey mailed from Pinkham Notch. I asked Marilyn if she could check the post office for me next week and bump them ahead to Manchester Center, Vermont. There was rain and snow in the forecast in the next week. I thought I'd end up buying a new pair. But Marilyn loaned me a pair of hers. I was living on generosity and kindness.

We went for a walk through town right on the Appalachian Trail which was indicated in markers lodged in the sidewalk. I was able to get fuel, batteries and a new journal. It was a glorious fall day and I had a nagging feeling that I should be hiking. But they offered such fine hospitality and my body wanted a rest. I had a long phone conversation with my parents and got caught up on emails.

That night Win and Marilyn went out to a dinner party, but before they left they introduced me to the Brownings, another couple who lived in their complex who took me to dinner in the dining room. We filled our plates at an elegant All-You-Can-Eat buffet and sat at a table under a chandelier. Of course, I went back for seconds.

They were from Maine and had hiked many places I'd just seen. After dinner I went back to the apartment to read. Getting ready for bed I weighed myself again, 125 pounds. I smiled.

That night I didn't sleep well. I awoke at 4:30 thinking about all I needed to do to get back on the trail. I checked the weather, emails, tried to clip my bangs and sorted through my care packages. I packed as much as I could, put together a box to mail ahead and still had some goodies left as a thank you gift for my hosts who'd been so good to me.

Win took me to the trail, dropping me off in the middle of town at the Hanover Inn. He pointed out the oldest building at Dartmouth just across the green, a classic old hall painted white against a clear blue sky. It was another bright, crisp autumn day as I started toward the Connecticut River and crossed the bridge. Now, I was in Vermont!

I walked a mile and entered Norwich, Vermont, a quintessential New England town. All the houses looked at least a century old. A church steeple stood at the end of the village green hovering above a canopy of golden leaves.

The trail goes right down the main street and then turns on Elm. I missed the turn, but spotted the post office because there were two blue mail bins out in front of a two hundred year old saltbox building. I stopped and scribbled a post card to Kelly and mailed it. Then I saw the hardware store that Win and Marilyn had told me about, Dan and Witts.

I made up an excuse to go in and looked around. It seemed like an ordinary small town hardware store to me. So I sheepishly asked the manager for a tour. He showed me the "secret entry" beside the meat cooler, that lead to the extensive back room with garden tools and hardware and just about everything you can imagine. It was like going into Narnia through the wardrobe. He said there was an upstairs, too, but I got the idea. I loved this whole town, so quaint and down to earth.

He steered me back toward Elm Street and I followed the white blazes past lovely homes where deer nibbled the fallen fruit from old orchards. The trail led up a hill and into the woods.

The landscape was beautiful, rolling hills, dry leaves, fields, farms and woodlands. It was late morning when I passed Podunk Road and headed into West Hartford, another tiny town. I saw a man raking leaves in front of an old home with a plaque that said it was a 150 year old school house. When he saw me he stopped raking and offered me water from the outdoor spigot. I thanked him and filled up my water bottles. He went into the house and came out with an apple and a banana. Yes, please, and thank you. I ate the banana as we talked. He took the peeling inside and came out with two chocolate bars and asked if I'd like a glass of tea. Those rockers on the south facing porch sure felt nice, but I had to make some miles. I thanked the man and moved on.

I walked two doors down and saw a man with a pack coming from the backyard. Duct Tape, another thru-hiker, had just been offered the same kind of generosity at the neighbors. I realized I'd met him in the Hundred Mile Wilderness, but at that time he was hiking with his fiancé and his trail name was Butterfly. As we walked on together he explained that she didn't like his snoring at night so she made him wear duct tape over his mouth, thus the name change. He went on to say that they had split up back in Hanover. But he wanted to finish the trail so now he was hiking solo. I told him he didn't have to keep the name Duct Tape if he didn't want to.

We stopped for lunch at 3:00. His enormous pack slid from his shoulders with a thud. It seemed packed solid. As I settled down in a thick layer of leaves and pulled out my lunch fixings, so did he. I smeared peanut butter on crackers and watched while he made a Dagwood style sandwich with garlic, ginger, cucumber, tomatoes, meats, cheeses, lettuce, onions, peppers and mustard on a thick bagel. My lunch was just about done by the time he'd finished constructing his masterpiece.

I checked my trail guide to see how far I was from the Cloudland Shelter where I planned to spend the night. I complained that it was a half mile off the trail. Duct Tape told me about a man he'd met hiking through the Whites who lived right on the trail not far ahead and had invited Duct Tape to sleep in his barn. He thought I'd be welcome there, too. The place was twenty miles from where I'd started. When Duct Tape began to build a second sandwich I checked my watch and decided to push on. It was 3:30 and I wanted to make seven more miles before dark. He said he was comfortable walking at night. I was not. I'd seen several turns on the trail I'm sure I would've missed in the dark. Heck, didn't I miss the turn on Elm Street that very morning in broad daylight?

My Bride Suggests...

The terrain was gentle so I made good time. At dusk I came out on a paved road, but didn't see a barn. So I walked in search of a light in one of the nearby houses. I knocked at the door of a stately home. Judy greeted me and led me into the kitchen where she was cooking dinner. Between her and her husband, Stu, they figured out where I'd intended to go. They knew Michael Ambrose but I'd passed the road to his house a mile back. By now it was dark so Stu drove me around to a dirt road with a modest home and a barn. I remembered having an intuitive feeling when I'd crossed that road. I'd ignored it. Now here I was back again.

The family was just finishing their dinner. I introduced myself to Michael and Nancy, their two kids, and the dog. Michael was confused. He remembered meeting a man and woman on Franconia Ridge and inviting them to sleep in his barn, but I wasn't either of them. I explained that if he wasn't here yet, Duct Tape, aka: Butterfly, would be coming along any minute now and that his girlfriend would not.

Michael walked me over to the barn and started up the stairs into the loft where a light had been left on. It was a bare bulb hanging from a cord near an open window. From the stairs we could hear buzzing and as we peered into the loft we found a swarm of bees circling the light. It was chilling down and they were seeking warmth. Michael stared at the swarm for a minute in silence.

I offered to sleep at the other end of the loft, but Michael said the bees were seeking the warmest spot. When we turned out the light, the warmest spot would be me. I said I could sleep with the light on. I found a broom and began to clear a spot to sleep. Michael went back to the house. In a few minutes I heard an engine start up and a van pulled in next to the barn. Michael stepped out and came into the barn.

"My bride suggests that you sleep in our VW Camper."

I was delighted. I'd always wondered how these campers worked. Michael showed me how to raise the roof and I threw my pack inside. Then he went back into the house. Just as I laid my sleeping bag out he returned.

"My bride suggests you come in for some leftover soup from dinner." I gladly accepted. I was really beginning to like his "bride". As I followed him into the kitchen I asked how long they'd been married.

"Twelve years," he said. "I used to call her my ex-girlfriend but that just confused people."

She had gone upstairs to help the children with their homework. Michael dished up a bowl of soup for me and saved some for Duct Tape. He washed the dinner dishes while I ate at the kitchen counter.

I asked if he was a beekeeper. I could tell by the way he'd looked at that swarm in the barn. He gave me my first lesson in beekeeping and let me sample some honey comb. I stirred some honey into a mug of hot tea as we talked. He'd worked for Outward Bound and NOLS (National Outdoor Leadership School) and led river rafting trips before settling down to raise a family. He'd soon be working at the nearby ski resort. We settled into easy conversation until 9:30 when the house grew quiet and I said goodnight. As I climbed into the camper I put a sign in the window for Duct Tape but he never showed. I slept cozy and warm in the loft of the camper. No bees allowed.

In the morning I made oatmeal on my camp stove in the driveway. The dog started barking at me and Michael stuck his head out the front door to call him back inside. It was 6:00 a.m. I ate breakfast and packed my bag so I'd be ready to catch a ride. Michael offered me a cup of tea but I was more interested in getting back to the trail with a stop to re-supply if possible. I asked if I could take his picture by the van but he insisted on taking mine instead. It was the most unique shelter so far.

I caught a ride with Nancy, his bride, as she hustled the kids off to school on her way to work. She dropped me off at an old general store at the end of the road. It didn't have much in the way of trail food, but I got some juice and a banana. There I met Stu on his way to play tennis. He offered me a ride back to the trail. It was 8:00 and I had another twenty mile day ahead in order to reach Killington, Vermont.

I met a few others along the way, three women day hikers. Two had been trying to complete the Appalachian Trail for eighteen years in short segments. The third was a woman from Edmonds, Washington. I passed a NOBO thru-hiker. Katahdin would close for the winter in a week. He knew he wouldn't make it, but didn't seem to mind. I saw a couple of smiley faces like the ones Red B used to carve into the trail with his hiking stick. I wondered where he and his short legged wonder dog might be.

After a full day of ups and downs I was getting tired. I began to think about where I'd spend the night. As the afternoon wore on I figured I didn't mind the hiking, but sleeping out in the cold this time of year with the wind, rain or snow, was something I'd rather avoid. I had the number of a friend of Al's, but then I remembered Feather and Firefly telling me about staying at a hostel in Rutland run by a group called the Twelve Tribes. They had a farm outside of town, a health food restaurant in town and a hostel upstairs. They welcomed hikers who would work for their stay. So I set my sights on Rutland.

When I reached Kent Pond my ankles and knees were tired. I followed dirt roads and was grateful for the smooth surface. Cresting a hill I came upon some guys and a woman in the road tossing a Frisbee. They said they were part of the Green Mountain Trail Crew. I asked about the trail ahead. It seemed to do a big loop and come out on the other side of Kent Pond. I shook my head.

It was getting late as I approached the highway. I didn't want to stick my thumb out on a major road. Just then a car pulled up to the stop sign next to me. The driver rolled the window down and offered me a ride. He'd lived there thirty years, said he'd picked up hikers often and knew the way to the hostel. As we rode I got a view of the peaks I'd be crossing next. We passed the Long Trail Inn and he pointed out the trailhead across the street. A huge red sun was just setting over the hills.

He drove me into the bustling town and stopped right in front of the health food restaurant. He pointed out the hostel door and said I could get checked-in by any of the staff who clustered around tables outside.

Grateful and tired I was soon climbing a flight of stairs to a long hall. I was shown into an empty bunkroom with polished floors and woven rugs. My feet were sore. I got a long, hot shower, with lavender scented soap, put on my cleanest clothes and hobbled down to the restaurant for dinner.

I'd been told meals were free in exchange for a half day of work. It was all vegetarian and that night's special was pumpkin ravioli Alfredo. I was famished. I placed my order and wrote in my journal while I waited. Streams of people came in. The smell of good food filled the air with a warm, thick, seductive lure. The windows fogged up as darkness fell. When the food arrived I fell passionately in love with the steamed broccoli, carrots and squash. The pumpkin ravioli was rich and creamy. The fresh pressed cider was sweet and crisp. I was in ecstasy!

A lone woman hobbled in and I knew I had a roommate. She picked me out of the dinner crowd. She introduced herself as Lakota and left me to continue writing as she took another table. But I noticed she was outside on her cell phone during half of her dinner.

Later in our bunkroom she told me that she was hiking the Long Trail. After a week she had blown out her knee and had a cold. She planned to take a day of rest but still hoped to reach the one hundred mile mark. "What we do to our bodies," I thought. I had planned to do some work for stay after dinner but my feet ached and demanded to be propped up so I promised to work the next day.

First thing in the morning, a Twelve Tribe member gave me the most recent weather forecast. That day, and the next, there'd be rain. Friday it would be cloudy. There was no mention of snow, but cold and rain in the lower elevations usually means snow on the peaks. I walked outside where a strong wind blew the flags straight out. The next stretch of trail would lead up and over 3,000 to 4,000 foot peaks where the wind would be stronger still. Add rain or snow to the mix and you have a nasty day for hiking. So my feet would get their way. I'd stay and work this morning and spend another night in Rutland. It's the second largest city in Vermont so there were plenty of services, supplies and nice places to spend the afternoon.

After a morning cleaning out a store room, I had a good lunch with the kitchen crew, then I went out to run errands. I found the library and went in to check my emails. Sue reported the results of her tests.

They said she was as healthy as a horse except for this tumor in her breast. But there was no sign of the cancer spreading. Soon she would start chemo therapy.

On my way back to the hostel, I found the transit center and asked about bus service to and from the trail. I was considering doing a slack pack, leaving most of my gear here, hiking the next stretch and then returning for the night. They said I could get a bus to the trailhead first thing in the morning. At the end of a 16.5 mile hike I could walk an extra mile on the road to catch a bus back here in time for dinner. It would be a little risky. If I missed that bus, I wouldn't have my gear to set up for the night. But I'd been walking twenty mile days and didn't think I'd have a problem.

When I went in and told Lakota what I had planned, she got a better idea. We could hike the 16.5 miles together and ask her mom, who lived in nearby Manchester Center, to bring us back here. Then we could all have dinner together. We'd hike together again the next day so Lakota could finish her one hundred miles and I'd have a warm, dry, place to spend the night after hiking in the rain. Besides I wanted more of the best food I'd eaten on the entire trail. Lakota's mom would be happy that she had a hiking partner, at least for a day.

Later that afternoon, I walked around the neighborhood and found a convenience store that would have hot breakfast food ready early in the morning. The Twelve Tribes are really great cooks, but after serving and cleaning up their dinners, they were slow to start the next day.

When I returned to the hostel I was told another hiker had come in. Duct Tape! We greeted each other warmly and I introduced him to Lakota. He hadn't made it to Michael's barn, but had stayed in a stable at Cloudland Road. When he stopped at Michael's the next day he was offered a sandwich. I couldn't help but wonder how it compared to Duct Tape's culinary creations.

After he got cleaned up, the three of us met downstairs for dinner at the big round table at the back of the restaurant. It was pizza night for the staff and they brought out five or six different kinds of pizzas, two at a time! Delicious!

I got up at 5:00 the next morning and left the women's bunkroom to find Duct Tape in the hall. His roommates were asleep, too. We went down to the convenience store together, got some breakfast and headed back to the hostel. Duct Tape stayed to do a work for stay while Lakota and I caught the bus to the trailhead. It took twenty minutes to reach the trailhead and twenty minutes more for her to get ready to go from there.

She was a futzer and by the end of the day I suspected she was a bit of a hypochondriac, too. She was also a talker or maybe I was just used to hiking alone. Once we got going the day went well. The predicted rain only came down for forty-five minutes. I threw my poncho over my pack and kept going. We crossed Killington Peak and Pico Peak in a cloud, but it cleared later and we had a nice afternoon. The walking was pleasant and we kept up a steady pace. She had some indigestion, and then tripped and hurt her ankle, and near the end of the hike, her knee gave her some pain, but she kept going.

About a mile from the end of the trail we passed a shelter where a man was sitting. I waved but he didn't. I wondered if it was Chase. I couldn't tell with him wearing a hooded raincoat. I knew from shelter logs that he was about a day ahead. We also met the three ladies I'd met on the trail the day before, Pearl, Rosie and Rita, with another friend, Annie. Pearl was a doctor and gave Lakota some advice and a bandage for her knee. It was good to see them again.

Lakota's mom was waiting anxiously for us as we finished our hike. As a light rain fell she brought us back to the hostel. She waited for us in the restaurant while we showered and changed for dinner. While Lakota was getting ready, Duct Tape and I made a run across the road to buy cards and mailing envelopes for my best friend and little sister who both had birthdays the next week. Then I bought some scented soap from the Twelve Tribes to send to them and we joined Lakota and her mom for dinner.

Duct Tape had been invited to join a prayer meeting with the Tribe that night. I think they'd been pressuring Lakota to join, too. I hadn't felt any pressure, just genuine kindness.

After a big bowl of corn chowder, good bread and tea, I retired to my room and packaged up my gifts to mail. I planned to get back on the trail the next morning after another hour of work and some breakfast. Lakota's mom said she'd host me when I got to Manchester Center in two days.

Friday the 13th of October and I was glad I wasn't hiking with Lakota who says she attracts bad luck. Her mom confirmed it. She was planning to hike with Duct Tape from the Long Trail Inn. My bus left a half hour before theirs. There was no sign of the Twelve Tribe members and no sign of breakfast. But they gave Lakota some muffins for us the night before and I got some tea at the coffee shop around the corner. The timing was tight as I had to get packed, then called the Killington Post Office to make sure I didn't have mail there, and the Manchester Center Post Office to ask if they'd let Lakota's mom pick up my packages there and still rush over to the Rutland Post Office to mail the birthday packages for my sister and Kelly. And my bus was leaving at 8:45.

I began the day writing a letter to a friend. It started like this:

"I am sitting on a toilet at 6:00 a.m. in order to get good light and not disturb my roommate. There are three good things about this statement. There is a toilet, a light and a room."

I had stayed at the Twelve Tribes for three nights. Before that I was inside in Hanover at Win and Marilyn's for two, and in between I'd been offered the luxury of a VW Camper for a night. But now I was heading back out on the trail and planned to stay at the Big Branch Shelter after hiking sixteen miles.

When I arrived, I pulled out my Thermarest and sleeping bag and said, "Hello old friends." I felt like such a wimp sleeping inside whenever I got the chance. Perhaps I was tiring of the trail. I could smell the finish line and imagined being with my family, cooking for Sue, staying for Thanksgiving, sleeping in a comfortable bed, getting hot showers, eating good food again. My fantasies took me back to Washington. I was looking forward to settling into the house-sitting cottage back on Whidbey Island, visiting old friends, writing, playing my banjo, making soup, drinking tea with honey, maybe starting a new job.

I had hiked roughly 1,800 miles but still had 375 more to go. I was in Vermont and still had to walk through Massachusetts, Connecticut and back into New York. And then I'd have to go back and cover the 125 miles I'd left undone in the Shenandoah's. My feet had been giving me unexpected shooting pains. I thought the new shoes would alleviate that. I was hoping they wouldn't break down before I finished the trail. That day I had shooting pain through my whole back. I think that was a result of the soft bed at the hostel. So it was probably good to sleep on a hard shelter floor again.

I went to fill my water bottles in the river. On my return I noticed that someone had carved a message in the side of the shelter. It read, "I Am Here." Someone else added the word, "Now". It reminded me to stop speculating so much about the future and be more present. I signed up to do the whole trail and I should value every mile of it.

The weather cleared a bit and the next day's hike over Baker Mountain and Peru Peak were joyous. I stopped for lunch sitting in a soft pile of dry leaves leaning up against a tree with my face in the sun. I was drifting into a nap when a family came along with three young boys. They were very curious about me sitting alone in the woods like this. They asked where I lived and where I slept.

"Right here seems like a fine place," I said

His mother interjected that I was walking the Appalachian Trail which goes from Georgia to Maine. One boy asked how many states I'd walked through. Counting on my fingers I named them, one by one.

"Georgia, North Carolina, Tennessee, Virginia, West Virginia, Maryland, Pennsylvania, New Jersey, New York, Maine, New Hampshire, and Vermont. Twelve States and two to go!" I looked up and saw the boy's mouth wide open and a look of amazement in his young eyes.

"I could never walk that far," he said.

"Oh, yes you could," I told him, "but probably not today."

His parents laughed and they moved on.

Hiking over Bromley Peak, I realized I was within a mile of the trailhead and started looking for someone with a cell phone that I could use. I was just outside of Manchester Center where Lakota's mom had offered to put me up for the night.

On the summit were six young adults, but when I asked to use a cell phone, none of them had one. Imagine that.

Another couple sat just down the hill so I approached them.

"Hello. Would either of you happen to have a cell phone I could use?" The woman reached for her phone.

The man looked at me and asked, "Maribeth?"

It was surreal. I didn't recognize him and he wasn't using my trail name. He introduced himself.

"Jamie," he said. When I still looked puzzled he added, "Country Walkers." I was flabbergasted. I'd worked for Country Walkers leading hiking tours in the Pacific Northwest for over a decade, but had never visited their home office in Vermont. They had walking tours all over the world and Jamie was my regional manager. Though we'd exchanged many emails and had many phone conversations, we'd never met. He had recognized me by my voice.

I couldn't believe it. He just happened to be visiting his friend who lived nearby, a two hour drive from his office. They just happened to be out for a hike on this very peak, when I just happened to be walking by. The six young adults didn't have a cell phone with them which was surprising, so I happened to ask Jamie and his friend, Vicky. It all seemed beyond coincidence, another magical moment of AT serendipity.

They offered me a ride. After sitting for a while admiring the view, the three of us walked down together. At the truck I called Lakota's mom, Sandy, to ask for directions. Jamie, Vicky and I climbed into the truck. Jamie said I seemed relaxed, in a good mood. I said, "I'm in

Vermont!" which I thought was enough of an explanation. He reached into his glove compartment and gave me a Vermont sticker as a souvenir.

We arrived at the house just as Sandy was heading out to pick up Lakota from the bus station. Lakota had hiked one more day before coming home. Sandy told me to go in and get cleaned up for dinner and they'd be right back. Her husband showed me to Lakota's room upstairs and retreated to watch the news.

The room looked like a little girl's dream, twin beds with matching pink quilts and baby dolls all over the place. How sweet, I thought. I got a shower and changed, and a few minutes later Lakota arrived and did the same.

We had appetizers before dinner. I tried to show restraint, though I didn't see any reason to postpone dinner one second longer. I listened to Lakota and her parents interact. In one hour she complained of a bum knee, twisted ankles (which I could relate to) but then added stomach and intestinal ailments, diarrhea, heart palpitations, low blood pressure, Crone's disease, acid reflux, asthma and allergies. Miraculously, she had made it back home all in one piece.

After dinner I did laundry and checked my emails. Friends on Whidbey Island let me know that my car had been stolen. They'd left it overnight in a commuter parking lot on the mainland. When they came back the next day, it was gone. The police knew where to find it. It had been taken to an isolated ravine nearby and cleaned out. They took my stereo, iPod, jumper cables and everything else including the gas cap. The car itself was undamaged. I was glad to get my car back but there was one item I'd left in the backseat that could not be replaced, a satchel that contained my journals from the first leg of my AT hike. I kicked myself for not storing them somewhere more secure. I had little hope that someone would find them and somehow return them to me. More likely, they were thrown in a ditch, or a dumpster, and the satchel was sold for drugs. At least I'd been sending emails, like journal entries, for the duration of my hike.

In the morning, Lakota drove me to the trailhead and we hugged good-bye. I crossed a bridge over a rushing river and started hiking. I put in another twenty mile day stopping at Story Spring Shelter. The next day I planned to go just eighteen miles and stay with a friend of Al's in Bennington, Vermont.

It was a beautiful day, clear and cool. The sun shone boldly in the autumn sky. Plowing through dry leaves up to my ankles sounded like walking through rooms full of potato chips. Living in Washington, the

Evergreen State, I had forgotten how noisy dry leaves underfoot could be. There was no chance to sneak up on wildlife or anyone else for that matter.

At mid-day I stopped for a leisurely lunch at Goddard Shelter, a nice, new, well built timber frame with benches and a porch facing south. It had a nice feel and I imagined building a little cabin like it somewhere. I wrote in my journal while I ate enjoying the sun on my face.

After lunch I found a box with the shelter log and with it I found a laminated page with a young man's picture on it. It said, "Don't weep for me." The story typed out on the page told of a young man who climbed to the nearby mountain *and though he loved his family, another hand had reached down to help him up the last few steps*, and that he was happy, and it was a wonderful place.

It wasn't spelled out but it sounded as if the young man had ended his life here on the mountain. He looked to be about twenty years old. What a shame, I thought, but he had picked a beautiful place to die. I wondered why every hiker that came to this lovely mountainside should become aware of this tragedy. Does it console the family to have strangers share their grief? Was this paper like carving a headstone for him here, a way to mark his passing? For me it cast a shadow on the beautiful day and the loveliness of the place.

When I arrived at the road it was almost 6:00 p.m. and getting dark but a nice woman stopped to give me a ride the five miles into town. I found a phone near a coffee shop and called Al's friend, Meg. I'd tried to call her two days before, but the line had been busy and I couldn't leave a message. Then I tried from the shelter the night before using another hiker's cell phone, but there was no reception. So I was hoping I hadn't come into town on a night when she wasn't home. This time I got an answering machine and left a message telling her where I was. I got a cup of tea and picked up a paper to read while I waited. An hour later I went to a restaurant and got a burger, and then tried calling her again at about 7:30.

This time she answered, but seemed flustered. I'd caught her in the middle of something. She said she'd come get me in an hour. I said I could wait. That seemed like a long time for me as I'd been "going to bed with the chickens" as my mom would say. But I was in a comfortable pub on a cushy couch and she was kind enough to host me, the least I could do was be patient. I got out my trail guide and planned the rest of my hike through New England. I could do it in just ten more days!

Meg walked in and we spotted each other. She was a big, strong woman. She shouldered my pack and threw it into her Jeep. She'd been pressing cider she told me and had a family over for dinner. They'd just sat down to pear pie when I called. She talked about all the squash she'd harvested, a real Earth Mother who also worked as a nurse. Her folks owned a large farm across the road from her single acre. They'd had big harvest parties there and Pete Seeger had come.

I asked how she knew Al.

"I don't," she said. "He's a friend of my brother's."

"Where does your brother live?"

"New Mexico."

She thought she might have met Al once at one of the harvest gatherings.

In her small cluttered cabin, baskets of onions and braids of garlic hung from the rafters. Baskets of squash, apples and pears sat on the edge of the stairs. We had a cup of tea and she served me a piece of pear pie while we got to know each other. She was a single woman who had raised a half black son on her own in a conservative New England town. She was tough as nails and had a filthy mouth that I found entertaining, friggin' this and friggin' that. She showed me a little banjo she'd found in the family attic. I tuned it and played a little but it was well past my bedtime. After a shower I climbed into the loft with her cat Felix.

Just before dawn I got up and packed my things. We met in the kitchen. She asked what I'd like for breakfast. I asked if I could make it myself.

"Sure," she said and watched amazed while I cracked her farm fresh eggs into a bowl and poured oil into the skillet on the stove. I made a cheese omelet with salsa while she made toast from homemade whole grain bread. We topped the toast with homemade jam and poured cups of fresh pressed cider and mugs of tea. I topped it off with a piece of pear pie with a banana on the side. She offered a couple of apples from her orchard and drove me to the trail by 8:00. She gave me a bear hug, wished me luck and watched as I climbed the steep slope. At the top I looked over my shoulder and shouted down.

"Tell Al I only have 298 more miles to go!"

"Holy shit!"

All Time Low

There'd been a red sky at dawn so I walked fast trying to beat the rain. It started in late morning so I didn't stop all day. The wind was tossing the treetops around. My wet pant legs wicked moisture up to my thighs. At twelve miles I passed the southern terminus of the Long Trail (which overlaps the AT through most of Vermont) and entered Massachusetts, my 13th state, but could not stop to celebrate. I ate almonds, a snack bar and drank a bottle of Meg's delicious cider as I hiked. In the wind and cold rain I had to keep moving to stay warm.

With just a few miles to go, I passed through Williamstown and hoped someone would invite me in for tea. Under darkening skies the homes and buildings looked dark, a little run down and the few people I met were like me, moving quickly, holding umbrellas or newspapers over their heads, darting for a doorway to get out of the rain. Water gushed down the streets and sidewalks as the wind whistled in the clotheslines and telephone wires. I rushed through town like an invisible ghost pushed along by the merciless wind.

Leaving town, I climbed into the hills another three miles toward the crest of Mount Prospect. The wind grew fierce. The trees danced wildly. Branches clashed like swordsmen overhead. Spear-like branches were hurled to the ground. I pressed on and made it to the Wilbur Clearing Lean-to just before dark.

Another hiker had already settled in and seemed shocked to see me out in the storm. He saw how wet I was and offered to make me a cup of hot cocoa. I gratefully accepted as I quickly put on more layers and unpacked my sleeping bag. By the time the cocoa was ready I was snug inside my bag, but it took a while for me to warm up.

The man asked how far I'd come that day.

"Twenty-one miles," I said.

"I hate you," he teased. He was a section-hiker who'd just started his month-long hike. He'd logged seven miles that day and seemed discouraged. I told him it would get easier, but wondered, this late in the year, if that were true. I was glad to have his company and his report that the weather was supposed to clear.

It rained and blew all night, pounding on the metal roof of the shelter. It was still raining when I woke the next morning. The wet clothes I'd slept in were now dry, but my shoes were still soaked. The section-hiker continued north, while I packed up to go south, but I wasn't anxious to get going. I felt like I'd gotten up on the wrong side of the shelter.

At 8:00 a.m. the rain stopped, but by then it was getting late. So I decided not to push it. Instead of going to Dalton, another twenty mile day, I went just as far as Cheshire and began my search for food. The lady at the post office said the only place to get food was at the gas station that I'd already passed. So I went back.

It was disappointing, the antithesis of the home grown food I'd had at Meg's house. After considering all the options, I got two hot dogs, some Fritos and a plastic bottle of cranberry juice. It was the best I could do. I ate outside, sitting on the curb in the cool wind.

Twenty minutes later I had an ice cream sandwich at the hardware store where I bought fuel. The store owner showed me post cards from other thru-hikers that had stopped there. They were on top of Katahdin in a victory pose. I looked forward to finishing the trail myself.

A church in town offered shelter for thru-hikers, though there were no showers or bunks. I called J.C., another friend of Al's who I'd met working on the schooner *Adventuress* years before. No one answered so I left a message and told him where to find me.

After putting my pack in a classroom in the church basement, I explored my surroundings. I was getting cleaned up in the bathroom when I found a tick on my belly. The area around the bite was red, a bad sign. I pulled it off and tried to save it in a Zip-lock bag. (I'd need to keep the tick to test for Lyme disease.) But I dropped the tick and couldn't find it on the floor. I returned to my pack in the unheated classroom and sat on a cold metal chair. When I checked the hiker's log I found my sister's logo, the Tortoise, and her typically brief "In for the night" dated August twenty-fourth.

J.C. came for me around 5:30. His young daughter, Willow, was with him. They'd been to the Farmer's Market, but this late in the season there wasn't much there. I didn't realize they lived in North Hampton, an hour from the trail. He explained his wife, Annie, was in school and he hoped she'd be home with dinner ready by the time we arrived. No such luck. The big old house was dark.

J.C. showed me upstairs to their spare room. There was a mattress in the middle under a bare bulb dangling from the ceiling. The room was full of storage boxes and garbage bags full of stuff. Though it wasn't the most inviting guest room, I was thankful for the hospitality. I put my sleeping bag out on the bed and took my clothes downstairs. I got a shower while J.C. started dinner. Annie arrived just as I was throwing my clothes, and theirs, into a washing machine.

Willow and I set the table. J.C. called from the kitchen asking, "Is there anything you don't eat?"

I answered jokingly, "Brussels sprouts," which was exactly what he was bringing forth in a big, steaming bowl. So I quickly added, "But those look really good!"

They actually did. I'd grown up eating canned Brussels sprouts which were slimy, sour and detestable. But these were fresh from the Farmer's Market, lightly steamed and sautéed in olive oil, a huge improvement. It felt like what my body really needed. The beans and tortillas were good, too, though not typically eaten with Brussels sprouts. "Why not," I thought. As long as it wasn't trail food I was happy.

After dinner I was able to check my emails and phone home. Dad told me that Sue had started chemo that day. She'd get small doses each week hoping the side effects would be minimal. She intended to keep working as much as she could.

Then he told me the insurance company wouldn't cover the cost of the stereo or iPod that were stolen from my car.

Mom said, "You didn't need that stuff anyway."

I knew I didn't NEED them, but when I was home I used them and enjoyed them and would miss having them. I'm afraid my tone betrayed my irritation. It wasn't her fault that those things had been stolen or that the insurance company wouldn't cover the loss, or that I had eaten hot dogs from a gas station for lunch, or found a tick on my belly, or was about to go to sleep in a store room. It was all starting to get to me.

Mom had sent a care package, but it wasn't what I'd asked for. It didn't have my chai tea mix (my favorite hiking treat). Instead it had some weird Halloween sucker toy which I gave to Willow, and a dried brown leaf on a twig. Perhaps it had been some bright color when she'd put it in the box. She'd included some snack bars and a disposable camera which was good. Dad had thrown in a train schedule from NYC to Harpers Ferry, West Virginia which I would need soon.

When I started my hike from Maine, I'd sent a box to my parents with four bags inside. I had asked my parents to forward them to me as four different care packages on my hike south. They included vitamins, chai tea mix, and trail food among other things. But when I asked Mom to send them, she sent the first one to the wrong post office. She sent grapes in another box which had turned to wine by the time they reached me. And she hadn't included the things I'd supplied. I wondered if she'd forgotten about the package I'd sent her in September or if she just didn't want to climb the stairs to get them. I was grateful for the warm clothes they'd sent to me in Andover, but much of the rest seemed random, a mystery.

No matter, I wasn't relying on care packages anymore. My body was rejecting trail food. Oatmeal made me nauseous. I'd been taken in by so many good people along the way, and there were lots of little towns near the trail in New England where I could shop for supplies.

Mom asked me when I thought I would finish. I told her it would be the first week of November, just as I'd predicted when I got back on the trail in September.

"Well," she said, "your sister, Carolyn, will be visiting that week. She'll be here until the seventh, so we'll drive up to get you after that."

Maybe she forgot what I'd told them about my finish date. Carolyn lived near Nashville, Tennessee. She and my folks visited each other two or three times a year. I would be finishing the Appalachian Trail once in my life. Couldn't they make other arrangements with Carolyn? I suggested that they bring Carolyn along but Mom said no. Mom hadn't even mentioned to Carolyn that they had offered to pick me up in Shenandoah National Park that week. There was no public transit there so what this meant for me was that it didn't matter how hard I hiked, or how cold and wet I got, I would still be on the trail until Carolyn left my parent's house on November seventh. I have a wonderful family, but just like any family, we have our idiosyncrasies.

The next morning after breakfast, J.C. took me to get the supplies I needed and put me back on the trail in Cheshire. I'd only go thirteen miles that day and planned to stop in Dalton for a burger in late afternoon. It would be just three more miles to the next shelter.

I enjoyed the walk. It was dry for a change which put me in a better mood. The trail goes right through Dalton where people had decorated their homes for Halloween. Jack-o-lanterns and ghosts made of bed sheets adorned the front porches of big old houses. Red and amber leaves rushed out to greet me as I passed on the sidewalk.

It was mid-afternoon when I stepped into a near empty tavern and ordered a burger. A big flat screen TV was my only companion, if you can call it that.

When I arrived at the shelter, I found someone had left some Aquamira, which is what I used to treat my water. They didn't carry it at the outfitters in North Hampton or anywhere in Cheshire and I was reluctant to use the Iodine tablets again. So this was a great find.

I shared the shelter with a fellow named Gary who had worked in several National Parks. He'd also taught English as a Second Language in Thailand and other places. He was a transient with a couple of weeks between things so he came out to soak up the fall colors. I fell asleep to the sound of the stream below and the distant highway.

In the middle of the night it began to rain. Not just an ordinary pitter pat. It was like the fire brigade had circled the shelter and turned on their hoses full force! It was still raining in the morning and not quite light at 7:00 am. Fall was swiftly giving way to winter. I wondered when to switch my watch to daylight savings time and how that might affect me.

I had 253 miles to go and estimated one more week on the trail in New England. I had just one more state, Connecticut, to cross before getting back to Stormville, New York where my northbound hike had ended in June. From there I planned to visit Kelly's folks in the Catskills. Then I'd return to Harper's Ferry, West Virginia and hike south 125 miles into Shenandoah National Park. The end was near. I would actually finish the trail. But first I had to put on my wet socks and shoes and get going, even in the cold and rain.

October Mountain

I stopped short after just nine miles instead of the eighteen I'd planned. The rain kept up all morning. When I stopped for lunch at October Mountain Shelter I decided it would be drier here than sleeping on the porch of the Upper Goose Pond Cabin that would be locked up for the season. I'd passed some NOBO's that said there were some SOBO's just ahead of me. I'd rather not reach the cabin porch and have to share it with others while this roomy shelter was empty. Here there were four bunks, a loft, a floor and a picnic table under the overhang. I wondered if Duct Tape would catch up.

I felt a little guilty about putting in only nine miles. I'd only done thirteen the day before, and the day before that just eleven. But other people I knew took the whole day off when it rains, why not me?

I got out my Thermarest and sleeping bag, put on my clean, dry camp socks and sat back to read an AT Journeys magazine that I'd picked up at the Highlands Center. North Carolina had a new license plate that featured the AT and Mom and Dad had said they were getting one for Martha for Christmas. I wondered if she'd been walking in the rain as I had. It was depressing. I just wanted a week of dry weather so I could get this leg done.

I'd worn my waterproof socks that morning and walked right through the lake-like puddles on the trail. My shoes were soggy and my feet got cold but they actually stayed dry – miraculous. I'd been using those socks to cushion my camp stove inside my cook pot for months until I'd totally forgotten about their intended use. When I finally remembered and put them on my feet, the results were amazing!

Still my pants were damp. At first there were just drips from the trees with very occasional wet spurts. But when the rain began to come down steadily I put on my poncho. My hair was wet. I got tunnel vision from the hood slipping forward. I felt like I'd been underwater since I'd left Bennington.

As the afternoon wore on the wind kicked up and the rain poured down. Trees shot branches down like spears and acorns hit the metal roof like bullets. Thunder and lightning blew in and by 3:00 p.m. it was almost dark. I no longer felt guilty for stopping early and was glad to be in an ample shelter.

At this rate I had to recalculate the next week on the trail. I hoped the storm would pass because it was twenty-three and a half miles to the next shelter. With the shrinking hours of daylight, I'd have to get up and out by first light. I ate dinner, cleaned my pot and climbed into my sleeping bag in the loft to read by the light of my headlamp. I was asleep by 8:00. The rain lightened up, but the wind howled all night.

What was that? The wind had been pitching branches and acorns at the shelter all night but this was a different sound. Voices. Men's voices. It was pitch black. I checked my watch. Almost midnight. Men were approaching the shelter. I turned on my headlamp and bravely welcomed them, asking how many to expect.

Three Boy Scouts and four adult leaders came in out of the storm. I pointed out the wet bunks where the roof had leaked. Two leaders took them. One had a cot and the other had a space blanket that was incredibly noisy. Two other men took the other two bunks and the three young scouts climbed into the loft with me.

I asked if they'd found the banana that had slipped out of the strap on my pack that day. Yes, they had and stabbed it with their walking sticks. "Oh, my poor banana," I thought, "to reach such a cruel and torturous end." It would be a while before I would see another.

As the leaders talked, I gathered that one car full of scouts and gear had missed a turn in the darkness and rain and got lost. The other car load waited at the trailhead which gave them a late start. Still, it seemed to be a conscious choice to start their hike after dark in the middle of a storm.

The boys were exhausted and quietly climbed into their sleeping bags. The one nearest me let out a loud, unguarded sneeze. I turned to face the wall. They were soon fast asleep. Not so for their leaders.

I've slept alongside a lot of hikers, but these were the most restless with which I'd ever had the misfortune to share a shelter. They sorted their gear, hung up wet things, made cocoa, cooked pasta. Sometime in the wee hours they finally got settled and quiet returned to the shelter.

I didn't feel at all guilty when I got up at 5:30, made breakfast and packed to go. By the time I left an hour later, one of the leaders was making espresso and offered me a cup. I was glad I'd been a Girl Scout.

Attitude is more Important than Altitude

Twenty-three and a half miles in nine hours. There was a lot of blow down and plenty of puddles on the trail, but it was too cold to stop all day. I hesitated at Upper Goose Pond. It was enchanting. The sun was shining on a rock by the shore beckoning me to rest. But when the sun went behind a cloud and a chill wind blew, suddenly it was bitter cold. I kept moving.

Late in the day, after putting in about twenty miles, I was climbing a steep hill when I came upon a lovely woman and her golden retriever coming down the trail. I petted her dog. She asked about my hike. I told her I was getting tired. She said it was because I was going uphill, but I meant that I was tired of hiking day after day by myself, sleeping outside in cold, damp shelters. She wasn't wearing a pack and must have been out for a short stroll.

"But isn't it beautiful," she said as she walked on with her dog.

"Sure." I thought sourly, "Its beautiful when you can take an afternoon stroll downhill, without a pack, with a nice dog, and go home to a hot shower (though she probably doesn't need one), a good meal and a warm home. I need a shower but won't get one, craved a good meal but have to eat trail food again, and will spend the night in a ratty old shelter with no heat, no soft bed, no reading lamp and not even a dog for companionship."

Then I looked around and started to notice. It really was beautiful. I thanked her inwardly for reminding me. I'd passed many delightful scenes that day. There were ten or twelve pretty little brooks I'd crossed, intricate stone walls, some picturesque fields rimmed with golden birches, and now I looked down over a huge red barn complex with a cupola on top that held my attention for a while. Though it was often cold, windy and rainy, New England really was beautiful in the fall.

Jug End

I had to congratulate my feet. I had regular conversations with various parts of my body and you can believe they talked back. Now that I was in New England with its rolling hills, and even some level places, they spoke up less and less. But I still praised them for the fine work they were doing.

The weather had improved and my feet had brought me forty-five miles in the last two days. It took the same amount of time to walk yesterday's twenty-three and a half as today's twenty-one and a half, because the morning was so lovely and I kept stopping to take it all in.

In the past week I had been in the hometown of Norman Rockwell, Robert Frost and W.E.B. Dubois. I could see where they got their inspiration.

Also, I knew I wasn't going as far so need not hurry all day. Massachusetts is merciful, but the trail tended to throw in a big climb in the last five miles of a long day. Today it was Jug End.

I had crossed a number of roads and lost track of which was what so I had little idea of how much farther I had to go. I'd just passed a marker commemorating Shay's Rebellion when I came upon an older couple at a trailhead parking lot. I asked if they knew which road this was and they slowly opened their car and took out three different maps. I answered my own question but the man kept me there waxing poetic about the views on Jug End. I was getting antsy. There was rain in the forecast and I still had seven miles to go before I'd reach the shelter.

After thanking them, I hurried back to the trail and met four more people on a boardwalk who started asking silly questions.

"Where does the trail come out?"

"Georgia." I replied.

"Where are you going?"

"New York." I had no time for this.

I stepped around them and called back over my shoulder to ask the couple in the parking lot, they have lots of maps.

There were a lot of cars at the trailhead to Jug End. I counted couples coming down as I climbed the steep hill and subtracted cars in my head. I hoped there wouldn't be a crowd at the shelter. The views were great but I'd seen terrific views from the ledges that morning and again at noon. By this time, with the smell of approaching rain, I was more interested in seeing a shelter.

I crossed the Housatonic River, again. I think I'd crossed it four or five times already. To get to know this river one would have to get in a canoe and travel in its flow for a long time.

I'd passed some beautiful farmhouses and fields and walked through some lovely woodlands on my hike that day. I liked Massachusetts. I had dry feet for most of the day. In the late afternoon, I worked on finishing some songs as I walked. I wrote them down when I reached the shelter. As I ate another pot of pasta, I studied my trail guide and realized the next day I'd cross the border into Connecticut, my last state.

Connect | Cut

It was a beautiful walk on yet another blustery day with dark, moist clouds looming just overhead. I crossed Mount Everett, Mount Riga, Bear Mountain and hiked on over to the Lion's Head, all rocky ridges with spectacular views of the autumn countryside below. I passed through woods and into the lovely Sage's Ravine where I crossed from Massachusetts to Connecticut and let out a "Yeehaw!"

I was entering my fourteenth state on the Appalachian Trail. The ravine was beautiful with colorful foliage and a gushing, cascading river down the middle. There aren't many Appalachian Trail miles in Connecticut. The trail just nips the northwest corner of the State, but crosses the highest peak, Mount Fissell, at 2,380 feet. There, a rock monument probably increased the elevation a few more feet for anyone that scrambled to the top. I stopped to read the plaque on the exposed summit, but the clouds started to sputter sleet so I hurried down. A class of school kids were scampering up the trail wearing cotton t-shirts and light jackets seemingly oblivious of the cold. I wondered if I had ever been like that. Maybe it's my Southern blood but I have a low tolerance for cold. I'd learned long ago that it's easier to stay warm than to get warm, so I always carried extra layers. But then, I thought, I had many miles to go and they would soon be back inside their heated vehicles headed for their warm homes.

By 1:30 I'd arrived at a road crossing with Salisbury, Connecticut, just a half mile away. I walked by a charming hotel. My trail guide said they'd charge thru-hikers $90 a night and would allow several hikers to share a room. But I was alone. It also listed a local woman's phone number who charged just $35 for thru-hikers. I kept that in mind. But my highest priority at the moment was food. There were several quaint shops on the main street. I found a grocery store and went to the deli counter inside. I got a "Thanksgiving dinner" lunch special in a Styrofoam tray, but had to go outside to eat it in the cold. I ate fast. It was filling and good.

As I ate, shoppers came and went. One woman said hello as she entered the store. I had finished my meal by the time she came out. She was heading to her car. I was carrying my fuel bottle in search of a hardware store. We were walking side by side on the wide sidewalk.

She asked, "Are you thru-hiking?"

"Yes."

"Where are you staying?"

I told her I hadn't decided. She invited me to her house. Just like that. Out of the blue. She went with me to fill my fuel bottle, get packages at the post office, stop by the drug store and even drove me to the next town to get batteries for my headlamp. Then she took me home.

Betsy and Rick lived in an old farmhouse in the country full of clutter and photos of family. Two old portraits hung above an antique buffet in the dining room. When I asked about them I got a thirty minute answer.

Her great grandfather was a cousin of Robert E. Lee (though, she was quick to add, he was against slavery) and her great grandmother was Elizabeth Blair who lived across the street from the White House. The Blair house is famous for hosting many presidential parties and esteemed dignitaries. Betsy threw in a lot of American history as she told me of her ancestors. Great grandmother Elizabeth wrote daily letters to her husband who worked as an oceanographer on distant seas. Her letters were recently published in a large volume I saw on the table. The Blair's country home in Maryland was torn down but the banister was brought to this house, so I was leaning heavily on the same stair railing as Abe Lincoln and many others.

Betsy's husband was a hiker and always wanted to hike the Appalachian Trail. He was pleasantly surprised when he came home and we were introduced. They invited another hiking friend for dinner whose daughter hiked the AT twenty-five years before. There was a lot of lively conversation swapping stories as we ate crisp salad, steaming butternut squash and pork chops.

I washed clothes and strung them on the line in the basement near the furnace to dry. They let me use their phone so I called Sue. She told me about her chemo treatments and invited me to go with her when I got off the trail. I left a message for Kelly's folks in New York warning them that I'd soon be in their neighborhood, and talked to Kelly back in Seattle, too. As I climbed into a real bed, with a grateful sigh, I pulled out my trail guide. Four more days, I figured, before I'd be back to Stormville, New York and done with this leg of my hike.

The next day, after breakfast, Betsy took me back to the trail. I had an easy day walking through colorful woods over gentle hills and tiny streams. That night settling into the shelter, I felt sorry for the kids I'd passed a few miles back, seventh and eighth graders at the mercy of two young adults. They were planning to get to this shelter, but were going too slow. They'd decided to stop at a campsite a few miles back. The wind has picked up a little and the temperatures were going to dip below freezing, so I hoped they had time to get their tents up and have a good dinner before dark.

This little shelter wouldn't have held them anyway and the only available water is from a beaver pond, a questionable source. Someone had left a pumpkin with a face drawn on it. It was a nice, homey touch, but not really part of the "leave no trace" ethic. I saw it as bear bait, so after dinner, I put it in the privy with my own food bag and wedged a log against the door. I tied my tarp across the shelter entrance to cut the wind.

There was plenty of animal activity on the roof of the shelter. It sounded like the squirrels were playing soccer with acorns. Wind-blown leaves, sticks, even branches were dropping on the tin roof hard enough to make me jump!

I read in the shelter log that the Librarian stayed here two nights before and that she had just 160 miles to finish her thru-hike. I recounted and found I had just 170 more myself. I'd been able to reach Kelly's folks by phone that morning. They said they were looking forward to hosting me in the Catskills. J.C. had given me a contact number for the nearby *Clearwater* office so I could line up a ride to their house. This time, I wouldn't have to risk hitch-hiking. Things were falling into place.

About an hour after dark I was reading in my sleeping bag when an older woman and her husband arrived. They were a retired couple from Connecticut. They apologized for coming in so late and said they'd had a late start. They explained their elaborate schedule of meeting friends and relations at trailheads, shuttling cars and coordinating slack packs, so they had to stay on schedule even if it meant hiking in the dark.

The woman was talkative and pleasant while her husband hardly spoke at all. She asked me why I chose to hike the AT and I found I couldn't really answer. It was getting late. I was tired. So I turned the question on her.

"That's easy," she said. "It's been my husband's lifelong dream and we always do everything together."

I gave that some thought. It was a romantic notion, but having just gone through a divorce, I wondered, was it love or fear that motivated them to hike the AT together? It was too late in the day for this sort of thinking. And it was absolutely none of my business. I closed my book, turned off my headlamp and was soon fast asleep.

In the morning they left the shelter before me, but I passed them an hour later. She was huffing and puffing up a steep hill while he waited patiently at the top.

Housatonic

The next afternoon I got to hike alongside the Housatonic River for a couple of hours. The trail followed a lovely old bridle trail, smooth and wide, that ran by the river for miles. The Appalachian Trail rarely takes such an easy route. I was highly suspect, certain the trail would lull me into a happy reverie alongside the river, and just as my mind wandered, it would cut suddenly upslope on a sketchy path and leave me meandering mindlessly in the wrong direction. But each time I thought it had been too long since I'd seen a white blaze, I would see another one up ahead leading me on. It was such a lovely afternoon. This was too good to be true which made it hard to relax and enjoy it.

The Housatonic and I kept crossing paths, like bumping into an old friend on the street. But I couldn't cross it without going out of my way to take a road bridge. Like most friendships, it required some effort. I'd jump over several small streams each day that were chatty and singing, but the Housatonic was quiet and deep. I thought I needed more time to get to know it, which I did that day. I walked about as fast as the current and began to hear its voice, deeper and richer than the other streams. I began to feel like I was walking with a friend.

In late afternoon the trail left the Housatonic and climbed steeply up to Saint John's Ledges and on to rocky Caleb's Peak. It was an abrupt change from the bridle path I'd been following, steep and rugged, which reminded me of being back in the White Mountains. At a road crossing near Kent I threw my pack behind a boulder and walked the half mile into town. I walked fast thinking how darkness falls so early now in mid-October, but the next shelter was less than a mile away.

Kent is home to a large prep school and had some cute but pricey tourist shops. I found a bakery where I got a bowl of hot chili, a root beer and a chicken and cheese burrito for lunch the next day. The peanut butter crackers I'd eaten that morning barely made a dent in my appetite. I craved real food, good, hot food. I got a ride back to the trail with a local lady and reached the shelter just before dark.

At ten o'clock I was awakened by Jay Bird, a "yoyo". He'd been hiking the AT back and forth for the last two years. He used to live with his mother until she died. Then he started hiking, completing his first northbound thru-hike in a quick four months. Then he turned around and went south. He stayed with his sister for a few months and then headed north again. Now he was heading south. He confessed he was getting a little trail weary. He pitched a tent because, he said, he snores. But that's nothing new. He seemed like a lost soul.

I didn't hear Jay Bird snore but the animals on the roof were plenty noisy. I awoke several times that night. Once I turned on my head lamp and looked around. I was very dizzy, like my eyes were rolling around in my head. I went back to sleep.

Just before dawn I woke up and went to the outhouse, but I felt like a drunkard weaving my way there and back. Maybe it was something I ate. Maybe I was dehydrated. After breakfast I began to recover.

I started hiking at first light with a plan to hike twenty-two miles. I climbed and grew warmer as the sun and I reached the top of a ridge. It was pleasant walking through the woods at the top of the forest. Just before I turned to come down I startled a coyote. It went leaping through the woods with terrific speed and grace. It didn't look like the scrawny gray coyotes I'd often seen in the West. This one was large, healthy and handsome with a reddish tint to his dark, bushy coat. Later, I passed a local on a day hike and described the animal to him. He nodded saying, "They look like German Shepherds around here." By the way this animal moved you could tell it was wild.

It was a clear, bright day with a strong, cold wind. I got to hike on a bluff overlooking the Housatonic. As I rounded a bend, the deep, calm water grew frothy with white rapids. It roared, resounding through the forest and then grew quiet again. This was an aspect of the river I hadn't seen before. When I crossed Ten Mile Creek I realized the trail would turn away from the Housatonic, so I sat down for lunch.

"This may be the last time I see you old friend." I watched the constant, mesmerizing movement of the water as I ate. We had been moving in roughly the same direction at about the same speed for days. It had been good to have this big river as a traveling companion, but this was where we would part. I wished it well. Before leaving, I pinched off a piece of my chicken burrito and made a small offering to the river. Then, with one last look, I shouldered my pack and climbed the next hill.

Later that afternoon I crossed a road to find the Appalachian Trail Railroad Station. I was now in the State of New York and these tracks led straight into Manhattan. I found a man nearby who was kind enough to take my picture as I stood on the platform under the Appalachian Trail sign. But I had no intention of catching that train. Instead the man and I walked on together.

He was conducting research on turtles. I had heard about this study when I worked for the zoo in Seattle. It was part of a school program I used to teach and here was the research biologist himself, Michael Munsik, out looking for his radio-tagged turtles! We were both surprised and delighted to meet out there in the woods. Turtles move slowly and turtle researchers more slowly still, so I left him to his work and moved on at a slightly faster pace.

At another road, I found the Dover Oak, supposedly the largest tree on the trail, though that title is also claimed by the Kiefer Oak in Virginia.

I hiked on across a wetland and came upon four more hikers. One, named Ralph, was a local man who maintained the trails in this section. I told him I would finish my Flip-Flop tomorrow at NY52 and planned to go celebrate with a pizza at a nearby deli, the same one where I had dined with Red B and his dog back in June. He asked what time.

"About noon," I said and wondered if he would be there.

After walking another mile into the woods I came to the shelter and found Hi Tech with a good fire going. Someone had pulled several dead saplings up to the fire pit and burned the ends. It left ugly remains across the campsite. We determined to burn them until they would fit into the fire circle. It was a fine evening watching the sun go down with our fire burning warm and bright. He said he'd hiked the trail but was coming back to fill in a few spots he'd missed. We found we were both originally from North Carolina. I sang him some of my trail songs. He somehow tolerated them, both laughing and crying at appropriate lines. It was a fine night on the trail and felt like a celebration.

We both woke at 6:00 am. Our fire still had some hot coals and we huddled around them for warmth. Hi Tech shared his box of four cinnamon rolls with me. What a treat! The morning before I had tried to finish my oatmeal, but could barely keep it down. I couldn't think about food afterward without feeling nauseous. We swapped emails and I started off with just eleven miles to go.

Crossing the Finish Line

My last day in New York was sunny and beautiful. I had a big grin on my face all morning as I hiked the last eleven miles to Highway 52. I had plenty of time and wanted to enjoy the day so I relaxed my pace. The leaves were dry and crisp and I kicked them as I walked. At mid-morning I took out a snack bar and sat on a rock in the sun to eat. When I found a tick crawling up my pant leg, I decide it was time to go.

Just before I reached the next road I came upon a Zip-lock bag tacked to a tree with a Snickers bar and a note inside saying, "Scout, Drink More Water!!!"

Deja vu! There were also two rocks inside, one from Katahdin and one from Springer Mountain, Georgia. There was a phone number with a note that said, "Give me a call."

It was from O. D. Green, the trail angel that I'd met at Harriman State Park last June. He'd followed my Trail Tale emails and had figured out that I'd returned to New York, and was almost done with my hike. His offering was a delightful surprise!

When I arrived at Highway 52 it didn't look familiar. There was a big cement bridge that I didn't remember at all. This wasn't the same place where I'd left the trail in June. I studied my trail guide and found I had another half mile to go. It was a beautiful walk. I crossed a little brook and then came upon a huge oak tree with a white blaze on it. I gave the tree a hug as a goodbye to the trail and a thank you to all the white blazes that had led me for over 2,000 miles. Then I walked through a field and some woods and came out by a road. I saw a man with a bike. It was Ralph, the trail maintainer I'd met the day before.

"I had a feeling you'd be here," I said.

Ralph lived nearby and didn't think I should finish the trail alone. He gave me a hug, a bottle of Gatorade and a Snickers bar to celebrate. Then we walked together up the hill to the deli and he bought a large pizza for our lunch. He'd just finished leading a walking tour the day before. I told him I also led walking tours. He had written a book and a weekly column about hiking in the area. He was fit and trim and had a lot of energy and enthusiasm. He was good company and I appreciated being with someone who seemed as excited as I was to finish my Flip-Flop, though I still had to fill in that section in Shenandoah National Park to complete my hike.

J.C. had contacted the *Clearwater* office in Poughkeepsie to ask if someone could give me a ride to the Catskills. Ron had responded with an email saying he could take me. So after Ralph took off on his bike I called Ron and told him where I was. Ron said the deli was too far out of his way. So if I wanted a ride to the Catskills I would first have to find a ride to Poughkeepsie by the time he got off work at 5:00.

I asked at the deli counter, but there was no public transit in Stormville and no, they didn't know anyone that was heading that way. I'd taken quite a chance hitch-hiking to the Catskills last June, a risk I didn't want to repeat. So I called Ralph. He had already been so kind and generous I hoped he wouldn't mind offering a little more trail magic.

He arrived a few minutes later in a sports car wearing jeans and a black leather jacket. He told me Poughkeepsie was a tough town. After a twenty minute drive we arrived in Poughkeepsie and found a phone booth. While I called to get directions, Ralph stood next to me posing as a body guard. The *Clearwater* office was just a few blocks away in an old, Victorian house with a fountain across the street. Ralph said he'd been in three bike accidents in that intersection.

He took his role as guardian seriously. Not only did he drive me to Poughkeepsie, he walked me into the *Clearwater* office to meet Ron. Clearly the trail meant a lot to him and he knew this was a momentous day for me. Ron was surprised that I could get there so fast. I explained that I had angels. I gave Ralph a hug and watched him walk out to the street. Superhero, Angel, whatever you want to call him, I was grateful we'd met.

I went to a quick mart nearby and got a bottle of juice and snacks and settled down in the corner of the waiting room to wait. When Ron got off work he gave me a ride right to the door of Suzen and Brian's home in the Catskills. Suzen gave me a quick hug and sent me directly to the bath tub upstairs. I had a nice long soak and then slipped into some of Suzen's clean clothes when I got out.

We lounged in front of the fire with grapes, Italian bread and cheese, living large. Just before dinner Kelly called from Seattle. Her father answered saying, "We gave at the office," and then passed the phone to Suzen who told her about the bald eagle she'd seen that day. We all wished Kelly a happy birthday. I told her I would sit in as her proxy for this birthday dinner. It was a good night to celebrate.

We sat down to a gourmet meal, chicken, salad with figs and goat cheese, and my new favorite, Brussels sprouts sautéed in olive oil and garlic. We topped it off with blueberries marinated in Tequila for dessert! Needless to say I slept very well.

In the morning we made my remaining oatmeal into oatmeal cookies. I had no problem eating them.

New York, New York

I'd made it just in time. As soon as I'd arrived in the Catskills, torrential rains turned the babbling brook out back into a raging torrent. On Sunday there were snow flurries and high winds. It made the couch by the fire that much more cozy.

Though I'd crossed one finish line I was not yet done with my hike. I still had to complete the 120 miles in the Shenandoahs. If weather permitted I'd finish in less than a week. The storm had passed, but it was still cold. I hoped it would be warmer in Virginia, but I'd be at higher elevations. I prayed for clear skies. If it weren't warmer, perhaps at least, it would be dry.

I called O.D. Green. We arranged to meet at a Dunkin' Donuts just outside New York City. Suzen and Brian weren't thrilled about the idea of me meeting up with a man I barely knew whose nick name was O.D. which they suspected stood for *over dose*. I tried to reassure them and they reluctantly agreed to drop me off on their way back into Manhattan.

O.D. took me to meet his family and pack a few snacks. We went for a walk at a Boy Scout camp, his old stomping grounds. We hiked to the top of a ridge, sat on some rocks and soaked up the late autumn sun. We could see the skyscrapers of New York City in the distance.

We talked trail talk and O.D. filled me in on his summer. He had hosted over thirty thru-hikers in his modest home. I was the first, but after I left, he got his system down. He would meet them at Harriman State Park and give them a ride to his home in Mahwah, New Jersey. He could accommodate several hikers at once, but they were all expected to work together to get the chores done, wash clothes, cook meals, shop for supplies.

At the end of the summer the small cottage he'd rented for cheap was razed and a large, new duplex was built in its place. O.D. had moved back in with his folks until he could find a new place.

We walked down the hill through the golden brown leaves until we came to a stream. With the recent rains it had flooded and braided into three streams. We looked upstream and down searching for the best way to cross. Finally, we pulled a smallish log over to span the stream with the far side on a boulder. O.D. dared me to try it. I borrowed his walking sticks. It bounced a bit. In the middle there was a small waterfall on one side and the corresponding underwater hole on the other. It was deep and the pole sank in a long way. I had to bend over to reach the bottom on the right while on the left the current pushed hard against the pole. But I made it over and tossed the sticks back for O.D. to follow. It was like waking up out of a sleepy afternoon nap, the only challenge of the day.

We met O.D.'s friend, Erin, at a coffee shop in Allendale, New Jersey. The three of us went to see a house nearby that was decorated for Halloween. It was incredible with plastic heads hanging from trees, skeletons springing out of coffins, monsters vomiting green stuff and others spitting up red stuff. One skeleton dressed in a worn out tux spoke with a Jersey accent, "What-choo looking at?" It was well over the top and had a steady stream of cars stopping and people gawking.

We went back to O.D.'s house where we met his friend, Adam, who had been asked to help us drive in and out of New York City. O.D. had only done it once before. I was no help at all, so we needed someone with experience.

We piled into O.D.'s little car and drove through two traffic jams and the filming of *The Sopranos* and then right by the corner where we should have turned. I spotted it as we passed so we circled back. I tucked a ten dollar bill into O.D.'s trail guide for gas, slipped out of the backseat and hugged them both goodbye.

Suzen runs a cooking school and test kitchen in Tribeca, so the loft is mostly a commercial enterprise. I arrived in time for some leftovers, an apple salad, curried rice and some Kentucky Fried Chicken. KFC had used the loft that day for a press conference to publicize their "No more trans fats" policy. The staff were cleaning up and preparing for the next day. I tried to stay out of the way.

I ate some gingerbread and rum raisin ice cream with caramel sauce while sitting in the cluttered office in front of a computer screen. I checked the forecast for northwestern Virginia. Clear and cold weather was predicted for the next week with temperatures dropping into the low twenty's at night. But it would be dry. I got packed and inflated the air mattress I would use for a bed in the large dining room. At 10:00 I pulled the shades on "the city that never sleeps" so that I could.

Southbound Train

I'd changed my watch from daylight savings time, but my body didn't catch on so I woke up at 4:30. It took a minute in the dark room to remember where I was. Then a car horn reminded me. I was in one of the largest cities on earth.

I felt like I had been away from home a long time, sleeping in cold shelters, or on someone else's bed or couch or floor. It had been a year since I'd left my own home to start house-sitting on Whidbey Island. It had been nine months since I started hiking the trail in Georgia. I'd been taken in by many kind and generous people, but I longed to be in a home of my own. Though I still didn't know where that might be, I had a general idea.

It was 6:30 when I went into the commercial kitchen to forage a little breakfast. There was plenty of food, but it all seemed to be designated for a certain dish and a particular event. I was eating some berries when Suzen came in sleepy eyed and offered me a loaf of French bread to take with me. We exchanged hugs. Then I shouldered my pack, grabbed my walking stick and headed down to the busy sidewalk.

This day would start much like the day last June when I'd made my way from New York City to North Carolina, but this trip would stop short of my home State. I made my way to the subway station. The city was just waking up. I took one last look around before going underground.

The subway took me to Penn Station where I bought my ticket and sat with my pack to watch people come and go. Everyone was moving at a fast clip. It wasn't long before I boarded a train and traveled south along the eastern seaboard. We went through Philadelphia and Baltimore to Washington D.C. under sunny skies.

When I arrived it was seventy degrees in the capitol city. What a shock after the snow in the Catskills two days before. I set my face toward the sun outside the monolithic Union Station. My fleece was too warm. I strapped it to the top of my pack. Getting lunch in the food court I had a dizzying array of appetizing options. Finally, I settled on fried rice and Asian chicken sitting at a tiny table on a tall stool. I wrote Martha a post card telling her how far I'd come and where I was going. We'd be much closer now.

Later, I caught a commuter train and headed out to Harper's Ferry, West Virginia. It was amazing how quickly the views changed from urban to woodland. I gazed out the window as we came alongside the Potomac River.

I disembarked in Harpers Ferry just before dark and climbed the stairs to the main street of this historic town. The lights were still on in the outfitters so I went in to refill my fuel bottle.

"Scout!" The clerk surprised me with his enthusiastic greeting. It was Garlic Man. I'd met him in May, five months before when I came through and bought new shoes. He'd given me a ride to the hostel. I told him he had a great memory. He confessed it was my sister Martha's recent visit that spurred his instant recall. "Tortoise" had signed the register two weeks before on her way south. This is about as close as we would get on our simultaneous thru-hikes.

Darkness fell as I climbed the hill into the center of town to get a room at the historic Hilltop Hotel. Perched on a bluff overlooking the Potomac River gorge, the setting was breathtaking, though the hotel had seen better days. I dropped my pack and went in search of a clerk. They had "special rooms" reserved for thru-hikers he said. The bed was old and squeaky, but the shower was hot. I went out to find some dinner. The pizza parlor served good calzones. I got an extra one to take with me.

It was Halloween. The old homes and store fronts flickered with glowing Jack-O-Lanterns. I strolled up the sidewalk watching the trick-or-treaters making their way from door to door. It was a warm night. Two women sitting on a porch called me over.

"Are you hiking the Appalachian Trail? Take some candy," they encouraged me. "Take more," they said. I took enough for my last week on the trail, a good supply of chocolate.

Back in my hotel room I washed my few clothes in the sink and hung them to dry overnight. Settling into the lumpy bed, I enjoyed reading by electric lights until I could no longer keep my eyes open. It was 8:30.

In the morning I was up well before dawn. The nights were long and with the change from daylight savings time I was waking up at 4:00 am. I read for awhile enjoying my heated room and reading light. At 6:00 I walked down to the post office and knocked. My trail guide said they'd open early for thru-hikers who came to the back door. Besides my package of trail food, I had three letters that had taken weeks to catch up with me, and a small package from Jeff, the organic farmer I'd met on Mount Washington. I took my loot back up the hill to the hotel. It was fun opening the packages and reading my mail. Jeff had sent a real treat, dried home grown tomatoes. They would go well with my pasta.

I read my mail over breakfast at the elegant but aging hotel dining room. The view was spectacular! The autumn leaves were peaking, the river gorge was stunning, and the sunshine burned through the early morning mist making everything look fresh and radiant.

I stopped by the Appalachian Trail Conservancy office to deposit the trail food I just couldn't stomach anymore and used their computer to check emails. They had some post cards that said, "Been There, Done That" with a map of the whole Appalachian Trail. The historic buildings in the morning light captivated me. I took pictures as I made my way through town before finally crossing the bridge over the Shenandoah River and following the trail south into the hills.

I didn't plan to go far, so I took my time and met a few other hikers on my way. The day was warm and I was sweating as I climbed. At Keys Gap there was a scribble on a fence post that said there was a store .1 miles away so I went. I was fully stocked but got some refreshing iced tea. The walk was enjoyable weaving back and forth between the Virginia and the West Virginia border. But the crisp leaves hid the sharp rocks and roots beneath them. The acorns rolled underfoot like ball bearings. After walking the sidewalks in New York City, Washington D.C. and Harpers Ferry, this was a bit of an adjustment.

Late in the afternoon I arrived at the Blackburn Center, a hostel run by the Appalachian Trail Conservancy. It looked like a classic mountain lodge with a wide porch around three sides. On the fourth side there was a young man placing large, flat stones on the ground creating a patio. His mass of red hair explained at least part of his trail name. Weather Carrot pointed me in the direction of the empty bunkhouse. I threw down my pack and went to take a solar shower.

Though it was November first, it had been a sunny day and I was optimistic. The water was lukewarm, but it was better than taking a sponge bath in a cold creek. I washed out my hiking shirt and hung it up in the bunkhouse where there was a wood stove that I would light later that evening.

As I sat on the porch writing in my journal, a pregnant woman approached from the house and invited me to dinner. In the big kitchen Hopeful introduced me to her husband, Red Wing, as we passed pork chops, mashed potatoes and green salad around the table. I told them of my trail family and they remembered Firefly and Feather who had stayed there back in May. My sister had also stopped there two weeks before and Weather Carrot knew her boyfriend, L.A. Bear.

Hopeful and Red Wing were expecting a baby in three weeks. They hoped to continue living in this mountain retreat, but didn't know how well that would work with the demands of next spring's thru-hikers and a new baby. Red Wing cleared the dishes away as Hopeful pulled a tray of hot brownies out of the oven.

In an effort to simplify his life, Weather Carrot told me, he had no bank accounts, no driver's license, no insurance. He worked here in exchange for room and board. I could see the advantages, but he said it was a trade off. It limited him in many ways, but also freed him up. I'd met others on the trail like him, flying beneath the radar. I found it fascinating and had to rethink my ideas of *simplicity*.

I loved the simple life on the trail. Though I would not miss the long, cold nights in the shelters, I dreaded going back to certain aspects of *the real world*. But for now there were warm chocolate brownies and good companions. I'd light the wood stove and spend the night in a warm bunkhouse. The trail kept me in the present.

Blindsided

I'd forgotten how easy it was to hike in Virginia, especially in the Shenandoahs. All the next day I walked south along a high ridge, my face heading toward the sun. It was dry but cold that morning. After I started hiking it took forty minutes for my frozen toes to warm up. At noon I found a spot among the rocks at the Bears Den, in the sun but out of the chill wind. I wrapped up in my fleece to eat lunch, peanut butter on Suzen's good bread with my oatmeal cookies for dessert. I'd been sitting there relaxing for ten minutes before I saw it, a bear's face peering up at me from the rocks. Someone had painted it there. Very subtle. I smiled.

Late in the day, I'd just come down off a ridge and crossed a stream when I saw a man in the woods. He was sitting on his pack chugging some yellow colored drink from a plastic two liter bottle. He looked overweight and worn out. I called, "Hello," but he didn't answer. I thought perhaps he hadn't heard me over the sound of the stream so when I halved the distance I said "Hello" again. He looked left and right as if expecting someone to come and answer for him. Finally, I stood directly in front of him and said "Hi."

"Hi," he said but kept looking around. His eyes seemed open too wide and rocked this way and that. I asked if he was expecting someone.

"Yeah," he said. "I'm expecting an eagle to fly over and drop a stone on my head to put me out of my misery."

I laughed a little and asked where he was headed.

"Rod Hollow Shelter," he said.

"So am I."

"Good," he said, "I'll have someone to talk to."

"I'll see you there," I said and kept going at a good pace. It was nearly dark. I wondered if he would make it and kind of hoped not. He seemed odd and made me a little uneasy.

I had settled into the shelter and made dinner by the time he arrived. This time he seemed more normal and talkative. He explained that he was legally blind but had hiked most of the trail in sections. He ran a snack bar in the State capitol building in Lansing and took hiking vacations when the legislators were out of town. He talked a lot about his hikes and offered me food, fuel and even cash. I said all I really needed was a spare headlamp battery, but his were a different kind.

After dinner and conversation I got into my book. My shelter mate wrestled around with his gear for a long time. All night he twisted and turned in his sleeping bag. There was a bright, full moon which made all outdoors restless. I must have woken up a dozen times before I got up at 5:30. He was already up, sitting in his bag with a cup of coffee.

I made breakfast in bed and then packed to go. Before I left, he passed me a chocolate bar. I wished him luck and started out at 7:30. As I hiked, I tried to imagine walking the trail with his poor eyesight, alone and at this time of year. Was he brave or crazy? Surrounded by politicians at work would certainly make me crazy. He probably doesn't fit in well in that environment, but on the trail odd fellows can find their place.

At mid-morning I came to Ashby Gap where a hand written sign pointed the way to a diner and I turned off trail to have a second breakfast. Food was easy to come by in the Shenandoah. It was nearly a mile alongside a four lane highway, a little farther and noisier than I normally ventured for a meal, but on those cold mornings it was worth it. I thought of it as pulling into a gas station. I needed fuel.

By the side of the road I saw a dead owl and thought about his collision with the full moon the night before, traveling at sixty miles an hour. It was beautiful and fascinating. I took advantage of its death to study it as I'd never be able to in life.

At the diner the breakfast crowd had left so I sat at the counter alone. The cook passed me a menu and I asked about an unfamiliar dish.

"What's scrapple?"

With a sideways grin he showed me a loaf of spam and offered to make me some. He assured me it was a local favorite.

"No thanks," I said and he laughed.

After my eggs, bacon, home fries, toast and jam, orange juice and hot tea, I walked back to the trail with the cold wind at my back and a warm sun in my face. As I entered Shenandoah National Park I felt immediate relief. I'd been wearing a little orange vest to alert hunters that I wasn't a deer, but the sound of shots not far off the trail had continually warned me that it was hunting season. Now I was in the National Park and it seemed the deer, bear and I were all happy to be off limits to hunters. I saw more wildlife in that park than in any of the States I'd crossed... unless you count mice. There were mice all along the trail.

That night I stayed at the Jim and Molly Denton shelter, a big, new, nicely kept shelter with a deck, benches and a picnic table. Instructions were left to cook, eat and hang food bags at the pavilion on the other side of the clearing. I could understand why with all the bears about, but the cold wind was blowing toward the pavilion. As the sun headed over the horizon temperatures fell. I wanted to make dinner while in my sleeping bag in the shelter. But I compromised and cooked sitting in a wood shed trying to stay out of the wind while soaking up the last rays of that November sun.

I hung my small tarp around a bunk in the shelter for any added warmth it might offer and climbed into my sleeping bag with almost all my clothes on. I threw my rain coat over the end of my bag and hunkered down deep inside. The temperatures dipped into the low twenties on that long, cold night.

In the morning I stayed snug in my bag until the sun was up, and then warmed some leftover hash browns for breakfast. The ink was frozen in my pen as I struggled to make notes in my journal. Owls and crows called around me. The sun was slow to warm the woods. My only furnace was inside me. I finally got going and hiked on a gentle uphill grade. One fellow I passed said it had been twenty-eight "on top" at mid morning.

"On top of what?" I had to ask.

"Compton's Peak," he replied before hiking on. I didn't notice any peaks. Still, it was wonderful to walk facing south in the sunshine all day.

Since entering the park I'd seen a lot more people. The hiking was easier and there was more wildlife. Deer were around every turn. As I neared the shelter after nineteen miles, I came upon a half dozen people pointing and aiming cameras into the woods. There was a small bear, probably this year's cub, about sixty feet off the trail. I looked around but it appeared to be alone. I remembered seeing a tiny cub in the park last May, the smallest I'd ever seen. This could be that same bear, growing into an adult after a long summer of foraging.

At the Gravel Spring Hut a father, grandfather and twin girls were making a big fire, gathering enough wood to keep it going for hours. I was grateful for their efforts and the warmth. They were quiet and courteous folk who seemed accustomed to camping. Another group came by but moved on to occupy some tent sites nearby. And last but not least, a young couple from Washington D.C. arrived. They seemed to be new to each other and the outdoors. The man cooked dinner for his sweetheart while she stood in front of the fire.

The fire radiated heat and light and brought people together. We stood within its sphere, roasting one side, and then the other. After dinner the group in the shelter was puzzling about how to store the food and trash overnight. I suggested the outhouse. The last one to use it that night rolled a big rock in front of the door.

I apologized in advance for my early waking hour. I planned to hike twenty-four miles the next day and had limited daylight hours. They said grandpa wakes early, too.

I went to bed at my usual time after getting dinner, washing my pot, getting water for breakfast, and hanging my food bag all before dark which was at 5:30. I got into my bag to read. The family played cards in front of the fire, a homey scene. I turned out my headlamp at 7:00.

At 10:00 I was awakened by the D.C. couple in the bunks above me. The woman was all stuffed up. She blew her nose loudly and tried to flip over in her sleeping bag which sounded like a seal on a dock. The man gave her some water. She woke me a few more times as she flipped and flopped in her sleep. He snored. It was a rough night.

At 4:30 I heard deer approaching the shelter. They stopped at a distance and snorted as deer do when they smell danger. Overhead I heard the woman say, "What was that?"

"It's just a bird, an owl," he answered.

At 5:30 I woke and began cooking breakfast in my corner of the shelter. I loved my silent stove. I cooked up some oatmeal Zama had sent me with coconut and cranberries. There was a promising red line on the horizon as I began to pack. Grandpa got up and stirred the coals of the fire back to life. I left at 6:30 with just enough light to see the trail.

As I got to the top of the hill and joined the AT, I startled several deer. The park is teeming with them. I'd heard coyotes in the night and an owl near dawn. It was nice to be in a National Park. Some of the deer I met just watched me walk by. The morning hike was smooth and lovely. I got to Elk Wallow about 9:00 and smelled bacon. My trail guide had said the wayside store was closed for the season, but my nose begged to differ. I couldn't resist. I got there just as the doors opened and ordered an egg "mac" something-or-other and hot chocolate, another good second breakfast.

It was sunny and cold all day. I was hurrying to cover twenty-four miles in ten hours of daylight. The angle of the sun can be misleading. In the morning it's low. Plowing through the treetops, it made me think time was passing very slowly. Then I realized it was noon and I had to move fast. After 2:00 it sinks low again. "Not long before sunset," I thought.

There were a lot of day hikers on the trail. As I neared a parking area I saw a plump couple standing about 100 feet from their vehicle. The man had a camera and they were staring intently into the woods. I looked around, but didn't see anything that caught my attention. As I approached they asked if I'd seen any deer.

"Yeah, lots of them."

"Where?"

"All over the place."

"When did you see them?"

"I saw a lot when I first started hiking around seven this morning."

The woman rolled her eyes and said, "Yeah, early in the morning."

I walked on.

Coming upon a sign that said Gravelly Spring Hut was 11.5 miles away, I checked my watch. It was 11:30. I'd covered almost half the distance for the day in less than half the time so I was making good progress. But clouds gathered as I hit some steep climbs after lunch, Mary's Rock, Byrd's Nest and the Pinnacles. The miles were catching up with me. At 3:00 I had to sit down and eat a couple of snack bars to refuel. Then I thought I could make it.

Moving along a smooth stretch of trail through a quiet wood, a young woman hiker approached. She moved quickly and effortlessly, carried a light pack, and wore a hiking skirt. We passed without a word, but our eyes met for an instant, then she was gone. A moment later it hit me. She was a thru-hiker. I'd not seen another thru-hiker in a while. After walking among day hikers and tourists, she stood out, like seeing that coyote leaping through the woods in Massachusetts. It looked like a German Shepherd, but I could tell by the way it moved with speed and grace, it was definitely wild.

My mind wandered every which way, from planting fruit trees in front of my house, to a fellow I was fond of, to my sister Sue and her fight against cancer. But after a twenty-four mile day, I'd made it to Skyland Resort by 5:00.

It was all hustle and bustle. The parking lot was full. The gift shop was busy. The nearby Big Meadows Lodge had just closed for the season. It was a Sunday, a school holiday was on Monday, the fall colors were spectacular and the sun had been shining all week. Shenandoah National Park is within a day's drive of some of the most populated cities on the east coast.

I took my place in one of the two lines waiting to check in at the hotel. I caught people in both lines stealing glances in my direction. Was it that I smelled like stale sweat and campfire smoke? Or perhaps it was because I was the only one wearing a pack. I didn't really care. I just prayed that Dad had been able to make a reservation for me since I called him last week. With darkness falling outside and miles between me and the nearest shelter, I had no other place to go.

When I reached the counter I asked if they had a reservation for me.

She clicked away at her keyboard and without looking up said, "Yes ma'am. Will that be for just one night?"

The idea of staying longer was tempting.

"Oh yes, one night. And would that room, by any chance, have a bath tub?"

"Yes," she said, looking up and handing me the key.

I smiled, "You've made me very happy."

On the way down the path to my room I thought, "Forgive me father for I have sinned. It's been five days since my last shower."

It's a good thing there are no mirrors in the woods. When I got to my room I could understand why people had stared as I checked in. It had been cold but sunny all week, and I'd been walking south right into the sun as it slinked low across the horizon. My cheeks were sunburned, wind chapped and in desperate need of some lotion. But first I ran hot water in the tub.

I spent a good half hour soaking my worn out muscles, washing my hair and scrubbing the dirt from between my toes. I might have stayed longer, but I felt the mighty tug of a good meal in the dining room.

While I dried my hair in front of the heater, I watched a little TV and polished off the last of Suzen's bread with some cream cheese I'd bought at a deli the day before. I put on my cleanest clothes and climbed the path up the hill to the dining hall. There was a line for the restaurant so I took a seat in the lounge and ordered a salad, a burger and fries. The lounge filled and the wait staff struggled to keep up. So as soon as I had finished I left my seat and returned to my warm room, looking forward to a good night's sleep in a comfortable bed.

In the morning I woke up groggy. I realized I'd eaten a lot of fat the day before. There was bacon on my egg sandwich at the wayside store. I'd had cream cheese before dinner and had eaten bacon on my salad, with blue cheese dressing, bacon on my burger and greasy French fries. Then I'd slept in a warm room. My face looked puffy with deep bags below my eyes. But I felt well rested. At breakfast in the restaurant I passed on the bacon and opted for pancakes with berries and juice.

I called my folks and thanked Dad for the room. We were planning to meet in two days. Mom said they wouldn't be able to leave Chapel Hill until my sister Carolyn left. It was a five hour drive for them. So they wouldn't arrive in the park until about 3:00 the next day. I had only twelve miles to cover that day. I'd be done by 1:00 if I took it slow. But the only way to stay warm is to move fast. Rain was in the forecast. I really didn't want to end my thru-hike shivering by the road for two hours in the rain in near freezing temperatures. I decided that if they weren't at the trailhead when I finished my hike, I would hitchhike back to the Resort instead of fighting hypothermia waiting for them. After all, I'd read somewhere that I was responsible for my own happiness.

Before I left Skyland Resort, I stopped by the front desk to ask for a room near the main lodge for when my parents arrived two days later. Mom didn't like climbing hills. I asked them to hold a bag of non-essentials for me and they agreed. Then I headed outside. Frozen rain was coming down. The forecast had said it would hold off until nightfall. I hoped it was not an omen.

I had twenty-eight more miles to finish. Passing under rock cliffs I looked up to see ten foot tall icicles dangling above my head. I hurried by as the sun came out and heard the crashing of ice spears hit the trail behind me. The day warmed as clouds moved in and rain threatened. By the end of the day I was hoping to reach the Bear Fence shelter before the rain. But where was it? I should have seen the turn off by now.

It was almost dark and still I had not found my shelter. Coming over a rise I stopped short. A large, black bear was rumbling up the hillside ahead of me. It had heard me coming through the dry leaves. It disappeared into the woods as I walked on cautiously until I came to a stream crossing the trail. "I probably scared it away from the water," I thought. I needed some, too. I stopped to fill my bottles, keeping a sharp eye out for wildlife, and then walked on.

I was beginning to think that my trail luck had run out. This was my last week on the AT. I was in Shenandoah National Park and no one I'd encountered imagined I was a thru-hiker. No one offered food.

No one had left trail magic. It was freezing cold at night. I could smell rain in the air.

"So this is how it will end," I thought, "alone under my small tarp in the rain and cold."

Just then I saw a sign post ahead. I hurried over to it. It told me I'd passed the shelter 2.5 miles back. Drat! By now it was almost dark. I checked my guide book. There was a cabin not far away. These cabins in the park are locked up, but maybe this one had a porch where I could stay for the night, so I went ahead.

Approaching the cabin from the back, I noticed smoke rising from the chimney. Then I heard happy voices. Coming around the corner I found three fathers and three ten year old sons on the porch in the midst of a pile of gear and food. I greeted them and told them of my plight asking if they'd allow me to sleep on the porch. They looked at each other. There was a long pause. Finally one man spoke up.

"No," he said, "you can't sleep on our porch... but there's a bunk inside that's available if you don't mind sleeping next to the wood stove."

"Oh, no," I said, "being warm is not a problem."

So I spent my last night on the trail in a comfortable cabin with six entertaining and hospitable fellows. One father and son had already walked about 350 miles of the Appalachian Trail in sections. They were champion scouts and inventive camp cooks. As we made our dinners outside on the picnic table a fire roared in the outdoor fireplace. They told me some of their favorite recipes including chocolate pudding that was mixed inside a ball they tossed around camp before dinner.

After we ate, we moved inside. The cabin could sleep up to twelve. It had a wood stove and a table where the kids gathered around a Coleman lamp to play a trivia game. I got a bunk with a thick mattress and settled in with my book, but continued to be entertained by their animated conversation.

Every so often one of the men would step outside and stir the fire. A mouth watering aroma emanated from the coals. I could hardly believe my good fortune when they served up some hot pineapple upside down cake from their Dutch oven and offered me a piece. My, oh, my! What a great way to spend my last night on the trail. My trail angels were with me still.

Red Sky in the Morning

At dawn the next day we watched a spectacular sunrise and one of the boys reminded me, "Red sky in the morning, sailors take warning." So on my last day on the trail I left my companions soon after breakfast and headed out for the final ten miles to Hightop Shelter. It was an easy stroll with plenty of opportunity for my mind to wander. I thought about the highlights of my thru-hike, my trail family and what might come ahead. When I came to a smooth patch of bare ground I drew my last heart in the trail in appreciation for the opportunity to hike the entire AT. I gave thanks for my safety and health, for the strength of my body, mind and spirit and for all the support I'd received from so many people, friends, family and strangers.

As I climbed up to Hightop Peak, a light drizzle turned into steady rain. By the time I reached the summit, the wind had grown brisk. I stopped long enough to take a last photo of myself with my arm stretched out and a grin on my face. A few minutes later I reached the shelter. I had finally reached the point I'd left in May. I'd finally finished the trail.

I stepped under cover remembering the day I had hobbled in with an infected blister. Firefly had sat across from me at this picnic table. Feather and Silver had slept on either side of me in these bunks. Two locals had cooked fresh-caught fish over the fire. Though I was alone in the shelter now, I could see them all here very clearly, hear their laughter, feel their warmth.

I checked the shelter log and found Tortoise had signed in two weeks before. Then I took up a whole page writing a big "YAHOO!" and drawing a picture of myself jumping up and down. I wrote a huge "Thank You to the Angels" and then signed off. I took out the Snickers bar Ralph had provided for my finishing treat and took a big bite. But sitting still, I began chilling down. With one last look around I walked out through the rain, headed for the trailhead just a mile and a half away.

When I got to Skyline Drive it was noon, raining hard and getting colder with a chill wind. I wrote my folks a note saying, "Gone to Skyland, too wet and cold here." I folded it, stuffed it into a Zip-lock bag and wedged it into the gate that closed the service road where we'd agreed to meet.

My feet were soaked so I started walking fast to stay warm. The clouds had moved in and visibility was poor. There was very little traffic. I'd walked about a mile when I rounded a bend and saw a clearing in the trees up ahead where the wind blew more briskly and the rain shot sideways. I hated to stop but needed more layers. I'd just pulled my poncho on when a jeep came along and I stuck out my thumb. A young man pulled over.

He was a local fellow who had the day off. He said he had nothing to do and would be happy to take me all the way to Skyland, twenty-five miles away. On the way he said he'd always wanted to hike the Appalachian Trail and liked helping thru-hikers whenever he could. At the resort, I wished him well and watched him drive away hoping that he'd get his chance someday.

I got checked in and immediately went to the restaurant for their lunch special, chicken pot pie. Then I went to the room. I ran a hot bath, washed out my clothes and hung them up above the heater. Then I got into the tub myself. After getting cleaned up, I leaned back in bed with my book. My folks would be arriving within the hour.

The hour passed and the next was well underway. I was beginning to worry about them when they finally appeared. They had arrived sooner than expected and took a nap in the car while waiting for me. After a while they started to wonder if they were in the right place. Dad left Mom there with her umbrella while he drove to the next trailhead. Since Mom was out of the car she strolled over to the gate and poked at the note in the bag. She'd thought it was a note left by park staff. Upon closer inspection she saw the words OPA and OMA framed by a heart.

They arrived at Skyland an hour later with a bottle of bubbly, crackers and cheese to celebrate. We popped the cork and toasted the trail from inside a warm room while watching the storm building outside. *T'was a dark and stormy night*, but this time I wasn't in it.

Epilogue

It's been a decade since I hiked the Appalachian Trail. Now I have a home of my own on Whidbey Island. My house sits at the edge of a forest with a big window facing east. I look across a twenty acre field and beyond that to a valley with horses and barns. Toward the south there's a distant view of the bay. My sister, Martha, calls it my "big screen TV" and complains that I only get two channels, the Weather Channel and the Nature Channel. I often have deer in my yard. Hawks, herons, eagles and ravens fly over the fields. A host of songbirds sing from the shrubbery. At night I hear owls call and coyotes howl. We all feel at home here.

Most mornings I see the sunrise, bold and bright in summer, or through a heavy cloud cover in winter. Majestic moons rise over a ridge of spiny evergreen trees. Storms come off the water. Clouds race across the sky like ships on a tumultuous sea. Some days the rain streaks the window, mist covers the valley and I watch the History Channel, flashing back to my hike on the Appalachian Trail.

I finished my hike on November 7, 2006. I spent a month with my family in North Carolina. On Thanksgiving Day my knees were strong enough to run a 5K with my niece and her husband before eating turkey and sweet potato pie with my extended family.

I went to chemo appointments with Sue and cooked and cleaned for her. She responded well to her treatments, and in time fully recovered.

On December first I returned to the Northwest. After a divorce and almost a year of hiking, it took a lot of time and effort to put my life back together. There were many job applications and many rejections. I spent several months house-sitting here and there and substitute teaching, living in limbo, waiting for things to fall into place. Many thru-hikers have a hard time returning to "normal" life. It's like a sugar high after indulging in too much sweet stuff, and the inevitable crash that follows. It was almost exactly a year from the day my thru-hike ended to the day I started a new full time job as an outreach educator that gave me fulfillment and support for years to come. I developed a romantic relationship with my old friend, Ben. My renters left and we moved into my home together and got a dog. I was happy, full of life and energy again.

Like on the trail, there were steep ups and downs. In 2009 I was diagnosed with breast cancer. I started chemotherapy just before Christmas and lost my hair. In April my mother was diagnosed with terminal pancreatic cancer. Because of my illness, I was able to take leave from work. I arranged to get treatment in my home town so that I could be with my family in North Carolina for her final months of life. It was a very tough time for us. My mother died in June. I returned to the Northwest after her funeral to start a new round of chemotherapy. My relationship with Ben was strained. Later that dark, rainy winter, we split up. He moved across the country and took our dog. The weight of my grief was almost unbearable. But one thing I'd learned from the trail was that I could make it, if I just kept putting one foot in front of the other. With the help of many friends, day by day, week by week, month by month, I pushed on. I got a gym membership so I could walk indoors while it was dark and stormy outside. If I didn't have the energy for the treadmill, I could at least take a sauna. My hair grew back. Finally, I felt spring's warmth and light returning. Snow melted, the first flowers appeared and I was able to get up into the mountains and hike. Over the summer I was able to gradually shed the weight of my sadness and grief.

In the next few years there were more terrible losses, more struggles, but there have also been more adventures. Eight years after discovering it, I returned to bike the Great Allegheny Passage and C&O Canal on a five day trip from Pittsburgh to finish on the Appalachian Trail in Harpers Ferry. I go backpacking to my favorite places in Olympic National Park every summer to see herds of elk, black bears and wild flowers. As long as I can keep getting out into wild places and soak in the beauty, I'm happy. I travel light and keep my closet stocked with supplies ready to go whenever I get a chance.

My early morning two mile walk to the bus is my favorite part of the day. I walk down through a wetland and then climb a big hill by pastures and woods where I often encounter wildlife. It reminds me of hiking the Appalachian Trail, especially when there's a brisk wind, and I smile.

I appreciate my snug little house, my car, my job and being part of a wonderful community. When I watch winter storms bending the tall trees in a frightening dance, I'm happy to be warm and dry inside.

Still, I remind myself that when I felt most alive was when I was on the trail. I was strong, relaxed, in a state of constant discovery. Each day I had wondrous encounters and experiences, hiking through a blizzard, joining a hoe down in a general store, meeting a tiny bear cub or a moonlit moose, laughing with my trail family, dancing with newts, all gifts from the universe.

Though it's been years since I walked the Appalachian Trail there are things that it taught me: the difference between *want* and *need*; that it's best to travel light; the value of fine companions; and of good health.

I'd wanted to hike the Appalachian Trail since I was a kid but it took me nearly four decades to actually do it. Almost every day on the trail I met someone who said, "I've always wanted to do that." There was a glimmer of hope in their eye, while at the same time their tone of voice said, "But I probably never will".

Never say never. I had to wait until the time was right for me, and when the opportunity came, I went for it. Now I can sit back in my easy chair and watch the Nature Channel, the Weather Channel and the History Channel without regret. And from the comfort of my snug home, by the fire with a cup of tea, I can plan my next adventure.

Made in the USA
Monee, IL
12 August 2025

23137887R00177